ANIMAL WELFARE
& HUMAN VALUES

ANIMAL WELFARE & HUMAN VALUES

ROD PREECE & LORNA CHAMBERLAIN

Wilfrid Laurier University Press

WLU

Canadian Cataloguing in Publication Data

Preece, Rod, 1939-
  Animal welfare & human values

Includes bibliographical references and index.
ISBN 0-88920-227-3 (bound)   ISBN 0-88920-256-7 (pbk.)

1. Animal welfare – Moral and ethical aspects.
I. Chamberlain, Lorna, 1945-   . II. Title.
III. Title: Animal welfare and human values.

HV4708.P74A65 1993   179′.3   C93-093988-3

Cloth edition
Copyright © 1993

Paper edition
Copyright © 1995

Wilfrid Laurier University Press
Waterloo, Ontario, Canada
N2L 3C5

Cover design by Jose Martucci, Design Communications, using the photograph, "Laboratory Cruelty You Were Not Meant to See," by Brian Gunn.

Stock photographs supplied by Design Communications.

∞

Printed in Canada

Animal Welfare and Human Values has been produced from a manuscript supplied in camera-ready form by the authors.

This book is dedicated to the staff of the Ontario S.P.C.A. (Ontario Humane Society), the Canadian Federation of Humane Societies and the Sarnia and District Humane Society. It has been written in memory of Demon, Nicholas and Oliver and in enjoyment of Blue, Brie and Tyler. They are all a part of our family.

Royalties from the sale of this book will be donated to the Caring Campaign of the Ontario S.P.C.A.

Contents

Acknowledgements

In writing this book, broad in scope as it is, we became indebted to many persons from a variety of sources—authors of previously read and often unrelated books who helped inform our values, passing acquaintances whose insights triggered further thoughts of our own, friends who encouraged us and opponents who decried our ideas but persuaded us to believe all the more that the book was necessary. There are many such persons, but the identity of a number is unknown and some others are perhaps best left unrecognized.

There are a number of people, however, whose contributions have been such that we owe them a special debt of gratitude: Sandra Woolfrey, director of WLU Press, who first suggested the book be written and then continued to offer helpful advice; Dr. Anthea McQuade, the queen of commas, who valiantly attempted to improve our syntax; Stephanie Brown, former president of the Canadian Federation of Humane Societies, who afforded us trenchant criticism of the first draft of our chapters on animal experimentation; Judith McKibbon, who scoured the daily press for relevant material for the book while continuing to think us unfair to aboriginal Canadians on the trapping issue; Maura Brown, managing editor of WLU Press, who saved us from several embarrassments, made numerous valuable suggestions, often pointed out what we should have thought of ourselves—and switched to eating only free range eggs as well!

To two persons our debts are more than is customary: Dr. Mathias Guenther, a Wilfrid Laurier University anthropologist; and Dr. David Porter, chair of the Department of Biomedical Sciences at the University of Guelph and former chair of the Steering Committee for the University of Guelph Centre for the Study of Animal Welfare. They were employed by WLU Press as readers of the submitted manuscript to help determine whether publication was appropriate. They put so much effort and expertise into their evaluations, offering much justified criticism along the way, that we were encouraged to refine some of what we had first written and avoid a number of pitfalls. We doubt that many other authors can have been so fortunate in a publisher's choice of appraisers.

While we remain entirely responsible for the contents of this book and while we are aware that we will not have satisfied all the concerns of those who offered us valid and valued criticisms, we also know that without those friendly criticisms we would have produced a somewhat different book. Even though others may not bear the responsibility for the book's failures they share substantially in any value it may have.

Both the Canada Council and the Wilfrid Laurier University Research Office have helped fund the publication of this book. We are duly grateful. Without assistance from public sources, much that needs to be expressed would remain unheard. In Canada public funding remains a prerequisite of intellectual freedom.

Finally, we would like to thank Helen Paret and Sherry Howse for their smiles and for their proficiency and goodwill in the typing and preparation of the manuscript for publication. We are happy that the book gave them an occasional chuckle, sad that they had to be sometimes sickened by reading of the cruelties civilized humans inflict on other species.

Rod Preece
Lorna Chamberlain

Summer Solstice, 1992

Introduction

We set out to write this book out of our concern for the animal realm. We have been in turn puzzled, exasperated and horrified at humanity's inhumanity to its fellow sentient beings. As chairman and vice-chairman, respectively, of the Ontario Society for the Prevention of Cruelty to Animals we are constantly being made aware of the atrocities committed in the more than 400,000 square kilometres of the Society's jurisdiction—an area of extensive hunting, trapping, intensive farming and family farming, animal experimentation and pet-keeping. As the most populous province of Canada, Ontario is a microcosm of the animal welfare issues which beset Western civilization.

Equally, though, this book is a reaction against the arrogant fanaticism of some of the animal liberationists who imagine there are simple moral solutions to complex social problems. Unfortunately, much which appears on behalf of the animal liberation movement, while well meant and straight from the heart, is little more than pious sentimentality, sometimes in the persuasively pretentious guise of academic philosophy or behavioural science. Of course, they also count several reputable philosophers and scientists among their numbers. On the other hand much which appears on behalf of the fur industry, animal experimentation and intensive farming involves a significant degree of self-serving rationalization. Each side to the disputes about such issues customarily talks past its adversary. There is no common ground, no consensus, no meeting point from which a meaningful debate can begin and from which practical and beneficial compromises can be reached.

Let us immediately acknowledge where we stand. We stand squarely on the side of the animals. But we do not believe that compromise is an evasion of principle. It is instead the most effective means to implement principle. The animal liberationists, as well as their adversaries, paint only half a picture, give us only one side of the story. Animal liberationist criticisms of the existing state of affairs are frequently valid. But criticisms are easy, whereas solutions are not. The liberationists make the unwarranted assumption that the mere elimination of what is wrong will produce what is right. In our view solutions are not that simple—they are to be achieved by working *with* others involved with animals and *with* governments at local, provincial and national levels to move toward humanitarian goals in a pragmatic and piecemeal manner. Solutions are not achieved merely by slandering those who do not always share one's philosophy.

It is one of the unfortunate facts of life that it is the fanaticism of the extremists which receives the most attention. And this fanaticism has at least served to arouse public indignation against some of the most blatant animal exploitation. Such fanaticism encourages almost

1

idolatrous adherence on the part of the sympathizers. But it also encourages ridicule and dismissal on the part of others, especially those who have a direct influence on animal welfare.

In our humane society work we have found that at least some of those who make their livelihoods from animal husbandry are not the callous and indifferent abusers of animals they are sometimes made out to be. We have certainly found that the executive members of certain farming organizations are people from whom we can learn and with whom we can co-operate. Such co-operation is to be encouraged rather than destroyed by emotional diatribes against their occupations.

This does not mean that in the conclusions of this book we have merely taken a position half-way between the opposing sides. On some issues we are decidedly and incontrovertibly committed to one side. On others we are rather more accommodating. What we have tried to do on all issues is to give a fair hearing to those who do not always share our commitments. In this way we hope to have produced arguments which, in turn, will be given a fair hearing by animal experimenters, hunters, farmers and governmental decision-makers as well as those committed to significant improvements in the lives of the members of the animal realm.

This is a book for those who want to think seriously and fairly about complex issues. It is not a book for those who want a cause to follow blindly. There is a cause, and an eminently worthwhile one, but it is to be pursued with common sense, with diligence, with goodwill, and with a recognition that there are human as well as non-human interests which do not always coincide. Moreover, there are legitimate and honourable differences of opinion which reason rather than unbridled emotion may help us to reconcile.

We realize that this book may alienate some of those who are committed to the radical implementation of animal rights. We respect their commitment and we would regret the alienation of their empathy. We realize also that it will be anathema to many animal users. But we believe that common sense and compromise are the surest paths to the goal of animal welfare. It serves neither justice nor progress to talk of one's own views as "transspecies democracy" and those of one's adversaries as "biological fascism," as does one of America's leading proponents of animal rights. He demonstrates in fact that he understands neither democracy nor fascism. More important is that the use of such emotive language, such uncontrolled invective, leads us further away from, not toward, relevant solutions. If we are to make meaningful and rational progress on animal welfare issues, the language of diatribe and invective must be eliminated from the discourse. While we stand firmly on the side of the animals we have attempted to ensure throughout that we have weighed animal interests against human interests where they are in conflict. It is our view that justice is best approximated by holding in balance the inexorably and unequally competing interests of all living creatures.

We wish to emphasize that the views expressed in this book are our own. They should not be interpreted as necessarily those of the organizations to which we belong.

The issues discussed in this book are the most contentious in animal welfare disputes—animal experimentation, fur-farming and trapping, the use of animals for human entertainment and the conditions under which animals are raised for human consumption. Our conclusions suggest that however necessary cold logic and objective data may be to an impartial consideration of these issues none of them may be resolved by reason and facts alone. At the end of the day solutions can only be found in the refinement of human sensibilities.

> Unaccommodated man is no more but such a poor, bare, forked animal as thou art.
>
> — *King Lear*, III, iv

> The best lack all conviction, while the worst are full of passionate intensity.
>
> — W.B. Yeats, *The Second Coming*

> Vociferated logic kills me quite; A noisy man is always in the right.
>
> — William Cowper, *Conversation*

Chapter One

The Status of Animals:
From Human Origins to Humanism

Had he only made one species of animals, none of the rest
would have enjoyed the happiness of existence;
— Addison, *Spectator*, October 25, 1712

To understand the early history of *Homo sapiens* is to understand
humanity's early relationship to other species. Animals were first hunted
for food and clothing, then domesticated to ensure a more dependable
supply and finally employed as beasts of burden. Moreover, early in
human history animals became both objects of worship and pets. It is
no exaggeration to recognize our relationship with other animals as a
principal source of population expansion, accumulation of wealth and
the benefits of civilization itself. Strange as it may seem, non-human
animals have played a major role in determining the specific forms of
humankind's divergent cultures. Humanity is not only itself a part of the
animal realm but also a species whose history has developed directly out
of its relationship to other sentient beings. Without the relationship to
other animals human history would have been quite different.

Human development owes a great debt to other species. Yet, at least
in Western civilization, a self-conscious humane respect for the interests
of other species is a relatively recent phenomenon, and one which even
today is only in its infancy. Historically, Western civilization has placed
humanity external to, and above nature, rather than within nature.
Moreover, Western history is not one of a consistent, gradual extension
of consideration to animals but in some respects, at least until the
nineteenth century, sometimes the reverse—despite the fact that there
have always been some who have been willing to swim against the tide.

By contrast, Oriental cultures, especially those influenced by Taoism,
Hinduism, Buddhism and, to a lesser degree, Confucianism, have viewed
humanity as within and subject to nature. It was not humanity's task to
dominate nature but to accommodate itself to it. Understanding
humanity as one animal among many species was never alien to the
Oriental mind. Oddly, though, as Western culture in the last century
and a half has moved toward a greater interest in and respect for the
animal realm, the very reverse has occurred in the East.

In early human history, cultivators, hunters and gatherers developed
tools and weapons for more effective hunting, skinning and food
production and thus furthered the process of making human life

5

distinctly different from the lives of other species. The need to develop more effective means to acquire sustenance and shelter honed our constructive skills. The hook and line was developed for fishing. The bow, the first composite mechanism, was invented, as was the spear-thrower. Both are mechanical devices which increase the range and accuracy—and consequently the success—of the chase. In addition to wood and stone, humans began to use animal parts as weapons. Reindeer antlers, for example, were sharpened to become effective harpoons. Bones and ivory were honed to make knives and cutting implements. Tents were constructed from animal skins. In the absence of wood, animal bones were burned. If necessity is the mother of invention, many of the needs were satisfied from our use of animals for food and some of the inventions employed the inedible parts of the prey—both to improve hunting skills and to provide more efficient shelter, clothing and warmth.

Early religions, in the form of magic rites, developed to promote the availability of game and success in the hunt. It is also conjectured by anthropologists that fertility rituals served as prayers for the abundance of prey. The famous animal cave paintings of France and Spain were undertaken by deftly skilled artists perhaps either to conjure up in reality what was depicted in art or to appease and claim the souls of the game. It is estimated that these ritualistic and highly skilled works of art are some 20,000 or more years old.

Certainly there is an intrinsic connection between the human-animal relationship and the development of the earliest religious practices. Moreover, there are strong indications that some 80,000 or more years ago the practice of animal sacrifice as appeasement to the spirits already existed—some of the proceeds of the hunt being so dedicated. Early ornamentation also displayed a decided animal orientation. Hunting tackle was embellished with animal engravings. Shells and animal teeth were strung together as necklaces. Bracelets were made from mammoth ivory.

Animals were first domesticated in the middle stone age. Not surprisingly, the first animal to be domesticated was the dog, which has continued its close relationship with humans for the ensuing 12,000 or so years. Probably for a few thousand years before that the wolf and jackal ancestors of the domestic dog had been tolerated as scavengers around human habitats. Eventually the dog was domesticated to help in hunting small game, from the red deer to the boar and hare. In payment for its services the dog would be rewarded with the less desirable meat of the prey. It was through such domestication that we began to treat the animal in part as an end in itself and take the first steps toward the closest interspecies association—that between human and companion animal. Indeed, a recent discovery in a Middle Eastern tomb suggests that the purely companion dog—not just a hunting aid—arrived on the scene some 11,500 years ago. And the cat as pet has a history of at least 4,500 years.

Although human pre-history is clouded in the mists of time, enough can be gleaned from the available evidence for us to be able to recognize that the origins of our habits, skills and modes of societal organization lie substantially in our relationship to the animal realm.

———————

In the neolithic period—beginning some 12,000 years ago—humans began to cultivate the soil. While men hunted, women gathered the seeds of wild grasses, the forerunners of our wheat and barley. Then they began to sow the seeds and cultivate the land, thus producing a more stable and predictable food supply, and through the creation of surpluses providing the potential to support a growing population.

With the stubble and husks of the grain plots it became possible to provide uninterrupted sustenance for wild animals—sheep, goats, cattle and pigs, allowing humans to domesticate these species. This tame game provided reserves of food and clothing—what Gordon Childe called "living larders and walking wardrobes."[1] Not only did such animals provide meat and skin, but they were also permanent suppliers of milk and wool. Villages were now from 1-1/2 to 8 acres in size and housed from 8 to 35 families but were apparently insufficiently complex to permit any division of labour other than by gender and age. Village sites were chosen in part for the suitability of the land for cultivation, whereas for people who remained predominantly engaged in hunting the proximity to game and wild fowl was more significant.

Generally, though, as the activities of grain-growing and stock-breeding developed, hunting was relegated to a lesser significance in the neolithic economy. The mixture of grain with stock was doubly beneficial—stock could graze on cleared plots and provide fertilizer to enrich the soil to produce new and healthier crops over time.

It is a perhaps surprising reflection on the propensity of a significant proportion of the male populations of Western civilizations to continue to hunt for game today to note that the economic necessity of the hunt was beginning to wane some 7,000 years or so ago. If, for some, sports activities have sublimated the psychological drives appropriate to the chase, for others the killing of game remains an essential part of 'manly' activity! Indeed, the word 'game' itself reflects the fact that all sports—'games'—find their origins in substitutes for hunting.

The invention of the plough some 5,000 years ago brought about the most fundamental change in the human-animal relationship. The arrival of the plough encouraged the invention of the yoke and the harness,

———————

1   Gordon Childe, *What Happened in History* (Harmondsworth: Penguin, 1960), p. 54.

which allowed oxen rather than humans to till the soil—the age of the beast of burden had arrived. The plough not only changed farming from plot cultivation to tillage, but united the tasks of grain-growing and stock-breeding. It also deprived women of their control over the cereal crops and hence reduced their economic significance. The yoked employment of the oxen soon spread to drawing sleds over trails and snow, and thus the long history of the animal as a means of transportation was begun.

Soon—at least 'soon' measured in terms of several centuries!—asses and horses were no longer merely sources of meat and milk but of transportation too—the asses as pack animals and the horses at first as drawers of two-wheeled carts (or chariots) and later with the rider astride. Somewhere around the same period camels were also being tamed and put into service.

Horse-drawn chariots were, of course, used in early warfare, as a little later were the elephant and the camel. However, domesticated animals were certainly not primarily used for destructive purposes but instead helped produce economic surpluses—the very prerequisites of civilization—and were themselves, particularly horses and cows, reckoned as wealth. The horse and the camel especially were instrumental in making trading between distant parts feasible, at least when it was not possible to undertake all or most of the journey by water. And it was trading which helped diffuse knowledge and create wealth, especially in the last millennium B.C.

Moreover, the horse above all helped spread and acquire learning—thus, for example, the Greek philosophical historian Herodotus was able to visit Mesopotamia, Babylon and Egypt in the fifth century B.C. The journey must have covered some 6,000 miles and involved about a year of travelling time. The Persians constructed the 'royal road' from Sardis to Susa, a 1,700 mile journey covered by horse in about 90 days. Travel brought new knowledge with practical implications for agriculture and animal husbandry—to take but one example, the Persians introduced alfalfa to the Mediterranean regions and acquired rice from India.

The acquisition of learning itself brought a more systematic understanding to farming and our awareness of the animal realm. Thus around the eighth century B.C. Hesiod, himself of farming stock, wrote, in his *Works and Days*, verse which contained practical advice to farmers, and in the sixth century B.C. or thereabouts Aesop wrote his fables, some three-quarters of which involved animals. In the fourth century B.C. Aristotle, no slouch as a traveller, gave lectures on zoology and botany along with producing his currently better known treatises on politics, ethics and logic. He even created a private but substantial menagerie on which to base his research.

Just as developments in metallurgy and the invention of the wheel had the profoundest effects on social and economic organization, so too, the ox-cart and the pack-ass, the horse and the camel, changed the very foundations of human life. If, in the earliest of human history, as it is sometimes conjectured, other species were treated with a certain respect, sometimes awe, any such respect must have dissipated along with technological development. As increased mastery over nature diminished respect for nature, so the refinement of ethical sensibilities became necessary through the development of moral education to counter the effects of technology itself.

It is undoubtedly true, as ecologists constantly remind us, that we have gone too far, especially since the Industrial Revolution, in our mastery and domination of nature. Nonetheless, it should be recognized equally that the wisdom which now permits us to recognize the crimes we have committed against the environment, including the animal environment, is itself a product of a civilization which could not have been constructed without some degree of mastery over nature.

If leisure was the prerequisite of the development of the arts and sciences, it was no less the occasion of outright cruelty. The most systematic and blatant cruelty to animals was to be found in the circuses of Rome. Circuses of today that ignore the needs of animals and debase and demean their natures pall into insignificance when compared to the horrors committed to titillate the palates of the Roman throngs.

There were some 70 amphitheatres in the Roman Empire which witnessed four centuries of the gravest atrocities committed primarily against non-human animals—but the barbarism extended to humans, too, primarily aliens and slaves. Eight thousand animals were slaughtered on the first two days following the opening of the Colosseum in Rome itself. Eleven thousand were killed to celebrate Trajan's conquest of Dacia (modern Rumania). Nothing of stature was left unharmed in the spectacles offered by the *circus maximus* in the following years. Elephants, hippopotamuses, rhinoceroses, crocodiles, chamois and giraffes were all butchered, along with the more customary lions, tigers, bears, bulls, leopards and deer—just for the fun of it! And if we find this heart-rendingly sickening we must perforce remember that for the vast hordes of Romans eager to be spectators at such events the killing was culturally acceptable. It was merely a display of the warriors' skills and courage—their dominance over nature. When Augustus claimed, in the document attached to his will, that he had exhibited 8,000 gladiators and 3,510 wild beasts in the circus he was boasting, not confessing.

When these cruelties finally came to an end around the fifth century A.D. it had nothing to do with any awakening to the sheer inhumanity of the events. It was because of the collapse of the Roman Empire and the coming of the feudal period of relative economic decline when such extravagances could no longer be afforded. Although they were called the dark ages, they must have seemed a little brighter to the animal realm. Unfortunately, the Roman circuses had already succeeded in decimating the larger animal population of the surrounding territories. The vicarious pleasures in the slaughter and the unadulterated hedonism of many Romans were prime symptoms of the destruction of the Roman character which led to the downfall of their Empire.

The leisure that was necessary to afford humans the opportunity to develop the skills which led to civilization also obviously had its dark side. Leisure also allowed time for entertainment, sometimes directed toward the very lowest of human appetites. Little wonder that philosophers from Plato through Machiavelli to Rousseau and Montesquieu insisted that the most effective of societal organizations are without merit if they fail to instil virtuous character in their citizens. Moral education is the prerequisite of justice. In the last two decades in Western society the most effective educators on justice toward animals have been the animal rights activists. However much one may deplore their excesses and doubt the extravagance of their claims one cannot doubt that they have aroused a justified public moral indignation. They have achieved some significant successes in limiting a number of the more blatant animal abuses— especially in Europe. Without the animal liberationists the current plight of the animal realm would be even worse.

Although animals were massacred in their hundreds of thousands in the gladiatorial combats of Rome they were, in total contrast, the objects of worship elsewhere. But the benefit to the animals was not always what one might imagine—though distinctly preferable to being the disparaged objects of infamous sport! We must look to Egypt for the most extensive deification of animals; but the attitudes which brought this about are to be found in early hunting history. When hunters first dared to challenge wild beasts to provide the next meal for themselves and their families, the animals proved to be worthy foes and indeed sometimes emerged the victors. Wild bull, bison and boar, for example, were formidable foes as well as kindred beings possessed of power and courage. They had to be treated with caution; they deserved to be treated with respect by those who fought them for food and raiment. While there was respect for animal life in general, the greatest reverence was reserved for those animals which possessed the courage which the hunter needed to conquer his adversary. Early humans could rarely ignore the fact that they were animals not very different from the species on which they preyed. For most of the time the hunters and gatherers felt themselves an intrinsic part of nature.

This awe for the adversary stimulated stone age peoples to devise spiritual means to acquire mastery in combat. They forged imitative masks to don, some claim, the courage of their foe, and painted images to claim his spirit. Some species attracted especial reverence and became totemic symbols of the traits necessary for human success or even as symbols of the ancestral figures from which the tribes thought themselves to be descended.

While paleolithic tribes claimed a particular species as their own totemic symbol, the Egyptians went further and sanctified a host of diverse animals. Not only did they worship Sekhmet, the lion-headed goddess of courage, but through her, Bastet, the domestic cat, the virgin goddess and mother (the source no less of the symbolism of the Virgin Mary).

The Egyptians also offered undue reverence to the leopard and the hippopotamus, and, perhaps more surprisingly, to mongooses, scorpions, frogs and dung beetles. In and around Egypt among one or more tribes at one time or another we find the inhabitants praying to gods which resembled crocodiles, antelopes, rams, falcons, ibises, baboons and snakes. The reverence was undue because it did not treat the animals with respect for what they were but attempted to make them what they were not. For the sanctified animals it meant that no one dared harm them—other than the priests, apparently. So many skeletons of young and apparently healthy 'worshipped' animals have been found in human graves in Egypt that it is surmised that the animals must have been acquired in the neighbouring territories specifically for the purpose. In most instances their necks were skilfully broken—presumably by the priests who performed the burial ceremonies. If being worshipped proved less than healthy, the prospects for the non-sanctified ani-mals—or those animals worshipped by people other than one's own—were far worse. Great cruelty was not only permitted but customarily expected.

William Wordsworth, the doyen of the English lake poets, wrote of "primal sympathy," reminding us of the inner relationship between human and nature, a concept notably lacking in influence in the written history of Western civilization. And Alexander Pope told us ironically of:

> The poor Indian! whose untutored mind
> Sees God in clouds, or hears him in the wind;
> His soul proud science never taught to stray
> Far as the solar walk or milky way;
> Yet simple nature to his hope has giv'n,

Behind the cloud-topped hill, an humbler heav'n.[2]

If the arrogance of the scientific mentality drew Western thought inexorably away from "primal sympathy" can we find a more worthily imitable attitude in other earlier cultures? On the surface Oriental thought seems to have a lot to offer. Yet Victorian descriptions of Oriental life—Mrs. F.A. Steel's *On the Face of the Waters,* for example—suggest that it rarely approached the behaviour recommended in its religious ideologies. And as the noted Orientalist philosopher Alan Watts wrote in mid-twentieth century, "Less and less has the 'wisdom of the East' anything to do with modern Asia."[3] Nonetheless, while Western civilization may have little to learn from Oriental practice about appropriate behaviour toward non-human animals there is rather more to be gleaned from their philosophies on the relation of human to nature.

It is not at all uncommon to find animal liberationists proclaiming the virtues of Taoist or Hindu or Buddhist attitudes to animals while castigating those of Christianity and Western civilization. While there is some justification for that view the matter is far from being as simple as it is sometimes portrayed.

It is rather more difficult to make categorical statements about Oriental thought systems and religions than about our own. In part that is because of the difficulties of translating concepts which lie at the very core of thought of one culture into the language of a quite alien culture. In part too it is because, for example, in Buddhism and the Vedanta, the centre lies in experience which is non-verbal and ineffable, and in Taoism truth lies in 'inwardness' which is both mysterious and inscrutable. It is difficult to express Oriental ideas in Western languages, if in any language at all. Nonetheless, most Oriental religions express some kind of identification of the human with nature. All of life is to be respected. Only occasionally is this made explicit. Nonetheless, in Hinduism's Bhagavad Gita we read that "we bow to all beings with great reverence in the thought and knowledge that God enters into them through fractioning Himself as living creatures." And in his "Sermon on the Turning of the Wheel of the Law" delivered at the deer park at Sarnath in India somewhere between the fifth and sixth centuries B.C., Gautama the Buddha forbade harm to any living creature. This certainly had the consequence of encouraging vegetarianism and a distant respect for, if not a relationship with, the animal realm. But Oriental religions seemed to encourage monastic orders,

---

2   Wordsworth's words are from "Ode on Intimations of Immortality," *The Poetical Works of William Wordsworth* (Edinburgh: Nimmo, no date), p. 304; the lines from Pope are from *An Essay on Man* (London: Methuen, 1970), Epistle, 1, 99-104.

3   Alan Watts, *Nature, Man and Woman* (New York: Vintage Books, 1970), p. 15 (first published 1958).

which lived their religious beliefs independently of the population at large. Moreover, Oriental religions tended to be quietist rather than activist. That is, a temperament of equanimity was encouraged, a resignation to things as they are was approved. Harm to others, including animals, was to be avoided, but one had no responsibility to be actively involved in creating a society which would respect the interests of others. In short there is often a relative indifference to the world as it is. It involved abstention rather than commitment, the avoidance of private evil rather than the doing of public good. This quietism underlay Taoism and Confucianism, influenced Hinduism but was rather less prominent in Buddhism. All in all this encouraged each individual to develop a respect for all living things—or give alms to the monk to have him do it for you—but did little to create a societal order in which there was any *requirement* of ethical treatment for animals, any punishment for cruelty. If Oriental religions encouraged a healthy respect for the animal realm, in the final analysis they did very little to bring about a world in which animals would be respected. Lao Tze admonished his followers to "Love the earth as yourself, then you can truly care for all things" but little was ever done by Taoism to make the admonition a reality. Perhaps, though, this is not so different from the Western tradition. While the Romans gleefully sacrificed gladiators, Christians, and animals, they expressed due reverence for the Stoicism which preached virtue and claimed in principle to treat each individual equally.

Animal liberationists have tended, on the one hand, to glorify Oriental pantheism, and on the other, to condemn Aristotle as the founder of classical speciesism. Speciesism is what Peter Singer has described as "a prejudice or attitude of bias in favour of the interests of members of one's own species and against those of members of other species."[4] While it is certainly true, as the animal liberationists tell us, that Aristotle did not share the respect for animals we find in Pythagoras or the members of his school, nonetheless it is easy to misrepresent Aristotle's view. We are told that Aristotle thought slavery both right and expedient (the animal liberationists don't bother to mention that Pythagoras thought so too) and that Aristotle's attitude to slavery is indicative of his attitude to animals. What we are not told is that Aristotle's attitude to slavery was a quite progressive one for the Greece of his time. Greek custom held that anyone taken in conquest could be enslaved, but Aristotle insisted that only those inferior in nature could be justifiably held as slaves. While we would, of course, condemn all slavery we must not fail to recognize that Aristotle's practicality was more likely to improve the lot of slaves than any

---

4 Peter Singer, *Animal Liberation*, 2d ed. (New York: New York Review of Books, 1990), p. 6.

outright condemnation of slavery. Moreover, according to Aristotle, the master has an inherent duty both to treat slaves with justice and to instruct them rationally rather than by command. For Aristotle, slaves must be ruled so that the best interests of the slave are served—again a principle not dissimilar from that of Pythagoras, and again something which is not mentioned by the animal liberationists.

What animal liberationists do tell us is that Aristotle ignored the interests of animals. In *The Politics* Aristotle writes:

> Plants exist to give subsistence to animals, and animals to give it to men. Animals, when they are domesticated, serve for use as well as for food; wild animals, too, in most cases if not in all, serve to furnish man not only with food; but also with other comforts, such as the provision of clothing and similar aids to life. Accordingly, as nature makes nothing purposeless or in vain, all animals must have been made by nature for the sake of men.[5]

We must presume that the animal liberationists are not objecting to the statements about usage, food and clothing for they are incontrovertible statements of fact. The objection is, and should be, to the idea that animals exist for the sake of humans. Yet this, too, must be understood in the context of other statements. Aristotle not only recognizes the human as a social animal with similar if more advanced characteristics to the beast—about pleasure and pain for example—but also he recognizes that humankind can descend below the level of the animals. "Man, when perfected," Aristotle tells us, "is the best of animals; but if he be isolated from law and justice he is the worst of all."[6] He tells us further that "Tame animals have a better nature than wild, and it is better for all such animals that they should be ruled by man because they then get the benefit of preservation." Moreover, "the use which is made of the slave diverges but little from the use made of tame animals."[7] Given the requirements of the just treatment of slaves and the recognition of the interests of self-preservation among animals which deserve consideration we can only conclude—despite the paradoxes in Aristotle's writings—that Aristotle considered the ethical treatment of animals a responsibility—even if not one of the highest—of human behaviour. Aristotle was among those who took the initial steps to diminish the exploitation of both humans and animals and to recognize that humans shared a great deal with the animal realm. He knew that to demand everything was to gain nothing politically. To

---

5   Ernest Barker, ed., *The Politics of Aristotle* (London: Oxford, 1952), VIII, 11, 12, p. 21
6   Ibid., II, 15, p. 7. On pleasure and pain, see II, 11, p. 4.
7   Ibid., V, 6, 8, p. 13.

press for piecemeal improvements was to succeed. But if we are to think more kindly of Aristotle than do the animal liberationists, we should not fail to recognize that when Thomas Aquinas and other Roman Catholic thinkers borrowed freely from Aristotle they did so without regard to the nuances of Aristotle's thought.

Neither Judaism nor Christianity has served animal interests well, though perhaps the former rather better than the latter. Judaism, forming its ethical foundations earlier than Christianity, retained some of its recognition of the primitive condition of the human as one animal among others. Nonetheless, the belief in the Jews as the chosen people of God served effectively to deify man and raise him above his animal origins.

As Desmond Morris reminds us, "One of the great weaknesses of the Bible is that, between its covers, it is possible to find a quotation to justify almost any attitude."[8] We might add that the same is true of many religions, including the paradoxes to be found in Taoism and Buddhism, among others. Although there are undoubted discrepancies in the Bible, if any kindness at all toward animals is to be found it is almost exclusively in the Old Testament. To be sure, St. Paul is sometimes quoted as the exception. He referred to "One God who is Father of all, who *is* above all, and through all, and in you all."[9] Using a different translation, the animal liberationist Michael W. Fox offers "within all" as the concluding words, thus suggesting a kind of pantheism. Indeed, Fox explicitly refers to it as such.[10] Not only would a pantheistic interpretation be inconsistent with the 'man' dominance of Christianity, but also the idea of God as within each human rather than animal sits better with the general tenor of biblical exegesis and with St. Paul's renunciation in 1 Cor. 9, 9-10 of the Mosaic law on consideration for the interests of oxen.

According to Genesis, humans began as vegetarians (1, 29) but God also gave them dominion over all animals, vegetation and earth (1, 26). However, since God saw that His creation of the beasts and the earth "was good" (1, 25) we might be inclined to the view that "dominion" referred to our human responsibilities rather than our power to use as we wished. Humans may have begun as vegetarians, but they are

---

8 Desmond Morris, *The Animal Contract* (London: Virgin, 1990), p. 34.
9 Eph. 4, 6.
10 Michael W. Fox, *Inhumane Society* (New York: St. Martin's, 1990), p. 251. Fox actually calls the doctrine "pan*en*theism" and uses the term on several occasions. We do not know whether he is merely mistaken about the word or is referring to a doctrine other than pantheism of which we are unaware and to which we can find no reference.

depicted as meat-eaters immediately after the Fall, Adam and Eve being clothed in animal skins, Abel being a shepherd, and Noah and his sons being explicitly carnivorous. "Every moving thing that liveth shall be meat for you; even as the green herb have I given you all things" (9, 3). However, since Isaiah condemned animal sacrifices and indicated that at least in some visionary future all animalkind will treat well with each other (11, 6-8), and since Moses required a modicum of consideration for the welfare of oxen, it might be acknowledged that there was some minimal requirement of consideration for the interests of sentient beings. Indeed in Proverbs we are told explicitly that "A righteous man regardeth the life of his beast" (12, 10).

Christianity borrowed from Stoicism the idea of the inherent dignity and equality of all humans and united it with the concept of the uniqueness of humanity that it inherited from Judaism. The consequence was not beneficial to species other than human. While we should rejoice in the consequent recognition of the sanctity of all human life we must regret its dismissal of consideration for the interests of other species. Only humans had souls and only human life was sacred.

Jesus himself sent the 2,000 Gadarene swine, filled with the spirit of devils, hurtling into the sea to their destruction (Mark 5, 13). Now while we should be mindful of the willful and unnecessary destruction of innocent animal life, we should also recognize that pigs were themselves considered unclean and thus deemed one of the lower forms of animal life. The destruction of swine should not necessarily be regarded as carte blanche permission to give no consideration to the ethical treatment of animals at all. Unfortunately, that was often how it was interpreted by the Church Fathers.

St. Augustine refers to the "superstition" of refraining from "the killing of animals and the destruction of plants." He tells us that we share "no common rights" with the animals and plants and offers Jesus' destruction of the swine and the withering of the fruitless fig tree as justification. We should be mindful, though, that if there was a superstition there must have been some who were superstitious and thus cared for the animal realm.

While some of the Roman Stoic contemporaries of Jesus, notably Ovid and Seneca, showed a greater compassion for animals than the founder of Christianity, the Greek Plutarch (A.D. 46-120) was the first to advocate ethical treatment for animals as ends in themselves rather than merely because they may be the repository of human souls (as Pythagoras had argued). There were also unusual semi-Christian groups such as the Manicheans to whom the killing of animals was forbidden, but who also thought of women as the allies of Satan! A few of the early Christian saints (Basil, John Chrysostom, Isaac the Syrian and Neot) seemed more to follow Plutarch than Christ in their advocacy and practice of kindness to animals, and the founder of the Franciscan Order of Friars, St. Francis of Assisi, expressed the most complete (though not vegetarian) pantheistic identity with the larks and oxen—but also with the sun, moon, rocks and plants. But it was St. Augustine who held the centre of the stage and who prepared the path mainstream Christianity was to follow, at least until evangelical Christianity turned its attention to the abomination of slavery and the care and protection of animals and children in early nineteenth-century England.

Illustrators and distant monks had a greater respect for animals than did prominent theologians. That magnificent Celtic illuminated manuscript, *The Book of Kells*, dated by Sir Edward Sullivan at somewhere near but perhaps a little later than the close of the ninth century, contains such warm depictions of animals—in the Evangelical Symbols and the Genealogy of Christ, for example[11]—that one cannot but be impressed both by the significance of the animals to the illuminators and the occasionally alarming (so one might describe the creatures seen in the portrait of St. Matthew) but always sensitive miniatures. And while Professor Westwood in his *Palaeographia Sacra Pictoria* describes with some justice the drawing which includes the Virgin's dog-head throne as "puerile" it is not without a childlike appreciation. There is, in fact, an unresolved debate about whether the throne is based on the depiction of a dog or a lion since, as Sullivan has it, the "dog in the Bible had a notoriously evil reputation, being 'unclean' under the Old Law." But if the dog was esteemed less the lion must have been esteemed more. The use of animal representations throughout the manuscript must lead us to a positive conclusion both about the animals' perceived relationship to humankind and their general estimation. Nevertheless, one must be careful not to exaggerate the estimation of the animal realm. Animals were still predominantly instruments through which to exemplify human virtues and vices rather than ends in themselves.

St. Francis and *The Book of Kells* remained without practical influence on the thought of mainstream Catholicism. It was instead St. Francis's thirteenth-century contemporary, St. Thomas Aquinas, who married the works of the recently re-discovered Aristotle with Christian theology—without looking into the nuances of ethical treatment for animals to be found in Aristotle's writings.

Certainly, St. Thomas countered the pessimistic predominance of St. Augustine's influence in Christian teachings. He recognized the polity as a force for potential good rather than maintaining the prevailing view of the state as a necessary evil. He acknowledged that life on earth was

---

11 Edward Sullivan, *The Book of Kells* (New York: Crescent, 1986) (reprint of 2d ed. of 1920), Plates 4, 5, 12, 17.

a good in itself rather than merely a preparation for the afterlife. And he understood that there were goods which pertained to each individual as a person as well as those which pertained to membership in a community. The stage was set for a much more optimistic, benevolent and compassionate view of human nature. Unfortunately, that compassion did not proceed beyond the relationship of human to human.

Following Aristotle, Aquinas recognized that animals experience pain, but the only possible reason humans might have for kindness to animals is because it might promote the taking of pity on fellow humans. Moreover, we have no duty of charitable behaviour toward animals, in part because we can "have no fellow feeling with them." What a pity St. Thomas never met St. Francis!

If our passions might move us in some direction toward consideration for the interests of animals, according to Aquinas, our higher faculty, reason, requires us to resist the temptation:

> It matters not how man behaves to animals, because God has
> subjected all things to man's power and it is in this sense that
> the Apostle [St. Paul] says that God has no care for oxen,
> because God does not ask of man what he does with oxen or
> other animals.[12]

If that is the conclusion of reason it is no wonder that the Romantics elevated feeling over rationality! Oddly enough in a 1988 publication of selected writings of Aquinas on ethics and politics all reference to his views on animals is omitted. It is difficult to know whether the omissions are because animal issues are considered irrelevant to ethics or because the selector preferred to forget the Thomist line.

It is certainly going too far to condemn St. Thomas's views as a justification of man's dominant role in the world, and hence slavery, as do a number of animal liberationists. Christianity generally, and Aquinas particularly, proscribed slavery, though one might argue that the prevailing serfdom was merely a form of economic slavery. Still, it is unjustified to accuse Aquinas, as again do some, of being the influence which caused "the Christian Church" to embark "upon centuries of sanctified torment, torture and murder."[13] After all, St. Augustine had taken the same line eight centuries earlier. At worst Aquinas was only confirming the prevailing view.

There can be little doubt, however, that the opinions of St. Thomas contributed to the public torment of animals that was once again becoming popular with the gradual increase in economic prosperity which had been slowly returning since the eleventh century—although nothing ever again would repeat the atrocities of the Roman circus.

---

12 St. Thomas Aquinas, *Summa Theologiae* (Turin: Caramello, 1952), II, 1, 102.
13 Morris, *The Animal Contract*, p. 35.

Bull- and bear-baiting, dog-fighting, cock-fighting and bull-fighting have been among the more popular and debasing pastimes. But equally the treatment of domestic animals left a great deal to be desired. Oxen and asses were sometimes worked until they dropped. Farm animals were often fed no more than necessary. Even horses—with which humans have had such a close relationship—were treated predominantly as objects which had a task to perform for their masters. Nineteenth-century Romanticism eulogized the feudal and medieval age of chivalry, but it did so without any awareness of the cruelty perpetrated on the animal realm. The stories of idyllic associations are but legends, even if there were a few significant exceptions.

Bull- and bear-baiting involved tethering the wretched animals, which were then set upon by dogs trained for the purpose. The outcome was wagered upon by the avid spectators. At such events additional 'entertainment' was provided by baiting 'mad asses', setting alight fireworks attached to dogs, bulls, bears—or whatever other animal might be handy. City ordinances—in Leicester in the English midlands, for example—forbade butchers to slaughter bulls before they were baited. Royalty put on displays of such barbaric cruelties to titillate their courts and entertain ambassadors. Not until the seventeenth century were voices raised against the 'sport' and then with rather more concern for the manner in which it debased the human spirit than for the cruelty inflicted on the beasts—Samuel Pepys describing it as "a rude and nasty pleasure" and another diarist, John Evelyn, calling it a "rude and dirty pastime." In his *History of England* the nineteenth-century Whig historian Lord Macaulay tells us that the seventeenth-century "Puritan hated bearbaiting, not because it gave pain to the bear but because it gave pleasure to the spectators. Indeed, he generally contrived to enjoy the double pleasure of tormenting both spectators and bear."[14] In fact it was not uncommon for Puritans to kill the bears to prevent the baiting! In the few years when Puritans held sway in mid-seventeenth-century England they determined to punish adultery with death, outlawed wrestling matches, Maypoles, 'theatrical diversions' and looked ill on horse-racing, bowls and puppet shows. The playhouses were torn down, spectators fined and actors whipped. But bull- and bear-baiting were never outlawed.

Bull-cults were common in the centuries immediately before and after the advent of Christianity. They involved the demonstration of heroism and courage against the fearsome foe, culminating in the ritual killing of the animal to demonstrate the human conquest of nature. These 'sporting' events continued during the medieval period, with knights lancing the bulls from horseback. A sixteenth-century papal edict prohibited the practice—not, of course, because of the cruelty to

---

14 Lord Macaulay, *History of England* (London: Longman, 1854), 1: 161.

the bulls but because it decimated the ranks of courageous warriors available for dynastic and ecclesiastical ambitions. Somehow the knights evaded the ban, but after another edict in the eighteenth century bull-jousting was effectively prohibited to the aristocracy.

Bull-fighting was introduced to Spain by the Moors—probably as early as the eighth century—and ultimately became the Spanish national pastime, rivalling and sometimes surpassing soccer as the symbol of national pride. As a consequence of Spanish and Portuguese influence bull-fighting has also enjoyed a wide popularity, along with cock-fighting, in South America. In Spain 4,500 bulls or more are killed in the ring in a single year.

In Portugal laws prohibit the killing of the bulls in the ring, though they are butchered in the slaughter-house shortly after their taunting in the arena. Shamefully, bull-fighting in the Portuguese manner has recently been introduced into Canada and to date the efforts of law enforcement officers have failed to curtail this infamy. The courts have not so far concluded that bull-fighting is cruel! Indeed a 1991 Ontario court judgement declared bull-fighting a legitimate expression of the multiculturalism promoted by the Canadian government.

Chapter Two

The Status of Animals:
From the Age of Humanism
to the Twentieth Century

> We and the beasts are kin. Man has nothing that the animals
> have not at least a vestige of, the animals have nothing that
> man does not in some degree share . . . animals are creatures
> with wants and feelings differing in degree only from our own,
> they surely have their rights.
> — Ernest Thompson Seton, *Wild Animals*
> *I Have Known*, 1898

Human history is not merely a history of inhumanity to other species.
It is also a history of inhumanity to other races, other cultures, other
nations. From classical Greek xenophobia to the lunacy of the Nazi
Herrenvolk some have thought of themselves as superior in kind—in
intelligence, in culture, in blood—to others of the human world. Oddly,
perhaps inexplicably, increases in knowledge and learning have not
always served to diminish such attitudes. To the contrary, they have
sometimes fuelled them.

As the new learning, the impetus to the Renaissance and the age of
science, was emerging in the thirteenth century, one might have
expected the nascent humanism to espouse humanitarianism. It did not.
The most famous professor at the newly founded University of Paris,
Albertus Magnus, teacher of Aquinas, asked himself *utrum pygmaei sint
homines?* (whether pygmies are men?). His answer was a decided 'no'!
Although they had the faculty of speech, since they possessed neither
art nor philosophy, lacked societal organization and a moral code, at
least according to Albert, they could not be counted as people. The
obvious implication was that since they could not be counted as people
they could not have the rights of people, nor expect to be treated as
people. If such was the attitude to pygmies—who, incidentally, Albert
had never seen and quite obviously knew nothing about—what hope
was there for the animal realm?

Fortunately, for at least some animals, the scholars had less
influence than they might have hoped. Some people do not appear to
have followed their reason—their reason according to Aquinas that
is—but instead succumbed to the temptation of listening to the
inclinations of their passions. They treated their animals with a
modicum of decency, at least in France. The magnificent miniature

21

paintings of the prayer book (*Les Très Riches Heures*) of the Duc de Berry give us a rather different view of the reality of animal conditions from what one might have expected from a reading of the philosophers. Sometimes a picture is truly worth a thousand words.

These wonderful works of art, painted by the Limbourg brothers in the early years of the fifteenth century, include depictions of animals in a variety of functions. In the January painting of a gift-giving ceremony we see the duke's pampered miniature dogs roaming the table, another well-fed larger hunting dog is being lovingly tended by a servant. In the wintry February farm scene we are offered a laden ass being driven to town—burdened, but clearly not over-burdened. Some three dozen sheep are huddled in a sheepfold, purposely built to protect them against the elements. The roof of the fold is in some disrepair and the fold is only just sufficient in size to house the sheep. A pet dog lies at the feet of farm-workers, sharing the heat of the fire with them. March depicts an ox pulling a plough—a well-fed and contented-looking ox, mind you. In the distance a shepherd is jovially encouraging his dog to tend the sheep. Almost all the paintings of the months portray contented, well-treated animals, although the September oxen show their ribs and the October rider of a horse drawing a small furrow rake wields a whip. These certainly are not the scenes one would expect if the philosophers had been taken seriously. Perhaps it was a boon beyond measure that only a very select few could read!

Now one might want to retort that the duke was a rich man who could afford to be kind to his animals and that the artists would want to flatter both reality and the duke who paid their commission. Quite possibly. But we should recognize that even if the paintings are a little less than honest—and personally we doubt it, given the Limbourgs accuracy of detail along with the depiction of the whip and ribs—they would still indicate that there was an awareness that animals ought to be treated with consideration. After all, the February farm scene showed there was some concern for the well-being of the sheep. The sheepfold lies within a stockaded area from which they could not have wandered. The fold was obviously built for no other purpose than to provide them with a place to eat and sleep, where they could be protected against the worst that winter could offer even if the fold was not adequately maintained. This may not be a representation of the best of all possible animal worlds, but it does show both that animals played a major role in the lives of humans and that there was some natural propensity toward a consideration of their comforts. As Sir Francis Bacon put it, "The inclination of *Goodness* is imprinted deeply in the nature of Man; insomuch, that if it issue not towards Men, it will take unto other living creatures."[1] To the extent that human interests are

---

1 Francis Bacon, *Essays* (London: R. Chiswell et al., 1706), p. 31 (written ca. 1600).

not threatened, so humans have a natural propensity to respect the interests of other sentient beings—so long as gamesters, theologians and philosophers do not divert them from their propensities!

Of all the major figures of the new humanism it is the artist, sculptor and engineer Leonardo da Vinci who most dissented from the prevailing anthropocentrism, going so far apparently as to become a vegetarian. Giorgio Vasari, da Vinci's first biographer, writing in 1550 some 31 years after the Florentine's death, tells us:

> He was so pleasing in conversation, that he attracted to himself the hearts of men. And although he possessed, one might say, nothing, and worked little, he always kept servants and horses, in which latter he took much delight, and particularly in all other animals, which he managed with the greatest love and patience; and this he showed when often passing by the places where birds were sold, for, taking them with his own hand out of their cages, and having paid to those who sold them the price that was asked, he let them fly away into the air, restoring them to their lost liberty. For which reason nature was pleased so to favour him, that, wherever he turned his thought, brain, and mind, he displayed such divine power in his works, that, in giving them their perfection, no one was ever his peer in readiness, vivacity, excellence, beauty, and grace.[2]

We should not only delight in da Vinci's deviation from the prevailing philosophic mentality. We should note equally Vasari's remarks about nature's pleasure and the divine power. We should recognize Vasari's pleasure at da Vinci's humanitarianism and the expectation that his audience will too. This tells us that there was a common recognition that it was natural and in accord with God's will to treat the animal world kindly.

Unfortunately, when we read further in Vasari, we find that da Vinci was not always as kind as his reputation would suggest:

> Leonardo carried to a room of his own into which no one entered save himself alone, lizards great and small, crickets, serpents, butterflies, grasshoppers, bats, and other strange kinds of suchlike animals, out of the number of which, variously put together, he formed a great ugly creature, most horrible and terrifying . . . and so long did he labour over making it, that the stench of dead animals in that room was past bearing.[3]

---

2 Giorgio Vasari, *The Great Masters*, ed. Michael Sonino, trans. Gaston Du C. de Vere (New York: Park Lane, 1988), pp. 93-94.
3 Ibid., p. 96.

For da Vinci, the beautiful animals were to be admired and respected, 'ugly', creeping, crawling, slithering creatures were not. For da Vinci, as for later generations, including our own, there is a natural hierarchy of animal value relating to beauty and complexity. Indeed throughout human history there has been a degree of paradox about attitudes to animals even among those who show them the greatest respect. It is a paradox which the animal liberationists have overlooked in their depiction of Western civilization as a history of human cruelty to animals and which the defenders of the naturalists have overlooked by portraying their kindness alone.

Sir Walter Scott, the most widely read author of the nineteenth century—"the troubadour of the times," Balzac calls him—was an avid hunter. Yet he said of the porpoises, "what fine fellows they are! I have the greatest respect for them; I would as soon kill a man as a phoca."[4] Indeed, in Scott's *The Antiquary* there is a notable battle in which the porpoises emerge the lauded victors over Captain McIntyre.

This paradoxical attitude is not a rarity but a common occurrence among naturalists. Gilbert White, the author of the first detailed ethological study, *The Natural History of Selborne*, of 1789, kept stuffed specimens of the animals he studied. Yet he was described by his editor not only as the "Father of Nature study" but also as a "sincere lover of Nature."[5] (He also planted four lime trees in front of his home to hide the view of the butcher's yard opposite!)

John James Audubon was not only an outstanding naturalist but a committed hunter. He described himself as "fond of shooting, fishing and riding, and [as having] a passion for raising all sorts of fowls"[6]—to be shot, of course! In all his renowned bird paintings Audubon demonstrated an affinity for the objects of his study. Yet he also amused himself by killing many of them for sport. He also slaughtered squirrels, raccoons, opossums and reptiles as decorations for his home (he was in fact at one time employed as a taxidermist). It offends our modern sensibilities that he shot the birds of his studies in order to paint them.

Nineteenth-century novels—Disraeli's *Endymion*, for example—are replete with stories of country clerics collecting examples of the objects of their naturalist interest. "The rector had written an essay on

---

4 J.G. Lockhart, *Memoirs of the Life of Sir Walter Scott, Bart.*, 7 vols. (Edinburgh: Cadell, 1837), 5:25. Phocae are in fact seals, but it is clear that chief commissioner Adam, who reported the statement, and Lockhart himself thought that porpoises were meant, even though Scott himself in chapter 30 of *The Antiquary* makes it clear that he knows phocae are seals. Porpoise or seal, the point remains.

5 Gilbert White, *The Natural History of Selborne* (London: Cassell, 1908), p. 4. The editor's name is not given.

6 Quoted by Sheila Buff in John James Audubon, *Audubon's Birds of North America* (Secaucus: Wellfleet, 1990), p. 3.

squirrels," Disraeli tells us, "and showed them a glass containing that sportive animal in all its frolic forms." Yet Disraeli insists that the rector possessed a readily recognizable "love of nature."[7] That such wanton destruction of life abounded should not surprise us. What should astonish us—a fact which requires explanation rather than mere condemnation—is that it was those who had the greatest interest in, and apparent respect for, these creatures who perpetrated such frivolous acts of destruction upon them. Keith Thomas, the author of the renowned *Man and the Natural World*, describes the family home of the great historian George Macaulay Trevelyan as "reflect[ing] the nature-loving preoccupations of its owners" and offers as evidence the home's contents, which included books on natural history, paintings of flowers and "stuffed birds." Thomas, despite his own affection for the natural world, does not notice the contradiction.

Those who engaged in the nefarious hobbies of butterfly collecting and bird-nesting—popular pastimes at least to the midst of the twentieth century—thought of themselves as demonstrating a great affinity for nature. At the close of the nineteenth century voices began to be raised long and hard against these practices. But well into the twentieth century J.A. Henderson in his *Nest and Eggs* still thought it appropriate to remind his readers that "A mere collection of faded eggs, lying in a drawer with labels on them, is not a very interesting thing; and the getting of it together is inevitably fraught with some suffering to the birds, for of course their loss is far greater than the collector's gain."[8]

Much as it may surpass the comprehension of most of those dedicated to the interests of animal welfare, we should be mindful of the fact that many of those who engage in sport hunting today talk of the awe and respect they feel for their adversary while dedicated to its murder. There can be scarcely a single book on hunting or angling which does not make reference to the love of nature, the beauty of the deer or the admirable characteristics of the prey. But such ambivalence is not restricted to the hunting community. It is amply demonstrated, for example, in Richard Jefferies's *The Open Air*, an early twentieth-century work ostensibly written to glorify the wonders of nature. After describing the "handsome" but dead hare "overtaken by the cartridge," Jefferies tells us that "Even in the excitement of sport regret cannot but be felt at the sight of those few drops of blood about the mouth which indicate that all this beautiful workmanship must now cease to be. Had

---

7 Benjamin Disraeli, *Endymion*, 3 vols. (London: Longman's Green, 1880), 1: 231, 287.

8 A.H. Blaikie and J.A. Henderson, *Nest and Eggs* (London: Nelson, undated but probably ca. 1915).

he escaped the huntsman would not have been displeased."[9] Traditionally, affection for horses and hounds accompanied the hunting of foxes—and even enduring the wiping of the bloody brush across one's face. The term 'sportsman' was once reserved for those who waged an unequal war against the prey—rarely did the 'sportsman' lose his life, almost always the 'game'. Given the term's connotation one might have hoped for a 'sportsman' to choose a level playing field! Hunting as a 'sport' is like a game of baseball in which only one side gets up to bat.

In his mid-nineteenth-century *Homes and Haunts of the British Poets*, William Howitt considered the "sweet and glorious spirits" of the finer poets as encouragement to lesser souls to "live, not as mere material machines; not as animal existences, as brutes." Such literary luminaries are deemed "as essential to the aliment and the progress of our intellectual being as the light, the morning dew of summer, the morning and the evening star."[10] Nature is glorified but, incomprehensibly, the animal realm is not recognized as a part of nature! Animals are likened to material machines, mere existences; they are but brutes. Indeed, generally when several of the Romantics lauded nature they thought rather more of the lakes, the trees, the mountains, the sky, the sea and flowers than they did of animal wildlife.

It is indeed a curious fact that the earlier history of book publishing, especially of the illustrated variety, contains a great deal more devoted to flora than to fauna, although that may merely reflect the importance of plants as primitive medicine. The history of animal welfare, of improving attitudes to our animal relatives, is itself a paradox. Progress is not achieved lineally. But, as Polybius, Hegel and Marx all recognized, change is dialectical, successively including and transcending contradictions. The fact that contradictions still exist should encourage attempts at comprehension rather than despair. Indeed current contradictions among hunters, anglers, and animal trophy collectors cry out for the research of some ambitious doctoral student in psychology.

If ambivalence pervades the times closest to our own it was of somewhat greater scarcity in the Renaissance. Da Vinci was in a decided minority among intellectuals in giving any serious consideration to the interests of animals. The Renaissance was far more concerned to rescue man from his dominance by the Church hierarchy and its theologians. If man was to be made the centre of nature and of the universe there was little time to waste on inferior beings. To be sure, there were occasional exceptions to the general rule. Giordano Bruno, for example, deemed both human and animal of but little significance in comparison with the infinity of God. And Michel de Montaigne

---

9   Richard Jefferies, *The Open Air* (London: Chatto and Windus, 1904), p. 127.
10 William Howitt, *Homes and Haunts of the British Poets*, 3d ed. (London: George Routledge, n.d.), p. 292 (2d ed., 1847).

thought cruelty to animals a wrong in itself, quite apart from any effect it might have on promoting cruelty among humans.

If life was less than idyllic for the animal realm before the seventeenth century it then took a decided turn for the worse—thanks in no small measure to the scientific method of René Descartes.[11] The new science of mechanics was proving so successful for the study of matter that it was convenient to assume that by applying its principles to the understanding of human behaviour similar advances could be made. The very problem with the treatment of humans as 'matter' is that the human then has to be understood as a machine, as a being whose behaviour has causes rather than motives, a brain but no mind. It was left to Thomas Hobbes in the middle of the seventeenth century to take such a thoroughgoing materialist view of human as matter to its logical conclusions.

Descartes, earlier in the century, hypothesized a duality of matter and spirit. Descartes suggested that while the rest of the universe consisted of matter, human beings were conscious, and since consciousness could not originate in matter, the human, and only the human, had a soul, which was given by God. For Descartes, since animals had no immortal soul they could have no consciousness, thus—contrary to all experience!—they could experience neither pleasure nor pain. They were mere machines—complex machines made by God, of course, but machines nonetheless. Thereby was solved one of the great theological problems—how could God have animals suffer if they had neither participated in Adam's sin nor had any expectation of an eternal reward? The answer was simple—they did not suffer. They experienced no pain!

Descartes claimed that his opinion was "not so much cruel to animals as indulgent to men ... since it absolves them from the suspicion of crime when they eat or kill animals." While we might recoil in horror at the unpalatable conclusions of Cartesian science we should not fail to notice the bright side. If Descartes felt it necessary to offer a justification there must have been at least some who believed that cruelty to animals was unacceptable. If there was the suspicion of a crime this suggests that there was a latent propensity to recognize that humans bore some responsibility for the just treatment of the animal realm.

Since animal experimentation was just in its infancy and since anaesthesia was unknown, the researchers had a ready-made explanation for the abominable cruelty they appeared to be inflicting on the animals they were vivisecting. Their consciences were appeased because what seemed like pain wasn't pain at all! They were merely triggering a

11 For our understanding of the significance of Descartes we are indebted to Singer, *Animal Liberation*, pp. 200ff.

spring in the machine on which they were working! Descartes himself
was a vivisectionist in the furtherance of his anatomical studies. And
Cartesianism gave both himself and his fellow researchers a convenient
justification.

An eye-witness account of experiments at the Jansenist seminary at
Port-Royal in France at the end of the seventeenth century tells us that
the scientists:

> administered beatings to the dogs with perfect indifference,
> and made fun of those who pitied the creatures as if they felt
> pain. They said the animals were clocks; that the cries they
> emitted when struck were only the noise of a little spring that
> had been touched, but that the whole body was without feeling.
> They nailed poor animals upon boards by their four paws to
> vivisect them and see the circulation of the blood which was a
> great subject of conversation.[12]

Horrendously cruel as we must find such behaviour let us again not fail
to notice not only that at least one contemporary felt it necessary to
speak out against the barbarism but also that there must have been a
sufficient number "who pitied the creatures" to evoke a Pavlovian
response from the experimenters.

Nor should we fail to note that while such cruelties were practised
in France nascent America was taking a different route. If Puritanism
was unkind to bears in England it nonetheless decreed in the Massachusetts Bay Colony in 1641 that "No man shall exercise any Tiranny or
Crueltie towards any bruite Creature which are usuallie kept for man's
use." Moreover, beasts of burden were entitled to a rest period during
their labours. Even earlier, in 1616, a proclamation was issued in
Bermuda "against the spoyle and havock" perpetrated against the
cahows threatened with extinction in particular, but also to protect all
birds subject to "stoneing, and all kinds of murtherings." A law was
passed to protect nesting birds in 1621 but to no avail. By 1629 or
thereabouts, the cahow had disappeared.

From the seventeenth century onwards the mechanistic view of
humankind has retained its force—but in somewhat peculiar and quite
divergent ways. There are still a number of social scientists—increasingly less common we suspect—who do their utmost to
make their research as mechanistic as possible (calling it 'science' not
mechanics), who treat humans as objects whose behaviour is to be
explained rather than understood, announce that all values are relative

---

12   Quoted in Singer, *Animal Liberation*, pp. 201-202.

and without objective foundation—and then with the most palpable contradiction proceed to denounce as unjust this or that government measure, this or that policy of some group or other—all of which is not allowed to them on the 'scientific' principles they espouse!

One of the expected consequences of treating humans as "matter-in-motion" (Hobbes's phrase) is that all living phenomena come in principle to be understood as essentially similar. Thus the human and the animal can be readily acknowledged as of a kind, all their behaviour being subject to explanation in terms of the pursuit of pleasure and the aversion to pain.

Reason, for Hobbes, is subsidiary to the passions. Its sole purpose is to enable the passions, which determine our ends, to achieve their goals. Ideas are merely "Scouts and Spies to range abroad, and find a Way to the things Desired." For the Classics and the Scholastics it was the faculty of reason which differentiated man from the beast. Hobbes, and scientism, relegated human reason to a subsidiary function, rendering humans closer to the animals. Unfortunately, the humans were no longer humans; they had become machines.

Hobbes talks about rights as emerging from our self-preservation in the state of nature. 'Good', 'beautiful' and the like are merely names we apply to what is pleasing to us. 'Good' and 'beautiful' do not exist in nature. There is, then, no objective moral sense, merely rights we possess in relation to our primitive condition. Again the human was but an animal, and a not very appealing one at that.

The problem was that, at least in the early part of the age of science, very few philosophers bothered to draw such conclusions. Instead of recognizing the similarity between human and beast (albeit at the lowest possible level) the new age of science concentrated all its attention on 'the individual' it had just emancipated from the fetters of feudal oppression.

In part this was due to the distinction Hobbes made between humans and animals. Whereas animals are naturally social creatures humans are not. Humans act from individual self-interest. Society for humans is artificial, not natural. Humans drive to excel and thus to achieve pre-eminence over others. Individuals thus only have private ends by nature, whereas animals have communal ends by nature. In part this serves as an explanation as to why some humans dominate other humans and all humans other species. But it also serves as a justification. If this is what humankind is by nature it cannot be changed. It must be accepted. Thus, in a roundabout way, the legitimacy of human refusal to consider the interests of other species is thereby justified.

Although the scientism of Hobbes proved ultimately less than persuasive as a philosophy, it remained, in slightly more sophisticated form, the basis of liberal hedonist ideology until very recently, and probably still dominates cynical intellectual circles. Such scientism, while initially serving but to continue the prejudice against the animal realm, provided the intellectual basis for the version of utilitarianism which contributed to the emancipation of the animal.

If the age of Enlightenment spawned the Reign of Terror in France it also produced a somewhat less arrogant and rather more tolerant attitude in Britain. Even in France, though, the tyranny of Robespierre was tempered by the eminent humanity of Voltaire, who called the animal experimenters "barbarians" and proclaimed, "Answer me, mechanist, has Nature arranged all the springs of feeling in this animal to the end that he might not feel?"[13]

It was in Britain, though, that philosophical attitudes began to change sufficiently that they had an impact on legislation itself. The Scottish conservative utilitarian David Hume, writing in 1751, expressed a growing sentiment, occasionally muted but always present in some degree in societal history, when he wrote that we are "bound by the laws of humanity to give gentle usage to these creatures." Unfortunately, some animal liberationists have reacted rather unkindly to Hume. While they acknowledge that Hume's view reflects a greater benevolence to animals, they seem to think that Hume's apparent approval of the 'use' of animals implies treating them as means rather than ends.[14] Yet Hume's "usage" is not equivalent to 'use' in the sense of employing an object for a purpose but has the meaning of customary treatment. Hume is instructing us that it should be our custom to treat animals with kindness.

The animal liberationists, or at least some of them, reserve their loudest applause for the liberal utilitarian Jeremy Bentham. While Bentham's philosophical system retains all the problems of a materialistic hedonism—epistemologically Bentham is no improvement on Hobbes—nonetheless Bentham was moved to recognize the tyranny imposed on animals throughout human history. In his *Introduction to the Principles of Morals and Legislation* of 1789 Bentham wrote: "The day *may* come when the rest of the animal creation may acquire those rights which never could have been withholden from them but by the hand of tyranny." Bentham reasoned that if "the blackness of the skin" does not give us a right to exploitation, neither does the number of legs, the amount of reason or the degree of conversability:

> A full grown horse or dog is beyond comparison a more
> rational as well as a more conversible animal, than an infant of
> a day or a week or even a month old. But suppose the case

---

13   Ibid., p. 202.
14   Ibid.

were otherwise, what would it avail? The question is not, can they *reason*? nor, can they *talk*? but, can they *suffer*?[15]

Now, Aristotelians would respond that it was the potential for reason rather than its immediate presence that mattered, that it was the purpose, the telos, of nature that placed the human above the beasts. But in fact the issue was becoming less a philosophical one than a practical one. Bentham was the philosophical mentor of an influential group known as the Philosophical Radicals, led by the Scottish Presbyterian James Mill, a reputed philosopher in his own right and the father of John Stuart Mill. He was also a committed disciple of Jeremy Bentham. This group held considerable sway among a minority of influential parliamentarians—though we should not imagine that animal issues were high on their agenda (nor on Jeremy Bentham's). Such issues as penal and parliamentary reform were of far greater significance to them. Still, the tide was turning.

In fact the Philosophical Radicals had no monopoly on the recognition that animals were entitled to consideration. A generation earlier the conservative Edmund Burke had in fact gone somewhat further than Bentham and hinted at an acknowledgement not merely of individual animal rights but of a communitarian relationship between humankind and animal. For Burke, the source of the relationship was beyond comprehension but it was nonetheless a part of God's reality:

> When other animals give us a sense of joy and pleasure in beholding them (and there are many that do so), they inspire us with sentiments of tenderness and affection toward their persons; we like to have them near, and we enter willingly into a kind of relation with them, unless we should have strong reasons to the contrary. But to what end, in many cases, this was designed, I am unable to discover; for I see not greater reason for a connection between man and several animals who are attired in so engaging a manner, than between him and some others who entirely want this attraction or possess it in a far weaker degree.[16]

As Burke understood, there is indeed a relationship between human and animal but not equally with all species, as the life of da Vinci so graphically demonstrated. Nor was da Vinci's experience an uncommon one. As Estelle Hurll, in her biography of the animal painter Edwin Landseer wrote, he "looked upon most animals with the eyes of the

---

15 Jeremy Bentham, *An Introduction to the Principles of Morals and Legislation*, ed. Burns and Hart (London: Methuen, 1982), 17, 4, b, p. 282.

16 Edmund Burke, *A Philosophical Enquiry into the Origin of our Ideas of the Sublime and Beautiful* (London: Rivington, 1812), p. 67. (First published 1756.)

artist, the poet and the natural historian, but the dog alone he painted
as a friend."

What Burke appears to recognize is that which Aquinas and Richard
Hooker had explicitly denied—that there is some kind of community of
sentient beings. Following St. Thomas, Hooker had insisted that:

> Between man and beasts there is no possibility of sociable com-
> munion. The chiefest instrument of human communion . . . is
> speech, because thereby we impart mutually one to another the
> conceits of our reasonable understanding. And for that cause
> seeing beasts are not hereof capable, forasmuch as with them
> we can use no such conference, they being in degree, although
> above other creatures on earth to whom nature hath denied
> sense, yet lower than to be sociable companions of man to
> whom nature hath given reason;[17]

Today we would, of course, acknowledge that animals do indeed
possess sense and reason. What Burke understood was that lack of a
common language was no bar to a relationship. Community stems from
affection, from identity, not from linguistic communication per se. After
all, infants are not excluded from human bonding prior to learning to
speak. It is indeed community with other beings, not necessarily
conversing with them, which increases our obligations to them. The
abstract utilitarian individual 'right' is less important than the
communitarian belonging. The one requires responsibilities by virtue of
an abstract moral concept, the other by virtue of a common relationship.

In 1800 a vain effort was made in the British legislature to outlaw
bull- and bear-baiting. The time was not yet ripe. Not only were the
parliamentarians far more concerned with the war with France, but they
could not understand the purpose of the measure. They treated it not
as a move to protect the welfare of animals but as yet another Puritan
attempt to interfere with the time-honoured pleasures and pastimes of
the English.

In 1792 Mary Wollstonecraft wrote her *Vindication of the Rights of
Woman*, the first serious attempt since classical Greece to provide a
philosophical justification for according equal rights to both genders. In
response a Cambridge academic, Thomas Taylor, wrote a *Vindication of
the Rights of Brutes*. If women were entitled to be treated equally with
men, Taylor argued, then exactly the same arguments could be used to
justify rights for horses and dogs. Of course, Taylor was not suggesting
that animals should have rights. Gender equality was so preposterous
an idea to Taylor and most of his contemporaries that it could be

---

17   Richard Hooker, *Of the Laws of Ecclesiastical Polity*, I,X,12, in *The Works of Mr.
   Richard Hooker* (Oxford: Clarendon, 1865), 1: 194-95. (First published ca. 1597.)

readily dismissed by comparison with an idea even more preposterous. Still, if woman was not yet the equal of man, woman's influence was increasing. A kinder, gentler, more humane attitude was beginning to be felt. Women writers were coming to be regarded as legitimate, though it was thought that they should restrict themselves to writing for the young, preferably on topics of religious and moral education. Charles Lamb, for example, acknowledged "the deep personal and artistic communion" between himself and his sister, Mary. "Lamb always maintained, and justly, that she wrote the best stories in *Mrs. Leicester's School* and her share in the delightful *Poetry for Children*," so we are told by R. Brimley Johnson in the Introduction to Talfourd's *Letters and the Life of Lamb*.[18] But Mary's "best stories" were, of course, only written for children.

In the vein of moral enlightenment for the young, Priscilla Wakefield wrote a remarkable little book known as *Instinct Displayed*. But the full title is more instructive: *Instinct Displayed, in a Collection of Well-Authenticated Facts exemplifying the Extraordinary Sagacity of Various Species of the Animal Creation*. The book may have been written for children; the preface was not. It exemplifies the philosophical conundrum into which the scientism of Descartes and Hobbes had led the human mind. Moreover, it hinted at how the conundrum could be resolved—allowing the faculty of reason to animals. It is worth quoting the preface at some length:

> The distinction between reason and instinct are difficult to ascertain: to define their exact limits has exercised the ingenuity of the most profound philosophers, hitherto without success. Nor can the learned agree as to the nature of that wonderful quality, that guides every creature to take the best means of procuring its own enjoyment, and of preserving its species by the most admirable care of its progeny. Some degrade the hidden impulse to a mere mechanical operation; whilst others exalt it to a level with reason, that proved prerogative of man. There are, indeed, innumerable gradations of intelligence, as of the other qualities with which the animal kingdom is endowed; in like manner as the different orders of beings approach each other so closely, and are so curiously united by links, partaking of the nature of those above and those below, that it requires a discerning eye to know what rank to assign them. . . . Reason and instinct have obvious differences; yet the most intelligent animals in some of their actions, approach so near to reason, that it is really surprising

---

18 R. Talfourd, *Letters and the Life of Lamb* (London: Sisley's Ltd., undated), pp. vii-viii.

how small the distinction is. . . . My motive has been to excite
attention to the propensities of animals, as a powerful antidote
to treating them with cruelty or neglect, so often practised by
the ignorant and thoughtless. . . . If by this small collection of
instances of animal sagacity, I have added a book of entertainment to the common stock, that neither corrupts the minds,
nor vitiates the taste of the rising generation, my endeavours
will be rewarded.[19]

Animals have intelligence and sagacity even though they do not have
reason! It is certainly no great step from there to conclude that
intelligence is but the capacity to reason and that sagacity is the union
of reason with experience. If the time was not yet quite ripe for Charles
Darwin, the attitudinal preconditions were present, especially since the
direct biological relationship between human and animal was now
openly and freely acknowledged. The distinction between mind and
matter, consciousness and unconsciousness, no longer predominated.

But if the time for Darwin had not yet come, the time had come for
legislation to protect animals and establish societies to enforce the
legislation. It was in 1824 that the first animal welfare society was
founded—the Society for the Prevention of Cruelty to Animals
(S.P.C.A.) established in Britain by Richard Martin, M.P., customarily
known in parliamentary circles as 'Humanity Dick'. It was he, too, who
managed to have the first modern animal cruelty act legislated—and
even then only after his first attempt was roundly ridiculed by his fellow
parliamentarians and was defeated. His second effort—which succeeded
in 1821—demonstrated greater practical wisdom. The bill was presented
as though it was designed to protect the interests of animal owners
rather than the animals themselves.

The success of the measure had little directly to do with any
influence of Benthamism and the Philosophical Radicals. Instead the
legislation stemmed directly from the humanitarian impulses which lay
behind the evangelical protestantism of the period. William Wilberforce,
one of their number and the force behind the abolition of slavery both
in Britain and the Empire, was one of Martin's strongest supporters.
Nonetheless, the influence of the Philosophical Radicals on the thinking
of the time encouraged a parliamentary success which otherwise could
not have been achieved.

The function of the S.P.C.A. was both to prosecute under the new
animal protection laws and also, as Martin said, "to alter the moral
feelings of the country." In 1824 alone 63 offenders were prosecuted,
mainly from London's Smithfield Market. Due to the efforts of Martin

---

19   Priscilla Wakefield, *Instinct Displayed*, 4th ed. (London: Harvey and Dalton, 1821),
     pp. vii-xii.

and his allies, legislation to protect bulls, domestic animals and cab horses followed in the 1830s which in effect improved conditions in slaughterhouses and outlawed bull- and bear-baiting and cock-fighting. In 1838 occurred the first fatality among animal legislation enforcers, when S.P.C.A. Inspector James Piper died from injuries he received in trying to stop an illegal cock-fight in progress at Hanworth in Middlesex. In 1840, Queen Victoria, who had given her support to the society in 1835 when she was still a princess and when the legitimacy of animal protection services were only slowly beginning to be recognized, conferred the 'Royal' prefix on the society.

In 1840 there were five full-time inspectors, all based in London. Following a bequest of £1,000 two years later, four branches each acquired an inspector (two in the west of England, one in the midlands and one in the northeast). By 1990 there were 208 branches throughout England and Wales and 270 inspectors.

The United States had to wait until 1865 for a similar organization, when Mr. Henry Bergh founded the New York Society for the Prevention of Cruelty to Animals. Returning from a diplomatic appointment in Russia—where he had been noted for his "active," if unofficial," interference on behalf of the right of animals to kind treatment"[20] according to a contemporary newspaper—he became acquainted en route with the Earl of Harrowby, president of the R.S.P.C.A. Based on the British model, his society was given the power of prosecution and arrest by statute in 1866. Between 1866 and 1869 nine other animal welfare organizations were instituted elsewhere in the U.S.A. In 1870 the Missouri and then the Washington, D.C. "Humane Societies" were chartered, thus beginning the use of that term in North America for animal welfare organizations.

In Canada the first organizations were in Montreal in 1869, in Ottawa in 1871 and the Ontario S.P.C.A. in Toronto in 1873—they were all S.P.C.A.'s. In 1887 the name 'Humane Society' was given earnest consideration at the founding of the Hamilton animal welfare society but was rejected on division. Later in the same year the Toronto Humane Society was founded, the first Canadian organization to bear the epithet 'humane'. The Calcutta, India, S.P.C.A. was probably the most effective in the world. In 1886 it prosecuted 7,125 cases and secured 7,042 convictions—indicating, of course, that the supposed Hindu concern for animal welfare was more aspiration than reality if there were that many instances of cruelty.

After 1874 some North American animal welfare groups expanded their objects of concern to include the welfare of children and occasionally women and the elderly. Thereafter a number of existing organizations changed their name to 'Humane Society' and many new

---

20 *Boston Transcript* (March 1888).

ones adopted that name rather than S.P.C.A. In 1877 the International Humane Association (later the American Humane Association) was chartered following a meeting in Cleveland. By 1922, 307 of the American Humane Association's 539 active member societies were involved in child as well as animal welfare, though as governments took over the children's welfare functions that number gradually declined. Today no animal welfare organizations are engaged in child protective services.[21]

Although animal welfare organizations pervaded the Anglo-Saxon nations in the second half of the nineteenth century they had less success in the Roman Catholic world in general (although there were advances in the Netherlands, which had a small but significant Catholic minority, in Germany, half Catholic, and in France, predominantly Catholic).[22]

Pope Pius IX (1846-78) prevented the opening of a proposed animal welfare centre in Rome on the grounds that it would divert attention from human welfare concerns. The *Catholic Dictionary* of 1897 stated unequivocally that animals "have no rights. The brutes are made for man who has the same right over them which he has over plants and stones. . . . [it is] lawful to put them to death, or to inflict pain upon them, for any good or reasonable end . . . even for the purpose of recreation."[23] Had the world stood still for Catholicism in the more than 200 years since Descartes and Port-Royal? For the Catholic Church the pain of animals still seemed to be, as Descartes's researchers believed, unoiled machinery creaking.

In fact it was not two centuries but three. As late as 1984, Pope John Paul II avowed, "it is certain that animals are intended for man's use," reiterating Immanuel Kant's claim that "Animals are not self-conscious, and are there merely as a means to an end. The end is man." Kant and the Catholic Church were reiterating what had been conventional wisdom in the Tudor and Georgian periods. By 1987, however, a change of direction was in evidence. The Papal Encyclical "On Social Con-cerns" advocated "respect for the beings which constitute the natural world." No longer were animals solely intended for human use. Instead, we are told, "one cannot use with impunity the different categories of beings . . . simply as one wishes, according to one's economic needs. On the contrary, one must take into account the nature of each being and its mutual connection in an ordered system."

---

21 Much of the information on which the preceding three paragraphs are based was kindly provided by Phil Arkow of the Humane Society of the Pikes Peak Region, Colorado.

22 See, for example, Thomas Jackson, *Our Dumb Companions* (London: S.W. Partridge, n.d. but ca. 1867), p. iv.

23 Quoted in Morris, *Animal Contract*, p. 36.

In 1859 Charles Darwin published his *Origin of Species*. By common consent among most animal supporters it was the book which presaged a revolution in human thinking about our relationship to other animals. For example, Michael W. Fox tells us with perhaps some exaggeration that, "As the concept of human superiority is, as Charles Darwin emphasized, logically and ethically untenable, then the only grounds for contending that it is humankind's right to exploit animals are based on custom and utility."[24] Even more significant for our understanding of our biological and evolutionary relationship to other animals were Darwin's *Descent of Man* (1871) and *The Expression of Emotions in Man and Animals* (1872).

Important as Charles Darwin's writing was, it should be understood both that his theories were not quite so novel as is sometimes imagined and that some of the consequences of Darwin's ideas were in some respects quite detrimental to the animal realm. Moreover, Darwin did not escape the limitations of prevailing scientism quite as completely as his admirers suggest.

Charles Darwin's grandfather, Erasmus Darwin, published his *Zoonomia* in parts from 1794-96. In it he explained organic life according to evolutionary principles, and it was on the basis of these findings that Charles Darwin began collecting his natural history data during his five years as naturalist aboard the *Beagle*. Evolutionary concepts can be found among a number of classical Greek authors including Thales, Empedocles, Anaximander—who deemed humans to be descended from fish—and Aristotle but from Roman times until the middle of the eighteenth century the Christian belief in the special creation of human and each other species held predominant sway. The great Swedish botanist and taxonomist Carolus Linnaeus, in his late-eighteenth-century writings, showed a clear indication of his acceptance of the idea of the mutability of species; and at around the same time the French naturalist Comte du Buffon was noting that use and/or disuse influenced the retention or obsolescence of vertebrate organs. It was, however, Buffon's naturalist associate Jean Lamarck who first developed a thoroughgoing evolutionary theory of the origin of species in his 1801 work, *Système des animaux sans vertèbres*. Unfortunately for the reception of the evolutionary theory it was associated with a theory of acquired characteristics being passed on to the offspring. With the effective repudiation of the environmentalist part of the thesis by the famed French naturalist Baron Cuvier the significance of the evolutionary aspects of the theory were lost. Nonetheless, in his preface to his novel *Père Goriot* of 1842, Honoré de Balzac noted that the teachings of Leibnitz, Buffon, Needham and Bonnet, if not evolutionary, all led to the same conclusion, "There is but one animal. The Creator used

---

24 Fox, *Inhumane Society*, p. 232.

one and the same principle for all organized beings." It is a matter of no small significance that such matters pervaded the literary as well as the scientific mind and that they were present prior to the acceptance of evolutionary theory.

Immediately prior to Charles Darwin's announcement of his discoveries, A.R. Wallace submitted an almost identical theory based on his studies of comparative biology in Brazil and the West Indies. Both Wallace and Darwin acknowledged the importance for their ideas of Malthus, the noted population theorist, and Charles Lyell, the Scottish geologist who relied on the findings of James Hutton concerning the geological development of the earth.[25] What distinguished Darwinism was the dynamic process of natural selection. In short, Darwinism was a doctrine with a long evolutionary history of its own—and it was predicated on the kind of scientific methods associated with Descartes and Hobbes which had proved so unkind to the animal world. The irony was that Darwinism was, or at least was interpreted as, a direct affront to the cherished Christian beliefs of most of those directly involved in the work of the societies protecting the interests of animals. Almost all the publications and pamphlets put out by the early S.P.C.A.'s and Humane Societies—and they were legion—have a very strong evangelical Christian bent. And Darwinism was viewed as incompatible with Christian thinking and morality. Ironically, it was those who repudiated Darwin's elevation of the status of animals who, in practice, did most to protect the interests of animals.

Certainly, though, Darwin indicated a very real concern for the interests of animals, not merely by showing how similar in every respect, including that of the possession of a moral sense, humans were at least to the primates, but also by castigating, for example, the cruelty of the trade in fur. However, the means by which he indicated the similarity between human and beast was by relying on traditional Hobbesian and utilitarian analyses of behaviour in which our moral sense is derived from utility—from enlightened self-interest rather than any altruism or compassion.[26] Nonetheless, he does quote Herbert Spencer to the effect that through our "experiences of utility, consolidated through all past generations of the human race" we have come to acquire "certain faculties of moral intuition which have no apparent basis in the individual experiences of utility."[27] This is, of course, itself quasi-utilitarian and directly Lamarckian; and contrary to our current

---

25 In his introduction to the later editions of *The Origin of Species* Darwin notes 30 previous writers who had contributed to the theory of evolution—or "transmutation" as Darwin called it. Even then, Darwin was accused of lack of generosity!

26 See, for example, Charles Darwin, *The Descent of Man* (New York: A.L. Burt, n.d. but reprint of second edition of 1874), pp. 110-39.

27 Ibid., pp. 139-40.

understanding of heredity. Nonetheless, it did allow Darwin to transcend the very real limitations to a genuine awareness of the rights of others implied by contemporary scientific suppositions about the understanding of behaviour—i.e., all behaviour involves a self-interested maximization of pleasure and a minimization of pain. Indeed, in Darwin's own altruistic concern for the animal realm he demonstrated the inadequacy of the philosophical method on which he relied.

If Darwin himself transcended in some degree the limitations to utilitarian scientific methods his disciples did not. Darwin wrote of the evolution of all life from a common ancestral origin by the process of adaptation to environmental conditions. The Darwinists wrote of the competition among beings for scarce resources with the resultant survival of the fittest (and, of course, humans, especially male white Anglo-Saxon humans, were the fittest!). Darwin gave humans and animals a greater affinity. The Darwinists—more properly, the Social Darwinists—made humans (especially certain types of humans) once again the pinnacle of nature, deserving of far greater consideration than all other sentient beings.

It is customary to comment that Darwin is without responsibility for the views of his Social Darwinist disciples. Unfortunately, that is not quite true. Not only did Darwin retain a close intellectual association with Herbert Spencer, who coined the phrase "survival of the fittest"—which Darwin himself adopted in later editions of his work—with its aggressive anti-egalitarian implications, but racist overtones were to be found in Darwin's writings directly. Thus, for example, we read in his discussion of the various races that their "mental characteristics are . . . very distinct; chiefly as it would appear in their emotional, but partly in their intellectual faculties."[28] Nonetheless, Darwin was also responsible for creating the intellectual climate in which humans would come to recognize their responsibilities to animals, not as was customary as a consequence of human benevolence to creatures different in kind but because such beings were in all relevant respects similar to ourselves. The idea of a community of sentient beings with common interests can be derived directly from Darwin's writings.

Unfortunately, the immediate political implications of Darwinism were less palatable. Darwin was appalled to read in a newspaper that he had proved that might was right and therefore that "every cheating tradesman" was right! It was this 'Darwinian' consciousness that inspired Thomas Carlyle to write his infamous article on 'The Nigger Question' in which he eulogized "the law of force and cunning," hero-worship and the natural domination of the inferior by the superior. Further, in a private letter, Canon of the Anglican Church and

28 Ibid., p. 191.

Christian socialist Charles Kingsley expostulated: "Sacrifice of human life? Prove that it is *human* life. It is beast-life. These Dyaks have put on the image of the beast, and they must take the consequence. Physical death is no evil. You Malays and Dyaks of Sarawak, you ... are the enemies of Christ, the Prince of Peace; you are beasts, all the more dangerous, because you have a semi-human cunning."[29]

Herbert Spencer wrote of the "purifying process" by which the animals kill off the sickly, the malformed and the aged, a process which was equally effective—and ought to be!—in human society.[30] It is certainly not that Darwin's writings necessarily inspired such thinking. After all, this jingoism and exultation of the benefits of competition would be ascribed more readily (if in less antagonistic form) to Cobden and Bright; and Spencer and Carlyle were shouting and touting their wares a decade before the publication of *The Origin of Species*. Rather it was Darwin's writings which gave a scientific justification to the ideas of the struggle for supremacy which dominated much of the second half of the nineteenth century. And if such ideas held sway, what hope for the protection of the lower species?

Fortunately for the animals the second half of the nineteenth century also witnessed the rapid development of humane societies, predicated predominantly on evangelical ideas of humane responsibility. Until the early 1700s the words 'human' and 'humane' were used interchangeably. Thereafter 'humane' began to acquire its current meaning—having the characteristics of compassion, kindness and tenderness. This humaneness competed with Social Darwinism for popular acceptance. Oddly enough, sometimes those who advocated ruthless competition and extreme nationalism were numbered among the enthusiasts for animal welfare! Even military officers played a significant role in humane development. In 1888 General Gonzalez, former President of Mexico and by then Governor of Guanaxuato, decreed the suppression of bull-fighting in that province—though admittedly it was primarily because he found the 'sport' financially wasteful and socially demoralizing. Nonetheless, one German S.P.C.A. numbered 3 generals and 23 officers among its members.

If Darwinism immediately failed to produce the benevolent and compassionate treatment of animals consistent with Darwin's findings on the significant continuity between human and other animal biology and psychology, it fared no better in the scientific realm. Of course, the theory of evolution was gradually accepted, but Darwin's treatment of animals as intelligent, complex, thinking and feeling beings (not always consistently with the scientific language he employed, mind you) was

---

29   Quoted in Walter E. Houghton, *The Victorian Frame of Mind* (New Haven: Yale University Press, 1957), p. 212.

30   Ibid., p. 209.

replaced by a behaviourist psychology which treated both humans and animals as insensate machines. Descartes and Hobbes still reigned!

Mechanism ruled the studies of animal psychology, largely because it was deemed more 'scientific', just as such thinking plays a predominant role in some of the social sciences today. In the early years of this century sociologists and anthropologists continued to deny that comparisons with other species could be scientifically relevant, but as they gradually began to accept the more 'scientific' mentality they reduced both human and animal to the level of machines rather than elevating the animal to the sensate level of the human. Intellectual arrogance has played a comic role. If our drives and interests, rather than our ideas and moral sense, play a decisive role in determining our behaviour, social scientists are presumably no more immune than others. And if that is so, the research of social scientists can reflect only their own drives and interests rather than an objective concern to understand reality! Even today such behaviouralism is not a rarity in the social sciences (including economics and political science) although its former pervasiveness is now spent.

Much of the problem arises from the scientific concept of *parsimony*,[31] the eminently sensible idea in principle that nothing beyond what is necessary for explanation should be added to the explanation. Unfortunately, in the case of animal studies, that led to the exclusion of the most relevant attributes of consciousness, purpose and emotion. The problem is thus not with the concept of parsimony per se but with its use to exclude all the relevant data. Not surprisingly, if you begin with the assumption that the object of your study behaves like a machine, à la Hobbes, you arrive at the not so remarkable conclusion that animals behave like machines! If one's model denies the relevance of the conscious and cognitive side of experience one can scarcely be astonished by conclusions which suggest that animals are instinctual rather than reasoning beings.

Thanks in no small measure to the fascinating research of such ethologists as Jane Goodall, Dian Fossey and R.D. Lawrence,[32] following the exploratory work of Niko Tinbergen, scientists are now coming to recognize that consciousness and intelligence in social animals have evolved in response to social problems. Animal behaviour involves learning from experience and conscious decision-making. What is now apparent is that animals plan their actions. They do not merely

---

31 For an informative discussion of this topic, see Mary Midgley, "Are you an Animal?" in Gill Langley, ed., *Animal Experimentation: The Consensus Changes* (New York: Chapman and Hall, 1989), pp. 1-18.

32 See, for example, Jane Goodall, *In the Shadow of Man* (Cambridge, MA: Bellknap, 1986); Dian Fossey, *Gorillas in the Mist* (Boston: Houghton Mifflin, 1983); and R.D. Lawrence, *In Praise of Wolves* (London: Collins, 1986).

respond by instinct to external stimuli. What used to be criticized as anthropomorphism—attributing human characteristics to non-human animals—is now coming to be recognized as legitimate. By combining scientific rigour with a subjective involvement with the species under study ethologists have demonstrated that the higher mammals are closer to us in behaviour, thought and emotions than even Charles Darwin ever imagined.

One unfortunate consequence of some of the outstanding ethological research is that the scientists themselves are not always willing to draw the conclusions suggested by their research. They have become so attached to the animals they study that they are blinkered by the reality. Thus in her fascinating decades-long study of chimpanzees Jane Goodall demonstrates the similarity between the chimps' and humankind's cognitive and affective faculties. She also notes that chimpanzees occasionally engage in murder, rape, and cannibalism, and are even known to go to war. She points out how chimpanzees make rational choices among the various alternatives before them. Inexplicably, she then concludes that "only humans, I believe, are capable of *deliberate* cruelty—acting with the intention of causing pain and suffering."[33]

Unfortunately, this smacks of an inverted speciesism (just as in our justified attempts to eliminate racism we permit ourselves castigations of the culture of the oppressors but deny ourselves the right objectively to describe negative features of the culture of the oppressed). The fact that a race, gender or species has been oppressed or treated unjustly should not blind us to its features. Justice requires the elimination of the oppression; truth requires that we do not paint a misleadingly generous picture out of empathy. Goodall allows herself a condemnation of humanity but resists the warrant to apply similar criteria to the behaviour of her chimpanzees.

It is in fact more consistent, and more in accord with Goodall's data, to conclude that there is both potential benevolence and malevolence in humankind's closest relatives ('closest' as measured by DNA comparisons). It is only when we draw such conclusions that we can truly recognize that both humans and chimpanzees are indeed alike (there is only just over one per cent difference in genetic structure). Only then can we recognize our genuine similarities to the remainder of the natural realm rather than our separateness from it.

Moreover, by drawing such conclusions, we can come to have sound evidence for doubting the unduly optimistic conclusions of those philosophers from Rousseau through Bentham to Marx who have imagined that the less desirable traits in human nature are the mere consequences of civilization, or ignorance, or capitalism, that it is the state or some other instrument of oppression which has brought about evil. Under-

---

33 Jane Goodall, *Through a Window* (Boston: Houghton Mifflin, 1990), p. 109.

standing our similarities to the chimpanzees allows us to recognize that the mere elimination of oppressive structures, or changes in education and socialization, or the replacement of competition by co-operation, will not prove the panacea to rid us of our negative characteristics—though such changes may be employed to make piecemeal improvements. No, both the bad and the good exist in our natures—as well as those of the chimpanzees. We may determine circumstances in which the one rather than the other may be given freer rein, but they cannot be eliminated—they belong to us as a part of our essence. It is in the recognition of this that we truly ally ourselves to the animal world, and ally the animal world to ourselves.

Over the centuries various criteria have been offered as the marks by which humans are in essence different from other creatures. Most commonly 'reason' was offered as the distinguishing factor, sometimes it was 'speech'. Rousseau suggested that it was the act of choosing which separated us from the beasts, Marx that it was the capacity for creative labour. Earlier anthropologists variously offered us game-playing, tool-using, and tool-making as the activity in which only the human species participates. Studies of cetaceans, apes and birds have now demonstrated all these suppositions to be false.[34] The differences between ourselves and other sentient beings are differences in degree, not in kind, although the degree is often quite substantial. It is high time that we eliminated humankind as the only malevolent species from the list as well.

If our latest research findings demonstrate the moral imperative of treating animals with respect and consideration, in part because of their similarity to ourselves, we should remember that throughout the history of humankind that view has never been entirely absent from human thought. Certain economic and social conditions throughout human history have influenced the degree to which the natural empathy of humans for other species has flourished or declined. And the prevailing philosophies have played a significant role in stimulating or rationalizing public attitudes toward other species. But throughout it all the underlying recognition of ourselves as but one species among many has been clung to by at least a few brave souls.

As the twentieth century comes to a close, there is no longer any excuse, circumstantial or philosophical, for failing to recognize, indeed rejoice in, the fact that the human is an animal. It is a fact of which we should be proud and upon which our behaviour toward other species should be based.

---

34 As well as the chimpanzees, certain species of bowerbirds and the Galapagos woodpecker are also tool-making animals. There are, of course, numerous tool-using animals, including the elephant.

Chapter Three

Animal Experimentation: Prologue

The senses and intuitions, the various emotions and faculties, such as love, memory, attention and curiosity, imitation, reason, etc., of which man boasts, may be found in an incipient, or even sometimes in a well-developed condition, in the lower animals.

> — Charles Darwin, as cited by the
> anti-experimenters

I know that physiology cannot possibly progress except by means of experiments on living animals and I feel the deepest conviction that he who retards the progress of physiology commits a crime against mankind.

> — Charles Darwin, as cited by the
> pro-experimenters

There is no more contentious animal welfare issue than that of animal experimentation. And it is perhaps the most difficult to come to grips with. Reading the divergent literature on the subject is a disheartening experience. It impairs one's confidence in the integrity of one's fellow human beings.

In support of the anti-experimental view one can read page after page about ill-conceived, repetitive, poorly conducted and outrightly cruel experiment after disgusting experiment. Moreover, none of the experiments is ever acknowledged to have produced beneficial consequences. Why, one is led to wonder, do the researchers continue their palpably futile experiments?

In support of the researchers one can read page after page about brilliantly planned and humanely performed experiments producing profound medical advances. There is no discussion of all the failed research because of the inappropriateness of animal models for the understanding of humans. Why, one is led to wonder, does anyone ever object to the experimenters' philanthropic efforts?

Each side distorts, deceives and denounces. It is sometimes difficult to escape the conclusion that they are doing it intentionally. They are blindly serving a cause to which they are committed. They appear to care very little for a complex truth. The end, quite simply, justifies the misrepresentations.

The one side develops an ideology to defend the interests of the oppressed. The other side defends the professional and economic interests of an elite in the guise of promoting public service. The one side paints a picture of mindless depravity—of "biological fascism" no less! The other sketches an image of public-spirited humanitarians working selflessly for a better world. Both are engaged in a purely political campaign. Both are genuinely honourable and caring. But both are blinkered.

This is not to say that *all* the literature is merely prejudicial self-service. There are a number of informative and thoughtful exceptions, although they too are almost never entirely fair. To read the anti-research material is to conclude that only a small fraction of the research undertaken relates to serious medicine. To read the pro-research material is to conclude that the vast majority of the research conducted is concerned with the elimination of the most serious diseases.

Perhaps surprisingly, given the high public esteem in which the medical and scientific communities are held, the majority of the more balanced assessments are to be found on the side of their opponents. But that is perhaps because the experimenters recognize that they are fighting a desperate battle against a changing consensus. All is fair in love and war. And the research community is under siege. Moreover, those in the ascendant can better afford magnanimity. However, while the more balanced assessments are to be found on the side of the animal liberationists, so too are the greatest calumny, invective and intemperance. It is a truly daunting task to find any legitimate consensual standards against which the appropriateness of research might be measured.

The language of the debate is itself instructive. Researchers do not tell us that animals are killed. Instead they are 'sacrificed'. Research animals never scream in pain. Instead, they 'vocalize'. There are no dead animals, merely 'mammalian preparations'; no electric shocks, merely 'aversive stimuli' and 'negative reinforcements'. 'Nutritional insufficiency' is the euphemism employed to describe death from starvation. Perhaps the scientists are not trying to mislead and obfuscate, to hide the fact that they too have some misgivings about their work. Perhaps they are merely duped by the pomposity of their own artificial scientific language, designed in these instances more to mystify and to impress than to elucidate. Or perhaps it serves to desensitize the experimenters to the unpalatable nature of their work. Whichever, it is clear that the language of the scientists hinders a fair and impartial judgement about the moral validity of their work.

Let us not assume, however, that this desensitization is necessarily some kind of heinous manipulation of employees by the scientific establishment. *If* the research is eminently worthwhile but involves necessary injury to animals, then the desensitization is equally necessary if the work is not to stimulate a debilitating trauma among the researchers. After all, every week countless humane society employees who care deeply for their charges are compelled by circumstance to help kill numberless stray and unwanted pets. It is a heart-rending but necessary undertaking. Naturally they 'euthanize' or 'put to sleep'. They do not 'kill'. If they do not succeed in desensitizing themselves to their actions they will become emotionally distraught. Desensitization is necessary for both researchers and humane society employees.

From the responsible adherents of the liberationist side the language is usually rather more objective, although one may occasionally encounter a phrase such as "*concomitant* legal rights" when the writer is unwilling to let us know what she thinks the legal rights of animals ought to be. In such instances words like 'concomitant' serve only to obfuscate. When we are told of the need for "a new moral agenda" in which "animals are acknowledged as legitimate objects of moral concern, and accorded concomitant legal rights"[1] we can only wonder what the 'concomitant' or 'accompanying' legal rights might be. Unfortunately we are never told explicitly. And until we are we can only guess at 'concomitant's' implications.

However, the failings of the animal liberationists lie far more in their unwillingness to acknowledge that significant gains in medicine have been achieved from animal experimentation. We are left confused by their writings—intentionally, we surmise—as to whether research involving pain is never justifiable, or sometimes justifiable, and if the latter what criteria stand as justification. They simply refuse to face the issue head on. Instead, some of them merely tell us of the need for medicine to concentrate on prevention rather than cure which, however true, is scarcely helpful; and anyway is nowhere more strongly believed than among the medical fraternity itself. The animal liberationists appear unwilling to concede, as our opening quotations to this chapter suggest, that one may have profound respect for other species and still believe that animal experimentation may be justifiable. Both sides quote Darwin ad nauseam but they are careful to select only that which supports their cause.

The favourite, and prima facie most convincing, argument of the researchers is that the awards of the Nobel Prize for Medicine and Physiology have demonstrated the major contributions which animal experimentation has made to scientific knowledge to alleviate human suffering which, they point out, in turn helps to alleviate animal suffering as well. Advocates on the other side have countered with the argument that the claims are exaggerated, that no distinction is made

---

1　Judith Hampson, "Legislation and the Changing Consensus," in Langley, *Animal Experimentation*, p. 220.

in the claims between in vivo (on intact animals) and in vitro (literally 'in glass', basically research using tissue culture) methods or whether vertebrates or invertebrates such as fruit flies were used. Indeed, we are informed by the anti-researchers that fully two-thirds of all awards went to research involving replacement techniques, i.e., techniques which employed alternatives to vivisection.

The rebuttal, or at least diminution, of the claims made on behalf of the animal research community is undoubtedly a sound one. Unfortunately, though, it does little to provide us with a satisfactory solution. We are still left with the evidence that significant medical research was undertaken which did involve experimentation on live animals involving pain and suffering, and which did provide effective cures for serious ailments.

What we need to be offered are criteria for determining when such research is justifiable. With the unwillingness of the disputants to offer criteria the task has been generally left to governments not merely to determine what is and is not permissible—which is, and indeed ought to be, their prerogative—but also to work their way through the conflicting arguments to develop acceptable criteria of discrimination. The combatants press competing claims, offering little of a constructive nature which might limit their moral imperatives and assist in the production of relevant standards.

Traditionally, of course, the prestige and power of the research interests have resulted in legislation—sometimes lack of legislation—favourable to their cause. In recent years, however, the balance of public opinion has shifted somewhat toward the anti-vivisectionist side and greater restrictions have been legislated. This is in turn encouraging the research interests to make far greater efforts to keep the public on their side. They have recently invested large sums in advertising, public education and lobbying.

Not surprisingly, the case for research on animals can be most convincingly made where such research is undertaken by physicians or well-qualified scientists to combat serious disease. And we have come to have such respect for the medical community that we are perhaps more hesitant to subject their claims to the same rigorous analysis we might take to the claims of lesser mortals. Their esteem interferes with objective decision-making. Yet the esteem of the profession is relatively recent and based in part at least on health improvements derived from factors for which physicians can scarcely claim responsibility—better sustenance, sewage treatment and sanitation for example. Moreover, such luminaries of the scientific establishment as Albert Einstein, Carl Jung and Albert Schweitzer display a far greater sensitivity toward the animal realm than is to be found in the relative indifference of at least some of the senior members of the current medical fraternity.

Einstein spoke of "widening our circle of compassion to embrace all living creatures and the whole of nature and its beauty." Jung wrote of our "unconscious identity" with the animal world as a part of our human essence. And Schweitzer informed us of the moral constraint "to aid all life" when we are able, to go out of our way "to avoid injuring anything living." For Schweitzer, "life as such is sacred." Of course, it does not follow from such statements that research is not justifiable. It merely indicates that if we are to take these admonitions seriously research on animals must only be undertaken if we can demonstrate that the most beneficial consequences follow. We must learn to disregard the recently established esteem of the medical profession in determining what is and is not justifiable.

Sound medical knowledge was very late in coming to Western civilization. From the Roman adoption of Christianity as the official state religion until after the Reformation, the Roman Catholic Church refused to permit the dissection of human cadavers. Since the Church was consistent in its view that God had made animals for human use it is perhaps surprising that animal vivisection was not widely employed to further medical knowledge. It was not. This must lead us to the conclusion that this resulted from a lack of intellectual interest in the natural sciences and, perhaps to an even greater degree, from an unhealthy respect, even total reliance, on the wisdom of the ancients. In Christian culture prior to the age of science the golden age lay in the past not the future.

Until the sixteenth century medicine was largely dependent for its knowledge of anatomy and physiology on the Greek scientist Galen (ca. 131-200 A.D.) who resided chiefly in Rome from about the age of 30 and was imperial court physician to Marcus Aurelius. Galen correlated extant medical knowledge with his own theories derived from dissection of animals, predominantly apes and pigs. His frequently inaccurate—and sometimes *quite* erroneous—conclusions remained the received authority until the publication of *De humani corporis fabrica* (*The Structure of the Human Body*) in 1543 by the Flemish anatomist Andreas Vesalius working at the University of Padua in Italy. Vesalius's research was based on human corpse rather than animal dissections and thus avoided the inappropriate analogies which sometimes had led Galen widely astray.

Writing in 1847 on medical training in the fourteenth century, the historian Charles Knight tells us of the early English physician that:

> His study, it appears was but little in the Bible, that is one negative fact; the positive information, if less amusing, is somewhat more direct and explicit. Chaucer gives us a catalogue of the books which the doctor *did* study. Esculapius,

> Hippocrates, Galen and Discorides are there, with Rufus, a
> physician of Ephesus during the time of Trojan; and we may
> observe that, in reference to these, that all our medical knowl-
> edge rests on Greek foundations.[2]

Having mentioned the Arab, Moorish and occasional European
commentators on the Greek anatomists, Knight instructs us that several
of these were also writers on astronomy which, according to the experimental scientist Roger Bacon at the onset of the Renaissance, "is the
better part of medicine." Astronomy even determined "the proper
hours" for the surgeon's operations. By the middle of the nineteenth
century the Victorians were appalled at how unscientific early medicine
had been, indeed had remained right up until their own times. Early
medicine was quackery, determined as much by our knowledge of
heavenly as earthly bodies!

As late as the eighteenth century the physician—the pejoratively
called Medical Mountebank—was depicted in engravings as customarily
accompanied by a performing monkey, usually a Barbary ape, peddling
panaceas at markets and fairs and extolling product virtues like any
other street pedlar. "Itinerant Galens," an anonymous but caustic writer
in *The Spectator* for 1712 calls them. It is only since the late eighteenth
century that the physician has been generally acknowledged as a serious
scientist rather than a pseudo-scientific charlatan—and even then as a
less than adequate one. Until then bloodletting and herbal remedies
were the nostrums and the barber was almost as effective a surgeon as
any.

It was the theorizing of Descartes, making a distinction in kind
between human and non-human animals with respect to the possession
of consciousness, which encouraged researchers to return to Galen's
methods of animal dissection. Paradoxically, despite the supposed
difference between human and beast, the anatomy and physiology must
have been considered sufficiently similar to permit extrapolation from
dogs and other complex mammals to humans.

But if the age of Cartesian science produced great advances in
anatomical and physiological knowledge, it did little to advance the
practice of medicine. As a consequence of his research on animals, the
English scientist William Harvey demonstrated the function of the heart
and complete circulation of the blood in his 1628 *Exercitatio anatomica
de motu cordis et sanguinis in animalibus* (*The Movement of the Heart
and Blood in Animals*)—something which had been known in ancient
China and India some 5,000 years earlier! Yet it was not until 1827 that
Harvey's theories were fully substantiated and accepted in medical
circles, despite the first blood transfusion being performed in 1667 when

---

2 Charles Knight, *Old England* (London: James Sangster, 1847), 1, III, III: 326.

a woman was injected with nine ounces of lamb's blood. The practice of medicine lagged the scientific basis of medicine by some two centuries.

In fact, around the turn of the nineteenth century several scientific investigators in Britain were involved in vivisectionist research into questions about the properties of blood—on the causes of its colour, for example—which were surprisingly little advanced beyond Harvey's findings, especially given the mid-seventeenth-century improvements to the microscope, the lack of which had hindered Harvey from understanding the capillary system. The writers of *The Edinburgh Review* for 1813 deemed this latest research on blood "not only interesting in itself, but connected with whatever is most important to human happiness, in as much as its improvement affords the best chances of solid advances in the healing art."[3] At least by the early nineteenth century the immediate relevance and application of scientific knowledge to medicine was readily recognized. And if it was recognized *in principle* in earlier times this did little to improve medical practice. By contrast, by the early nineteenth century medical practitioners were becoming serious research scientists. As an aside, it should be noted that the Edinburgh reviewers were delighted by the potential advances in healing, but the question of cruelty to animals was of insufficient significance to be raised in their writings.

In other areas animal research was proving of the greatest human benefit. For example, in 1796, Edward Jenner, a student of John Hunter, who was a pioneer in comparative anatomy, proved that cowpox provided immunity against smallpox by vaccinating an eight-year-old boy with the mild virus from a diseased cow. It was Jenner who developed the now common practice of vaccination against serious diseases. The vaccines are today prepared from live micro-organisms, from weakened or dead micro-organisms and from the toxic products of micro-organisms.

Despite Jenner's scientific and medical success the public appraisal of medical practitioners was such that it was quite some time before the benefit of cowpox immunization was publicly accepted. Again, a perusal of *The Edinburgh Review* is instructive. An 1810 article entitled "Pamphlets on Vaccination" reviewed 19 publications on the vexatious topic which saw the light of day in the preceding three-year period—and which, according to the author, was "but a small proportion of what has lately been written on the subject."[4] On the one side were arrayed the Royal Colleges of Physicians of London, Edinburgh and Dublin, the French Ministry of the Interior, and a "Physician to the Small-Pox and

---

3 Anonymous, *The Edinburgh Review* (Edinburgh: Archibald Constable), 63: 184. Home, Blande, Brodie and Young are among the researchers mentioned.
4 Ibid., 30:325.

Inoculation Hospitals," among others. On the other side of the issue the opponents of cow-pox innoculation complained of the "undue influence of professional men" pursuing their pecuniary interests, indicated significant distrust in the profession's integrity, and expressed total disregard for the claimed accomplishments and intellectual and practical abilities of physicians.

In his *Advancement of Learning* of 1605 Francis Bacon had suggested that there was, indeed, a reputable side to medicine but nonetheless "we see the weakness and credulity of men is such, as they will often prefer a mountebank or witch before a learned physician." Over two and a half centuries later, the learned physician was not much more 'learned' according to popular opinion.

A writer in *The Saturday Review* for October 11, 1862, tells us "that people have followed quacks because they have not found in the doctrines or the practice of the regular profession reasonable ground for confidence." Nor was this an isolated instance. In *The London Review* for January 24, 1863, we read:

> Can anyone at this moment seriously declare that there is such a thing as a science of medicine? What there is is this. There are a few facts—a very few—distinctly known, and beyond the reach of controversy; and the number of them increases but slowly, if it increases sensibly at all. There is a pharmacopoeia of drugs, about the use of which no three men agree completely. There is a vast amount of chemical research, which appears to bring more physiological difficulties to light than it serves to explain, and passes by a number of organic laws to which it is powerless to afford the slightest clue.

Yet in his Presidential Address on "The Public Estimate of Medicine" to the British Medical Association in the same year John Addington Symonds notes the tremendous developments in medical science over the previous 30 years—on the anatomy of tissues, on blood as a seat of disease, on cellular theory, on albuminuria, as well as on the treatment of pulmonary tuberculosis and pelvic diseases, in uterine pathology, and, most significant of all, on the use of anaesthetics. Still, all was not quite well with the public esteem of the members of his profession. He writes of the "speculative scepticism afloat as to the true character of medicine." Nonetheless, he noted also that the opinion of the profession had changed from its historical disapprobation. He is able to acknowledge "the public trust in our art," to write of "the often painfully touching trust reposed in [the physician's] skill."[5] The medical practitioner had begun his move from mountebank to demiurge. In the early seventeenth century Francis Beaumont and John Fletcher had

---

5   John Addington Symonds, *Miscellanies* (London: Macmillan, 1871), p. 353.

declared "the medicine worse than the malady." In the closing years of the nineteenth century medical advances were so rapid and far-reaching that the physician reached the apogee of public adulation.

It was well into the nineteenth century before the educated public began to express even the rudiments of the esteem in which physicians later came to be held. But with the increasing successes of medicine over disease physicians began gradually to emerge as superhumans with extraordinary abilities and powers which raised them above the level of ordinary mortals. Such was the public adulation of physicians by the close of the century that their word came to be accepted not only in the area of their expertise but even on the ethics of their professional practice in which they are no better qualified than educated laypersons. Physicians can make no legitimate claim to judge what research is ethically justifiable, although their knowledge of the research methods used is necessary to such judgements.

In fact the legal principle of Publilius Syrus, that no man should be judge in his own cause, repeated by Pascal in his *Pensées* and given permanent expression in English jurisprudence by the liberal John Locke and the conservative Edmund Burke, denies the right to the physician and the experimenter to a legitimate determination of what research is permissible. Some physicians and experimenters, however, claim that they and they alone should determine what is permissible and insist that research on animals raises no moral issues.[6] Yet even if most enlightened commentators would find such claims quite self-serving it should be noted that the British Animal Procedures Committee instituted to administer the relevant sections of the Animals (Scientific Procedures) Act 1986 consists by law at least two-thirds of medical practitioners, veterinary surgeons or biologists and up to half the membership may be practising animal researchers. And the British Act is touted even by animal liberationists as the most favourable legislation in existence!

Although there were numerous isolated instances of experimentation on live animals in the earlier parts of the nineteenth century it was not until after the publication of Claude Bernard's *Introduction to the Study of Experimental Medicine* in 1865 that the principle was established of the laboratory rather than practice as the foundation for medical knowledge. It was Bernard who convinced the medical community of the value of the artificial production of disease by chemical and physical means through reliance on animal models. Such models, according to Bernard, were "very useful and entirely conclusive of the toxicity and hygiene of man. Investigations of medicinal or of toxic substances are

---

6   See Singer, *Animal Liberation*, pp. 75ff.

wholly applicable to man from the therapeutic point of view."[7] It was in response to the abundance of laboratory work stimulated by Bernard and his followers that the anti-vivisectionist movement was instituted in the 1870s.

It is doubtful that any serious researcher would today be quite so readily convinced as Bernard on the suitability of animal models for conclusions about human diseases. Yet laboratory experimentation is still the favoured avenue of medical research. Since Bernard's time countless millions of animals have been killed in the service of scientific and medical knowledge—not to mention the countless millions more sacrificed to the principles of the counting house.

In recent years more and more critics have made the claim that such research is not merely morally unjustified but also scientifically wrong-headed. Such research, it is claimed, leads to unsubstantiated and often demonstrably false conclusions. Moreover, so it is said, such techniques have hindered approaches which would have been more scientifically and medically profitable. Such research, we are told, has wasted countless years of research activity—and has done so at the cost of hundreds of millions of innocent animal lives. If such claims are, indeed, justifiable, modern medical researchers are no less medical mountebanks than their eighteenth-century predecessors—sedentary rather than itinerant Galens! And if such conclusions are unpalatable the claims have now been made so often and with such clarity that they can no longer be merely dismissed with a shrug. Perhaps, however, a more realistic conclusion might involve a recognition of the physician as a very ordinary human with no greater claims to preferment than those of any other profession. In judging the physicians' performance we must ignore the physicians' public stature. If they were once denigrated, then adored, it is now time to treat them realistically.

———————

Physicians qua physicians are no less likely than members of other occupational groups to pursue their private rather than public interests. Physicians fought, and in places still fight, the implementation of socialized medicine. Where midwifery is not yet legal physicians campaign against its legitimization, despite the fact that midwifery is a highly respected profession elsewhere. It is not that the physicians are necessarily wrong on either issue. It is merely that we can confidently expect physicians (like any other group) to take the side on an issue which corresponds to their pecuniary and professional interests, regardless of the merits of the case. And they see continued extensive

———————

7 Quoted in Robert Sharpe, "Animal Experiments—A Failed Technology," in Langley, *Animal Experimentation*, p. 89.

experimentation on animals as conducive to their interests. As any other directly affected group would be, they are prejudiced on the issue and should have no more than a minor role in determining its outcome. In fact, of course, physicians and scientists have a preponderant role in making such decisions.

Lest we are tempted to imagine physicians less prone to self-service than others let us not forget the infamous Rabinovitch case in Montreal in the 1920s.[8] All the interns at the Notre Dame hospital, supported by sympathetic interns from other hospitals, went on strike against the employment at the hospital of a brilliant young Jewish physician, Sam Rabinovitch—on no other grounds than that he was Jewish. They were concerned, they said, that Catholic patients would find it repugnant to be treated, or even touched, by a Jewish physician! Rabinovitch resigned and it was 40 years before the hospital hired another Jewish doctor.

The point is not to castigate physicians or scientists but to point out that they are not entitled to any preferment in the determination of moral questions. Those most affected by the decisions personally and professionally—on any moral matter and with regard to any professional group—are the least capable of making objective and rational decisions.

At this point it is necessary to jump ahead of our story for a moment and more or less assert some conclusions which we will be discussing at length in the final chapters of this book. It is necessary to do that in order to offer some preliminary criteria against which the permissibility of research might be measured.

Utilitarian philosophers have argued that the customarily accepted ethical principle of equality requires that we treat the suffering of one being equally with the like suffering of any other being. There is, moreover, abundant evidence that animals, especially the higher species, experience pain in a very similar manner to ourselves. However, pain is not quite the same thing as suffering. Suffering involves the reflective faculties of the cerebral cortex, which is significantly more developed in humans than in other animals, while pain is located in the diencephalon, which is well developed in many more animals. Suffering involves thinking, while pain has more to do with a basic biological impulse. Any consideration of suffering must lead us to the conclusion that regard for the interests of different species must be differentiated, following the criterion of "like suffering," according to the degree of their mental capacity, i.e., of their capacity for suffering.

---

8 See Irving Abella, "The Making of a Chief Justice: Bora Laskin, The Early Years," *Law Society of Upper Canada Gazette* 24 (1990): 187-95.

If we accept these arguments—stated all too baldly here for the sake of brevity and without considering complicating factors such as the value of life itself and the sociability of the animal—it follows that we should give earnest consideration to the interests of *all* sentient beings but that we should give *more* consideration to the interests of those species with the greatest mental complexity.[9]

What follows from such a principle is either that we must be able to develop some objective measurement of suffering or that we must rely on informed judgements in the absence of precise measurements. And certainly, at least in our present state of knowledge, objective measurements are unlikely to be developed in the near future, if, indeed, they are ever even in principle attainable. The judgements will require constant weighing and balancing of human and other animal interests. And obviously the balance will vary according to the private sensibilities of those making the judgements and the prevailing public sensibilities which constitute the context in which the private judgements are made. Clearly, both public education, which influences the prevailing public sensibilities, and the choice of judges, are the significant variables which will affect decisions made according to the criterion of "like suffering."

Given prevailing public sentiment and our estimation of the state of 'informed judgement' we suggest the following starting points for laying down conditions for the justification of research involving harm to animals:

1. Research should be restricted to that which meets some significant human need, such as the elimination of serious illness, i.e., where informed judgement indicates that the pain and suffering inflicted on the animals are likely to be adequately compensated for by the relief of pain and suffering in humans and/or in other animals. During the period of research there should be a periodic reappraisal of the value of the research by a reassessment of the human benefits against the animal cost.
2. The research should be conducted on the lowest possible order of animal consistent with the objects of the experiment, i.e., on animals which informed judgement indicates are likely to suffer the least.
3. Research should first be undertaken on the most effective means to minimize the amount of pain and suffering inflicted.
4. Every avenue should be explored to discern alternative methods of research which do not involve the use of animals. This should be so even where the research does not involve pain or suffering, since the animal is entitled to its natural life unless some significantly greater benefit to a higher species can be confidently predicted.
5. No unnecessary repetition of research should be undertaken.

---

9 We propose to add some refinement to this principle in a later chapter. See below, pp. 301ff.

Certainly, the criteria here offered are not likely to be universally accepted. Some will consider them unduly generous to the animals, others will deem them mere verbal window-dressing, readily circumnavigated by the researchers. They should serve, however, as a significant point of departure for discussion. Moreover, it is distinctly preferable to have some criteria against which the validity of experimentation might be measured, even if we are required to amend them in the light of experience and changing public sensibilities. Further, it is useful to have criteria of discrimination already in mind when we come to consider the validity of the research presently undertaken—which is the subject of the next chapter.

The criteria we have adduced do not of themselves determine what may or may not be permissible. They indicate merely what the criteria of considerations might be. Everything depends upon the sensibilities of those who are required to make the 'informed judgements'. Accordingly, the most important consideration is the criteria we employ to determine the appropriate qualifications of those who are to be appointed to make the judgements. Let us be aware, though, that the implications of adopting such criteria involve the recognition that, if we were to be visited by extraterrestrial beings whose mental complexity was greater than our own, such beings would be entitled to greater consideration than ourselves. Human women could be milked to provide butter and cheese and to quench thirst, constantly impregnated by artificial insemination to provide offspring for food. We all would be a legitimate source of food or put into forced labour. We must either, it would appear, be willing to accept that or come to believe that all sentient beings are in principle entitled to a significant amount of protection independently of their level of mental complexity.

Clearly, some expertise is required if the judgements are to be sound. Equally clearly, if we rely on those who have the greatest expertise, i.e., the experimenters themselves, we will simply permit the experimenters to be judge in their own cause. Moreover, it would be unwise to allow the general esteem in which the medical or scientific profession is held to permit it an inordinately significant role in the determination of permissibility. Of course, the expertise of physicians and experimenters is important but it must not be allowed to preponderate. Some consideration must also be given to those on the animal liberationist side who have demonstrated their knowledge of research and alternative techniques. Again, though, they should not be permitted a majority voice (though, of course, in their case any voice at all is—unfortunately—more than they have sometimes been given).

Above all what is needed are well-educated and preferably trained amateurs who should be able to demonstrate a knowledge of the issues based upon an awareness of existing argument and evidence on all sides of the issues, who are uncommitted to a particular view, who are aware of current research methods and techniques, and who are open-minded to new evidence and argument. Further they should understand that while those in authority might lead a society forward they should never lead it by the nose. With Aristotle, they should understand that while public opinion should not alone determine what ought to be done it is always deserving of significant consideration. To move society in any direction it is necessary first to persuade significant proportions of the population that that is the direction in which they want to move.

Chapter Four

Animal Experimentation: The Debate

> Infliction of pain on an animal, then, amounts to cruelty when
> the pain is not compensated by the consequential good. The
> human good envisaged must be a serious and necessary good,
> not a frivolous or dispensable one, if the infliction of pain on
> animals is to be ethically acceptable.
>
> — Advisory Committee Report for the
> British Home Office, 1979

Ann McWilliam, information officer with the Canadian Council on
Animal Care, complains that animal rights activists "equate animal life
with human life."[1] Ron Calhoun, executive director of the advocacy
group Partners in Research, claims that "With their convoluted
thinking, the animal-rights radicals assign the same moral worth and
privileges to a rodent that they do to a human."[2] Kathleen Marquardt
of Putting People First equates Peter Singer's animal rights philosophy
with Nazism! McWilliam and Calhoun are mistaken, Marquardt
disingenuous. There is probably no notable animal rights advocate who
consistently holds the views ascribed to them. But it is scarcely
surprising that such conclusions are drawn.

The liberationists do little to make their views readily interpretable.
Peter Singer's *Animal Liberation* is by common consensus the philosophical starting point of the animal rights movement. Tucked away in
a footnote on p. 271 of the second edition Singer repudiates the view
that the insect and the mouse have the same right to life as a human
and he doubts that many, if any, animal liberationists subscribe to it.
Nonetheless, the reader is more likely to be influenced in his or her
interpretation by the title to chapter one: "All Animals are Equal." A
careful reading of that chapter would indicate that Singer's view is not
as egalitarian as the chapter heading would suggest but it is not always
easy to discern the practical implications of Singer's philosophy.

We read in Singer that "if we consider it wrong to inflict . . . pain on
a baby for no good reason then we must consider it equally wrong to
inflict the same amount of pain on a horse for no good reason."[3] We
might then be surprised to find Singer stating that "Equal consideration

---

1   Ann McWilliam, *University Affairs*, March 1990, p. 5.
2   Ron Calhoun, *Chatelaine* (June 1989), p. 36.
3   Singer, *Animal Liberation*, p. 15.

for different beings may lead to different treatment and different rights."[4] This raises innumerable questions to which we are never offered an answer. What are the criteria on which differentiation is to be determined? What constitutes "good reason"? How are differing treatment and rights compatible with "equal consideration"? And, of course, these are all the questions which need to be answered before rational decisions about animal welfare can be made.

The animal liberationists do not make it easy to determine where they stand. If the amount of pain is the sole determinant of consideration, as the quotation about infants and horses would seem to imply, then this would require us to differentiate our behaviour among humans on the basis of their respective potential for pain, a conclusion which Singer would not want us to draw. Clearly it would be inappropriate to conduct research on, say, disabled persons whose nervous systems are damaged, thus making them less susceptible to pain. The inherent dignity of the disabled would be at issue. Indeed, a good case could be made that such disabled people are entitled to more, not less, consideration. Of course, no animal liberationist would countenance such injustice toward the disabled, but, prima facie, that is the direction in which the sole consideration of pain would have us move. What is relevant is that since the animal liberationists do not make their position clear it is impossible to present their views adequately in terms which are comparable to those of their adversaries, those who hold clearly and consistently to the view that human rights are greater than those of other animals. What needs to be determined, of course, is that, even if the rights differ, how much weight should be given to each. And that, in the final analysis, is not a scientific question, nor even entirely a philosophical one, but a matter of moral judgement based on refined sensibilities. Conscience, moral intuition and natural law may not be popular concepts among scientists, or even a majority of philosophers, but ultimately it is these which provide us with the avenue to moral judgements, however difficult of comprehension and discernment they may be. As with so much of political radicalism, the animal liberationists excel at demonstrating the inadequacies and injustices of the current state of affairs, but they do so without being able to offer us anything of a philosophical or scientific nature which does not create even greater inadequacies of its own. What they do provide, however, is the groundwork of a debate in which we may all refine our moral sensibilities to make sound practical judgements. Had they not stimulated the debate it is highly unlikely that the recent progress would have been made at all.

The medical research establishment informs us that research on animals has helped produce such benefits as insulin, penicillin, polio

---

4   Ibid., p. 2.

vaccine, smallpox vaccine, cortisone, kidney dialysis, asthma medication, high blood pressure medication and artificial joints, etc. They also tell us that animal experimentation is indispensable to the discovery of the cause, treatment and prevention of cancer, atherosclerosis, Alzheimer's disease, multiple sclerosis, AIDS, cystic fibrosis and muscular dystrophy. They claim further that such research has helped produce a feline leukemia vaccine, thus curing an illness previously almost always fatal in cats. Moreover, dogs have benefitted from renal and heart research. Veterinary medicine uses the vaccines, drugs and surgical techniques developed from the use of animals in research to maintain the health and cure the illnesses of companion animals, livestock and zoo animals. They tell us that when the renowned ethologist Jane Goodall reported an outbreak of polio in her East African chimpanzee colony polio vaccine was flown in, administered to the animals concealed in food, and cured them. The Foundation for Biomedical Research has published a solid, well-documented book entitled *Health Benefits of Animal Research* (edited by William I. Gay, undated [though ca. 1988], and no place of publication) which provides 79 pages of significant medical advances.

Surely no one can doubt the benefits gained from research on animals. The pertinent questions, then, must relate to whether the cost in animal lives and suffering is a worthwhile price to pay, whether those major medical successes could have been achieved in some other manner, whether in future more successful and less invasive techniques might be employed and at what point on a descending scale of potential benefits research activity should be prohibited. It is certainly worth noting that the experiments currently permitted on animals are deemed totally unacceptable for performance on humans even where the greatest benefits to mankind may be confidently expected to be derived. We do not seem to consider the benefits to humans worth the intentional infliction of pain on humans through experimentation. And that is true even where there are no suitable animal models. In such instances the research is simply not undertaken, the potential benefits are forsaken. This suggests that humans are being treated as different in kind from other animals, not merely in degree. There is an absolute prohibition against invasive research on unwilling humans—and a significant degree of prohibition even on volunteers—but there is no similar protection for animals.

Where do the animal activists stand on such issues? Search as we might, we have been unable to find one example of an animal liberationist complimenting the research establishment on its successes. There are no unequivocal acknowledgements of the accomplishments. There is not even a "yes, but." All we find are lots of "buts." We have certainly heard prominent animal liberationists say that not one of their number opposes *all* animal experimentation. But we have been unable to find instances of particular research projects of which they approve. The number of which they disapprove, however, is myriad.

What, then, are the grounds for the concerns, either from the liberationists or from those who merely believe that there must be restrictions on the academic freedom to perform research? The objections fall into the categories of cruelty, inadequate concern for the interests of animals, the inappropriateness of animal models for the understanding of human behaviour, inadequate attention to replacement and refinement techniques, poor experimentation, repetition, triviality and insensitivity.

'Cruelty' involves difficulties of definition. One might initially be inclined to accept dictionary-type definitions such as "the act of inflicting pain or suffering." If that is, indeed, what cruelty is, then there can be little doubt that what animal researchers do is frequently cruel. On the other hand, the quotation from the British Home Office Report of 1979 with which we opened this chapter suggested that the infliction of pain involves cruelty only when it is not compensated by a serious and necessary consequential good, rather than a frivolous or dispensable one. If that is a more appropriate use of 'cruelty', then, of course, everything depends upon our judgement of what is necessary and what dispensable. And there are no scientific ways of determining answers to those questions. Indeed, scientific data are not even relevant to such determinations. Scientific knowledge is vital to the determination of appropriate means and the likelihood of success but can have no bearing on the ends.

Obviously, almost everyone today is opposed to cruelty—including animal researchers, whatever the animal rightists may say about them. Almost everyone, too, is opposed to the infliction of pain and suffering unless there is some adequate compensation. The difficulties arise around what is adequate, on which animals the pain is to be inflicted, and how much pain is necessary. Moreover, today most people will acknowledge that animals do indeed experience pain and that at least some of them suffer. There are, however, difficulties in determining the extent of suffering and the degrees of pain and, indeed, how far down the animal chain one has to go before one can be confident the pain does not exist—the fish, the cockroach, the flea, the amoeba? Moreover, should any particular class of animal be excluded from research altogether—perhaps the chimpanzee, whose genetic structure differs from the human by only just over one per cent, or the companion animal with whom the human shares a communal experience?

Attempting to find an answer to that last question will serve to indicate how difficult and inconclusive are almost all questions about animal experimentation. The state of Massachusetts forbids the use of pound or shelter animals in research. Thirteen other states prohibit pounds and shelters from providing animals for research, but animals from out-of-state pounds may be purchased from licensed dealers. In Britain the 1986 Animals (Scientific Procedures) Act, Section 10(3)(a) reads: "no cat or dog shall be used under licence unless it has been bred at and obtained from a designated breeding establishment." Most of Western Europe requires animals for research to be purpose-bred. On the other hand in the province of Ontario pounds are required by law, after certain conditions have been met, to release animals for research to licensed dealers. The price for a dog is $6.00, a cat $2.00. Most American states and Canadian provinces have either no relevant legislation or have laws analogous with those of Ontario.

The argument for the restrictions on research use for such animals relies on the fact that the pounds and shelters to which the animals have been entrusted have a special duty to the public not to betray that trust. If the animals are to be used as "tools for research" then the public will lose its confidence in the humane society shelters and the public pounds. They will prefer to release their unwanted pets in the countryside rather than give them the opportunity to be adopted if the likely consequence is that they will suffer pain on the operating table or be the object of some other invasive research. And as long as the stray or unwanted pet remains in the shelter it has a chance of being reclaimed or of finding a new home in which it can once again have a happy life. If no home is found at least it will have a humane and painless death. Moreover, once an animal has been a companion we feel more inclined to use individual rather than collective criteria of justice toward it—a point we will discuss at some length in later chapters.[5] In essence what this amounts to is that we owe more to an animal with which we have developed a familial kinship than we owe to animalkind in general.

Persuasive as these arguments may appear there are arguments on the other side. It is claimed that if pound animals are not used then double the number of animals will die. Since, customarily at least, animals are only released from pounds after they have been scheduled for euthanasia, if they are not then released a purpose-bred animal will have to be used instead. Consequently, either way, one will be used for research and may suffer but if the pound animal is not used then both the purpose-bred and the pound animal will die, one of them needlessly.

Further, researchers point out that the cost of a purpose-bred animal is some 10 to 12 times that of a pound animal. Figures vary enormously according to jurisdiction, what factors are built into the costing—and what the interests are of those who are issuing the statement! As with almost every animal welfare issue reliable estimates are difficult to acquire. But a typical estimate is $50.00 for a pound dog and $500.00 for a purpose-bred one. The cost of the animals is a significant factor

---

5   See below, pp. 245ff., 268ff., 286ff. and 300ff.

in the cost of the research project—15 per cent on average, according to the head of one laboratory—and, so we are told, a number of significant research projects designed to alleviate suffering have had to be abandoned because of the mounting research costs. Moreover, if pound animals are not used there is a danger that suppliers will return to the horrendous practice of dognapping to meet the research needs.

On the other hand, those who believe that unnecessary and sometimes repetitive work is readily undertaken in research laboratories, and that even where the research is important too many animals are used argue that the higher costs succeed in eliminating trivial research, encourage animal experimenters to seek alternative and perhaps even more effective research methods and persuade them to restrict their research activity to the numbers necessary for sound conclusions. Moreover, the use of purpose-bred animals allows for scientific controls impossible with the haphazard employment of companion animals whose genetic, social and medical history is not known. One Canadian National Research Council experimenter recently claimed that it would take 10 times the number of random animals to produce the same scientific validity acheived from purpose-bred animals. Accordingly, the use of purpose-bred animals rather than pound animals will not increase and may actually reduce the number of animals which are euthanized and will in reality produce scientifically superior research. Finally, we are told, it is not difficult to control dognapping. The requirement of effective source record-keeping by the suppliers and research establishments, together with hefty fines for breach of regulations, is sufficient, as the European experience indicates.

While it may be difficult to draw easy conclusions from such valid but conflicting arguments one conclusion should be clear: scientists cannot claim, as they often do, any special expertise in solving the dilemma; indeed, their interests preclude them from objective decision-making on such issues. If we value the lives of animals being used in research, committees which include a preponderance of knowledgeable people from outside the research community should have a significant influence on determining the source of the animals, the numbers used and the legitimacy of the research. We must be forever wary of those on either side of the issue who would have us believe that answers and solutions are easily come by. In the final analysis any rational decision depends upon the relative importance one ascribes to animal and human. Both sides may acknowledge the human more important than the non-human animal. What is at issue is how much more important.

In deciding whether and how much pain may in a given instance be justifiable one must first determine what pain is and which kinds of animals feel it. While no one—we suppose—would deny pain in some animals, it is still difficult to estimate the amount of pain felt by any animal or any species. And the problem is much more acute with suffering, since there is no common understanding of what suffering is.

Relying on the argument, evidence and conclusions of Margaret Rose and David Adams,[6] whose work was itself based on numerous previous studies, it seems that pain is a sensory function of the nervous system, requiring the activity of the brain, spinal cord, coaxial and spinal nerves together with their ganglia and end-organs. Pain thus exists in all vertebrate species. Evidence of pain-associated behaviour suggests strongly that it also exists in the more complex invertebrates, though here the evidence is somewhat less conclusive. The evidence for all components of pain is strongest in mammals but weaker, though not absent, for fish, amphibians and reptiles. Behavioural adjustment to pain perception by emotional and cognitive reaction can be readily demonstrated in mammals but is not quite so readily recognizable in lower species.

The evidence for suffering—understood as an unpleasant emotional response usually associated with pain and/or distress—is indisputable among the great apes and is seemingly present in all species that have a level of self-awareness, including members of the canine and feline families. The cries of such animals as, say, birds and squirrels to an injury to their offspring—when the parents themselves are clearly not in physical pain—are prima facie evidence of suffering, at least to those who are not wedded to a reductionist behaviouralism and quaintly imagine the cries to be the outpourings of neural templates. There is thus ample, if incomplete, evidence of both pain and suffering in animals at various levels. We conclude that the available evidence suggests that there is a gradation of pain and suffering in animals relative to their complexity. It is for this reason that we suggested at the end of the last chapter that experimentation, if necessary, should be conducted on the lowest species consistent with the object of the study. By 'lowest' we mean primarily least subject to pain and suffering. It must not, of course, be forgotten that even though there may be less pain this does not mean that pain in the lower species does not matter. Nor must we ignore the fact that there may be other considerations in determining the more appropriate 'tools of research'—the value of life itself and the characteristics of the particular species or individual animal, for example.

In a landmark book published in 1959 W.M.S Russell and R.L Burch introduced the principles around which discussion is now concentrated—those of replacement, reduction and refinement (the

---

6 Margaret Rose and David Adams, "Evidence for Pain and Suffering in Other Animals," in Langley, *Animal Experimentation*, pp. 42-71.

3Rs).[7] Wherever possible invasive animal research should be replaced by other forms of study; techniques should meanwhile be developed to permit a reduction in the numbers used and to refine existing methods so that pain and suffering are reduced. It is probable that many, if not most, responsible scientists accept the general legitimacy of those principles today, although, of course, there is significant disagreement on what is and is not possible, what is and is not appropriate. It is here that the expertise and specialized knowledge of scientists becomes indispensable. The educated layperson lacks the training of the scientist and cannot acquire it without becoming a scientist. Nonetheless, the scientist must be constantly reminded by the layperson of the importance of pursuing the objectives.

It is here that the radicals perform a decided disservice to the cause of the animals. Having successfully aroused public indignation against the worst features of animal experimentation they continue to castigate animal researchers per se rather than to seek out and denounce the irresponsible ones. Indeed, unwisely and counterproductively, the Toronto Humane Society unsuccessfully attempted to bar animal researchers and their spouses from membership (along with a variety of other animal users). They did not consider the invasiveness of the research, its objectives or the humanity of the researcher as relevant considerations. It was a blanket prohibition. In fact, of course, it is animal researchers themselves who have developed the less invasive alternatives to in vivo animal experimentation. It is the animal researchers themselves who have done a great deal to improve the lot of the research animal. To take but one recent example of the greatest potential benefit, Professor Jacob Sivak of the University of Waterloo, Ontario, received a $25,000 grant in June of 1991 to test industrial chemicals on eyes from cattle killed for meat. If the research is successful, and the indications are positive, then there would no longer be *any* justification for continuing the use of the infamous Draize and LD50 tests for cosmetics, home, industrial or agricultural purposes.

We do not want to leave the impression that the lot of the research animal is a happy one and that all problems are solved or are about to be solved. They are not. Indeed, Michael Balls and Jacqueline Southee have reported disturbing trends in the other direction.[8] Successes in replacement, reduction and refinement, however, depend upon co-operation with, rather than antagonism to, the research establishment itself. Unfortunately, the radicals make enemies of the researchers. The

7   W.M.S. Russell and R.L. Burch, *The Principles of Humane Experimental Technique* (London: Methuen).
8   Michael Balls and Jacqueline Southee, "Reducing Animal Experiments by Questioning their Necessity," in David Paterson and Mary Palmer, eds., *The Status of Animals* (Wallingford: CAB International, 1989), pp. 111-22.

researchers are constrained to take up the cudgel in defence to prove how right they always were. They are constrained to defend their traditional aims and methods. Moderates, on the other hand, work with the research establishment to bring about the appropriate changes. They are able to interact and persuade rather than drown in bombast. It is with such an approach that many improvements have already been achieved, and the scientists themselves have played an essential role in bringing this about.

In the United Kingdom from 1977 to 1989, inclusive, the number of scientific procedures using live animals reduced each year, reaching a figure of 3.3 million in 1989 (the last year for which data are available), a reduction of 5 per cent from the previous year. The comparable figure for Canada with somewhat less than half the British population is approximately 2 million. The British figure for 1984 was 4.5 million. Thus there was a reduction of some 26 per cent in a five-year period. Some 85 per cent of the animals employed in 1989 were rodents. Point four per cent of the experiments were for cosmetics testing—a great deal less than the radicals would have us believe—and 6.7 per cent were on safety testing of substances (0.1 per cent household products, 2.6 per cent industrial products, 2.4 per cent agricultural products). Seventy-one per cent of procedures involved "medical, veterinary, dental or other biological research," according to the British Home Office. Fifty per cent of all procedures were applied medical research, dominated by drug development and testing. Sixty per cent of procedures were carried out in commercial laboratories (mostly pharmaceutical companies) with universities (including medical schools) accounting for a further 23 per cent.[9]

A cynic may well want to question the meaning of 'other biological research', may well wonder how much was artificially constrained to fit the 'medical' category, how much was 'necessary', how much repetitive, how much merely because scientists and technicians have career requirements to satisfy and incomes to justify. Whatever the answers may be to such questions we cannot but be gratified to note the reduction in numbers and the high proportion in the categories more readily justifiable—especially at a time when industrial, technological and medical developments are on the rapid increase. These figures suggest that there is a growing recognition of the need to be concerned with the welfare of animals even though the figures for the U.S.A., the Netherlands and Japan—especially Japan—are not as comforting.

Some would argue that while improvements are being made they are nowhere near fast enough, and that far too little attention is being paid to alternatives. Scientists are still employing outmoded and unnecessary techniques. If that is so, effort needs to be concentrated on persuading

---

9   The source for most of this information is *Nature* 346 (August 1990).

the scientists to change. Like other professionals, scientists are motivated by the desire to accomplish, to be recognized for their accomplishments, to satisfy their intellectual curiosity and to receive tangible rewards for their efforts. At least some are also motivated by altruism—the desire to achieve something which will be of benefit to humankind and perhaps other sentient beings. When they are maligned for their efforts and are accused of the most heinous barbarism they are inclined to become defensive and resist change, for they know they are not the uncaring monsters of the radical portraits. If, on the other hand, rewards and recognition are offered for scientific work which follows the principles of the 3Rs, then much more humane work is likely to ensue. It is indeed the task of those committed to improvements in the welfare of experimental animals to help provide the appropriate intellectual and occupational climate.

The task is not always an easy one. Scientists who have achieved prior successes by the more invasive methods and those who pay scant attention to the physical *and* psychological well-being of the sentient animals at their disposal are loath to discontinue that which has earned them their rewards. They have little incentive to learn something new. Many are set in their ways, and learning new methods and approaches detracts from the time available to be spent on research itself. Indeed, the Secretary of the British Medical Research Council has expressed the view that it is impractical for scientists to be engaged specifically in devising alternatives as their prime activity, separately from engaging in research activities themselves.[10]

The traditionalist scientists have succeeded in desensitizing themselves to the more disturbing aspects of their work and have carefully rehearsed and internalized the defence of their procedures. Convinced that the public benefits derived from their research are beyond dispute, they defend themselves against those who denounce animal research per se rather than listening to those who openly admire the outcome of their research but suggest that there may be far less invasive ways of conducting it. In fact, in reaction against the exaggerated denunciations of radical animal rights groups, at least some prominent members of the research establishment have taken a much firmer stance in favour of continued and even expanded experimentation on animals than may have been warranted had more co-operative and conciliatory approaches been undertaken.[11] Indeed, as we know from the correspondence we receive, some of those who are actively involved in the search for

10   See Gill Langley, "Establishment Reactions to Alternatives," in Paterson and Palmer, *The Status of Animals*, p. 136.
11   See, for example, Dr. Bessie Borwein, Associate Dean of Research, University of Western Ontario, "Life is a Miracle—But is Threatened by Disease," mimeographed, October 1989, p. 4.

alternatives resent what they see as the unwarranted interference of humane societies in matters which, the researchers believe, should be left to determination by research scientists. Others who simply want to get on with their research resent even more the regulations now imposed upon them either by legislation or self-governing bodies. One researcher bridles at the review process, complaining of having protocols judged "by people who have little or no knowledge of [one's] field," as though it were the scientific quality not the ethics of the work which was being vetted! He complains of the bureaucratic hassles, the constant concern of considering animal interests.[12] What is perhaps more disturbing is that the experimentation advocacy group Partners in Research considers such self-serving arrogance as deserving of dissemination to those who request material from them.

It is encouraging, however, to recognize that many, especially the younger, research scientists, including physicians and veterinarians, have been converted to the 3Rs approach and are actively involved in encouraging their colleagues to adopt similar principles and in having institutional and national animal ethics committees require an at least formal commitment to these principles, with countless beneficial practical consequences. The cutting edge of scientific research is rapidly becoming the more humane approach. In fact, the University of Guelph, Ontario, has recently instituted a Centre for the Study of Animal Welfare whose established purpose is to conduct non-invasive research with the welfare of the animal as the end. Current research of the Centre focusses on alternatives to the use of animals in teaching; assessment of animal well-being; ethical issues of animal use; genetic engineering; humane husbandry systems; identification of animal suffering; relationship between animals and people; seal hunting; welfare of fur-bearing animals; and whaling. There are some 50 faculty actively associated with the Centre. It is unlikely that anyone concerned with the interests of animals would object to such research, given that its end is the welfare of the animal. It is, then, the invasiveness of research which is at issue and the ends toward which the research is directed.

Contrary to what many imagine, the scientific and industrial community is itself doing a great deal to change the climate of research involving animals. Research advocacy groups—and some researchers—are currently informing the public how vitally important is the research they undertake. What they rarely discuss is why it is necessary to conduct it in the manner they choose. And they are reluctant to consider alternatives, especially when the rewards may appear less easily achieved by non-traditional methods. To that end the Procter and

---

12 Alan Garbutt, "Biomedical Research: The Paperchase," *University of Western Ontario Medical Journal* 58, 2 (1989).

Gamble Co. offers up to $50,000 annually for up to three years (currently three such awards are being offered per annum) for the development and use of new methods for testing the efficacy and safety of drugs and consumer products that eliminate or reduce the use of animals or distress imposed on animals. There is a similar European Pharmaceutical Industry Award to the value of SFr 25,000. Bristol-Myers Squibbs Co. and Tom's of Maine Inc. help fund the Tufts University "The Alternatives Report," a bi-monthly publication. The Johns Hopkins Centre for Alternatives to Animal Testing lists 71 companies which make financial contributions to the centre, which is dedicated to the development of alternatives to invasive animal research. A number of industries have funded conferences on alternatives to animal testing and on discussion of ethical and other considerations relating to animal experimentation. There are several laboratory animal periodicals, including the Tufts University "Alternatives Report," the "Newsletter" of the Johns Hopkins Centre, "Lab Animal" from the Nature Publishing Co. of New York, and "Frame News" from the Fund for Replacement of Animals in Medical Experiments of Nottingham, England. All of these are devoted to reporting on progress made on replacement, reduction and refinement in animal experimentation. In Canada the Joseph F. Morgan Foundation was established in 1988 to promote research to reduce the use of animals in experimentation. What is of the greatest urgency, and what, co-operatively, such groups as F.R.A.M.E., C.A.A.T. from Johns Hopkins and the Joseph F. Morgan Foundation are committed to provide, is a computerized international data bank which will minimize the necessity for repetition and encourage refinement by providing information on extant results, methods, etc., though this will only reach its ultimate objective once the regulatory agencies of one jurisdiction permit acceptance of research findings developed in another. As it is, invasive research harming millions of animals is conducted even though the researchers know exactly what their findings are going to be. Such unnecessary repetition is not because the scientists want to do it but because national regulatory agencies require it.

While much remains to be done—some indeed to be begun—there is a growing awareness of the need to reduce and refine animal experimentation. Nowhere is this more apparent than in the growing importance of institutional animal care committees in universities (including medical schools) whose task it is to investigate the ethics of the research undertaken and of the national organizations instituted to inspect and evaluate the animal research undertaken in universities and other research establishments.

Nonetheless, especially among pharmaceutical companies, much scientifically unnecessarily repetitive experimentation is undertaken to meet legal contingencies. While such companies may often prefer to conduct in vitro research because of its often greater scientific reliability and greatly reduced cost and inconvenience, they find it necessary to repeat the experiments on intact animals. This is because extant case law in several countries requires such validation if the companies are to defend themselves against lawsuits if claims are made on the basis of inadequate experimentation in the production of their drugs. Legal systems and regulatory agencies are more responsible than researchers for delays to improvements for the research animal.

In order to make valid judgements on what steps ought to be taken with regard to animal experimentation a number of questions need to be raised. What has medical science contributed through research on animals which could not have been achieved in other ways? How much would we lose if we ceased or substantially reduced experimentation? How much, if anything, are we prepared to lose? Unfortunately, in their beliefs that those who question animal experimentation are vehemently opposed to all experimentation, medical research scientists are usually unwilling to engage in open and honest debate. Subject to abuse as they are, they feel the need to rationalize and obfuscate rather than to clarify.

Chapter Five

Animal Experimentation: The Alternatives

But tell us, O men! We pray you to tell us what injuries have
we committed to forfeit? What laws have we broken, or what
cause given you, whereby you can pretend a right to invade and
violate our part, and natural rights, and to assault and destroy
us, as if we were the aggressors, and no better than thieves,
robbers and murderers, fit to be extirpated out of creation.
From whence did thou (O man) derive thy authority for killing
thy inferiors, merely because they are such, or for destroying
their natural rights and privileges?

— Thomas Tryon, *Complaints of the birds and
fowls of heaven to their Creator, 1688*

Speaking in terms of animal rights is no novel radical phenomenon of
the late twentieth century. Indeed, as the above quotation indicates,
Thomas Tryon was already using such language in the year of the
Glorious Revolution, the year in which modern constitutional order was
firmly established. Just less than a century later, in the year of the
American Revolution, the English cleric Humphry Primatt published his
Dissertation on the Duty of Mercy and the Sin of Cruelty to Brute Animals
in which animal rights are again mentioned—if not in quite the flowery
prose of Tryon. Again, toward the close of the nineteenth century
Henry Salt wrote extensively in such terms, as did Ernest Thompson
Seton. The language of animal rights has a venerable history, and
currency is what gives language meaning. The question is not, nor ought
to be, whether animals have rights, but what rights they ought to be.
Animals may possess rights without it being imagined that those rights
are the same as human rights, without it being imagined that animals
are entitled to the same treatment as humans.

In fear that acceptance of the very idea of animal rights might imply
an end to all animal experimentation, pro-research sympathizers have
tried to argue that animals cannot possess rights, since rights are a
peculiarly human, moral, cultural and legal attribute. For example,
Herbert Lansdell, writing in the *International Journal of Neuroscience*,
claims that rights are "ordinarily said to be applicable universally,
without selectivity" and animal protection is and has to be selective,
preferring some animals over others, in that "the killing of vermin and

microbes is of high priority throughout the world."[1] Yet such time-honoured phrases as "the rights and privileges of an Englishman," "the rights bestowed upon graduation," etc. are quite meaningful and certainly not universal. The right is restricted to all who are members of a certain class, e.g., Englishmen, graduates, etc. Yet the notion of human rights does not preclude there being gay rights or vice versa. Thus a right may be applicable to all animals, to certain species only, or to animals with certain characteristics without it being doubted that there are animal rights—any more than the right of, say, only U.S. citizens to have an American passport should be thought incompatible with the idea of human rights.

Lansdell also insists that animals cannot have rights, since the possessor of rights must be able to claim them. But this would mean that it would be meaningless to talk of the rights of, say, an infant or the retarded. It certainly makes sense to argue that animals, or particular species, or homosexuals, or infants do not possess the rights ascribed to them, but to deny that they can possess rights is to try to win the battle by denying that the opponent is entitled to compete, to gain the victory by default. The title of Lansdell's article is instructive: "Laboratory Animals Need Only Humane Treatment: Animal 'Rights' May Debase Human Rights." But what is a 'need'? Clearly, it is something required to achieve a certain end, in this case the proper end of the animal. If we are required ('need') to treat the animal humanely, as Lansdell concedes, it would appear that the animal is entitled to humane treatment. And what is this entitlement but a right? The fact that animal rights may not be equated with human rights does not mean that animals do not have rights and may be treated merely as a means to human ends. Indeed, all civilized societies today have laws which prohibit cruelty to animals—which means that animals have a right not to be treated cruelly. Let us not fear the very idea of animal rights.

What should disturb us most of all about Lansdell's article, and the popularity it has engendered in research circles, is the justification it offers for humane treatment of animals:

> There are acceptable reasons for wanting farm and research animals, besides pets, to be treated with consideration for their welfare and to not be subject to unnecessary pain or discomfort. Among the reasons are: 1(a) research results are likely to be more worthwhile with healthier animals. (b) farm production tends to be optimal with healthy animals, and (c) presumably people are less likely to become antisocial if they can be

---

1 Herbert Lansdell, "Laboratory Animals Need Only Humane Treatment: Animal 'Rights' May Debase Human Rights," *International Journal of Neuroscience* 42 (1988): 171.

led to show concern about any mistreatment of the animals used by society.[2]

Lansdell mentions no reasons which pertain to the animals in themselves. What Lansdell is thus telling us is that animals are entirely subservient to man's use à la Kant. Humane treatment of animals is not for the betterment of animals but merely because it is in the human interest. We are astounded that a responsible researcher would write the article (the author is a primate researcher), even more astounded that a responsible journal could find referees to support it, and are despondent about the fact that research advocacy groups would subscribe to its views. We can only hope, and are inclined to believe, that fellow researchers, many of whom we admire in the primate field, have not recognized the implications of Lansdell's arguments. We even wonder if Lansdell himself means what he says, for what can be the import of 'mistreatment' in the last sentence quoted if only human ends are at issue? If Lansdell's views are widely held there is not only a gulf between the relative weight to be ascribed to human and animal interests but a chasm between those who think that animals matter for themselves and those who do not. On the whole, however, the evidence indicates that those who would deny intrinsic value to the animal are in a decided minority. Let us certainly hope so, for progress in questions of animal experimentation depends upon achieving some degree of consensus.

It is not uncommon for research advocacy groups to depict their opponents as 'animal rightists' and to suggest that those arrayed against them are bent on bringing an end to all experimentation tomorrow. In fact, as we have tried to show, one may believe that non-human animals may possess rights, that one should work toward minimizing the indignities inflicted upon the animal realm, and still recognize the importance and benefits of research conducted upon animals. What needs to be done, then, is to find the appropriate balance.

The questions for animal experimentation issues must revolve around the types and extent of rights possessed by animals. We must determine how we may best weigh human interests against animal interests. The questions would be significantly less difficult—even if appropriate measurements were available—if we could rely solely on the utilitarian view that pain and suffering are the only relevant criteria or on Gandhi's tenet that "the more helpless a creature, the more entitled it is to protection by man from the cruelty of man." We should not fail to note that Gandhi's view is the very antithesis of the utilitarian view advocated by Peter Singer and his followers. Appealing and compassionate as Gandhi's pronouncement may sound initially, its implications

---

2 Ibid.

are disturbing. It involves preferment for the flea over the dog, the micro-organism over the chimpanzee. Perhaps what Gandhi had in mind was the fact that all sentient beings deserve consideration and those that cannot protect themselves are entitled to more consideration than those which are able to look after their own interests adequately.

What should be clear is that there are philosophical disagreements among the different proponents of animal interests. What they share in common is the recognition that animal interests are presently less considered than justice would demand; what differentiates them is their intellectual attempts to come to grips with precisely what constitutes that justice. In fact, as with all moral issues there are neither simple answers nor even simple factors to consider. Life, sentience, purpose, reason, self-awareness and communal relationship are all elements worthy of consultation, and they are all in some measure in conflict with each other. And just as there are complex judgements to be made about human moral issues, weighing many conflicting considerations, so too in the case of animal experimentation rational determinations can be made only in the light of balancing several competing factors. Sometimes the philosophical complexities are greater than the difficulties of making judgements themselves. Lord Chief Justice Mansfield (1705-93), head of the English judiciary, advised his judges to "Consider what justice requires and decide accordingly. But never give your reasons; for your judgement will probably be right, but your reasons will certainly be wrong." While Singer and Gandhi differ in their reasons we feel confident that they would concur in their judgements. Moral decisions are often easier than ethical justifications. We do have a moral sense even though it may be difficult to express its rationale. In considerable measure ethical explanation is a raising to a level of consciousness what we already know by intuition.

Tempted as one may be to forget the reasons and rely on the judgements, that is only fruitful once a degree of consensus has been reached on what interests (and in what proportions) are entitled to consideration—and to date, of course, there is no consensus. Yet just as consideration of such issues as race and gender have brought out greater consensus by honing our intuitions through debate and reflection so, too, is this possible with animal issues. And the honing takes place by responding to questions. The types of appropriate questions with regard to experimentation include: How important are the ends of the experiment (what benefits are intended for human and animal)? How likely is the experiment to be fruitful? How much pain needs to be inflicted? Will the potential benefits and chance for success outweigh the pain inflicted? What methods are available which reduce the amount of pain? On which species can the experiment be conducted so as to minimize adversity without hindering the viability of the experiment? and, most important of all, What alternatives are there to the use of intact animals?

The chapter, "Tools for Research," in Peter Singer's *Animal Liberation* is replete with numerous examples of the most heinous, frequently redundant and rarely productive research performed on primates, ponies, dogs and several other species. Many of the worst cases reported occurred in the United States—where legislation is relatively weak and as many as 25-35 million animals are used annually for experimental purposes. The worst offender appears to be the U.S. military establishment. We do not consider it necessary to repeat any of the accounts here, either of those instances reported in Singer or in other studies devoted to the issue. Suffice it to say that they are a revolting indictment of humankind's inhumanity to our fellow creatures. If one wants the details a reading of Singer is to be recommended.

The customary response of research advocacy groups to the litany of crimes perpetrated against animals in research establishments is to claim that many of the accounts are inaccurate or tendentious, that significant abuses may have once existed but no longer do, and that modern regulations and site visitations have eliminated the possibility of abuses. It is undoubtedly true that many of the abuses which were relatively common at the time of the first edition of Singer's book (1975) are now a rarity. Indeed, in the 1990 second edition Singer acknowledges the improvements which have been made—while insisting that cruelty continues. Certainly, cases of trivial, questionable and cruel research continue to be reported by responsible scientists.

Clive Hollands has written a compelling account of inappropriate experimentation in agricultural research, toxicology, behavioural research in psychology (psychologists are frequently portrayed as among the worst offenders), primate experiments, weapons and safety testing, and medical research.[3] Hollands is an honorary associate of the British Veterinary Association, Secretary to the St. Andrew Animal Fund and a member of the British Home Secretary's Animal Procedures Committee, the body which advises the Crown on the implementation of the Animals (Scientific Procedures) Act 1986. Many of the examples of which Hollands writes are British and all experiments mentioned took place before the passage of the 1986 Act.

The importance of that legislation lies in part in Section 5(4): "In determining whether and on what terms to grant a project licence, the Secretary of State shall weigh the likely adverse effects on the animals concerned against the benefit likely to accrue as a result of the programme to be specified in the licence." The Home Office "Guidance Notes on the Administration of the New Act" require the responsible

---

3   Clive Hollands, "Trivial and Questionable Research on Animals," in Langley, *Animal Experimentation*, pp. 118-43.

cabinet minister to set limits to the degree of severity of procedures and to balance the predicted severity against the potential benefit—to conduct, in other words, a cost-benefit analysis. Moreover, in assessing the benefit, the public interest is deemed to include the interest of animals.

Clearly, the degree to which animal interests will be effectively considered will depend on the private sensibilities of the cabinet minister and/or the advisors, together with the prevailing public sensibilities that are the context that no wise government will ignore, even though it need not blindly follow them. The intent is at the very least to remove all possibility of blatant abuses of animals, and the indications are that it has succeeded to a commendable degree. What is as yet uncertain is how much further the administration of the Act will go in promoting the consideration of animal interests.

Perhaps not surprisingly, there are already complaints from both sides of the spectrum. Some scientists complain bitterly of unjustified intrusions into their research. On the other side, Judith Hampson, also a member of the Home Office Animal Procedures Committee, and who recognizes many of the benefits of the Act, bemoans the fact that "we cannot get there from here." The end of the exploitation of research animals, she insists, "requires nothing less than a gestalt shift in the evolution of human consciousness."[4] While one may be inclined to consider Hampson's concerns premature, perhaps she has a point. If the types of abuses which aroused public indignation have been eliminated, or at least significantly reduced, it may be more difficult in future to sustain public consciousness of the issues. After all, some 85 per cent (as much as 90 per cent in some jurisdictions) of experiments involve rodents, and it is notoriously difficult to arouse the public to the plight of rats. 'Smoking beagles' and apes with electrodes in the skull may stimulate public fury, but protection for rats could be more readily achieved if they were given furry tails, if they sat engagingly on their haunches to crack nuts with dexterity, and were called squirrels. They would still be rodents but rodents with a human appeal. The private sensibilities of government advisors cannot be effective if the public mind is not attuned. Public persuasion is the prerequisite of practical politics.

One of Hampson's prime concerns—and one which has implications well beyond the confines of the administration of the British Act—relates to the ends for which animal experimentation is permissible. Many of those involved in the development of the Act thought that Section 5(4) empowered the minister to determine the appropriateness of ends, i.e., whether the purpose of the project was ethical. Yet, according to

---

4   Judith Hampson, "Animal Experimentation—Practical Dilemmas and Solutions," in Paterson and Palmer, *The Status of Animals*, pp. 100, 109.

Hampson, "The Animal Procedures Committee has not yet decided whether it is within its brief to advise the Secretary of State not to grant project licences for work which might be considered unnecessary."[5] And if it does not so decide, much of what was thought to have been gained might be lost. It has not decided whether it has the legal right to recommend against animal testing for decorative cosmetics, tobacco, drug and alcohol abuse, maternal deprivation, pure (as opposed to applied) research and the like on the basis of the purpose of the research rather than the ethics of its procedures. A careful reading of Section 5(4) is not encouraging, for it refers to effects, not purposes. Similar problems exist in most jurisdictions, but it had been thought that the much vaunted British Act had overcome that limitation. Clearly, unless the purpose of the research is considered, the value of any cost-benefit analysis is seriously curtailed. It should be noted that in those jurisdictions covered by voluntary ethics committees rather than legislation such committees usually restrict themselves to consideration of procedures, since it would be considered ultra vires to restrict the ends of research not expressly prohibited by law.

Certainly, much research is in one sense unnecessary. When a pharmaceutical company has developed a successful drug and its period of legal monopoly has expired, other companies wishing to produce a similar product will have to engage in similar testing. It would be unreasonable to expect the initial developer merely to hand over its expensively acquired scientific knowledge and expertise. It is, of course, countless more animals who will suffer from the duplication. And when such examples as Thalidomide are suggested as indications of the inappropriateness of animal models for drug-testing, the research bodies reply that the example of Thalidomide clearly indicates the need for more, not less, testing on animals. Indeed, scientists themselves are frequently in disagreement as to how much testing is necessary to give a reasonable guarantee that a product does what is intended and does not produce other effects which may be harmful.

How appropriate is the animal model for application to the understanding of the human? Again there is no consensus. There is a host of conflicting material which the educated layperson may read, but in the absence of a detailed knowledge of toxicology it is difficult to make a reasoned and impartial judgement. It is in the field of toxicology that the most impressive advances are being made in the replacement of intact animals by tissue-culture analysis. It should be clear, however, that the use of animal tissue culture also presupposes the applicability of extrapolation from animal to human. It is not always easy to understand the position taken by the anti-researchers. Some tell us that animal models are inappropriate for human understanding but advocate

---

5   Ibid., p. 102.

the use of tissue-culture research as an alternative—and its appropriateness in turn depends on the validity of extrapolation from animal to human where human tissue culture cannot be used.

The quality of argument of the American research advocacy group, iiFAR, is even less satisfactory than that of the anti-researchers. On the limitations of computer modelling to replace animal experimentation we are told that the "airlines have been using computers to schedule flights for many years, but the latest figures indicate nearly half of all flights still arrive late."[6] It doesn't take a genius to recognize that the late arrival of flights bears absolutely no relationship to the inadequacy of computers to flight scheduling. It is no wonder that the person attempting to make a fair and impartial judgement is frustrated by the quality of evidence and argument offered.

Humans and other mammals do share certain features in common—which suggests appropriateness of extrapolation—yet in other respects are quite different—which suggests inappropriateness. For example, rodent stomachs differ sufficiently from human stomachs that it is difficult to assess, say, the effects on humans of common food additives which cause cancer in rats. Conversely, we know that other agents cause cancer in humans but not in most strains of rats. In such instances reliance on a rat carcinogenicity test would be, to say the least, foolhardy. Yet iiFAR, in discussing the limitation of tissue-culture research, tells us that the "Ames test . . . [a method for detecting the possible cancer-causing properties of compounds] cannot determine whether or not that particular mutagen will actually cause cancer—thus the continued need for tests on animals."[7] Do they not know that causing cancer in the animal is only a prima facie indication of cancer causation in humans? Or do they simply not care to tell us? Again the reader wanting to make a fair and impartial judgement is constantly misled by the arguments used by the advocates.

As Erik Millstone has pointed out, "there is evidence which suggests not just that our inferences from animals to humans are unreliable, but that they may be actively misleading."[8] On the other hand, John Gilman, former Executive Director of the Canadian Joseph F. Morgan Research Foundation and an advocate of alternative techniques, describes the "predictive ability" of in vivo methods as the "best

6 "Issues and Answers: A Discussion of the Animal Activists' Most Common Allegations Against the Use of Animals in Medical Research," mimeographed August 1988, p. 3.
7 Ibid., p. 2.
8 Erik Millstone, "Methods and Practices of Animal Experimentation," in Langley, *Animal Experimentation*, p. 74.

available" and of in vitro as still "under scrutiny."[9] It is very difficult for the layperson to make a reasoned judgement.

While drugs may certainly produce effects which are unique to a given species and while there are limitations to extrapolation from animal to human there can be little doubt that pharmaceutical products have been developed from animal testing which have proved to be of immense human, and, to a significantly lesser degree, animal benefit. When we read, then, that in carcinogenicity tests on rodents there is a less than 50 per cent chance of finding human carcinogens, we are led to wonder why such animal studies continue to be used. After all if they do not produce answers which help the pharmaceutical companies develop appropriate drugs, why would they waste their time, effort and money? The reality appears to be that such tests are less reliable than one might hope, but it is surely in the interests of the developers as well as the public to achieve increased effectiveness. We should certainly have cause for concern that the prevailing behaviouralist mentality we discussed in the second chapter encourages some scientists and research establishments to give greater weight to animal studies than to epidemiological and clinical data based on humans. We should be no less concerned that animal tests are sometimes used because they help negotiate regulatory hurdles rather than because they are necessary. Mice and rats are often used, not because they are biologically appropriate, but because they are readily available and there are standardized and relatively simple methods for dealing with them. On the other hand, choosing more biologically appropriate animals may well require the use of more complex, sentient and rational creatures.

At the very least we need more consistent and relevant rules for interpreting the data acquired from animal studies so that fewer repetitions will be necessary and the public more adequately protected. But let us not imagine that there is an easy route to the elimination, or even significant reduction, in animal experimentation in the foreseeable future. While there are vociferous public demands for decreased animal usage, there is also an equivalent demand for protective monitoring of health and environmental risks—which requires *greater* use of animal experimentation. Contradictorily, it is not unusual to find the same group of people making both demands!

We should in fact be gratified that animal experimentation has been reduced as much as it has. The past several decades have witnessed an unprecedented escalation in the number and diversity of chemical, physical and bio-engineering products which have entered the market, many requiring animal experimentation. The fact that the number of

---

9 John Gilman, *Report on Status and Trends in In Vitro Toxicology and Methodology Modifications for Reducing Animal Use* (Ottawa: Health and Welfare Canada, 1991), p. 1.

animals used in some jurisdictions has decreased significantly and in others remained steady or risen only slightly reflects the successes of the use of in vitro methods, employing tissue cultures rather than intact animals. John Gilman estimates that a rabies tissue-culture infection test saves 30,000 mice annually in Canada alone, while a procedure to replace the mouse in insulin batch tests saves 600 mice per batch.[10]

It would, however, be unwarranted to expect in vitro methods to replace all live animal testing for, while there is much to commend it in the field of toxicology in particular, there are many areas of experimentation where such methods are impossible to adopt. Nonetheless, we should not fail to note that it is epidemiological studies through occupational correlation, not animal tests, which have identified the vast majority of substances known to cause cancer in humans. Similarly clinical studies, rather than animal experimentation, have proven decisive in improving treatments for drug-overdose patients, even though regulatory bodies require animal studies to be conducted and even though such studies, while they might suggest appropriate treatment, are unlikely to indicate the effectiveness of the treatment.[11] This might suggest to us that there are significant limitations to both in vitro and in vivo studies, even though neither is dispensable.

In vitro systems are those that involve the culturing of cells, tissues and organs or organ fragments in a nutrient medium. In vitro technology can be applied to the study of practically every cell type, and the practical problems of growing specialized cells were effectively solved by the early 1980s. In vitro systems have the advantage of allowing for controlled studies of isolated systems, but this is also a disadvantage in that what occurs in isolation may not occur when the complex systems of the body interact. Thus while in vitro systems are very useful it would appear unlikely that they could ever replace in vivo system study in entirety. It is for this reason that iiFAR prefers to talk of cell- or tissue-culture research as "supplements or adjuncts" rather than as alternatives.[12] The obvious advantage from an animal welfare perspective of in vitro techniques is that the cells may be acquired from minimally invasive biopsies or slaughterhouses rather than live animals. Moreover, human tissue may also be used, which obviates the need to extrapolate from animal to human.

Vaccine production is in fact the way in which tissue-culture research can be most effectively used as a replacement for the use of intact animals. Numerous other vaccines have been produced in this

---

10   Ibid., p. 3. See also p. 5 on the escalation of producers.
11   See Martin Stephens, "Replacing Animal Experimentation," in Langley, *Animal Experimentation*, p. 155. We have relied extensively on Stephens for an understanding of replacement techniques.
12   iiFAR, "Issues and Answers," p. 2.

manner since the Salk vaccine broke new ground—and with the greatest medical benefits. Tissue-culture techniques are also in the forefront of basic research in biomedicine, especially in studies of the immune system, where cultures taken from one mouse now replace what took from 200-400 mice before.

Mathematical modelling via computer simulations is also proving successful as a replacement for animal experimentation, and this has the advantage over tissue-culture research in that it allows for the study of the whole and not merely of the parts in isolation. It has been used successfully in malaria and cancer research, and has been used with some success to attempt to duplicate the complex physiological system of the human body.

The advocates of the medical establishment acknowledge some of the advantages of computer-based research but are quick to point to its drawbacks. As iiFAR tells us, "a non-animal model cannot totally mimic the complexity of a living, breathing animal." But how much can a living, breathing rat tell us about a living, breathing human? Is it more or less than the computer? Why does iiFAR fail to comment on the drawbacks of the animal as a model? "Simulations," iiFAR continues, "have inherent limitation. The validity of information obtained from any simulation is directly dependent on how closely the simulation resembles the original."[13] Of course it does. But this begs the question in favour of animal experimentation unless it demonstrates how much more closely the animal resembles the human than does the computer simulation. While there are certainly limitations to the use of the computer as a replacement for animal experimentation, in at least our present stage of computer knowledge the prospects are hopeful, if not unbounded. But those prospects are too far off to save most experimental animals in the foreseeable future. Of course, it is not uncommon to encounter the view that the use of computers is limited because a computer can only give out what was fed in. If we feed in all the knowledge we have we cannot get *new* knowledge out. This is in principle true. However, the computer can synthesize the information entered in a manner which amounts in effect to an increase in knowledge.

Physical-chemical techniques are also now being employed to analyze the properties of drugs, toxins and body chemicals. They have replaced animals in assays for a number of vitamins and have replaced rabbits in human pregnancy testing. Moreover, liquid chromatography may be about to replace mice in testing the potency of insulin. What we should not fail to notice is that many of these alternatives have come about as a consequence of people, often research scientists themselves, caring enough to reduce the use of intact animals—although conveni-

---

13   Ibid., p. 2.

ence, cost and improved technology have also played an important if indeterminate role.

Many scientists are now coming to recognize the opportunities which have been missed by an excessive reliance on animal experimentation. Today many more are turning to epidemiological and clinical studies—of both human and animal patients. Moreover, there is a growing awareness of the moral need to use the least sentient beings consistent with the objects of the research. While many of the more established members of the medical and scientific fraternities retain their ardour for what they see as the tried and true they have many younger—and some not so young—colleagues who are seeking less invasive ways to achieve their worthwhile ends.

It should be the task of those who care for the dignity and welfare of animals to encourage the research establishment to find new ways of promoting medical and scientific knowledge which is less invasive and to persuade the business community to employ the new ways when they are developed. We should welcome government and industrial funding to such ends and press for more. Above all, we must help create a research climate in which every consideration is given to animal interests while not impeding the research. The most important of immediate ends lies in persuading governments to prohibit animal experimentation research on unjustifiable ends such as cosmetics and tobacco, alcohol and drug abuse—where the ends most certainly do not justify the means. Who would today believe that a new perfume is worth the torment of thousands of animals? And who would doubt that tobacco causes cancer? Surely these are areas in which the medical and scientific establishment could join with the animal welfare community to demonstrate their goodwill. And would that not in turn make us less suspicious of research establishment motives when they engage in genuinely beneficial research?

If animal experimentation is not an entirely failed technology, as some would have us believe, it has far greater limitations and far fewer successes than the research interests would have us believe. Let us insist that the truth be told rather than the evasions and half-truths we are currently offered. Above all, we should attempt to further the demonstration to the scientific community that consideration for the animal is consistent with, and indeed a prerequisite of, better science and more effective remedies for human and animal illnesses. And if that sounds like pious sentimentality, perhaps it is. What is important is that animal welfarists should be prepared to work with rather than against the responsible scientists in the interests of animal well-being.

Chapter Six

Animal Experimentation: Legislation and Assessment

The law is the last result of human wisdom acting upon human experience for the benefit of the public.
— Dr. Samuel Johnson in Piozzi's *Johnsoniana*

Good laws lead to the making of better ones; bad ones bring about the worse.
— J.-J. Rousseau, *The Social Contract*, III, 15

Justice, according to Plato, is giving everyone their due. According to Aristotle, it involves treating equals equally and unequals unequally. To be just to animals involves giving them their due, and determining, in light of their relevant differences from humans, precisely what their due might be. Good law is, in no small measure, the implementation of such justice.

Plato, it is said, defined man as a two-legged animal without feathers. Diogenes plucked a cock, took it to the Academy and announced, "This is Plato's man."[1] Here we have the contrasts of attitudes which have bifurcated Western culture for at least 3,000 years. On the one hand are those who emphasize the similarity between humankind and other animals. On the other are those who stress the differences. We can neither determine with confidence what is just, nor what the law ought to sanction, until we can find some accommodation between these competing conceptions. There is nothing more infuriating, nothing more vexatious, than the phrase given by Addison to his Sir Roger de Coverley when refusing to be decisive: "much might be said on both sides." Infuriating and vexatious as the phrase might be, there is much truth in the adage, especially when dealing with the issue of animal experimentation.

But this decidedly does not mean that what is just with regard to animal experimentation is merely a matter of opinion. Indeed, a consideration of the statements of the animal rightists' harshest critics would demonstrate that. We are told that animals kill other animals. The whole of the natural world consists of predators and prey. Nature

---

1 Diogenes Laertius, *Diogenes*, 4.

is cruel. And if nature requires that some kill others for sustenance, for survival, then surely we are entitled to the same rights.

The most common response by those concerned with animal welfare is that humans possess a moral sense which is absent in animals.[2] We suggest that is an insufficient response on two counts—(i) that animals do indeed have a moral sense, a topic to which we will return later;[3] (ii) that possession of a moral sense is unnecessary to the rebuttal. Animals, in fact, attack and kill others only for sustenance, survival and territorial protection, at least except in a few rare instances. If we thus accept the analogy with 'nature', humans are entitled to the destruction and use of other animals only to the extent that their survival and their safety depend on it. Moreover, to say that 'nature' is itself 'cruel' is to claim that 'nature' is less satisfactory than one would desire. The killing and harming of other animals is an 'unfortunate' necessity. Of course, the *understanding* of something as 'cruel' and 'unfortunate' does depend on the possession of a moral sense, but its *being* 'cruel' and 'unfortunate' does not.

If 'nature' gives the 'right' to animals to kill their prey under certain limitations (e.g., the necessity of survival) then the right for humans is similarly restricted. Moreover, the extension of a right within certain limits implies a duty not to exceed those limits. Restrictions in 'nature' of the killing of some by others implies the value of life per se which may only be harmed if those conditions are met. Thus if we follow the reasoning of the animal rightists' critics we will recognize that it implies that humans have a right to the use of animals only to the extent that their survival depends on it, or is furthered by it, and a corresponding duty, given the recognition of the value of life, not only not to exceed these limitations but to work toward the reduction and elimination of that use and killing when survival does not dictate otherwise. Just laws must reflect both the right and the duty. It should be noted, moreover, that this argument is not restricted to animal experimentation but is equally applicable to hunting, the fur issue and intensive farming. One might note further that the killing of animals by other non-human animals is usually conducive to a balance in nature. And animals often kill the weakest of other species (i.e., those unable to escape) whereas humans—in both hunting and animal experimentation—seek out the fittest.

If this line of reasoning from 'nature' is accepted it implies that justice requires the limitation of animal experimentation to testing which is likely to curtail significant human suffering and premature death, and requires equally that we seek every means to replace that testing with harmless or at least less harmful techniques. Moreover, it

---

2   See, for example, Singer, *Animal Liberation*, pp. 224ff.
3   See below, p. 251 and pp. 312ff.

requires that when harmless or less harmful methods have been discovered the more invasive methods must be abandoned forthwith. While this approach does not deal with the nuances of what refined sensibilities may or may not permit it should give food for thought to those who use the argument from nature to defend humankind's right to treat animals as subservient to our interests. One might hope—forlornly perhaps—that the advocates of minimally restricted experimentation will recognize that their own arguments do not support their conclusions.

We should not imagine that there should be fixed and immutable laws which apply to animal welfare issues. The development of technology and moral sensibility are relevant factors to the determination of appropriate rules. What may be appropriate when hunting is necessary for food and raiment, when poverty is rife, or when experimental methodology was in its infancy, may well be quite inappropriate as technology and related moral sensibilities alter. And given the speed of change in our modern era, laws need to be more flexible than was once appropriate. Enabling legislation is more effective than firm statutes. Rather than providing for firm and fixed rules, laws should now be more general in scope, allowing for variations in judgement as to what is and is not permissible as technology and culture change. The laws—which are difficult to change—should lay down general principles. Administrative bodies instituted by the legislation should lay down the regulations—which may be more readily changed in light of altering public perceptions and technological capability. Inflexible legislation enshrines and reinforces current public morality. Flexibility permits a timely response to changing mores and capabilities.

The first legislation to control animal experimentation was the British Cruelty to Animals Act of 1876. It has always struck us as ironic that the country historically renowned for its imperialism and the phlegmatic and complacent character of its people should have been the first to develop a society for the prevention of cruelty to animals (1824), to legislate their protection (1821, 1830s, 1849 and 1876) and to lead the way in both the nineteenth and twentieth centuries in the control of animal experimentation. It would appear that the British have a greater sense of commonality with the rest of the animal realm than do most other nations.

For its time the 1876 Act was remarkably progressive. It required licensing of experimentation and controlled, to a degree, the amount of pain to be inflicted, although anaesthetics did not need to be given, except for surgery, if they frustrated the purpose of the experiment. At the time of the passage of the Act animal experimentation was still in its infancy; only a few hundred animal experiments were performed annually, though following the publication of Bernard's *Introduction to the Study of Experimental Medicine* in 1865 and the success of Louis

Pasteur's experiments to produce a rabies vaccine, it was growing rapidly. As the number of experiments increased to over four million annually and as scientific needs and technology changed, so it became increasingly clear that the 1876 Act had outlived its viability.

The 1986 Act which repealed and replaced that of 1876 is, by common consensus, the legislation most considerate of the interests of animals and the standard by which other legislation and controls are to be measured. Yet it too accepts the legitimacy of animal experimentation, and not merely to cure serious illness, but to gain scientific knowledge for its own sake as well as permitting research beneficial only to human adornment. The Act in fact prohibits very little explicitly. It is enabling legislation which allows for the extension of stricter controls through its administrative machinery—primarily the Home Office Animal Procedures Committee, consisting at least two-thirds of medical practitioners, veterinary surgeons or biologists. No more than 50 per cent of the Committee may hold current experimentation licences or have held them within the previous six years. The remaining members of the Committee are laypersons among whom animal welfare groups must be "adequately represented" (4 out of 20 in 1989).[4] The Committee itself is invested by the Act with the power to investigate and report on matters it determines appropriate as well as responding to the initiatives of the Home Office.

Provisions of the new Act require that both the experimenter and the project receive a licence before testing can be undertaken. It also extends the concept of 'protected animal' to include all vertebrates from the halfway point of gestation in the case of mammals, reptiles and birds and from the point of capacity for independent feeding in the case of fish and amphibians. Further, it extends the areas of experimentation brought under jurisdiction significantly beyond that covered in the 1876 Act, e.g., production of vaccine, breeding for physical defects, etc.

A Home Office inspector interviews and assesses each applicant before granting a personal licence and in the case of a project licence the inspector may refer the matter to an independent assessor via the office of the Home Secretary or to the Animal Procedures Committee if the proposed research gives cause for concern or if it involves an area of research which the Committee has asked to have referred to itself. The willingness of the Home office to fund a team of qualified and trained inspectors is itself indicative of a greater commitment to the diminution of cruelty compared to, say, Canada where assessments are undertaken largely by volunteers.

---

4 We have relied extensively on Judith Hampson, "Legislation and the Changing Consensus" (in Langley, *Animal Experimentation*, pp. 219-50) for our understanding of current legislation in Britain and Europe.

Each project must be assigned a level of severity—mild, moderate or substantial—and researchers are required to demonstrate that they have given adequate consideration to alternatives to the use of protected animals. Moreover, where an animal has been subjected to severe pain or distress which cannot be alleviated the licensee is required to have the animal painlessly killed forthwith by an appropriate approved method. This is required whether the object of the experiment has been attained or whether the suffering is thought likely to endure. There is not yet any agreement on what constitutes 'severity' either for the level to be assigned to the project or the determination of the need for euthanasia, but it is expected that over time inspectors and experimenters will reach a common understanding. Clearly, those experiments with greater severity require greater deliberation and control.

All experimental and breeding facilities must be registered and are subject to periodic, usually unannounced, inspections. Each certificate of registration includes the names of three persons, one of whom has overall authority and responsibility for ensuring compliance with the requirements of the certificate; the second is responsible for the everyday care of the animals—"usually a highly trained chief animal technician or animal house curator"[5]—and the third is a veterinarian. The second and third are required to inform the personal licensee in the event that the condition of any animal is giving cause for concern, and, in the absence of the licensee, are given the authority to take the necessary steps to have the condition rectified or have the animal painlessly killed. Animals which have already undergone a general anaesthetic may be re-used, provided they are not kept for an undue period between procedures, a veterinarian has declared the animals healthy and the licensee has received the specific authority of the Home Office, which means in practice the Animal Procedures Committee. Such second tests must be under terminal anaesthesia.

The Animal Procedures Committee has referred to it all licence applications which the inspectorate deems unusually controversial or which present special difficulties of technique and procedure as well as those which are of particular public concern—e.g., all cosmetics and toiletries testing and all research on tobacco and its substitutes (unless carried out under terminal anaesthesia). It should be clear, incidentally, that such provisions indicate that the new Act continues to show a far greater concern for the elimination of pain and suffering than it does for the value of life itself.

Further responsibilities of the Committee include a review of all licences for the purpose of gaining manual dexterity in microsurgery. This is considered a matter of public concern, since the acquisition of surgical skills was excluded by the 1876 Act—which at least hints the lie

---

5   Ibid., p. 225.

to those who claim that surgical practice on live animals is essential for medical training, unless of course it is imagined that British surgeons have been less competent than their counterparts elsewhere. The Committee requires all such applications to be determined by itself and has only granted permission for procedures carried out on terminally anaesthetized rodents. It also reviews retrospectively all applications in the category of substantial severity and makes recommendations for restriction or modification of similar future projects. The Committee reviews general trends in research, advises on the system of inspection and prepares reports on areas of public concern. Moreover, its Annual Report is presented to Parliament where the relevant cabinet minister may be required to answer questions, particularly where the minister may have chosen to disregard the Committee's recommendations.

The prime function of the Committee is to attempt to seek a balance between the needs of scientific research and the welfare of animals. The Committee, as we noted earlier with regard to the cabinet minister,[6] is required to perform a cost-benefit analysis, though again it must be noted that there are no existing criteria by which the cost and the benefit are to be measured. Everything depends on the sensibilities of those making the judgements and on the public sensibilities which are the context in which the private judgements are made.

Section 19(2) of the Act reads: "In its consideration of any matter the Committee shall have regard both to the legitimate requirements of science and industry and to the protection of animals against avoidable suffering and unnecessary use in scientific procedures." The use of 'legitimate' and 'avoidable' are of the greatest importance in this section of the Act. What is 'legitimate' will vary according to the dictates of public conscience. As the public recognition of the illegitimacy of certain types of testing increases, so the capacity of the Committee to reject applications will increase. However, the preponderance of members of the scientific community on the Committee is likely to delay the response to the changing public consensus for, as we discussed earlier,[7] the scientific community is no less likely than any other body to defend its own sectarian interests rather than to pursue the public good. It is unlikely that the British Act will achieve its potential unless and until the lay portion of the Committee is significantly increased, and then only if the personnel are well trained in the issues. Nonetheless, the use of the word 'avoidable' as an additional qualifier to 'unnecessary use' in the legislation portends the greatest benefit (most legislation refers only to 'unnecessary'). If 'avoidable' suffering is to be eliminated then there is presumably a legal, not merely a moral, requirement to

---

6   See above, pp. 77-78.
7   See above, pp. 54-55.

employ alternatives and to pursue the least invasive methods wherever and to what extent they are available.

If only 20 per cent of the Committee membership represents animal welfare interests and up to 66 per cent represents research interests perhaps that reflects the balance between scientific and animal welfare interests that the drafters of the legislation intended—a higher than 3 to 1 ratio in favour of science. That, it seems to us, is an inappropriate reflection of the public interest (which, of course, must not be confused with the scientific interest, however much scientists attempt to have us believe that). Nonetheless, the British legislation gives a far greater representation than is customary to animal welfare interests. For example, only eight per cent of the membership of the Canadian Council on Animal Care represents animal welfare interests.

Generally, in the last decade or so, considerable strides have been made in Europe to develop legislation to cover animal experimentation, although no other country has quite matched the British model. In Denmark, though, legislation has gone further than in Britain to inhibit the use of animals for teaching purposes and in Germany weapons, tobacco and cosmetics testing is prohibited. It is accepted in Denmark that television, plastic models and computer simulation are at least equally effective teaching techniques. And Liechtenstein's 1936 Animal Welfare Act prohibits all vivisection although a recent amendment allows for experiments conducted by government agencies but only in exceptional circumstances.

The situation in Europe is both complex and in flux, some parts of Europe having entered a quasi-federation in 1992 and others having a tenuous relationship to the new union. There are 21 member countries of the Council of Europe but only 12 members of the European Community.

The Council of Europe finalized a European Convention for the Protection of Vertebrate Animals Used for Experimental and Other Scientific Purposes in 1986. However, individual member countries must ratify the Convention for it to be effective, and the Council has no machinery to enforce its provisions. Moreover, its provisions are weak, providing minimal standards for pain control, animal husbandry and record-keeping (intended in part to eliminate the use of stolen cats and dogs).

The importance of the Convention, however, lies in the stimulation it gave during its 16 years of discussion, debate and passage to member countries to enact legislation, which in many instances goes well beyond the requirements of the Council of Europe Convention, and to the Commission of the European Communities which enacted a substantially stronger Directive enforceable in the 12 member states of the European Community. Belgium, Denmark, France, Greece, the Federal Republic of Germany, the Netherlands, Luxemburg and the U.K. all passed national legislation during the period of consideration of the Council of Europe Convention. Eire still operates under the British 1876 Act and Italy under its 1941 legislation, while Portugal and Spain have no current legislation (though in the latter case a 1980 decree was prepared but requires authorization and a new decree is in preparation). Eire (minimally), Greece, Italy, Portugal and Spain will require changes to meet the requirements of the E.C. Directive.

The Directive's measures include adequate husbandry standards, limitations on pain and distress, a weighing of benefit against severity, and adequate training for experimenters and animal care personnel. However, they do not include the requirement of veterinary advice during experiments, there is no provision for an inspectorate, anaesthesia requirements are weak, there is no requirement for consultation with representatives of animal welfare bodies and the use of random-source animals is not prohibited (though the restrictions are greater than in most American states and in Canada).

The major limitation of the Directive is that its jurisdiction is restricted to matters involving trade between the member states, hence to the development and testing of products (including, of course, drugs). The Commission has no jurisdiction over scientific knowledge, education or medical and veterinary application. Nonetheless the Council of Ministers of the E.C. has passed a resolution whereby member states will be required to enact national legislation to cover areas of animal experimentation outside the E.C.'s immediate jurisdiction and that legislation must meet minimally the standards of the E.C. Directive.

If illegal and reprehensible behaviour by animal rights extremists has been greatest in the U.S.A.—in the last 10 years animal rights activists have broken into more than 80 research and educational institutions—it is perhaps because more animal experimentation is conducted in the U.S.A. than anywhere else, and the behaviour, ideas and attitudes of some of the members of the research community have demonstrated a deplorable lack of concern for the welfare of the animals in their care. Moreover, legislation in the United States is generally weak, confused, inconsistent and often not enforced. And while many British researchers were the strongest advocates of the 1986 Act and several were numbered among the prime movers behind it, many American scientists have long clung to the view that there should be the least possible restriction to free scientific inquiry. Fortunately, the evidence of the last few years suggests that this attitude is beginning to change, although it is also in the U.S. that research advocacy groups have been most instrumental in attempting to persuade the public that all is well in the field of animal experimentation.

Animal experimentation in the United States is controlled by the 1966 Animal Welfare Act as amended on three subsequent occasions and by state legislation in some areas. The federal Act does not itself deal directly with the details of animal experimentation but requires the Secretary of Agriculture to institute regulations governing experimental practices. The regulations have proved less than adequate.

The U.S. federal system of government, where individual members of Congress have significant influence and are subject to excessive pressure from political action committees (P.A.C.'s) and industry lobbyists, is less conducive to effective legislation inimical to the interests of the powerful and the wealthy than the parliamentary style of government. In the U.S.A. more than elsewhere money and lobbying expertise speak very loudly. The $27 million contributed in five years to election campaigns by the representatives of the research establishment (euphemistically called 'the health industries' to enhance their prestige) has played a significant role. The members elected by such funds continue to exert their influence on House and Senate Committees to persuade the Secretary of Agriculture to maintain the same minimal standards. As attorney Holly Hazard has written, "In the U.S.A. . . . no animal is too sentient and no experiment is too silly, painful or duplicative for the government to restrict its implementation."[8] If animal welfare interests are to succeed in the U.S. they will have to acquire the same lobbying expertise (though presumably without the plethora of funds) as their adversaries. Indications are that, against all odds and mammon, they are slowly but surely acquiring it.

For now, however, the American system is far from adequate. "Animal" is defined by the Act, as amended, "to include any warm-blooded vertebrate determined by the Secretary as being used in research and testing." Since the Secretary has excluded rats, mice, birds and farm animals from regulation under the Act we do not know whether they are cold-blooded, invertebrate or never experimented upon! For the Secretary to be in compliance with the Act they must surely lie in one of those categories. Moreover, the Secretary of Agriculture has exempted facilities using insubstantial numbers of animals from inspection. Clearly, the vested interests have persuaded the cabinet minister to evade the requirements of the law and his department has insufficient funds to conduct what minimal inspections there are left to do. After all, since more than 80 per cent of experiments are conducted on rodents, and rodents are exempted, four-fifths of potential inspections are automatically unnecessary. One would have hoped at the very least that would mean that the major facilities with higher order animals would be inspected more rigorously and more frequently. Perhaps this is so, for over 80 per cent of the facilities investigated by the inspectors of the United States Department of Agriculture in the late 1970s and early 1980s failed to meet even the

---

8 Holly Hazard, "Current Legislative Initiatives in the U.S.A.," in Langley, *Animal Experimentation*, p. 252.

basic provisions of a weak act—abuse or neglect was documented in all these cases.

Media attention prompted by public concern finally led to some improvements in the amendments enacted in 1985. It is comforting to know that if the public squawks loud enough and long enough and has expertise, reason and justice on its side then it is possible to make some inroads into the oligopolic influence of the vested interests. These amendments instituted Animal Care and Use Committees at each establishment conducting research (except on cold-blooded, invertebrate rodents, horses, sparrows and the like!). These committees must include the laboratory veterinarian and at least one member from outside the institution. They are required to review procedures, inspect animals and file a report with the Department of Agriculture. The amendments require consideration to be given to (but not requirements for) alternatives to animal use, regulated drug use and multiple surgery, the provision of appropriate veterinary care and promotion of the use of anaesthetics and analgesics. Primates are to be provided with an environment appropriate to their psychological welfare, dogs must be exercised and facilities are to provide training in humane experimental techniques. Department of Agriculture inspections are required annually and there are penalties for violation of the regulations.

The complexity of the situation in the U.S.A. is exacerbated not merely by the fact that there are state as well as federal regulations but also because the Department of Agriculture is not the only body to lay down federal ordinances. For example, a significant proportion of research in the United States is conducted with public funds received from the National Institutes of Health (N.I.H.). All institutions receiving grants from the N.I.H. are required to comply with guidelines issued by that agency and, following passage of the 1985 amendments, all other research facilities are also required to follow a strengthened version of those guidelines. Among the most important of the provisions is the requirement that the Animal Care and Use Committees review all applications for funding, including those using rodents (though such experiments are still not themselves monitored).

The consequences of these changes have included refusal to award research funds to non-compliant institutions, increased inspection of facilities (twice annually) and the requirement of reports on the training of personnel. On the negative side, the use of anaesthesia and analgesia is at the experimenter's discretion, there are few restrictions on research techniques and there is inadequate requirement for species-specific needs to be met. The greatest failing, though, is that the Care and Use Committees do not function as, or usually think of themselves as, ethics committees; hence, there is no requirement of cost-benefit analysis and little concern with the purposes of the research itself. Procedures involving severe pain or distress or even death during the experiment may receive approval if the researcher can demonstrate (which often amounts to little more than stating) that the purposes of the research cannot be otherwise achieved. Despite these modest changes, a heated debate still rages in the U.S.A. between the research lobbyists and the animal protection lobbyists. The one argues that the Department of Agriculture has acted ultra vires by requiring the Animal Care and Use Committees to review protocols. The other argues that the new rules conform to the intent of the Act and should in fact be extended to include rodents and farm animals which, they claim, were never intended to be excluded by Congress. Despite the modest improvements made, American animal welfarists constantly bemoan the fact that even when legislation is passed the strength of the research interests is such that the regulations to implement the legislation are constantly delayed and, when promulgated, are almost never as strong as the legislators intended. Indeed, seven years after the passage of the 1985 amendments they are still not being enforced as enacted, since the Department of Agriculture has failed to ask Congress for the necessary appropriation.

In Australia the constituent states have jurisdiction over animal welfare issues, although the federal parliament did establish a Senate Select Committee on Animal Welfare in 1983 which issued a finely argued, lengthy report on animal experimentation in 1989. Three of the seven states have instituted significant amendments to animal experimentation regulation in recent years—two (Victoria and South Australia) by making major revisions to Prevention of Cruelty to Animals legislation and one (New South Wales) by enacting special legislation to control animal experimentation. The other states and the capital territory are governed by the 1969 Code and Practice for the Care and Use of Animals for Experimental Purposes. The Code has recently been amended and all states now operate in a more or less similar manner, relying predominantly on the use of Animal Ethics Committees.[9]

Such committees are required to have at least one member from outside the institution and one with a demonstrated commitment to animal welfare. Since 1979 institutions receiving funds from the National Health and Medical Research Council have been required to have such committees which, as legislation has developed, are now mandatory throughout Australia. The primary duties of the committees include the examination of compliance with the Code of Practice in relation to the acquisition, housing, care and use of animals, examination of protocols for the use of animals in research and teaching (which they have the power to accept, modify or reject) and monitoring

---

9   We have relied extensively for our information about Australia on Margaret Rose, "Regulation of Animal Research—The Australian Experience" (in Paterson and Palmer, *The Status of Animals*, pp. 123-35).

of research activities. They are also responsible for developing guidelines on alternatives and ensuring the competence of relevant personnel. Animal Ethics Committees are themselves monitored by government-appointed inspectors.

Given the relative novelty and the paucity of information about the Australian situation, it is difficult to judge how effective the system is, or, more appropriately, is going to be. Nonetheless, it is encouraging to note that the 1989 Commonwealth (i.e., federal) Senate Select Committee Report stated explicitly that all involved in the practice, administration and control of animal experimentation need to be publicly accountable for their actions. It was also recognized—and this is perhaps the major drawback of all current systems—that a narrow spectrum of scientific views tends to be significantly less critical than where membership reflects both scientific and community attitudes. While the Australian report did not mention the appropriate proportion, there are good grounds for the belief that at least half the membership of animal ethics committees should come from the educated—and preferably trained—lay public. It is, moreover, highly desirable that such committees should be called, as they are in Australia, Animal Ethics Committees, for that is a constant reminder of their raison d'être.

Apart from Portugal, Spain (and technically Australia), Canada is alone among the Western liberal democracies in having no national legislation to govern animal experimentation, although there is legislation in 3 of the 10 provinces (Ontario, Saskatchewan and Alberta). Unlike Portugal and Spain, however, there is a fairly elaborate but voluntary (and uneven) system of assessment. Despite the lack of compulsion, the Canadian system has been acknowledged as responsive to changes in technology and public sensibility and as containing elements worthy of imitation elsewhere.

In its *Guide to the Care and Use of Experimental Animals* the Canadian Council on Animal Care (C.C.A.C.) states that the "fundamental concept on which animal care in Canada and its surveillance by CCAC is based, is that of control from within the institution exercised by the scientists themselves."[10] But who guards the guardians? From the perspective of animal welfare advocates it is the convicts who are running the prison. Ethical decisions are made by those who have neither the relevant expertise nor the interests of the public or animals as their prime consideration. Their immediate interests lie in the promotion, not regulation, of animal experimentation.

While there is in principle much merit to such a view, in practice the Canadian system is much more favourable to animal interests than one

---

10 *Guide to the Care and Use of Experimental Animals* (Ottawa: Canadian Council on Animal Care, 1980), 1: i.

might expect. Nonetheless, that is largely because of the qualities of the professional personnel who administer the system and the expertise and commitment of the animal welfarists who sit on the council and serve on the committees. The system itself leaves a great deal to be desired.

The C.C.A.C. claims "that the achievement of optimal conditions for animal care and use is more likely to be approached through the CCAC program which is considered preferable under Canadian constitutional conditions, to attempting national legislative control. Legislation has always tended to enforce only minimal acceptable standards. Historically, it has failed to involve or satisfy the concerns of the animal welfare movement."[11] These claims require a response. "Canadian constitutional conditions" are in principle no bar to legislation. Under the British North America Act—now officially called the Constitution Act of 1867 and still the closest Canada comes to having a formal constitution despite the Canada [Constitution] Act of 1982—matters not explicitly reserved to the provinces devolve to the federation. Provinces may legislate in areas not explicitly reserved to them and not explicitly deemed federal until and unless the federation acts. And there is no mention of animal welfare in the British North America Act or the Canada Act. It is possible that the courts may determine animal experimentation a matter of health or police or educational jurisdiction—which are primarily reserved to the provinces—but there is no probable reason to believe so. It is true that in 1990 the Federal Minister of Health claimed the matter to be beyond the jurisdiction of the federal government in the view of his advisors. But this seems only a convenient way to avoid a controversial issue. After all, the federal government has usually determined it has the right to legislate in areas where direct federal funding is involved.

While legislation may once have been thought to enforce only minimal standards and be difficult to change, the increasing use of enabling legislation overcomes those limitations. And while the animal welfare movement may not have been involved or satisfied traditionally by legislation there is every reason to believe they have been more satisfied *with* legislation than *without* it. Moreover, the British, Swedish and several other national experiences have indicated that legislation can increase both their involvement and their satisfaction.

There is no reason why legislation could not incorporate the existing peer review system and make it more effective by ensuring enforcement through sanctions (which are presently notoriously ineffective). It would eliminate the unevenness of the present system (some animal care committees take their responsibilities very seriously, others do not). By providing effective legal requirements for such committees it could mandate much more effective responsibility, operation and control. It

---

11 Ibid.

could extend the requirements to private institutions, which are presently unevenly administered, and ensure appropriate training and standards for animal technicians. Most importantly, it would require public accountability and a minister responsible to the parliamentary body. The public provides the funds for research through taxation. It is quite remarkable that the research establishment believes it owes no demonstrable responsibility to those on whom it is dependent for its funds.

The C.C.A.C. argument continues, "the implementation of legislation through a national inspectorate would be difficult where institutions are sparsely scattered and frequently isolated over many thousands of miles. Additionally, no government inspectorate could expect to enjoy the benefit of the scientific expertise presently provided, without honorarium, to the CCAC assessment program."[12] In fact Ottawa and the provinces already provide inspectorates in other areas which cover such territory and, anyway, the vast majority of research facilities are to be found within a 100 miles of the U.S. border, many in close proximity to each other. And surely the British inspectorate experience suggests that there are few difficulties with expertise, especially when there can be a national committee to which all problematic cases can be referred. Moreover, the experience of the inspectorate could rapidly make up for any deficiency in expertise.

The power of C.C.A.C.'s claims lies much more readily in the words "without honorarium." The Canadian federal government is unlikely to dig into its pocket for a single penny, especially when it already fails to live up to its legal responsibilities with regard to the provision of an inspectorate for inter-provincial animal transportation. On the other hand, however, the Canadian Federation of Humane Societies has argued that a legislated system should cost no more than the extant voluntary system. Unfortunately animals have a lower priority in Canada than they do in, say, Britain or Sweden, though probably higher than in the U.S.A. and certainly higher than in the Mediterranean countries.

Increased financial constraints hinder C.C.A.C. from performing its current mandate and certainly do not encourage it to think of doing more. Certain council members continue to have exorbitant travel budgets while there are substantial limitations to needed expenditures elsewhere.

In response to incipient public concern regarding animal experimentation, in 1961 the Canadian Federation of Biological Societies established a standing committee on animal care whose guidelines served as the basis for the use of research animals until the establishment of the Canadian Council on Animal Care in 1968, with the support of universities and government. It functioned as a standing

---

12   Ibid.

committee of the Association of Universities and Colleges of Canada until its independence in 1982. There are 21 agencies represented on the Council of 25 persons, only one agency (two persons) of which is not an animal user.

The Council has published a two-volume *Guide to the Care and Use of Experimental Animals* which, even though it is rapidly becoming dated and in need of overhaul, is commonly acknowledged as one of the soundest guides to animal experimentation and one generally favourable to animal interests, requiring constant consideration for animals and the diligent search for alternatives. The Council and its assessment personnel are committed to the greatest consideration for animals consistent with sound research. They demand allegiance to the 3Rs principle, as well as those of "good science, good sense and good sensibility" and "the right animal for the right reasons." Nonetheless, there can be little doubt that in any cost-benefit analysis the weight is more heavily in favour of the researcher over the animal than is the case in Britain and several other European countries.

The Council carries out its responsibilities through a nationwide assessment program involving previously announced site visits and conducted only once every three years or so (site visits are conducted at least annually in the U.S. by its American counterpart and often unannounced). The assessment panel includes the Director or Associate Director of Assessments from the council, usually three research scientists (chosen frequently from those with not only relevant expertise but also with greatest sensibilities) and one representative appointed by the Canadian Federation of Humane Societies (C.F.H.S.). Unfortunately, in invariably having to choose a representative from a C.F.H.S. member society in the locality of the research institution, the result is that the panel member sometimes possesses little or no experience and little knowledge of the procedures or issues. Training for such representatives is essential. Good heart and good sensibility are not enough.

If the institution is found in non-compliance or provisional non-compliance with the guidelines, an unannounced visit can be expected from the Director of Assessments, usually within a year, to see if the 'recommendations' (not requirements) have been implemented. If the recommendations have not been implemented, Council may "take such further actions as deemed necessary." Unfortunately, there is both very little that Council does do, and not much it can do. One university is notorious for its failure to comply, others are quite lackadaisical, especially with regard to the requirement for public participation in their animal care committees. In some institutions the members of the committee have never inspected the animals or their quarters! The lack of effective sanctions minimizes the effectiveness of the Council despite the very real commitment of its professional personnel to the welfare of experimental animals.

The failings of the system of review in Canada revolve around the lack of effective legislation. It is argued that a system of peer review is more satisfactory than legislation since scientists are more responsive to suggestions, recommendations and advice from their peers than they are to legislative control. Yet there is no reason, as the Australian experience suggests, why the peer review system cannot continue under effective, preferably enabling, legislation with effective sanctions for non-compliance.

A further drawback to current Canadian practice is the confidentiality of the assessment panel reports, which can only be made public by the C.C.A.C. or the institution assessed—and then only with C.C.A.C. approval. Indeed, that confidentiality has prevented us from reporting here matters we believe ought to be reported. The argument in favour of confidentiality is that the assessors are more likely to be effectively critical if they know they are not condemning the researcher publicly and the researchers are more likely to be responsive to private criticism. Were it to become public they would be more likely to dig in their heels and defend their practices. While there is considerable merit to that view, strong arguments can be offered against it. Not only does the public have a right to know what it is they are funding but researchers would be more likely to comply initially if they knew their work was subject to public scrutiny. They would know they would have to satisfy public sensibilities and not merely the sensibilities of fellow researchers with common interests.

The researchers argue, however, that if their research activities were in the public domain the more invasive research would make their facilities subject to terrorist activity from the lunatic fringe of the animal rightists. Yet there are very few such documented instances in Canada. To the extent that they may have occurred they have been based on rumour, which is surely far worse than fact. If the assessments were published, then at the very least it would be known which facilities needed protection and at the very best invasive research would not be conducted in a manner likely to give occasion to the legitimate concerns which such terrorists express in a totally illegitimate manner. Moreover, the most effective argument of the terrorists would be removed—that cruel invasive research is being conducted about which the public has a right to know. At the very least, critical assessment reports should be released if the offending institution has not responded appropriately within six months of the assessment panel report.

The unfortunate reality of the Canadian situation is that we do not know from any official sources how many animals are experimented on annually (the figure of two million is a "guesstimate") or what kinds of experiments are undertaken. There are no effective penalties for non-compliance. At any given time several institutions will have failed to comply with relevant standards but none has been punished for failure to meet these modest recommendations—a far worse record than even the U.S. In fact, although C.C.A.C. may request funding agencies to withhold research grants from non-compliant institutions, it has not once done so in its 23 years of existence. While the Canadian system has its merits through its use of peer review, such review needs to be incorporated into a more rigorous, evenly administered and legislated system.

Good judgement, as Plato knew, is better than good law. But, as Aristotle knew, since we cannot rely on people having good judgement, good laws are necessary. And their starting point must be prevailing public sensibilities. It is not an assumption that the public is always or even customarily right but rather that no legislator can afford to ignore the public mind if respect for the law and a sense of community are to be assured. If respect for the law is to go hand in hand with good law then the public mind must be in tune with the relevant ethical sensibilities. And only education, socialization, discussion and debate can refine those sensibilities.

If John Milton in his *Areopagitica* and John Stuart Mill in his *On Liberty* were unduly optimistic in their view that freedom of debate would inexorably lead to the truth, it is beyond doubt that education, socialization, discussion and debate are the prerequisites of the sharpening of the public mind. They are certainly imperfect, certainly subject to excessive influence by those with greater wealth, power and, above all, authority, but they are all we have. We must rely on the expectation that public discourse will lead to greater sensibilities.

Fortunately, history is on the side of progress most of the time, though sometimes dialectically rather than lineally. The history of the last two and a half centuries is in part the history of increased ethical refinement and, as ethics have been refined, better laws have followed. While it is undoubtedly true that humankind may be by nature excessively egotistical, we cannot fail to notice that when ethical issues have been effectively brought to public attention and repeatedly impressed upon the public mind, appropriate legislation has eventually ensued. It is one of the nobler features of humanity that principles may ultimately diminish the excessive pursuit of self-interest.

One of the most common criticisms of those who seek justice for animals is that they are the enemies of human progress, that they ought to be concerned with human rather than animal rights since so many humans are oppressed and deprived in the modern world. Yet history is not on the side of such critics. Many of those who fought for the abolition of slavery, improved penal conditions, factory legislation and race and gender rights were among those who demanded better treatment for animals. Jeremy Bentham, Voltaire, Lord Shaftesbury and Henry Salt may be better known for their humanitarianism than for their concern for the protection of animals, but concerned they were.

Conversely, the anti-vivisectionists Francis Power Cobbe and Walter Hadwen may be more readily recognized as opponents of animal experimentation but they were also influential in social reform and university education for women, and health and sanitation reforms, respectively. The question for them, as now for us, was not whether to choose the interests of humans over animals, but how to balance those interests when they are in conflict. As sensibilities and technology change, so we can afford to give greater emphasis than before to animal interests—not at the expense of human interests but because good science, humanitarianism and concern for all sentient beings are ultimately on the same side. Good science and replacement, refinement and reduction are not enemies but allies.

Let us not leave the impression that all is well, or even leading inexorably to a world in which animals are given their due consideration, in the world of animal experimentation. Continuing spinal experiments on cats, burn experiments on dogs and invasive experiments on monkeys make us shudder. But we are confident that replacements for such experiments can be found if we encourage the scientists to seek them, if we help refine their sensibilities, if we work with rather than against them.

It is not so much professors of ethics we need as scientists and laypersons of refined ethical sensibilities. And education, socialization, discussion and debate are the remedies. The engagement has only begun and progress is in its infancy. But history is on the side of the angels—angels engagé, mind you. When Condorcet and Turgot wrote of the inexorable nature of progress they did not believe that one should stand on the sidelines of history and watch progress occur. Progress has to be made, not analyzed. Sound decisions may sometimes be, as Edmund Burke tells us, a choice between evil and evil—in this case the evil of depriving the sick of a cure and the evil of harming sentient creatures—but with increasing scientific sensibility we are becoming increasingly able to find the cure without inflicting the harm.

Although we must rely on the scientist and the physician to increase their sensibilities to make better scientific decisions we should not rely on them for the ethical decisions. Aristotle distinguishes between *sophia*—scientific or philosophic knowledge—and *phronesis*—practical judgement derived from maturity and experience. The *spoudaios*—the person of sound practical judgement—will usually be neither the scientist nor the philosopher but the person whose general wisdom and knowledge make her or him the representative of the community's interest. It is the *spoudaios* we need on our animal ethics committees.

Chapter Seven

Hunting, Fishing and Fowling

'Unting is all that's worth living for—all time is lost wot is not spent in 'unting—it is like the hair we breathe—if we have it not we die—it's the sport of kings, the image of war without its guilt, and only five-and-twenty per cent of its danger.

It ain't that I loves the fox less, but that I loves the 'ound more.

> — Robert Smith Surtees,
> *Handley Cross*, 1843

Nature Through the Year,[1] a 1946 book dedicated to the glory and wonders of nature, also glorifies the English South Oxfordshire Hunt—and without any hint of inconsistency. Paradoxically, perhaps, hunters have sincerely thought of themselves as the most dedicated nature lovers—even though they may not love the fox less but the 'ound more. Shockingly, to some, today there are Humane Society managers who hunt raccoons with dogs, Humane Society inspectors who shoot deer for pleasure and Humane Society directors who engage in duck-shooting. The managers, inspectors and directors perform their responsibilities with diligence and dedication and show considerable concern for the protection of animals—except apparently where their own pastimes are involved. Both historically—as we tried to show in the first two chapters—and currently humankind has demonstrated a remarkable ambivalence toward our fellow sentient beings.

If hunting is an activity engaged in by those who otherwise show consideration for animal interests, it surely cries out for explanation. Indeed, hunters will often talk of the identification they feel with their prey while actively involved in bringing its life to an end. There is respect and admiration for the object of the hunt—but the consequence is the killing of the object of that respect and admiration! Now it is sometimes said that the hunting is necessary to eliminate predators or to promote a sustainable environment—but that is independent of the fact that hunters engage in the practice because they enjoy it, derive satisfaction from it, not because it is environmentally necessary. 'Environmental necessity' may be used as a justification for the behaviour but it is not an explanation of the motive. The very fact that

---

1 (London: Odhams Press), no author or editor given.

hunting requires a justification, and that hunters are constantly offering them, is itself instructive. One does not feel constrained to justify that which one is confident is right.

The hero of Surtees's novels, John Jorrocks, displays this ambivalent attitude with aplomb. "'Unting" is the "sport of kings"—Jorrocks acquires his stature and self-worth through his dominance over less powerful creatures. Jorrocks's attitude is not dissimilar to that of the poor whites who are (statistically) more racist than the middle class. Our sense of significance is affected by having some beneath us to whom we can feel superior. Dominance of the weaker is one of the ways in which we can achieve it. Thomas Hobbes may have exaggerated when he claimed that there was "a general inclination of all mankind, a perpetual and restless desire of power after power, that ceaseth only in death."[2] But we cannot doubt that it is a common feature of humanity after the age of science if not throughout history. And if we lack power over other humans we exercise it on animals.

For Jorrocks hunting permits "the image of war without its guilt." Men, it appears, derive satisfaction and glory from the conquest of others, although there is guilt attached if the enemy is in principle an equal—a fellow human being. The guilt evaporates if there are few moral restrictions against the hunting of lesser beings—and, of course, "the five-and-twenty per cent of . . . danger" is not because the fox might be the victor but because one's horse might stumble. In fact, the danger is a gross exaggeration, reflective of no other reality than that the hunter wants to be admired for the 'risk' he takes. It should not escape our attention that elsewhere in his novel Surtees has Jorrocks proclaim, "No man is fit to be called a sportsman wot doesn't kick his wife out of bed on a haverage once in three weeks." The dominance over lesser creatures has its parallel in superiority over 'the weaker sex'. Hunting is, to employ the modern idiom, a power trip. Let us not even bother to discuss how hunting may be deemed a 'sport' and its participants 'sportsmen'. Suffice it to say that while hunting may require a skill it is not a contest.

How, then, is there any ambivalence? Is this not simply a case of the unwarranted and unjustifiable slaughter of the weak by the strong? Perhaps, but Jorrocks's love of his 'ounds—and no less of his 'orses—should not be lightly passed over. It is, in no small part, the English love of hunting which contributed to their respect for the animal realm in general. While the fox—or the grouse or the hare or whatever was hunted—was treated without regard to its interests, a deep and wholesome affinity with the creatures who aided in the hunt was acquired, which in turn led to a general respect for the whole of the

---

2   Thomas Hobbes, *Leviathan*, ed. Michael Oakeshott (New York: Collier, 1962), p. 80. First published 1651.

vertebrate kingdom. It may be paradoxical, but it is certainly true, as we noted earlier,[3] that those who first displayed an interest in, and concern for, the study and understanding of animals also shot, stuffed, collected and proudly displayed them. But that does not constitute a justification of such practices today, for, as our ethical sensibilities are honed and as any sustenance and raiment justifications for hunting diminish, so too our moral responsibilities increase.

We are not sure whether our moral recognition of the rights of other animals is innate and tempered by custom and practice or whether it is something acquired as a consequence of refining and extending our moral intuitions beyond encompassing fellow humans. We are rather more inclined toward the former, even though it goes against the grain of what most modern psychologists instruct us is the nature of morals—though not against the Swiss psychiatrist, Carl Jung, who wrote of the unconscious identity we feel for our fellow creatures. It is worth repeating the adage of Francis Bacon, "The inclination of *Goodness* is imprinted deeply in the nature of Man; insomuch, that if it issue not towards Men, it will take unto other living creatures." For Bacon it was our nature to put human interests first but insofar as our human interests were not threatened we had a natural propensity to respect the interest of animals—which involves the requirement that we not harm them unless some significant human interest is at stake which we cannot meet by other means.

We remember as quite young children being taken on fishing trips and hoping against hope that we would not catch anything. Fortunately, our skills matched our ambitions. But we wonder whether our distaste for harming the fish arose from our innate sensibilities or whether we had received some mysterious socialization we cannot recall. The reason that the question may be significant is that, since some young children evidently do enjoy fishing, we wonder whether the natural propensity may exist in different proportions in different persons. Of course, we have no means of answering that question but we raise it as a possible partial explanation of why some are more reluctant to hunt than others. We remain convinced, however, that socialization is the predominant reason that some do hunt to test their skills, develop their prowess, and feel more self-actualized. And the means to deter that development lies in more effective socialization and education by those who recognize that hunting—at least that form of hunting commonly called sport hunting (mainly by the hunters themselves, of course)—is an unnecessary deprivation of the rights and interests of sentient beings with dignity, purpose, communality and reason.

In fact, the argument against hunting—or any activity opposed to legitimate animal interests—can be readily made not merely from the

---

3   See above, pp. 24-25.

interest of the animal but from the interest of humankind. Just as General Gonzalez prohibited bull-fighting in Guanaxuato because of its socially demoralizing effect on the Mexican province's population, so too hunting encourages and promotes humankind's baser propensities. It dulls our sensibilities, arouses our aggression and diminishes our caring. Nor can it be intelligently argued that aggression directed toward animals diminishes our aggression toward fellow humans. Cruelty toward animals has in fact been documented as a precursor of cruelty toward children. The development of soccer, baseball, target shooting and archery—all substitutes for the chase—can scarcely be said to have proven an inhibition against war. In his 1836 novel, *Rory O'More*, Samuel Lover ascribes Shan Regan's improvidence to "his love of debasing amusements—such as cock-fighting, etc."[4] In Lover's estimation, Regan was less, not more, of a man because of his involvement with activities destructive of animal well-being.

How, then, does the hunter defend his apparently unjustifiable behaviour? In essence the defence amounts to a desire to maintain those characteristics which occasioned humankind's development from a primitive to an accomplished animal and a claim that hunting is necessary to sustain the environment, defend the farmer against predators and to ensure the preservation of species.

It is certainly true that the psychological traits of the primordial hunter remain within us. The daring, the courage, the risk of life and limb, all contribute to an image of 'manliness', of providing for one's nearest and dearest without a thought for oneself. One could be proud of one's accomplishments, proud of one's potential self-sacrifice. It is an image appropriate to a warrior fighting a just war—if there are any just wars. But how appropriate is it to the hunter—with his high-powered rifle and telescopic lens? What courage, what 'manliness', what bravery is there in shooting a deer from 500 feet—or, for that matter, 'a man-eating tiger' or an elephant? We fail to see any courage in the hunting of moose or elk or . . . whatever. With primitive weapons there may have been a contest, with modern weapons there is only carnage. The image of the African big game hunters as giants among men is a fraud. "Boastful thugs" is what Desmond Morris calls them.

What, then, of the skill required in the operation of the rifle or, say, the crossbow? A skill it may be, and perhaps a worthy one, but it is a skill just as easily practised on moving non-living targets. And if one must employ one's skill in the wild why not choose a camera? The skill is greater and the photographic rewards are surely no less than that of a carcass. We are confident, in fact, that our photographs of birds, deer, seals, elk, moose and various other wildlife took every bit as much patience, skill and cunning as those of the hunter and are a more

---

4 Samuel Lover, *Rory O'More* (London: Daily Telegraph, undated), p. 94.

worthwhile keepsake than any trophy head. Try as we might to view things from the sport hunter's perspective we can reach no other conclusion than that he (usually 'he', infrequently 'she') hunts for no better reason than that he gets pleasure from killing. And that makes him less of a human being than he otherwise might be. Killing for fun is no fun for the animal, and for the human it is a fun derived from the very basest of human appetites.

One would have hoped that the refining of human moral sensibilities would have diminished the desire to slaughter—slaughter, we might add, without much risk (unless it is from a fellow hunter's carelessness with his weapon) and without courage. In fact it has in recent years brought about a new carnage, especially in North America—the game ranch, which is distinguished from the game farm in that the latter raises game for consumption not hunting. On the game ranch the intrepid big game hunter can fearlessly bag an unarmed but decidedly wild turkey for around $350 or go the whole hog and tame a ferocious zebra in its lair for around $5,000-6,000. Need it be said that such bravery comes from those with rather more money than derring-do?

While game ranches are only now becoming widespread they have in fact existed in Texas since the 1930s and today it is still Texas which has the largest and the most. Today they are common in a number of American states and in Canada, especially in Alberta, Saskatchewan and Ontario. While it is impossible to justify game ranches on the basis of the hunting—other than quite simply as killing fields—the ranchers themselves defend their sites as a means of conservation of the threatened species of Africa and Asia. They can thrive in Texas but will soon become extinct on the African and Asian continents, suffering the greatest depletion of wildlife through the uncontrolled explosion and consequent geographic expansion of the human population.

Human population explosion is indeed a far greater threat to endangered wildlife—and that not yet endangered—than the activities of any hunters. As the human population increases dramatically in many parts of Asia, Africa and to an only somewhat lesser degree in South America, so the habitats of wildlife are destroyed by the need to turn ever-increasing acreages of land over to agriculture. Indeed, while we all constantly concern ourselves about the very real danger to the environment caused by industrial pollution, the loss of the rain forests, the effects of the burning of the oilwells in the Gulf War and the Alaskan oil-spill disaster, the potential catastrophe from human population explosion is greater than all of these combined.

If the presence of African wildlife in North America is so beneficial why then is it hunted on the game ranches—which, being private, are exempted in some jurisdictions from seasonal hunting restrictions? The answer quite simply is a financial one. No one would have been willing to pay to have the animals brought from Africa or Asia in the first place if others hadn't been willing to pay even more for the debased luxury of killing some of them. The overall viability of certain species is promoted by the wealth of those who want to kill them! One is reminded of Adam Smith's providential invisible hand of the market place through which the economic interests of the weak are promoted by the economic self-interest of the strong. From a moral standpoint—beneficial to both the general public and the animals—wildlife game parks or zoo parks would be distinctly preferable, but until governments increase the relative priority they allot to animals those with the big bucks will continue to kill the big bucks. Until governments act, the big guns of American business will be both the individual threat to and the source of species protection for endangered exotic wildlife.

'Sport' hunters may appear the enemies of those who would protect wildlife, but the gulf between them is not unbridgeable. As Jorrocks's statement about the fox and hounds indicates the more responsible hunters give all animals consideration—the hunter's pleasure above all, the hounds second, and the fox a distant third. (By 'more responsible' we mean those hunters who feel [wrongly, in our view] in tune with nature when they hunt, make every effort to inflict no pain on their prey and do their utmost to remedy matters if they wound rather than kill.) Clearly, we would distance ourselves from Jorrocks, but only in the weight we would give to each interest, even though the shifts in weight would be substantial. These different weights, producing a different balance, involve a redirection of priorities and emphases, but not a complete change of the more responsible hunter's mind. It is thus that socialization, discussion and debate can alter human attitudes—if not always in this generation, then at least toward greater changes in the next. Vigilance and commitment are what it takes. And if there is a degree of respect for the animal, however paradoxical, stimulation of that respect can end the carnage.

Fishing is a 'sport' akin to hunting. But at least there is no pretence about the bravery. It is entirely a test of skill and the product is often consumed at the table—unlike the fox and the zebra—if not thrown back. But there is a mistaken and widespread belief that cold-blooded animals generally and fish particularly feel no pain. Indeed, as we saw in the previous chapter, American legislation on animal experimentation makes the assumption that cold-blooded animals are ipso facto less sentient than warm-blooded animals. We can find no justification for that prevalent belief. Indeed, fish are reasonably complex animals with a spinal cord and a nervous system. We can only assume that the belief that they feel no pain with barbed metal piercing their skin is because they neither cry out nor make anguished facial expressions in the manner of a mammal. Nonetheless, while there is little scientific evidence on the *degrees* of pain in fish, their physiological responses indicate beyond any reasonable doubt that significant pain is felt. While fish are evidently less sentient than the more complex mammals, there are good grounds to believe that fish are treated with significantly less consideration than they deserve. Indeed anglers have probably endangered more species than hunters. Even the magnificent sturgeon has been overfished to the point of extinction.

It is probably unfair, but we cannot resist the lines attributed to Dr. Samuel Johnson, "angling or float fishing I can only compare to a stick and a string with a worm on one end and a fool on the other." If there is skill in fishing it is rather more in fly-fishing than float-fishing and it is predominantly fly-fishing which is enjoyed for sport rather than food. And when it is primarily for sport it cannot be justified, for there is inadequate compensating good to justify the cruelty. Fool or cruel is the choice of those who fish.

Those who fish for 'sport' have never bothered to deny that their primary reason for fishing is pleasure. This is quite unlike the hunter, who usually hides his pleasure in a labyrinth of environmental justifications; yet the hunter acknowledges the sentience of his prey while those who fish do not. For example, Myron E. Shoemaker, in his 1942 book, *Fresh Water Fishing*, deems fishing analogous with "other types of sport—baseball, football, golf, hunting, basketball, and all the rest" and seems to consider the very purpose of fish "their inestimable value as a medium of recreation." The reason for understanding the fish in "their struggle for existence" is so that "we may wisely use [it] to a good advantage to protect the very thing we enjoy—good fishing."[5] As ever, Shoemaker talks of anglers as "the friends of nature," continually mentions the importance of conservation but never once considers that fish can be anything but entirely subservient to the interests of the "army of fishermen" engaged in their "wholesome, healthy, recreational activity."[6] Not once does Shoemaker ever question the right of humanity to kill fish for no better reason than recreation. He openly acknowledges that the primary reason for fishing is no longer, as it once was, to secure food. Good laws are always to protect the interests of the angler, never the fish. Either Shoemaker has no conception of the sentience of fish and the cruelty perpetrated by the lure or he simply doesn't care. Nature is there, Shoemaker frequently avers, sometimes explicitly, sometimes implicitly, solely for the benefit of humankind.

Things have changed in the half century since the publication of Shoemaker's popular book, but not for the better. Thumbing the pages of the *Ontario Fisherman*—or for that matter most similar magazines—one encounters the same sentiments again, dressed in the language of conservation. Any degree of scrutiny will demonstrate, however, that what is meant is the conservation of fish for the benefit

5 *Fresh Water Fishing* (New York: Doubleday, 1942), pp. ix, 2.
6 Ibid., p. 3.

of the angler alone. On page after page we read advertisements for the latest electronic gadgetry and modern technology to find the fish and lure them to their death. Modern methods make fishing even more one-sided, even less of a skill. Every effort is made to make fishing easier. Yet the anglers have the audacity to continue to call themselves "sportsmen."

Now we do not at all wish to suggest that hunters or anglers are somehow in their nature cruel or uncaring people—at least any more than humankind in general. We believe that, generally speaking, hunters and anglers engage in their recreation at least in the first instance without giving much thought to the consequences of their actions upon their prey. Hunting and fishing are legitimate activities within most societies—necessary activities for food and clothing in some—and are undertaken quite genuinely as outdoor recreation and viewed by the participants as "wholesome" and "healthy," to use Shoemaker's words. They are undertaken because it is not yet customary in our society to subject such activities to personal scrutiny, though it is clearly becoming increasingly so. The answer, as indeed to so much, lies in education, discussion and debate.

Education is, however, most effective as socialization. That is, it is the minds of the young which must be captivated, as the good educators have always known. That seventeenth-century cynic Thomas Hobbes told us that thoughts were but "Scouts and Spies to range abroad and find a way to the things Desired"—in other words our thoughts are rationalizations of our interests, not impartial attempts to discover the truth. As always, Hobbes exaggerates. But, as equally always, there is an important kernel of truth in Hobbes's declaration. We do tend to seek justifications for what we want to believe; we do look for arguments which serve our cause. Hence the importance of imparting ideas on those early in life. Once one has become committed to a cause—be it hunting or anti-vivisection—one tends to give far greater weight to arguments and evidence supportive of one's entrenched views and interests than to those which counter them. It is not that discussion and debate cannot influence the minds of the more mature but rather that it is far more difficult to persuade the already convinced than those whose ideas are open and uncommitted.

Let us not, however, be fooled by Hobbes into believing that it is in principle impossible to convince the hunter and the angler, but let us recognize with Hobbes that the task is a difficult one, our arguments must be overwhelming and we must state them repeatedly.

As we suggested earlier, the course of history is on the side of increasing recognition of animal interests, but history is dialectical in its progress, not linear. That means that there are momentary lapses in the historical march of the human mind; there are occasional regresses within the general progress. While the proponents of animal interests have done an effective job in capturing media attention on the problems of the whales, the seal hunt, animal experimentation and the like, they have lost the initiative with the young. Once the Bands of Mercy and the Jack London Clubs abounded. Humane Societies directed a very significant part of their activities to the education of the young. This is far less true today. If animal advocates were once again to concentrate on impressing the youthful mind, much of the difficulty of persuading the contrarily committed would be avoided.

Unlike anglers, hunters do not rely on the pursuit of pleasure as the justification for their activities. They tell us they are necessary to the protection of the environment and humankind's well-being, even necessary to the interests of the animals themselves. Mankind has historically been one of the predators, so the argument goes, and predation is necessary to maintain nature in balance. If hunting is discontinued, there will be a dangerous imbalance with the gravest consequences for the environment. Let us acknowledge that there is superficial merit in this view. But let us also indicate that the matter is not so simple as the hunter suggests. After all, the greatest change in man as predator occurred thousands of years ago as we became farm animal domesticators rather than primarily hunters. Even further back in the clouded early history of humankind on this planet we changed from vegetarian hominids to meat-eating humans. Neither of these momentous changes appears to have occasioned environmental calamities. Nature managed to adjust and maintain its balance.

Nonetheless, evolutionary change is relatively slow—or rather the change may occur suddenly in genetic structure but the preconditions of that change may take centuries or even millennia to evolve. And now that environmental change is so rapid—as a consequence of technological, industrial, and agricultural progress and, most of all, human population explosion—nature simply hasn't time to evolve to meet the new conditions. Paradoxically, the changes have resulted from humankind's excessive interference in the natural order of things, but this regrettably requires further interference, not less. We can neither undo what we have done, nor unlearn what we have learned. We must interfere once again with nature but now by attempting to redress the imbalances we have created and that, unfortunately, sometimes means that we must restrict animal populations, however distasteful that may seem.

It would be nothing short of a providential miracle, though, if that which hunters sought as their prey were that which a redress of the imbalance of nature required and in the numbers nature required. If Adam Smith's invisible hand works in the economy it doesn't in the ecology. After all, the hunter is not hunting primarily for food—more than adequately provided from other sources in the Western world—but for the pleasure of the hunt. To this end governments institute hunting seasons and species and number restrictions, although unfortunately the regulation-setting employees in environment or natural resources ministries are often hunters themselves whose knowledge of the hunters' interests is far greater than their knowledge of the requirements of nature. Still, the point is well made that there is an overabundance of some species detrimental to the vegetation and to other species and there simply is inadequate time to permit nature to find a new balance.

However, it should scarcely be imagined that government departments actually administer their jurisdictions with the overall interest of the environment in view, despite their protests to the contrary. In Ontario, for example, the Ministry of Natural Resources has sought to increase the number of deer to provide prey for the hunters, even though it is commonly acknowledged that an overabundance of browsing animals is destructive of the habitat.[7] While a case can be made for sport hunting if circumstances require it, surely no case can be made for a harmful manipulation of the animal numbers which necessitate it. In fact, as a consequence of the artificial manipulation by the Ontario ministry, hunting seasons were actually lengthened in several areas in 1990.

Nor should we be persuaded by the hunters' rhetoric that their purpose is to protect the environment and promote the long-term interests of conservation and the animals they hunt. The real voice of the hunter was expressed in the August 1990 issue of *Angler and Hunter* by its associate editor Ron Truman. "Ontario is up to its ears in whitetails," he rejoiced, "We deal with abundance, lots of venison on the hoof, lots of *super-duper sized antler-carrying road rats*."[8] Those are scarcely the words of a responsible, caring environmentalist who, at the very least, would want to root out the sick and infirm, not those which make the best trophies. Of course, one of the traditional arguments in favour of hunting is that the hunters kill the weak and infirm and thus improve the general stock. In fact hunters always seek out the biggest bucks, as Truman is here admitting—unless their permit restricts them to non-antlered deer.

Some local government authorities have been persuaded by hunters to pay bounties for wolves (even though such bounties have been illegal in Ontario since 1972). The fear is that the wolves will diminish the deer 'harvest'. Ignoring the fact that they have confused wolves with coyotes in reporting their pervasiveness, hunters who cared about nature and the environment would gladly let the 'wolves' act according to their nature. Their real fear is that the wolves will get the hunters' prey and

---

7   See, for example, R.D. Lawrence, "Conservation in Ontario: A Time for Change," in *OSPCA Animal's Voice* (Spring 1991):4-11. We are indebted to R.D. Lawrence for much of the information on which this section is based.

8   Quoted in ibid., p. 6. Emphasis added.

deprive them of their pleasure. Again we can come to no other conclusion than that hunters revel in the killing. There is also no reason to believe that the practices of hunters and governments elsewhere in North America are any better than those in Ontario.

Such criticisms are laid not at the feet of the worst hunters but the very best, the most responsible. The less responsible engage in poaching, grossly inadequate care of their hounds, which are frequently lost and left to starve, wilful and consistent trespassing, and cutting off the more valuable hind-quarters of slaughtered prey. Of course, the more responsible hunters are just as opposed to such practices as are the most adamant of animal welfarists.

If the government of Ontario were seriously concerned with the environment and animal interests, as it claims, a great deal could be *readily* done—and the same applies to other Canadian provinces and American states, for Ontario is certainly not even among the gravest sinners. Already little is done to enforce the existing weak legislation. For example, 245 conservation officers cover an average of 6,288 square kilometres each—an admittedly misleading figure, since so much of the far north is very sparsely inhabited. Still it is a far from adequate number to enforce hunting regulations, since their other more extensive and far more 'important' duties take up the majority of their time. However, 245 officers is 244 more than the province compensates to enforce the provisions against cruelty to animals—other than the provincial police force, that is, which prefers to leave such matters to Humane Society inspectors. Such inspectors possess police powers in these matters but are paid out of charitable contributions to the Humane Societies. Perhaps the differing numbers reflect the government's respective commitment to legal hunting and animal protection.

Poaching has reached epidemic proportions. Grouse hunters shoot from inside vehicles, venison is sold on the black market, and illegally acquired deer and moose antlers and hides are readily traded abroad for lucrative rewards, thus encouraging even more poaching—and all because the conservation officers have inadequate numbers and time to enforce existing provisions. But even if existing provisions were enforced, little would be done to restore the balance of nature, even though Ontario law has been amended to cover rare, threatened, and endangered species. However, there is no legislation to provide for the protection of endangered habitat.

Regulation is urgently needed to protect the black bear, which may be legally hunted in the spring as well as the fall. Since there are few ways a hunter can distinguish between a male and a female, either from a distance or from his perch up a tree, if he kills a female its cubs will almost certainly die from starvation. Spring hunting results in demonstrable cruelty, even if the target is killed painlessly. Why, one might ask, would one want to kill a black bear at all—if not from the senselessness of killing for its own sake? To protect moose? In fact, the answer lies in substantial profit. In the Orient, a bear's gall bladder may be sold for a few thousand dollars ($18,500 is the most recent estimate), its paws for over $100 a piece, and lesser parts such as claws and teeth for lesser amounts. Killing bears, legally and now more often illegally, has become big business.

One of the practices now current in Ontario and elsewhere is bear-baiting, as it is commonly called. The name of the practice is confusing, since bear-baiting was the name for the 'sport' of setting dogs upon, and tying fireworks to the tails of, bears from the Middle Ages until the practice was outlawed in Britain in 1838. Now the term covers the abominable practice of strewing a small area with carrion to attract the prey. The hunter waits up a nearby tree and shoots the bear when it enters the baited area. The skill required is somewhat less than that of a ten-year-old hitting a window with a baseball from about 15 feet. Surely, responsible hunters ought to be up in arms (to employ a suggestive metaphor) demanding that such practices be outlawed.

Are there, then, no cases where animal populations are excessive and need to be decreased? Indeed, there are. Often Humane Society members will trap such animals live and remove them to areas where there is a greater scarcity, although it is a practice fraught with danger to the animals if the participants are not skilled and knowledgeable. Fortunately, some are so skilled and are willing to devote considerable time and energy to the activity, although one must concede that available evidence suggests that most animals which are so moved (e.g., raccoons) die in the wild in a short space of time. However, that kind of movement, even when successful, is restricted to relatively small numbers and to animals which are not too large.

Elephants are clearly too large. We are constantly being made aware of the terrible plight of the elephant, which is threatened with extinction throughout much of Africa, partly by the nefarious activities of ivory poachers, partly by the population explosion which encroaches on their habitat. Ironically, and despairingly, though, there are parts of Africa where the elephant population has risen, and is rising, at such a dramatic rate that they need to be culled annually. For the elephant, if the hunter doesn't get you, the conservationist will.[9] Overall, the elephant population is halved every decade, yet in the countries which have been effective in preventing, or at least severely limiting, ivory poaching, the game rangers have had to kill many thousands of them—46,000 in a 45-year period in Uganda—just over 1,000 a year—and hundreds annually in Zimbabwe. Humankind has so upset the balance of nature that if elephants are allowed to breed unhindered

---

9 Our information on elephant data is derived from Morris, *Animal Contract*, pp. 74-76.

by the mendacity of ivory poachers they rapidly devour the available food supply, destroy the vegetation for other species, and starve to death. It is because of such situations that we cannot rely on the customary palliative of allowing nature to run its course and restore the balance. We have so upset the balance through our dominance of nature that only humankind can restore the balance by further but opposite manipulation—that is, if it can be restored at all.

The African elephant population reduced from 1.3 million to 740,000 between 1979 and 1988. Over 60,000 a year of those magnificent creatures were destroyed. While it is thus but a small proportion which are 'culled' or 'cropped'—less than three per cent of those which died and were not replaced—the thought of game rangers herding groups of 30-50 or so together and mowing them down with machine guns is sickening. It is sickening but without acceptable alternative.

On a less grand scale, the nutria—a muskrat native to South America—are overabundant and eating the Louisiana wetlands down to the mud now that they are no longer trapped for their fur as a consequence of decline in the fur trade. Here there is some hope that nature can respond, for an increase in the nutria population stimulates an increase in the alligator population which feeds on them. But how long can we wait while the remaining flora and fauna are decimated by the excess of nutria? And anyway it is agricultural expansion which has had more effect on the water level than the nutria.

A thousand years ago wolves and bears were indigenous to Britain. Hunters extirpated them. In Canada, hunters extirpated the great auk, the sea mink, and the swift fox (though in the last case poison was an even greater factor and the animal has now been reintroduced into Canada). Other species are under threat from the hunter—the eastern wolverine, the Newfoundland pine marten, the prairie long-tailed weasel, and the grey fox (technically 'rare' rather than 'threatened'). While the burrowing owl and the roseate tern are not hunted, their continued existence is threatened by the activities of hunters. In the U.S.A. the hunter has eradicated, among others, the passenger pigeon, the Eastern elk, and the plains wolf, while numerous other species are threatened.

Let us not, however, leave the impression that it is hunting which poses the greatest threat to wildlife. In Bangladesh, for example, rhinoceros, yak, and several species of monkey have been extirpated. Elephants, royal Bengal tigers, crocodiles, lizards, frogs, snakes, and dozens of species of birds are on the endangered list. In 1983 a ban was imposed on hunting threatened wildlife with up to ten years in prison as the penalty. While the ban has been ineffective, illegal tree-felling, depletion of underground water, natural disasters, and the huge human birth rate are even more significant factors in the animal population decline. And while Bangladesh has the worst record in Asia, other countries are not far behind. It is difficult to know how Bangladesh's enormous problems might be resolved, for whereas a 25 per cent proportion of forest is needed to maintain an appropriate ecological balance, only six per cent remains forested.

It is ironic that we face such contradictory problems. The Gulf War wrought havoc on all the indigenous wildlife both through the oil intentionally spilled in the Gulf by Saddam Hussein and the pollution of the air by the criminal burning of the oil wells. Elsewhere the plethora of certain species threaten others and the vegetation. For example, the vastly increased presence of ring-billed gulls on the Great Lakes has had a devastating impact on other species such as the piping plover. We must both restore and cull—the latter hopefully only when there is no viable alternative. In his classic *Wildlife in America*,[10] Peter Matthiessen depicted the damage wrought on our planet by the hunters. He wrote of the loss of the short-tailed albatross to satisfy the Oriental market for its feathers, the reduction in the hawk population, including the beautiful Aplomado falcon, "by that body of American gunners which regards the passing bird of prey as a fair target,"[11] the extermination of the deer in Massachusetts, and on and on. But he noted equally that the activities of the lumber, mining, and other industrial interests were prime causes of the early depletion of wildlife before our industrial and technological revolutions became the uncontrolled monsters of the present. We should recognize, though, that some early companies, such as the Governor and Company of Adventurers into Hudson's Bay (more popularly known in Canada today as The Bay), were at least as much benefactors as they were culpable through concern for the wildlife of their field personnel and their record-keeping of animals and their behaviour.

If we must cull on occasion, how is it to be done? The hunters, of course, claim that they are the appropriate ones to do it. Not only will they keep the excesses in check but they will even pay for the privilege through license fees. Moreover, they are a constant stimulus to the economy through their purchases of weapons and shot. Hunters insist they are truly public benefactors, for if they were not to eliminate the excesses it would be left to government to fund all the necessary extermination.

Prima facie the argument appears to have some merit. Or at least it would if we could have any confidence that the animals they killed were the ones which a consideration of ecological interests indicated were the ones that needed to be killed. There is in fact no shred of evidence that it is so. On the contrary, if deer are depleted, hunters demand the government take action to increase the stock. If abundant,

---

10   2d ed. (New York: Viking Penguin, 1987). (First published 1959.)
11   Ibid., 1987 ed., p. 47.

they claim their actions are necessary to maintain an ecological balance. Their purpose is the killing, not the health of the environment, as our discussion of the Ontario situation indicated. Of course, if a knowledgeable and caring government determines what may be hunted and in what numbers, then the hunters have a point—even though we would be quick to suggest that the destructive attitudes of the hunters encourage generally aggressive behaviour toward animals rather than a concern for their protection. The question must be whether governments make sound decisions in these areas. To date the answer appears to be that even if they had the will they self-confessedly lack the knowledge.

In January 1990 the Director of the Wildlife Branch of the Ontario Ministry of Natural Resources published a 60-page Report, *Towards a Wildlife Strategy for Ontario*. The report covers 'Wildlife Issues' and is the first of several projected reports arising from ongoing workshops throughout Ontario. One might initially wonder why it took until 1990 to produce the Report, since there has been public concern for half a century. But that would be a somewhat unfair criticism. Emotions abound, but knowledge is scarce. It would be unwise for governments to act in the absence of sound knowledge. But what is disturbing about the report is that even now it only raises questions and provides no answers.

Time and again we read, "we do not have the data base or knowledge required" followed by "Knowledge provides the basis. Knowledge is essential. Knowledge is critical." They acknowledge "confusion and misinformation," concede "we do not know what the habitat requirements (or interactions among habitats) are for the species we are to protect and manage." Further, "The impacts (positive and negative) of rehabilitated species on wildlife populations and human society must be determined." Most significantly, they confirm that they do not know what has to be known if they are to decide which animals and in what numbers need to be 'trimmed'. They tell us, "The present status of most wildlife populations (absolute population size estimates) is not known and the Ministry has no practical means of measuring most populations . . . [there is] the need for much more knowledge to arrive at [an] acceptable definition of 'optimal populations'." The Ministry thus openly acknowledges that it does not have the expertise to make the decisions regarding hunting seasons and appropriate target numbers or the means to determine between the potentially conflicting interests of bear and moose or wolf and deer—which really means the conflicting interests of humans with bear, moose, wolf and deer.

Culling or hunting, there is no one available to make sufficiently knowledgeable decisions. Nor should we imagine Ontario particularly backward. We have no reason to believe its "experts" any less expert than anyone else's experts. In fact, the admission of lack of knowledge may be a blessing. Just as Socrates knew that admission of ignorance was the first step to knowledge, so too the Ministry of Natural Resources' recognition of the need for knowledge as a pre-condition of sound decisions is infinitely preferable to the adamance of those who do not know they do not know. And that is what we have traditionally been served.

Of course, even if they knew, we are not sure that there would be easy solutions to problems. What if the offending superabundant creatures were, say, rodents? Who could they persuade to hunt them? There is a notable paucity of Pied Pipers around. It is remarkable that authorities seem to believe that if the offences to ecological imbalance are committed by creatures whom no one wishes to hunt then the ecology is capable of looking after itself quite satisfactorily.

Some of the omissions in the Ontario government report are quite startling. "Numerous human activities are damaging our environment," we read. "Decreases in the quality of air, land, and water due to global warming, acid rain, toxic wastes etc. affect habitat quality and impact on wildlife populations." Hunters and anglers are notable by their absence. Other than a hint that their range of activities might be increased to include hunting on Crown wildlife lands and the provincial parks, where they are presently prohibited, hunters do not get a mention until the last third of the Report and nowhere is it suggested that they may be a part of the problem rather than the solution. In the final pages of the report we are told, "There are many wildlife uses, and examples include hunting, fishing [the very first time fishing is even mentioned], photography, and viewing." Neither here, nor elsewhere, does the Report differentiate between the destructive and non-destructive 'use' of wildlife! Although the Report hints that wildlife might be a value in itself there is nothing in the discussion of wildlife uses which suggests they take that view seriously.

There are always, of course, at least two sides to a story, and much of the Report reflects a welcome awareness of the increased public concerns regarding sustainable development and the ecosystem approach to resource management. The Report indicates that there is an increasing sensibility to animals, though one is amused by the failure to discuss 'sensitive' issues. The shortest section of the Report is under "Consumptive Uses: (2): Recreational Uses." The whole section reads "Should some consumptive recreational uses be limited, such as hunting?" No further word follows. No answer is attempted, no discussion ensues. No wonder it can be rightly said that the Report raises questions and provides no answers. But it is an important step that the question is raised. It is up to animal protectionists to provide an answer and to ensure that government acts on it. In fact in September of 1991 the Ministry began to demonstrate a welcome increased sensitivity. It decided that the excess of deer at Rondeau Provincial Park in Southern Ontario required the culling of 80 per cent of the population. But instead of handing the tame deer over to the hunters it decided to have Ministry officials shoot the deer. Moreover, it determined that some of the remainder should be sterilized, thus reducing the likelihood of a recurrence.

We have so far discussed only 'sport' or 'recreational' hunting and fishing. And, of course, there are other types of hunting which are far more defensible. Thus when Canadian or other native peoples hunt for food and to a lesser degree clothing for themselves and their families and use all parts of the animal for some end or other, they are acting entirely within the legitimate bounds of nature—far more so than the eaters of domesticated meat. In fact, if Inuit were not to hunt meat they would quickly starve, for the areas they inhabit rarely have vegetation. Their diet is almost entirely animal.

A sound case can also be made that a farmer is entitled to protect his stock from predators. Owls prey on ducks, osprey devour trout from stock ponds, and we hear of wolves killing sheep and calves. In principle we can see no legitimate objection to farmers protecting their stock against predation. However, problems occur if, say, the predator belongs to an endangered species. And one is entitled to ask whether farmers have taken sufficient care to protect their stock by adequate fencing and accommodation. If we acknowledge the farmers' right to protect their stock we must also ask how it is to be accomplished. Far too often it is by trap-setting—and traps will frequently ensnare non-target animals and inflict the most barbaric cruelty on the trapped animal. Farmers who have a sensibility toward animal life—and a number do—will take every precaution, even though some may be expensive, to ensure that their stock is adequately protected from potential predators.

Around 8 per cent of Americans are reported to be involved in hunting and angling, and somewhat less than 4 per cent of Canadians. Americans have developed an image of themselves as rugged individualists tearing down frontiers to build the promised land. In Canada law, order, and administration preceded population settlement and Canadians have a much more composed and orderly conception of themselves. Canadians are rather less readily self-fulfilled through proving their mastery—be it over other persons or other creatures. Given, then, that only about 2 per cent of Canadians fish and a further two per cent hunt, it is quite remarkable how much time, energy and money is devoted to their interests by provincial governments—but that is minuscule compared to the United States.

Most hunting in the United States takes place on public lands—state and federal parks, forests and wildlife refuges—a rather inopportune use of the idea of a 'refuge' ("Come into my parlour," said the spider to the fly.) The maintenance of such public lands is predominantly at general public expense, although there are park entrance fees (payable by everyone, of course, not just hunters) and hunting licence fees. There are over 400 wildlife refuges in the U.S. and its possessions, over half of which permit hunting and trapping, and almost half of which contain threatened and endangered species. Almost 400,000 animals annually are killed on these 'refuges', according to official statistics which, of course, ignore all the unreported killings. It is known from ranger findings that at least 12,000 further animals are crippled annually and die later from their injuries or starvation. Not one of these animals—say four million a decade—was killed to serve any other purpose than to satisfy the hunters. Remember, we are talking of the wildlife refuges alone and are ignoring those killed on other lands and the hundred thousand a year killed by trapping on federal property. National Parks have historically forbidden trapping and hunting, but in some instances this regulation has been evaded by renaming them 'national recreation areas'—and the Ontario *Wildlife Strategy* Report has at least raised the question of whether the use of its own wildlife lands and provincial parks might be similarly extended.

Each year half a billion dollars is spent by the U.S. government, and about 25 million by the individual states, on its public land programs. Naturally, only a relatively small proportion of that covers hunting-related costs, but it is a great deal more than warranted by the eight per cent of the population who are hunters. Furthermore, some $65 million a year is paid by the federal government to the states to promote hunting—and these funds are used to burn, clear cut, bulldoze, flood and defoliate land for the benefit of the hunter and trapper. In addition, state and federal governments support programs financially to provide food for game animals, maintain lakes to attract fowl, and stock lakes with fish—out of all proportion to the taxes paid by hunters and anglers. This is in large part due to the effective lobbying of hunting and firearms advocates in the U.S. While the funds expended in Canada are proportionately a good deal less, they are still significantly greater than the four per cent of anglers and hunters could possibly justify.

Occasionally, if very infrequently today, one hears that it is necessary to hunt dangerous animals because of their attacks upon humans. Today most people recognize that wild animals attack humans only in rare circumstances—if they believe themselves, their habitats or their offspring are in danger, if they are starving, or if they mistake the human for their regular prey. Even the notorious shark prefers to avoid rather than encounter humans, though Australia and the idyllic Caribbean island of Curaçao still go to inordinate lengths to protect the foolhardy swimmer—in the latter case by the authorities feeding the sharks at one end of the island while the tourists bathe at the other! Certainly, the movies popular in the 1940s and 1950s depicting the glorious conquests of hunter over malevolent foe—whether it be lion, python or the vegetarian gorilla—were the product of directors' lively but warped imaginations as no less are the contemporary and almost comically careless shark films. And the nineteenth- and early twentieth-century novels which depicted, say, the brave white sahib rescuing the grateful Indian villagers from 'the man-eating tiger' (F. Marion Crawford's *Mr. Isaacs*, for example) were based upon prevalent but scarcely fact-based myths. Certainly, if a hunter attacks a prey without immediate success and in a careless manner there will be some reprisal—even though the bear or the wolf (or the docile deer or the doting raccoon) are not likely to be carrying modern weapons. Even apparently harmless creatures fight back in extremis. As far back as 1831 wounded whooping cranes were reported as "putting the fowler to flight, and fairly driving him off the field."[12] One cannot but recall that anonymous, poignant French epigram: *"Cet animal est très méchant. Quand on l'attaque il se défend."* (This animal is very wicked. When attacked it defends itself.)

"I was already beginning mentally to enter their world and to feel their dramas as my dramas."[13] So writes Desmond Morris of his watching pike and roach while he was a youth. Morris is not radical. He does not believe that animals and humans are equal. He is not a vegan or a vegetarian. But Morris does identify with animals, including fish. He feels an affinity toward them. We are different from them but we share common interests, a common habitat, often a common purpose. If hunters could extend their vision of the environment just a little toward the sensibilities of a Desmond Morris they would come to see animals as ends in themselves, not mere objects of humankind's recreation.

---

12 Quoted in Matthiessen, *Wildlife in America*, p. 253.
13 Desmond Morris, *Animalwatching: A Field Guide to Animal Behaviour* (London: Jonathan Cape, 1990), p. 7.

Chapter Eight

Frivolous Fur:
Veneration and Environmentalism

The reckless depletion of natural resources that has marked the development of North America was first exhibited by the fur trade.

— Edgar McInnis, *Canada: A Political and Social History*

Every Canadian has, or ought to have, a sentimental attachment to the fur trade in some degree, even if it is tempered by the recognition of how damaging to animal interests its consequences have been. Canada's early commercial and cultural history is based on it—Canada's youth escaped the seigneurie to become coureurs de bois and feel the freedom of the wild. The foundations of Canada's trading wealth were created by it. Even if Europe gained more by the trading, a stable indigenous merchant class was settled in what later became the major Canadian centres of commerce. For Americans, fur was somewhat important in the origins of commercial trading but it was never the centre of activity it became in non-maritime Canada.

For Europeans fur was a luxury commodity reserved to give expression to the vanity of the wealthy. For northern North Americans fur touched all and was often the determinant of comfort or poverty. For the native populations fur proved the one escape from poverty—and the route to cultural calamity. It is scarcely surprising, then, that the North American attitude to fur has been more resistant to change than that of the Europeans. North America, Canada especially, still has a viable, if decreasing, fur industry, providing employment and income to a small but not unimportant segment of the community. Moreover, the native population is more dependent than others on fur-bearing animals as a means of sustenance and subsistence. Much of the Canadian and American population, in its guilt about traditional mistreatment of aboriginal peoples and its historical failure to consider their economic and cultural interests, is thus sympathetic to their cause.

When the early explorers discovered to their dismay that Canada was not the ready route to Cathay, that it did not possess the wealth available to the plunderers of Mexico, it was commercial fishing, whaling and the fur trade which persuaded the Europeans to stay. Without the fur trade most of the Canadian interior would not have been worth colonizing, for whaling and fishing are by their nature maritime activities.

While the fur trade was initially a casual activity of fishermen, European fashion decreed the lavish use of fur for robe trimmings, cloaks, and above all the ubiquitous beaver hat—though the winter short-tailed weasel in its white or "ermine" phase was the most avidly sought pelt. European fashion was fickle, the vicissitudes of trade uncertain and the supply subject to interference. But since resources other than lumber were scarce—there was no coal in the interior and ore and minerals were later discoveries—and since agriculture was only productive in the more southerly lands, fur, which began as a sideline, became a staple of the economy.

In the twentieth century the portion of the Canadian gross national product derived from fur has substantially declined. Nonetheless, it is still considered sufficiently important that, following the collapse of one of the major fur auction houses in 1990, the federal government provided an unbudgeted $1.8 million to promote the fur industry. And in the summer of 1991 the socialist premier of Ontario spoke of the importance of trapping to the province's economy. While for Europe fur has become an almost entirely moral question, for Canada—and Russia, to a lesser degree the United States—fur is still partly an economic issue. And if one is to ask to whom the furs are to be sold, given the European and increasing North American reluctance to purchase, the answer lies in the Orient. As the economic might of Japan is felt throughout the world and as Korea follows in its footsteps, so the Oriental demand for luxury goods increases rapidly. And the sensibility toward animal interests is notoriously lacking in the Orient—despite the sensitivities of Oriental religions. The Orient is becoming a lucrative market for these furs—especially the more luxurious ones—which Western customers are no longer as willing to wear.

We once again encounter ambivalence. With the intent of maintaining the economic viability of a moribund industry and protecting what they see as the legitimate interest of trappers, while showing concern for animals, the Canadian Association for Humane Trapping (C.A.H.T.) still seeks vainly for a trap which will kill instantly or will trap without harming. And the Association does its utmost to persuade Canadian trappers to abandon the use of the steel-jawed leg hold trap which is so notoriously vicious that it is outlawed in most of the civilized—and almost all of the uncivilized—world. Sixty-eight countries have outlawed the trap, but not Canada, the U.S.A. or Russia. The Association in fact takes the traditionalist, and implicitly utilitarian view, that what is at issue is not the value of the lives of the trapped animals but cruelty alone. This view implies that humankind has a right to the use of other creatures to its own ends provided no cruelty—no avoidable pain or suffering—is inflicted upon the animal. Indeed, unless we take the vegetarian or even stricter vegan view, we have to concede some merit to the argument. (The vegan eschews dairy products as well as flesh and refuses to use products made from animal parts.) After all, as meat eaters, we must acknowledge that is precisely the requirement of good farm management. Farm animals are raised and tended for the sole purpose of providing human sustenance. While good ethics and good law insist that the animals be treated humanely during their life their ultimate purpose—without which they would never have had life—is to be the centre of the dinner table. The C.A.H.T. extrapolates from the ethics of farm management to the ethics of the treatment of fur-bearing animals, although, of course, one must question whether the purpose of each is genuinely equivalent.

The role of the C.A.H.T. is akin to the traditional role of Humane Societies—the elimination of cruelty to animals, and nothing more. In fact, that traditional role is often a hindrance to the more ambitious Humane Societies today, especially where the purpose of the prevention of cruelty to animals is enshrined in their letters of incorporation or in relevant legislation. For example, when Canadian Humane Societies choose to oppose fur-trapping or fur-farming or sealing they are subject to threats from farmers' organizations, from the Canadian federal government and even from other very conservative Humane Societies. Four Canadian Humane Societies were threatened with a loss of their charitable status in letters from the federal Department of National Revenue for engaging in quite minimal activity in opposition to the fur trade. The Ontario Farm Animal Council wrote to the Ontario S.P.C.A. in May of 1991 stating that opposition to fur-farming was beyond the Society's mandate, and a copy was sent to the Attorney General's office of the Ontario government. And one local Humane Society sent letters in April of 1991 to all other humane societies in the province and senior civil servants partly in an attempt to prevent the provincial Society from taking what the local Society saw as animal rights steps. The letter included a legal opinion from the local Society's solicitors which suggested that measures to support "animal welfare" were beyond the legitimate bounds of Humane Society activities! It should not surprise us that the local Society's senior employees are hunters and that some of the directors support trapping. It should surprise us no less that many of the more committed animal protectionists in Canada prefer to belong to organizations outside the restrictive Humane Society orbit and in some cases such organizations do not even seek charitable status so that governments will not attempt to interfere in their activities.

None of this should lead us to the view that supporters of humane trapping are somehow careless of the interests of animals. While to an extent the matter may be one of the relevant degree of sensibility, in greater part it is a question of whether one has a utilitarian or an 'end-in-itself' view of the worth of the animal. For the utilitarian it is the question of pain and suffering alone which is relevant. Indeed, as we saw in our discussion of animal experimentation, most legislation is designed to minimize pain, and where pain is deemed necessary, to measure it against the benefits of the research which inflicts the pain. The increasingly popular 'end-in-itself' view involves a recognition of the animal as being a dignified, purposive creature whose right to a natural life is worthy of consultation and which may not be treated as a means to humankind's convenience. We should be mindful of the fact—and this is certainly borne out in our experience of the representatives of humane trapping associations on Canadian Humane Society boards— that those who hold to the utilitarian view also have a significant sensibility on a host of animal welfare issues. In reality, while the utilitarian and 'end-in-itself' views may be philosophically distinct they are in fact intertwined in a complex and probably unravellable manner within the various personalities representing the competing views.

In order to confound the views of one's adversaries on animal welfare issues—or even to make up one's own mind—what one seeks are facts. And what has astounded us in our years in the animal welfare movement is the absence of reliable 'facts'. It is not that 'facts' are not offered. They are constantly available—but they almost always contradict one another, or are unsupported by any evidence. "What I tell you three times is true," as Lewis Carroll averred in the *Hunting of the Snark*. We are confident that competing advocates sometimes make up 'facts' as some kind of synthesis of desire and reality, others are persuaded to repeat them, and in time they become gospel. Unfortunately, there is not only a Bible but a Koran, a Veda, I Ching and Bhagavad Gita! 'Facts' are as difficult to choose as religious doctrine. And if religious doctrines are to be refined—and attitudes toward animals appear to resemble ideology or religious doctrine—then one needs facts as well as arguments. How long does it take on average for animals to die in a trap? What is the average annual income from trapping? How painlessly are animals killed on a fur farm? How significant is fur-trapping to the native economy?

The problem is not merely one of getting government statistics or reading Codes of Practice and discerning the degree to which they are followed—such information is rarely available. We lack in a surprising degree information about the very natures and behaviour of most animals which would allow us to acquire a felt rather than merely a philosophical or abstract sensitivity toward them. We feel for our companion animals because we know so much about them, share so much with them. But it is difficult for us to feel for a weasel or a ferret or a muskrat except in the most abstract of manners. We have lots of biological data but we know so little about the way they live their lives.

Of course, that is precisely the problem raised by the trappers and the farmers. 'City people', it is said, have a romantic and unrealistic view of 'nature' or 'the countryside' or 'wildlife'. They do not know the reality. In response the animal advocate may well point out that there are many rural inhabitants not involved in the exploitation of animals who share the animal advocate's view—including many ex-trappers finally revolted by a recognition of the unbearable cruelty they inflict. Moreover, the pecuniary interests of the fur-farmer and the trapper give them a jaundiced view of reality. Their experiences and interpretations are filtered through their search for profit.

Trained as a zoologist himself, Desmond Morris acknowledges that "It comes as a shock to some people to learn that we still do not have definite answers to many of the most obvious questions about animals."[1] And this is because of the naïve behaviouralist mentality of those who studied animals between the time of Charles Darwin and Niko Tinbergen. Sixty years of almost exclusively behaviouralist research may have taught us a great deal about the anatomy of animals and how they may behave in a laboratory or even a zoo but scarcely anything about their communal and purposive natures.

One of the principle purposes behind the founding of the Zoological Society of London (the creator of the first modern public 'zoo' at Regent's Park) was the "introducing and domesticating of new Breeds or Varieties of Animals . . . likely to be useful in Common Life." In line with Sir Robert Peel's 1835 Tamworth Manifesto, which presaged the primacy of 'useful knowledge' for the whole Victorian age, the Zoological Society of London's quest was to mould as yet unmoulded animals to human ends. (In fact, the only animal it ever succeeded in domesticating was the golden hamster!) Until Tinbergen, an Oxford University professor during the second quarter of the twentieth century, the study of animals was devoted primarily to an understanding of their usefulness to humankind. Tinbergen was followed by Louis Leakey, who introduced Jane Goodall, Dian Fossey and Biruté Galdikas to the ethological study of chimpanzees, gorillas and orangutans, respectively. It is only through ethological study—making and recording observations of wildlife in its natural habitat over lengthy periods—that we have come to have any worthwhile knowledge of animal behaviour at all. Yet many traditionalists still consider the Goodall type of study as anthropomorphic, interpreting animal behaviour inappropriately by analogy with human emotions and purposes. The reality, of course, as Charles Darwin knew so well, is that animal and human emotions and purposes are analogous. The development of ethological studies has stimulated an amazing amount of research into the behaviour of animals. Our knowledge is growing at an unprecedented rate, even though long-term studies of animals in their natural habitat remain a rarity. Still, as David Attenborough wrote in 1990 in his introduction to *The Trials of Life: A*

---

1   Morris, *Animalwatching*, p. 11.

Natural History of Animal Behavior, "ten years ago . . . we could not have witnessed many of the actions that I can now describe."[2] And if one believes that Goodall or Fossey or Galdikas became too personally involved with their research matter to provide objective interpretations, Christophe and Hedwig Boesch have undertaken research on chimpanzees in the Ivory Coast for 10 years in a manner which has avoided the personal involvement of Leakey's followers' methods. Despite all this we still know very little of the lives of the creatures whose furry skins we are tempted to wear on our backs.

It is remarkable how ostensibly impartial 'facts' influence one's conclusions—and that, of course, is because one is seeking the facts relevant to one's purpose. Whether one wants knowledge for its own sake, to use the object of one's study for human ends, or to understand the creature in and of itself as a sentient and purposeful being affects what one seeks to discover. As J. Bronowski wrote, "Those who think that science is ethically neutral confuse the findings of science . . . with the activity of science." If one's study of animals is devoted to their usefulness one is scarcely likely to discover anything about their purposive nature. The child who strokes the snuggling pet rabbit knows more about the animal as a communal being than any behaviouralist zoologist. The child and the animal have a relationship, the child experiences the rabbit's response to tenderness and warmth, while the zoologist possesses selectively acquired 'objective' data.

It is the facts possessed by the child upon which Tinbergen, Leakey and their followers built and which affect our sensibility toward animals. These are the kinds of facts we need if we are to understand wildlife—and it is a form of knowledge which the commercial trapper and the fur-farmer can never possess, for the knowledge of which they boast is merely subservient and useful knowledge.

In the world of Christianity the view of the animal realm has been—dare we use the word again?—ambivalent. In the first two chapters we sketched the progress of the animal under Christian tutelage. The difficulty Christianity has always had is that the underpinnings of its belief system appear to place humans not only at the pinnacle of nature but with everything subservient to them and their interest—at least to the extent that they were the interests sanctioned by God. And God sanctioned—or appeared to sanction—our dominance over nature. Yet evangelical Christians were among the most avid proponents of the early humane movement. Still, it was on the subject of cruelty they campaigned—and, as often as not, the purpose was to improve the behaviour of humans rather than to promote the interests of animals. While Christianity as a whole may historically have had a

2   David Attenborough, *The Trials of Life: A Natural History of Animal Behavior* (Boston: Little, Brown, 1990), p. 8.

hard time coming to grips with recognizing the animal as an end in itself there are notable exceptions among its ranks. Albert Schweitzer, of course, but also the Reverend Dr. Andrew Linzey, have made significant strides to overcome the apparent limitations inherent in Christian theology. In his books *Animal Rights, A Christian Assessment* and *Christianity and the Rights of Animals*,[3] Linzey has tried to square the biblical passages and interpretation customarily deemed inimical to the idea of animal rights with a more humane dogmatic, suggesting, for example, that Genesis 1 commands us to be vegetarians, indicating God's original will for creation, and only in Genesis 9 does God permit us to eat flesh under certain conditions. In fact some of humankind's progenitors were vegetarian and so still today is the ferocious and menacing gorilla which novels and the cinema have taught us to hate! The importance of Christian dogma to such animal welfare issues as the fur question lies in the fact that rural populations tend to claim a greater ongoing commitment to Christian principles than do urban ones. For them justification for attitudes to animal welfare is to be found in the Word, and the more traditionalist views predominate.

The famous Scopes monkey trial of 1925, in which a Tennessee school teacher was prosecuted for imparting the view to his students that humankind was descended from the apes, is instructive. The trial involved two of America's most accomplished court jurists: William Jennings Bryan for the prosecution and Clarence Darrow for the defence. At issue was less the literal truth of the Bible than human exclusivity from the rest of nature. Darrow lost the trial but crossed the threshold of winning the battle for the American public mind. He helped make the theory of evolution somewhat more publicly acceptable.

The importance of the theory of evolution lies in that its acceptance as fact encourages the recognition of ourselves as a part of nature different from other animals only by degree. And if we are different only by degree then our rights, interests, and essence differ only by degree. Of course, one might accept the theory of evolution intellectually, as many do, without allowing its implications to affect one's sensibilities toward animals. But if the *facts* of evolution are employed, not for the end of using animals to human purpose, as the Zoological Society of London would have had us do, but for our understanding that animals have similar if less complex purposes, rationality and dignity to humankind, then we cannot but fail to recognize animals' inherent rights. If, and only if, we understand animals in these terms will we be able to judge how they deserve to be treated. And if we

---

3 Andrew Linzey, *Animal Rights, A Christian Assessment* (London: SCM Press, 1976); *Christianity and the Rights of Animals* (London: SPCK; New York: Crossroad, 1987).

understand the kindness and compassion we owe to our companion animals, on what basis can we imagine that mink, or lynx or fox are in principle entitled to considerably less? If they are entitled to considerably less it is up to the animal users to demonstrate on what grounds they acquire the privilege to breach the responsibilities implied by a recognition of the values inherent in the theory of evolution.

On what grounds are the economic interests of fur-farmers and trappers, and the consuming interests of fur purchasers, to be preferred over the interest of the fur-bearing animal in keeping its coat? It is a question to which increasing numbers of Europeans and North Americans—a little more of the former—are prepared to give the animal the benefit of any doubt. The increasing antipathy to the wearing of fur has become a sufficient threat to the fur industry that it is engaging in a propaganda war against its opponents—including the mailing of intemperate and somewhat caustic letters to Humane Societies which take a public stance against the trapping and farming of fur. Indeed, it goes further and attempts to persuade individual Members of Parliament to intervene with the Humane Societies on the industry's behalf. The fur industry is in decline and under threat. And it attempts to fight back as any wounded animal would.

In an attempt to resurrect the fur industry's tarnished public image, the proponents of fur have attempted to align themselves with the ecology movement, insisting that fur-trapping contributes to a balanced environment and pointing out that unlike its synthetic replacements fur is biodegradable. Moreover, in the fur-producing economies it is argued that if fur is not consumed then this will likely diminish domestic employment and produce an outflow of capital. Such arguments appear generally persuasive to government, if less to the population as a whole, which is gradually switching from seeing the matter as predominantly economic to largely moral—even though the effects on the environment and the plight of the aboriginal peoples are an important part of the moral considerations. Certainly, it is easier for West Europeans to treat the matter as a unidimensional moral issue than it is for Canadians and Russians especially.

Along with lavish advertising to promote its products in the glossy magazines, especially those aimed at the upper fashion market, the fur industry is promoting its cause through the publication of articles dedicated to the defence of the fur industry's interests. One such article was published in the summer of 1990 in *Domino*, the magazine of *The Globe and Mail*. It thus reached the wide readership of Canada's national newspaper and, based on the evidence of private conversations, was convincing to a significant proportion of subscribers.

As in so many keenly felt disputes, the supporters and opponents of fur customarily talk past each other, finding no common ground on which meaningful rational discourse can take place. For example, it is the view of the Ontario Farm Animal Council that the consumption of fur should be treated as strictly analogous with the consumption of meat, the only questions at issue being whether fur farms meet appropriate standards for animal maintenance, slaughter and transportation. The question of the ends for which fur is raised is of no relevance. In such circumstances it is difficult, if not impossible, to reach any meaningful accommodations. On the other hand, if Humane Societies were to distance themselves entirely from such organizations they would lose any influence they presently have on the development and amendment of industry Codes of Practice. At present the Canadian Federation of Humane Societies plays a role in the development of national standards. The unfortunate price paid for such involvement is that the farm industry attempts to give the impression in its correspondence and literature that the Federation of Humane Societies is comfortable with the Codes developed. The Federation is on the horns of a dilemma—co-operation with the groups which set the standards is important to improve the standards but that co-operation is used by the farming organizations to justify the standards on which the Federation's influence may have been minimal (two members out of 24, for example, on the committee formed to rewrite the pork industry's Code of Practice. One of the authors of this book was a member of that committee and wholeheartedly endorses only a small portion of what was approved). Certainly, while the Codes of Practice of fur-farming are important to the welfare of fur-bearing animals, even if such Codes were beyond any measure of reproach and universally followed, that would have little bearing on whether fur-bearing animals should be raised for 'consumption' at all. There is an important distinction between the means by which such animals are raised and the ends for which they are raised. When the two are confused by the competing adversaries no common ground is even in principle achievable.

In similar vein, the proponents of fur will point to leather shoes or other leather or animal skin apparel, purses, luggage, and the like and suggest that if it is appropriate to use leather it is surely equally appropriate to use fur. They appear to remain singularly unimpressed by the retort that leather, suede, and pigskin are by-products of the slaughter of animals for human food whereas the use of fur, and certain other animal skins, is a purely luxurious use without any adequate compensatory benefits. Indeed, the use of leather can be promoted by the argument that if the animal is to be killed for a human benefit (an eminently important benefit, carnivores would add) then as little as possible of the animal should be wasted.

To be scrupulously fair to the proponents of fur it is necessary to give fur advocates a hearing, to let them speak for themselves. To this end we propose to treat the *Domino* article point by point. The article was written by John Barber and entitled "Trapped; The Fur Trade-off—Sacrificing Humans to Save Animals." And let us immediately acknowledge that if Barber can make his case, that if an end to the fur trade is truly sacrificial of humans for the benefit of animals his case is won. For while we adamantly espouse the importance of animals we are equally adamant that humans matter even more when interests are in conflict.

Using the example of the Louisiana nutria we mentioned in the previous chapter, Barber begins his argument with the claim that they are destroying coastal marshes now that their pelts are no longer in demand and the population is thriving. They are eating the marshlands right down to the mud and endangering the wildlife of the wetlands. The answer to the problem, he believes, is to encourage the wearing of fur again so that the nutria—a muskrat native to South America—would be worth trapping and thus reduced to its former level.

But Barber's solution to an admittedly very important environmental problem raises many equally important questions. Was the decline in nutria trapping occasioned by the decline in the fur trade or was it in part because, among furs, muskrat (or musquash, as it is called in Britain to avoid the negative connotation of 'rat') was one of the least popular? What if fur were popular again and muskrat remained without demand? Are we to leave environmental considerations to the vagaries of fashion? What if muskrat were to become among the more popular of furs? Should we permit its trapping to the level where the muskrat's food—aquatic animals along with the vegetation—became superabundant? Are there other ways of dealing with the problem without inflicting cruelty? Certainly, it should be recalled that when the muskrat was introduced into Europe it became "a serious pest"—to quote *The Columbia Encyclopedia*—but the problem was eradicated without encouraging an increase in the wearing of fur. The point is quite simply to suggest that environmental problems are complex, that our knowledge of how to deal with them is in its infancy, and that simple solutions are as often as not the foundations of the next generation's problems.

Barber writes of the unintended—and hence pernicious—consequences of the anti-fur campaign. And he is right to do so. Every social movement in history has had some detrimental consequences—from the Reign of Terror spawned by the French Revolution to the European migrations produced by the enclosure system which rationalized—and vastly improved—agricultural production, even though its immediate consequence was disastrous to the peasant populations. Given the limitations to human reason and our inability to predict the long-term implications of our actions, we are wise to act prudently and cautiously, minimizing excesses. But the argument about unintended consequences applies every bit as much to the introduction or extension or revitalization of trapping as it does to its abolition.

To avoid all unintended consequences we would have to refrain from acting at all. The question ought not to be whether there are negative consequences—there always will be—but whether the negative consequences outweigh the positive, and whether there are other ways of dealing with the negative consequences. We should indeed be mindful of Edmund Burke's prescriptions against precipitate actions whose consequences we are unable to discern. Yet the answer, for Burke, lies not in inaction but in action based upon veneration. As the Burkean Russell Kirk wrote, "The modern spectacle of vanished forests and eroded lands, wasted petroleum and ruthless mining . . . is evidence of what an age without veneration does to itself and its successors."[4] While, with Burke, we must be wary of that "delusive good intention . . . which is no sort of excuse for . . . presumption" we are convinced that actions which accord due reverence and veneration for our environment are less likely to produce harmful unintended consequences than the mindless depravity which has clear cut our forests, strip-mined our dales and endangered our wildlife. Now we do not wish to suggest ab initio that trappers, or the advocates of trapping, are, in principle, without due veneration. We are merely suggesting that the consequences of actions are likely to bear some relationship to the veneration for our environment with which they are undertaken. And if environmental protection is truly the cause of the trappers, if veneration for our landscape is their motivation, we should be sympathetic to their concerns. But is it?

What Barber has not told us is that in the United States over 50 per cent of the wetlands which existed in colonial times have now disappeared. The causes of wetland depletion throughout the world are various but can be generally linked to industrial and agricultural development. From the mid-1950s to the mid-1970s half a million acres a year were lost in the U.S., 90 per cent to agricultural development. Since the mid-1970s depletion has been diminished, though it remains potent. The Louisiana marshlands have been depleted by human population expansion not nutria population expansion, and most of the depletion occurred before there was any reduction in the demand for fur. *At most*, the nutria have played a very tiny part in the marshland depletion. There are no good grounds to believe that a revitalization of fur-trapping in Louisiana would have any appreciable impact on the marshes at all. We can only surmise that the fur industry's purported veneration for the environment is a self-serving subterfuge to promote its pecuniary interests.

The greatest veneration for our environment would be best exemplified by leaving nature to recreate its own new balance. This has been the traditional view expressed until recently by most responsible

---

4   Russell Kirk, *The Conservative Mind* (New York: Avon, 1973), p. 52.

natural scientists. But in the modern age, as we suggested in the last chapter, we are witnessing the most devastating effects of our lack of veneration, most threateningly ever since the onset of the Industrial Revolution, whose worst impacts we are only now experiencing. The destruction has been so complete that we must acknowledge our duty to repair our calamitous interventions. With the damage to the ozone layer, the loss of the wetlands and the pollution of land and sea we cannot afford nature's venerable time. We must repair, though we doubt our ability to do it, and deplore the lack of will for it to be done. We do not mean to suggest that there are ready solutions at hand if only we had the will. There are enormous, perhaps insurmountable, technical problems and there is inadequate expertise. Above all else we need to recognize that in the Western world solutions require major changes in our way of life which will be perceived as a reduction in the standard of living. Elsewhere it requires a diminution of the desire to live by Western standards and of the belief that one has a moral right to do so. As the West slowly discovers the folly of its excesses so the disadvantaged world acquires Western expectations! A vast and rapid decrease in the human population is only the necessary beginning to the solution.

Let us suppose, for the sake of argument, that we concede to Barber that there is an excess of nutria in the Louisiana wetlands. We would then have to point out that the very presence of nutria in Louisiana is itself an unintended consequence! They are not native but were accidentally let loose there half a century ago. We have to wonder how this artificial introduction was handled by nature. But handle it it did. It cannot then be argued that human predation is necessary to maintain the balance, since it was human introduction which created the initial imbalance. We are further led to wonder why only fur-bearers are deemed to cause the environmental problems and need to be thinned. If trappers or hunters play such a crucial role in wildlife management why don't voles and squirrels devastate the balance of nature? There's no one out there hunting and trapping them!

Are there too many nutria for the health of the wetlands? As our discussion of the wetlands problem suggested, no reduction in the nutria population will bring the wetlands back to life. Only major changes in human population and modes of agricultural production could do that. Still, if environmental interests required a reduction in nutria numbers how could it be achieved? Scientific research on the problem may help us determine a satisfactory answer. But it is clear that whatever answers environmental scientists may offer us will be very different from the numbers killed if furriers and trappers determine what should be done. And if the environmental scientists determine that no reduction in the nutria population will assist the wetlands' problem will the furriers readily concede that the nutria should be left alone? Are we unduly cynical to be inclined to doubt it?

Let us also not forget that significant 'unintended consequences' would occur if the nutria were again sought for their furs. Certainly, for example, the number of nutria will have a direct bearing on the alligator population which feeds on them. But if it could be demonstrated that the nutria were harmful to the interests of the environment, that it was sufficiently urgent that population eradication was necessary, *and* that the reduction in nutria would help restore the wetlands in measurable degree, then we would concede Barber his point. Even then we would want environmental scientists to make the decisions. We could scarcely leave it to the goodwill of furriers and trappers.

Even if we were to concede that there is an excess of nutria, requiring population reduction, we would still be suspicious of Barber's argument in that it attempts to generalize from a single instance. There is an excess of nutria, so the argument runs, nutria need to de depleted, trapping, predicated on the wearing of fur, can solve the problem, ergo trapping and the wearing of fur ought to be encouraged. Even if Barber were right in all his premises and arguments, and no other factors at all were taken into consideration, it would only *at most* follow that the wearing of muskrat fur ought to be encouraged. Is Barber then willing to concede, as his argument would imply, that in those populations which are stable or are diminishing, where the animals pose no threat to the environment, trapping should be prohibited and the wearing of fur discouraged? Again we doubt it.

We remain unconvinced of the argument that the anti-fur campaign has produced negative environmental 'unintended consequences' in any significant manner, though we are perfectly ready to concede in principle that there may have been some. Such unintended consequences do not dismiss the claims of the opponents of fur. Any disadvantages would have to be weighed against the advantages to the environment. And the primary advantage beyond those to the animals themselves is that those who would protect the animals possess that veneration, that respect, for the environment, which appears to be lacking in their opponents. We make that claim because the furriers and their advocates restrict their arguments in favour of environmentalism to those cases prima facie supportive of their economic interests.

We must concede, however, that the furriers make a telling point when they describe their product as biodegradable while people-manufactured products are not. The price of fur, however, excludes it from all but the wealthiest of markets and it is not a feasible replacement for everyday manufactured clothing. If the issue is one of environmental appropriateness because of fur's 'naturalness', then such products as leather, suede, and pigskin are to be preferred. They possess the 'naturalness' of fur while being a byproduct of animals raised for food.

The fur interests suggest that the killing of fur-bearing animals is no different from the killing of cattle or sheep or pigs for human consumption. While vegetarians and vegans may take the view that we are never entitled to kill an animal for human use, that view is completely unnecessary to those who would find the slaughter of fur-bearing animals inappropriate. The opposition to the trapping, farming, and wearing of fur is not based on the view that animals should never be killed for human consumption but on the much stronger moral claim that animals should not be killed solely for the vanity of human adornment. If cattle were bred for their leather alone the argument would apply with equal force. The opposition to fur is predicated on the belief that the life of the animal is valuable and may only justifiably be taken if the ends are greater than the loss incurred. And, quite simply, while the acquisition of meat may be considered a sufficient benefit, the opportunity to display oneself in a luxurious garment is not worth the lives of the numerous animals which are therefor skinned.

Why should any individual be entitled to sport a coat which cost the lives of numerous innocent creatures when we have the capacity to produce one equally effective with the cost to no life at all? And if the red herring about biodegradability is raised again one need only retort, even without mentioning the preference for leather, that the number of synthetic coats that it would take to replace the number of fur coats worn would have a negligible effect on the environment—but it would be a positive one! The fact is, as Ford Motor Co. research demonstrated, the production of a real ranch fur consumes 66 times as much energy as a fake fur. While the production of the supposedly environmentally friendly ranch fur uses the equivalent of 62 U.S. gallons of gasoline, the fake fur consumes just 94 per cent of one gallon. Even the trapped fur coat consumes over three and a half times as much energy as a fake fur. The fur industry's claims of environmental responsibility are quite unsupportable—as is the naïve insistence of the Canadian federal government that fur is "a renewable natural resource." Ignoring the non-renewable life of the slaughtered animals, fur-trapping has in many instances so depleted the resource that once abundant species are now scarce in the wild and fur-ranching uses significant non-renewable resources to achieve its ends. Both *Snark* and environment are harmed because the Canadian government has been told three times by the furriers that what isn't so is so.

But even if convenient myth were a reality, and even if the Canadian government wasn't so readily duped, given the relatively few occasions on which a fur coat is likely to be worn, the likelihood is that in many, if not most, instances the fur coat will not have to be replaced with another. Those who own a fur coat are likely to own several other coats, the most fashionable of which will prove an adequate substitute. And, as the wearing of fur becomes less of a status symbol and more of an occasion for surprise, if not scorn, the fewer circumstances there will be on which fur is worn. And surely the most common reason for the wearing of fur is to arouse admiration. If admiration is no longer aroused the fur coat will not be worn.

For each beaver coat 8-10 creatures must die needlessly. For Arctic white fox it is 15, raccoon 26-28, muskrat 30, sable 40 and ermine 125, and these figures reflect coats for smaller women. If the wearer of the coat thinks of herself as wearing the mothers of orphans, lost siblings and murdered mates she will be less likely to don her luxurious garb. But that, says the furrier, is just playing on people's emotions. And why not? It is, and ought to be, an emotional issue.

If the overall welfare of the animal population and environmental protection were the determining factors in the decisions of the fur industry with regard to which animals, and in what numbers, were to be killed, then the attitude of the population to the slaughter of fur-bearing animals may well be different. But, of course, these are not the considerations of furriers. Rather they are profit and elegant adornment—both of which have their rightful place. We recognize that substantial profits are the prerequisite of a sound economy and that without substantial profits employers, employees, and consumers would suffer alike. And we certainly believe that attractively attired people make the world a more enjoyable place. For the anti-fur movement the opposition does not have to be—as its detractors pretend—to profit and elegance per se but to the totally unacceptable price at which they are procured. And that price is the wholesale, and absolutely unnecessary, taking of innocent animal lives. How can we ever justify the killing of 10-12 lynx or 50 female ranch mink to produce one solitary coat, however elegant it may be?

Certainly, it is not inconsistent with the beliefs of those who are opposed to the fur industry to recognize that not all animal life must be preserved at whatever cost to the environment. The necessity of killing wild animals on some occasions and in some circumstances may be readily, if never happily, acknowledged—as the plight of the African elephants would indicate, and as, say, the spread of an infectious sickness in a bison herd might require. The relevant question is what criteria are appropriate to the decisions about killing—and the desire to wear fur can never be an adequate criterion. There are always insufficient compensatory benefits even to come close to a justification.

One justification which might carry weight if it were true is that trapping is necessary to prevent the spread of rabies. The suggestion is preposterous, but since it is often made it should be dealt with. A study in 1973 by the U.S. National Academy of Sciences concluded that trapping did not reduce rabies incidence. And when Massachusetts prohibited trapping for a year only one case of rabies was reported and that in a bat. Clearly, if there was a known rabies epidemic in a particular species then culling of the infected proportion would be necessary. But random trapping—and we haven't yet met the trap which can tell which animals have rabies and which haven't—is less likely to catch the infected than the healthy animal since the rabid animal is unlikely to be tempted by the bait. And if it is retorted that sometimes a rabid animal is caught one must ask if that is intended as a justification for the random killing of all potential rabies-carrying animals—just keep killing until one hits on a sick one!

Barber goes on in his article to refer to biologists and environmental scientists who believe that the efforts of the animal rights movement will lead to "brutalized landscapes and wildlife depleted and squeezed into tiny enclaves." Unfortunately, Barber never tells us who these scientists are and on what grounds they make the argument. Certainly, if Barber is telling us that those who oppose the elephant killing in Uganda or Zimbabwe, or those who think we should never cull the infectious sick animals in a herd to protect the healthy, are seriously misguided, he has a point. But we simply cannot imagine how the argument may be intelligently applied to the killing of fur-bearers for commercial purposes. It is not the animal rights movement which has brought about "brutalized landscapes," has depleted wildlife and "squeezed it into tiny enclaves." It is the population explosion and the over-consumption of natural resources with their attendant depletion of the forests and destruction of the wetlands which have brought about these calamities. And whatever the excesses of the animal rights movement may be, its proponents surely possess more of that needed veneration for the environment and its wildlife than do those who manipulate environmental concerns for no better reason than to defend their economic interests.

Chapter Nine

Frivolous Fur: Trappers, Clubbers and Farmers

> The most commonly used trap in Canada is the notorious leghold, the trap described by Charles Darwin as the most diabolical instrument of torture ever devised.
>
> — Ann Doncaster, *Trapped*

> Some who reflect upon this subject for the first time will wonder how such cruelty can have been permitted to continue in these days of civilisation, and no doubt if men of education saw with their own eyes what takes place under their sanction, the system would have been put to an end long ago.
>
> — Charles Darwin, "Essay on Fur"

In the hundred odd years since Darwin's essay little has changed in the manner of trapping fur-bearers. Yet many of those who go no further than a repetition of Darwin's adages are treated as though they were at best naïve, unknowing simpletons, and at worst the destroyers of the environment and even civilization. The denigration of adversaries is one of the most common tactics of the fur industry.

After an initially constructive, if ultimately unconvincing argument about the environmental effects of the anti-fur campaign, Barber takes this all too common approach of demeaning the opposition, of descending to the level of personal invective in his diatribe against what he calls "the lunatics and terrorists" among the anti-fur activists "who are addicted to the pleasure of moral disapproval and, as all the old orthodoxies crumble away, turn to fur for their fix." He acknowledges that there are "respectable and sincere" members of the movement but leaves the entirely misleading impression that they are in a small minority and possibly even dupes.

What Barber intends is that the reader will deplore the excesses of the so-called "lunatics and terrorists" and oppose their cause by dissociation from its supporters rather than by an informed analysis of their arguments. If you can discredit your opponents by employing ad hominem arguments against them you might be able to convince the reader to dismiss their position. Yet to attempt to discredit the anti-fur argument by attacking the excesses of the extremists is like opposing votes for women because of the purportedly outlandish behaviour of some suffragettes. If we were less than sympathetic in the introduction to this book to the vitriol of some of the animal liberationists we are equally offended by the stratagem when employed by their adversaries.

Barber next quotes a trapper, to the effect that 98 per cent of all fur-bearers trapped in Canada die instantly or within a few minutes. Barber acknowledges that federal officials would discount that figure—though he fails to tell us by how much—and doesn't seem to think that the readily admitted "few minutes" of suffering matter one iota. If one were to spring a steel-jawed trap on the leg of a domestic animal and watch the excruciating suffering inflicted for a "few minutes" before the welcome escape of death there would be no doubt in the observer's mind that this was a deplorable act of cruelty punishable at law. If the animal is wild the law suddenly changes. Not only is it not an offence to inflict the pain but it *is* an offence in Ontario to release the trapped animal from its torture.

The amount of pain inflicted by a trap would not likely be permitted even in almost all animal experimentation to alleviate human suffering. It is improbable that the Canadian Council on Animal Care would condone the infliction of an equivalent amount of pain in an important medical experiment—even the highly unpleasant burn experiments on dogs require anaesthesia. In Britain the skills of microsurgeons must be developed on terminally anaesthetized rats. And surely medicine and microsurgery are of higher priority than a frivolous fur. The horrendous suffering inflicted on fur-bearers is thus unwarrantable when the sole accrued benefit is one small part of one fur coat. No cost-benefit analysis would possibly deem the benefit matched by the cost. Even if we accept Barber's dubious 98 per cent figure the cruelty inflicted by trapping must be deemed unacceptable in any society which has any pretensions to being civilized.

In fact, we cannot know how long the suffering lasts. No one is around the traps to tell us. Much depends on what type of trap is used, how often the trap lines are visited—varying from daily to six times a year!—and how the trap is set. Trappers know what proportion of animals are still alive when they inspect their traps—the California Trapper Education Guide recommends the use of an axe-handle or iron pipe to finish off the survivors—but we cannot know what proportion perish in indescribable agony, succumb to starvation or simply freeze to death. The conclusion of the British Parliament's 1951 Scott Henderson committee was that only one in ten died instantly when the steel-jawed leghold trap was used. Our guess is that some three-quarters die within the euphemistic "few minutes." Even for those that die instantly the suffering of their parents and offspring cannot be measured. For many of the ensnared the torture lasts for days or even longer—until the release of death or unconsciousness or until the animal escapes by gnawing off the trapped limb. It is called "wring-off" and is an occurrence far more frequent than furriers will concede. The 600,000 a year estimate of the anti-fur activists may well be an exaggeration. But even if it is only one-third of that, we should recoil in horror. The pain can only be imagined. Of the amount of psychological suffering we have inadequate capacity to know. But if we simply compare, say, a bobcat or a beaver with a beagle—surely not an inappropriate comparison in terms of respective complexities—we would have little difficulty in recognizing the mental suffering our companion animals would undergo in similar circumstances. Why would we imagine it any less for the lynx, beaver, fox or coyote?

Different types of traps are employed for different purposes and different targets—though all at least occasionally capture a non-target animal. Such captives are termed "trash" in the trade, and include 'worthless' non-fur-bearers or domestic animals. So much for respect for the conservation of wildlife and the animal realm in general. We are inclined to doubt as hyperbole the activists' 1.25 million estimate of 'trash' animals trapped annually in Canada, but we doubt it could be less than a couple of hundred thousand. Some 30 per cent of land-trapped animals are caught in snares which are designed to strangle by suspending the animal until the struggling victim is overcome by the tightening of the wire around its neck. Awful as that may be, often enough the animal is inadequately suspended and a lingering death ensues, though the snare lock has reduced that problem. The leghold trap has been adapted to catch semi-aquatic species such as beaver, mink, muskrat and otter and to kill by drowning. The horrendous hook trap is baited and hung, and when the unsuspecting target leaps for its meal it is left dangling, hooked by the steel barb until the merciful release of death—fortunately that system is now largely illegal.

But surely, one is entitled to suggest, there must be more merciful, more effective, ways of 'harvesting the crop'. And certainly a great deal of time, effort and not inconsiderable money have gone into attempts to develop a humane trap. Animal activists will, however, tell you that the very idea of a humane trap is arrant nonsense. If the word 'humane' means something broader than just 'painless' they are right. And even if it is restricted to 'painless' they are certainly right to note that there are at present no humane traps. Equally though, one cannot doubt that some traps inflict less pain than others, that improvements to trapping methods will reduce the amount of pain and suffering, and that conditions will improve for the animals if governments are persuaded to require the use of the least painful methods available. Of course, if animal advocates refuse to acknowledge the possibility of a humane trap they lose their potential influence to effect improvements. In essence it is their belief that if improvements are made they will make trapping more acceptable and thus delay if not prevent the elimination of trapping altogether. They are on the horns of the dilemma faced by progressive social and political organizations throughout history. The achievement of minor successes may dim the public ardour to press for more. If the worst cases of animal experimentation are eliminated, who will care about the rodents? If the most blatantly cruel aspects of trapping are diminished who will care if millions of fur-bearers are painlessly—or less painfully killed?

The Canadian Association for Humane Trapping is in an unenviable position. It has been traditionally castigated by the more radical animal protection groups as offering legitimacy to an illegitimate enterprise. More recently, it has come under attack from 'humane trappers' themselves, most notably from the British Columbia Trappers Association which has accused the C.A.H.T., among several other things, of misinforming "the public about the modern fur industry and the positive efforts made by the [Fur Institute of Canada] to advance humane trapping methods." The actions of the C.A.H.T. are seen "as a direct attack on trapping and not promotion of humane trapping systems using the most humane traps available to the trapper." C.A.H.T.'s sin was to promote improvements and recommend deadlines for implementation for which the trappers themselves are far from ready. The tightrope which C.A.H.T. walks is precariously slack. If they offend the more progressive trappers' associations they lose their influence to promote the changes they deem desirable. If they do not offend such associations they fail in their endeavour to minimize the current cruelty. C.A.H.T. was threatened with expulsion from the Fur Institute of Canada for being too concerned with the animals' interests. It is no longer a member of the World Society for the Protection of Animals because it is thought not to be concerned enough!

Over the years C.A.H.T. has successfully promoted trap research, education for trappers, the exchange of less offensive for more offensive traps with the trappers themselves, and, most importantly, the implementation of trapping regulations. They have been instrumental in having many provincial governments prohibit the use of hooks and traps with metal teeth, in requiring locking devices on neck snares, in restricting foothold traps to targeting of certain species, in mandating training for first-time trappers, in prohibiting the use of steel-jawed leghold traps for bears, in requiring daily trap inspection in some jurisdictions, etc. Their primary focus lies in having the steel-jawed leghold trap outlawed, in encouraging use of the padded leghold trap and the conibear trap where it is appropriate—both of which they concede are still inhumane but distinctly preferable—in promoting non-invasive holding traps and, in general, encouraging research on quick-killing traps. There can be little doubt that there is less wildlife suffering in Canada today as a consequence of C.A.H.T.'s gargantuan efforts. Certainly, in part because of the work of C.A.H.T., many of the most critical comments that were made in 1988 about the types of traps used and the horrors they inflicted were no longer valid by 1991. No doubt, the changes resulted at least in equal part because of the decline in the industry due to public outrage at the methods used. If the trappers didn't act quickly they would be out of business.

Barber continues his defence of trapping with the claim that no fur-bearing species in Canada is endangered or even threatened by trapping. Barber is technically correct, though trapping is a significant factor in the disturbing population reductions of wolverines, the grey fox, the Newfoundland pine marten, and the long-tailed weasel and, with hunting, has proved a serious threat to a great variety and number of fur-bearing species throughout the world.[1] Given that most Canadian species are widespread it is extremely difficult to extinguish any species, but slightly in excess of three million fur-bearers have been trapped annually in Canada. Trappers offer two responses to that statement, one contradicting the other. The first is that the depleted stock is rapidly replaced by the growth in population which naturally rises to meet the available food supply. The second is that population control is necessary to reduce starvation and disease. Trappers must choose what they believe, but they can't hold to both. Again, if such 'resource management' is so necessary for beaver, raccoon, fox and mink why doesn't it apply to marmot and chipmunk, to vole and shrew? We wonder how fur-bearing animals managed for hundreds of thousands of years without the resource-management skills of trappers when human population was scarce. So far as we can tell the same natural laws still apply.

Species extinction is not at issue here—though it is in other instances a matter of grave concern—but the unnecessary and unjustified taking of animal life. Logically, the denial of species endangerment amounts to a justification for killing many by proudly announcing that one is not killing all. Genocide is the most heinous of crimes but to claim that one is not practising it is scarcely a justification for mass murder.

Barber next lauds the trappers and hunters, proclaiming them the true environmentalists, the ones who are the first to complain about pollution or oil spills or clear-cutting. The argument is the reverse of the one he used on those he called the extremists. Readers having been asked to dissociate themselves from the fanatics, are now expected to associate with the trappers. We are expected to believe, without any evidence being offered, that because trappers have a responsible attitude to the environment they must be equally right about trapping.

In reality, of course, Barber is telling us no more than that hunters and trappers have some admirable qualities. Yet those qualities have little bearing on the question of whether hunting and trapping are

---

1 For a lengthy list, see Barry Kent MacKay, "Let's Be Reasonable," in Ann Doncaster, ed., *Skinned* (North Falmouth: International Wildlife Coalition, 1988), pp. 216-18.

themselves admirable. Moreover, there is no reason to fear that the demise of hunting and trapping would harm the environmentalist cause, as Barber implies. There are tens of thousands of other individuals deeply committed to a healthy environment with certainly no less sincerity, integrity or expertise. Indeed, Barber's admonitions should give us cause for concern about the integrity of the hunter and the trapper. Is he really saying that if they no longer hunt and trap they will cease to care about the environment? If so, we must doubt their commitment and question whether their environmental concerns are mere rationalizations for their hunting and trapping interests.

As for the "luxury furs," Barber tells us that fur is not a luxury to the trappers because they are among the lowest paid groups in Canada. To which we respond that if they are so poorly paid it would be no great hardship for trappers to turn to a more financially rewarding way of life. If it is then suggested that it is the way of life rather than the income which is the reward one is perforce led to wonder about the nature of people who satisfy their needs through killing when there is so little extraneous compensation. Certainly one would have cause to question the veneration, the commitment to wildlife, which they claim. In fact a comprehensive U.S. study by S.R. Kellert has indicated that American trappers possess an above-average concern to dominate and a below-average commitment to the welfare of animals. If we were methodological behaviouralists we would be tempted to conclude that the wildlife commitment claims of the trappers were nothing but a sham.

Who, then , traps and what are their incomes? Reliable information is hard to come by. From one source we read of the good commercial trapper earning $17,000 a year, from another source we discover that the average trapper income for a good year was $735.01, from a third that generally it is just over $1,000 and from a fourth $650.00. What these figures tell us, assuming they are not grossly inaccurate, is that if commercial trappers are making several thousand dollars a year then there must be a very large number of part-time 'sport' trappers who engage in the activity for pin money and pleasure. In fact, it would appear that the cost for the 'enthusiast' of snowmobile, traps, fuel, weapons, ammunition etc. far exceeds the income which can be expected.

Other data indicates there are just over 100,000 trappers in Canada, approximately 0.4 per cent of the population, or one in every 250. According to one report 29 per cent of trappers are aboriginal, according to another it is close to 50 per cent. Each province has its own trappers' association, and although it is unclear what proportion of trappers have membership, clearly most of the membership comes from commercial trappers. Most commercial trappers require additional sources of income. Fur-farm production is only 50 per cent that of trapping but equal to trapping in revenue. Total revenue from fur in Canada has been approximately $600 million a year, of which high estimates suggest $85 million went to trappers (which would give us yet another figure this time, of $830 per trapper) and around $300 million to fur farms which produce predominantly mink and fox although there have been a few recent attempts to diversify to lynx, marten and coypu. The total number of animals killed for their pelts has amounted to around 4-1/2 million animals annually though that figure has been in decline in the last few years.

Fur, then, may not prove a luxury for the trapper but it is clearly a luxury for those who have reaped the over $500 million which did not find its way into the trappers' hands and a luxury for those who can afford, or choose to afford, the several thousand dollar price tag of the more expensive garments. For Barber to tell us that fur is not a luxury is a thinly disguised attempt to manipulate the issue, however impoverished the trapper may be. The argument that fur is a luxury has nothing whatsoever to do with the income of trappers—or for that matter of furriers, wholesalers, tanners or whomever—but refers to the fact that any necessary function provided by fur can be provided more than adequately by materials which do not require the unnecessary and unjust taking of animal lives. Residents of the most northerly extremities find manufactured garments superior to fur in protection from the bitterest elements.

Not all fur-bearers are trapped for the fur market. A significant proportion are raised on farms—slightly in excess of one-third of the total market. A few are hunted. At the height of the seal hunt's popularity the Total Allowable Catch of 186,000 seals was being clubbed (or gunned or netted) to death for its fur.

At the end of 1987, in response to European pressure, the Canadian government yielded and announced that the participation of ships in the commercial hunt was over and the killing of white coat pups—those under 16 days old whose fur is the most avidly prized—would be prohibited for commercial purposes. But had it yielded in fact? Or was this subterfuge? A bit of both seems to be the answer.

The slaughtering of the infants was ended—at least for commercial purposes. And ships could no longer be used, though boats could (i.e., those less than 65 feet in length) and the Total Allowable Catch was not altered. The ban on the ships was a hollow gesture, since it was uneconomical to use them if the seal-pelt market was destroyed. New markets would have to be found, given the European Community (E.C.) ban on importation. The Orient is in some measure providing that market, both for aphrodisiacs and seal leather: some 70,000 young harp and hooded seals were marketed in 1988, a figure which had dropped to 54,000 by 1990. There is still no prohibition against clubbing, though netting—by which the pups are drowned—ended in 1991 except by natives. The proponents of the fur trade argue that clubbing is the most humane form of killing for seals. Of course, any consideration of the 'most humane' form of slaughter can only resemble a discussion of the advantages of hanging over gassing over lethal injection for capital punishment. The reality is that the seal hunt is far from over and the increasing wealth of the Orient will stimulate it further.

Nonetheless, we hear constant complaints of how the abolition (!) of the seal hunt has depleted the fishing to a dangerously low level. Of course, anyone who cares to investigate would know that the depletion is caused largely by the overfishing by European and Canadian trawlers. The Canadian government in fact receives constant complaints from east coast fishermen, on whom quotas are imposed, when the Europeans customarily overfish the waters. Moreover, toxic waste, oil discharges and other debris from tankers play a substantial role in killing the fish. We do not have adequate information on which to judge the role that seals play in depleting stocks but it is highly unlikely that they are the major culprits. The seals do not devour the young breeding stock, which is devastatingly extracted by the trawlers.

Surprisingly little information is available on fur-farming in Canada. We know the numbers sold—about one and a half million pelts a year—and we can read the industry Code of Practice. We can note that the Canadian Federation of Humane Societies was involved in developing that Code. But there are few details available about farm conditions. We should recognize incidentally that the Federation of Humane Societies was simply trying to get the best deal it could for those animals. It certainly does not believe that the conditions of fur-farming are appropriate, merely that *any* improvements must be of *some* benefit to the animals. Nonetheless, the Ontario Farm Animal Council attempts to justify fur-farming practices by proclaiming them as supported by the C.F.H.S.

A lifetime of incarceration in a small wire cage is scarcely a worthwhile life at all. Even the trapped animal gets to live a full and natural life until it is snared. Conditions on fur farms are a great deal less than satisfactory—and to make them 'satisfactory' by any humane standards would be to drive the fur farmer out of business. In Switzerland there are fairly rigorous standards for fox farms with regard to cage size, shelter, veterinary treatment, nutrition and killing. There are no longer any fox farms in Switzerland. In Iceland there are virtually no standards, and fox farms abound.

If Canadian fur-farmers are to compete in the international market they simply cannot afford to implement standards which give any serious consideration to the nature of the species they raise. As long as there are no rigorous international standards strictly adhered to by the industry worldwide the lives of ranched mink, fox, lynx or marten will remain abysmal. Indeed, we wonder why the E.C. is so concerned to discourage, if not ban, the sale of furs produced from animals killed by the leghold trap while permitting ranched fur. The life of the animal killed by the trap is distinctly preferable until the inexcusably agonizing time of death than that of the ranched animal. Were we to be given the choice of a full and natural life but with the possibility of an horrendous death over a short life of total incarceration in a very restricted space with the certainty of a somewhat painful death we would have no hesitation in choosing the former. It couldn't be that the E.C. is considering the economic interests of its own fur-farmers over those of foreign trappers, could it?

Fox and mink are in fact particularly unsuited to being caged. They are very active and highly strung animals. When incarcerated they are subject to compulsive pacing—much like excessively restricted zoo animals—to self-mutilation and neurotic behaviour. Although statistics are not available there is prima facie evidence that a captive lifestyle produces disease and early mortality. Genetic defects occur frequently, cannibalism is not uncommon, and the young are deprived of maternal nurture at about six weeks of age. The natural long-term familial behaviour of fox and mink is prevented by their mode of shelter. They are served a less than adequate diet by comparison with what they eat in the wild and they are intensively bred to produce a variety of unnatural but marketable colours. Their mode of death is usually by gas, electrode or cervical dislocation. If law mandated the purchasing of fur we would have no hesitation in choosing wild fur over ranched fur. The ranched mink or fox may be treated in death with a little (though only a little) more respect than the wild fur-bearer, but the captive life, if it can be called a life at all, is treated with utter disrespect for every aspect of its nature. The ranched animal is nothing more than a fur-producing machine.

There is an industry Code of Practice but there is neither enforcement nor penalty for non-compliance. One must have some empathy for those who adhere strictly to the Code for it increases their business risk while diminishing their profit. Nonetheless, no Code of Practice could justify fur-ranching, for it is an activity which treats animals completely and utterly as a means to human convenience.

But what if all fur production were to cease? Would the effects be damaging to the Canadian economy—or the American, the European or the Russian? No Canadian could relish the loss of $600 million from the annual gross national product with some $280 million being foreign earnings at the trade's peak (though $160 million was also spent on imported fur). But, to put it in perspective, that amounts to a loss of around $25 for each man, woman and child, just over four hours of work at the Ontario minimum wage. The loss would be regrettable but not insurmountable. Still, it is significant that the economic loss is deemed important when we consider the fur industry but is never suggested as a relevant factor when, say, we hear indignant voices raised against the pornography industry. Such voices rightly tell us that the moral issue is too great to allow economic considerations to outweigh it. Much of Canada is an ideal place to grow marijuana and the cash crop income would presumably exceed $600 million a year if it were legal. Certainly, economic considerations are not deemed sufficient to permit them to outweigh the moral imperatives.

Changing concerns about tobacco have proved a serious threat to the interests of the tobacco industry, changing customs have decreased the consumption of liquor, movie theatre attendance rapidly decreased with the advent of television. We take all these things in our economic stride. It is the nature of economics to respond to supply and demand. We earnestly regret the dislocation to furriers, fur-farmers, and trappers if changing public sensibilities interfere with their mode of earning a living, just as we empathize with tobacco farmers and liquor company employees. But just as we consider the public good from not smoking a greater benefit than the interests of tobacco farmers, so too the greater public good (which, to refer to the British animal experimentation Act again, includes the interests of animals) requires a reduction in, and ultimately elimination of, fur consumption.

Barber's arguments in favour of the fur trade arouse the greatest public response when he turns to the issue of the destruction of aboriginal cultures in Canada. He claims that hunting and trapping are intrinsic aspects of the aboriginal way of life and that the destruction of the fur trade is deeply injurious to them. Let us immediately acknowledge that this is an issue about which all who oppose the skinning of innocent animals should be deeply concerned. It is certainly worth remarking in response that Indians, and later, Inuit, were introduced to fur trading—as opposed to hunting for self-consumption—by the fur industry. Prior to the arrival of the Europeans the aboriginal peoples did not engage in fur trading. And it is equally important to note that fur-farming has been more detrimental of late to Indian fur trading than perhaps any other single factor. For example, the fur industry's development of ranched white fox—with its superior pelts—has severely depressed the market for wild Arctic fox. The average 1989 price for a ranched white fox pelt was just under $62, for the trapped white variety just under $13. But the fact that the present fur industry is itself partly responsible for the damage to the native economy should not persuade us to ignore the very real problems faced. Even if we recognize that the traditional economic exploitation of the native peoples by the fur interests is now being replaced by an exploitation in which the fur interests use the plight of the native peoples to bolster their own cause let us not forget that the native predicament is a very real one.

It is ironic to witness the fur industry today rushing to the protection of the native peoples and would be amusing if it weren't so deceitful.

The arrival of the first fur traders in the sixteenth century began the destruction of the Indian[2] culture—and introduced the way of life now defended as the Indian culture! Traditional native culture was based on subsistence patterns of hunting and fishing, which were sufficient for food and raiment. With the arrival of the fur traders this pattern changed, and animals were hunted for furs to trade. No longer was the whole animal used. Indians' reverence for the animals they hunted was diminished by the commercial practice in which they now engaged. The furs were traded in exchange for guns, ammunition, powder, iron pots and occasionally beads and other baubles. Their own crafts—pottery, bow and arrow, their own ornaments—were replaced by 'superior' European items, including, of course, firewater. The hunted fur-bearers diminished in number and the Indians fought among themselves for territory in which to hunt and trap the prey they now needed for their foreign—not indigenous—way of life. Diseases they had never known—from influenza to syphilis—accompanied the trading. The Indians changed their traditional dress whenever they could to European wool and cotton. Through the hunting of buffalo for pemmican to feed their employees the fur traders managed to deplete the stock on which the Indians relied. They thus became dependent on the fur trade, and at times when the fur trade declined—whether from supply or demand—on the Canadian government for charity.

We should recognize that when native people—never more than 400,000 or so—hunted for food and raiment alone the animal population remained relatively stable. When they hunted for commerce it declined. This alone should give us cause to wonder about the 'resource management' statements used by trappers to justify their slaughter of three million fur-bearers alone. It should also force us to recognize that the fur trade was entirely detrimental to the culture of Canada's native peoples. It is unconscionable now to defend the fur trade as a necessary part of the Indian and Inuit way of life.

Of course, it could be intelligently argued that if fur trading was not the original native culture it has become so over the last four centuries. And so it has. But in that case it cannot be treated as something

---

2 Today the use of 'Indian' to describe North American aboriginals has come into disrepute since the word reflects nothing more than the fact that the Europeans who first came to North America mistakenly believed they were in India. Unfortunately, none of the alternatives is much better. 'Natives' refers, of course, to all those born in North America, not just aboriginals. 'Native peoples' fails to differentiate between the Amerindians and the Inuit—to the chagrin of both—and ignores the fact that both were themselves immigrants, albeit earlier. If possible, it is preferable to refer to the relevant nation, e.g., Sioux. Where the context does not permit that, most of the Amerindians we know personally are content to be called Indian—provided it is with respect. We have employed all the currently used terms interchangeably in this book.

deserving of some kind of special consideration as traditional native culture. It must be subject to the kinds of arguments we would use about any other group in North American society.

Moreover, if the alienation, suicide rates, alcoholism and crime among native populations can be ascribed to the destruction of native culture by European commerce one wonders why anyone would now want to defend native reliance on the fur trade. The only possible justification is that Indians and Inuit often live in abject poverty and that the destruction of the fur trade makes them poorer still. But surely if that poverty has been occasioned by dependence on European culture it would be foolhardy to become even more dependent upon it. If it is the economic circumstances in which they live, rather than cultural maintenance, which is the prime concern of the Indians and Inuit then the answer lies in assimilation. If assimilation is not desired then the Indians and Inuit should desire a break from the fur trade which has occasioned their downfall.

Let us not pretend that keeping the fur industry alive would rescue aboriginal culture from the gradual decline it has faced for nigh on four centuries—a decline which is so thorough that it is increasingly difficult to recognize any authentic culture at all, except in those areas where natives have limited contact with other Canadians. That decline is an intrinsic result of the incompatibility of aboriginal culture with the individualist, commercial and industrialist culture of white North America. There are certainly important remnants of the aboriginal culture which have not been totally destroyed—the kinship system and the modes of political decision-making, for example. And there is a decided will among the native peoples to resurrect their culture. But whether they recognize it or not that can only be accomplished by a withdrawal from the fur trade.

It must be conceded, however, that the decline of the fur trade has been detrimental to current native economic interests, as well as to those of the trapper, the fur-farmer and the fur retailer. It is for this reason that Barber insists that animal rights advocates are saving animals by sacrificing humans. Plausible on the surface as that may appear, it cannot be justified by any serious consideration of the matter. Anti-fur people—not all of whom consider themselves 'animal rightists' despite Barber's attempted identification of the two concepts—pit the *very* life of the animal against the *way* of life of the human. The question is whether it is better to change the way of life, the means of subsistence, or maintain the killing of animals for unjustifiable ends. And the question can only be determined by how highly one values the very life of the animal compared with the value one places on fur-trapping, farming and merchandising. Nonetheless, at no point is it necessary to the anti-fur argument—or, for that matter, the animal rights argument—to put the life of the animal ahead of that of the human.

The argument that trapping is a part of the aboriginal culture and must therefore be maintained would not be very convincing even if one were to acknowledge trapping as an indigenous part of native culture. After all, no one would argue that infanticide, according to most historians once a practice of certain groups within aboriginal culture, is today justifiable. If that was deemed worthy of change on moral grounds then why not other aspects of aboriginal culture? The general argument about the sanctity of culture is no better than arguing that a class-ridden society is acceptable if it is a part of the accepted belief system or that, because it was once believed that women were intellectually inferior to men, gender equality of education should never have been introduced. Consider for a moment the not unusual and sometimes valid claim that non-indigenous North Americans have a lot to learn from the natives. That could only be true if we did not regard 'white' culture as sacrosanct. And it would be inconsistent to consider native culture sacrosanct and 'white' culture not so.

An unjust practice cannot be immune to criticism merely because it is a part of a particular culture. To argue that committing acts of violence against animals is to be tolerated because it is endemic to a culture is little different from arguing that larceny is acceptable if it contributes to the well-being of the thief. Moreover, we should recognize that violence toward animals in native culture was introduced by the acceptance of European commercialism. The native traditional belief was to show a significant respect for the animal realm. Commercial trapping has severely harmed that respect. If the aboriginal peoples are to return to their traditional ways, including a revitalization of their reverence for nature, it is essential for them to abandon commercial trapping.

It is commonplace to encounter the argument that individuals from one culture cannot legitimately criticize the belief system or practices of another culture by their own standards or that two different cultures cannot be judged by the same criteria. And there is a certain limited truth in these assertions. But if we were to treat such assertions as predominantly true it would imply there are no adequate criteria for condemning the atrocities of Nazism, the hostage-takings by Moslem fundamentalists or Saddam Hussein's pollution of the sea and air of the Persian Gulf. If such judgements are legitimate—or, indeed, if any general moral judgements are legitimate—it must be conceded there is a moral law common to humanity rather than one restricted to each culture. As the celebrated Dr. Johnson once said of the ethical relativist, "If he really believes there is no distinction between virtue and vice, why sir, when he leaves our homes let us count our spoons."

In the final analysis one's attitude on the fur question, as with most animal welfare issues, corresponds to the *degree* with which one is in accord with Albert Schweitzer. In his *Civilization and Ethics*, Schweitzer asserted that "a man is really ethical only when he obeys the constraint laid on him to aid all life when he is able, and when he goes out of his way to avoid injuring anything living . . . to him life as such is sacred." Few of us could possibly go as far as Schweitzer in our views, and even less in our practice. We would have to permit the mosquito to bite us. We would not drive anywhere since we are all aware of the insects which splatter on our windshields. We would not kill the fleas or parasites which invade our canine friends. At the very least, we would be vegans or vegetarians. If Schweitzer's ethic is impractical, the adoption of that ethic as the basis for the cost-benefit analysis is not. Life is indeed valuable in and of itself and may only be taken if the benefit outweighs the value of the life. For those who support the fur trade the value of a mink life must be deemed to be less than one fiftieth of the importance of a mink coat.

According to Barber, people living on the land, close to nature, cannot afford the "cozy view" of the urbanite—or, we might caustically suppose, the "cozy view" of Albert Schweitzer, who was living at a field hospital in French Equatorial Africa! Again Barber is trying to score points against the fur trade's adversaries by making derisory points about *them* rather than their arguments. But let us take Barber seriously for a moment. Presumably he is telling us to have no respect for the views of the Canadian government (predominantly urban by residence) when it sides with the Canadian fur industry. Presumably he is telling us to pay no heed to the views of the retail furrier or the Canadian Fur Council (again predominantly urban). Of course, what Barber is really trying to tell us is that urban views which do not coincide with the rural views which support the fur interests are the ones to ignore!

When Barber tells us the kinds of views he considers appropriately 'rural' we are confident much of the rural world would be appalled by them. He cites as an example of 'natural' cruelty the Inuk dog which, when it grew too weak to pull a sled, "was cut loose and left to freeze on the tundra." Rural people know that "there is no such thing as old age in the animal world, that every wild animal meets a horrible, often violent death." Of course, Barber's statement implies that nature is exceedingly cruel, and when trapping is cruel then that is only in accord with the laws of nature, and how lucky animals are that we are not even more cruel when we so readily could be! Barber's statements could be used to justify *any* act of outright cruelty.

It takes very little knowledge of nature to know that Barber exaggerates greatly about violent death in the wild, and it takes even less knowledge of ethics to be repelled by the implications of Barber's statements. Every school child knows—even if somewhat misleadingly—

of the aged elephant leaving the herd to wend its way to the elephant graveyard. And what of the orca, dolphin, grizzly, wolverine, fisher, puma or the star-nosed mole—all Canadian and all with few predators other than man. Of course, nature consists substantially of predator and prey but many do survive to perish of old age. However, the subject of non-violent death has been scarcely broached in ethological research. It is an area about which relatively little is known but what is known does not support Barber. Even if Barber were right about the universal lack of longevity, his implied conclusions would not follow. In nature predators usually take no more prey than is necessary to their survival. They are environmentally efficient in their predation. Not so the trapper, who takes as much as the market or government quotas will bear. And what he takes is in no way necessary to survival as is the death of prey in the wild. Clearly, Barber is vainly trying to provide a justification for the cruelty of the trapper and the furrier by acknowledging the fact of cruelty. But that contradicts the claim that trapping in Canada is humane, that the trapper respects the animals and is concerned with their long-term environmental interests. Could we imagine anyone with a genuine veneration for nature attempting to justify cruelty, even in such a surreptitious manner?

The rightly renowned Ernest Thompson Seton avowed that the "life of a wild animal always has a tragic end" and it is perhaps he who is the source of the common misconception. But it must be remembered that Seton was every bit as much a storyteller as a naturalist and was making more of a literary than a scientific point. Anyway Seton was writing at the end of the nineteenth century when so much less was known about our fauna. Certainly, anyone who reads Goodall or Boesch on chimpanzees, Fossey on gorillas, Galdikas on orangutans, or Cynthia Moss on elephants can read both of death from old age and death from violence. And should anyone be rash enough to point out that animal life expectancy in the wild is less than in captivity—which it is—one need only retort that human life expectancy in Japan is far greater than in Ethiopia but many Ethiopians still die of old age.

More importantly, it takes very little insight to recognize that an Inuk's dog is a domesticated, not a wild animal and thus Barber's excuses for the Inuk's cruelty would not apply even if they were valid. What totally invalidates Barber's argument is that it takes no great moral sensibility to recognize that if the dog has performed its tasks honourably and dutifully then the owner owes it, on the simplest of contractual grounds, the reward of a comfortable retirement unless *perhaps* the cost of the maintenance of the dog constitutes a dire threat to the well-being of the Inuit community. To conclude otherwise is to treat the animal as nothing more than a means without the least intrinsic value in itself. Indeed, if what Barber is telling us about the

Inuk is a common occurrence we will have to reappraise the much vaunted reverence for nature among the native peoples.

Continuing the use of invective by the proponents of fur, Barber accuses his opponents of racism—for promoting policies detrimental to the interests of native groups. It would in fact be more appropriate to judge Barber guilty of that sin in implying that we should apply different criteria in judging the behaviour of an Inuk than we would in judging humanity in general. The claim that something is justifiable merely because it exists in a particular culture, or is characteristic of a particular 'race', implies that no argument for change can ever be justified, that nothing can ever be deduced as legitimate criticism. It is comical how often those who hold this view condemn the moral position taken by others even though to do so constitutes a direct contradiction of their own argument. This is true of all those who hold to a simplistic ethical relativism, but it is especially comical now that the majority opposes the wearing of fur. If Barber took the logic of his own argument seriously he could not support the wearing of fur because it counters the prevailing belief system—the culture—of modern North America!

To argue that those "close to nature" cannot believe in the "cozy view" of treating an animal as an end in itself rather than as a means is to fail to recognize the relationship between the shepherd and his collie, the Hindu farmer and his cow or the mahout and his elephant. Who ever heard of the shepherd condemning his dog to death because it had gone lame after a lifetime of herding? Of course, the dog would be given a just reward of a leisurely retirement. And if it were not, the shepherd would be roundly and rightly condemned by his own community. Northern English farmers used to trade stories about the lack of compassion of the Welsh shepherds toward their retired sheep-dogs—without evidence as far as we can tell (and since one of us is of Welsh heritage we probably would refuse to believe it anyway!). The consequential animosity toward the Welsh shepherd was acerbic. Yet according to the logic of Barber's argument the English farmers should justify the practice as a Welsh cultural characteristic! In the final analysis the argument from culture amounts to 'whatever is, is right'. Clearly, the shepherd, the Hindu and the mahout live every bit as close to nature as does the Inuk hunter but their attitudes to the animal realm are morally superior.

The only circumstance which might permit us to avoid that judgement would be dire poverty that would hinder the Inuk's ability to deal compassionately with the animal. Even then, at the very least, the dog should have been painlessly destroyed, not left to die in the snow. If Barber's portrait of the native peoples is accurate—and our experience leads us to doubt it—the fur trade has another sin to repent, the destruction, and not merely diminution, of one of the most admirable characteristics of the historic native community—its fellowfeeling with the animal realm.

Although aboriginal peoples are threatened more by anti-fur successes than the remainder of the Canadian community it is not because they live close to nature but because of their poverty and the changes being imposed on what remains of their traditional culture. Most importantly, it is because of the limited alternatives available to them in adapting to new moral recognitions—which are anyway quite consistent with their now diminished traditional moral recognitions. When Europeans first encountered North American natives they found them treating moose, bison, wolves, bears and birds as pets—no domestic dog would have been left to die in the snow. The young were even sometimes suckled by the women though as often as not to provide workers rather than companions. (Traditional Amerindian 'pet-keeping' was not quite the same as our own. Pets were 'educational toys' for the children, aids to teach them hunting attitudes and skills. Sometimes the pets were used as target practice and often ended up in the pot. Nonetheless, they were also often the objects of affection.) The identity of the traditional Indian community with nature is not what it was, and that is because of almost four centuries of involvement with a rapacious commercialism.

Even if the decline of the fur industry had not even further harmed the aboriginal economy the traditional culture would still have been waging a losing battle against the dominant commercial and progressive culture with which it shares the continent. Since the average annual income from trapping for native hunters can scarcely have ever exceeded $1,000 per trapper, even the economic harm to the aboriginal communities has been customarily exaggerated by those with a vested interest in so doing. The portrait of aboriginals as driven to drink, despair, penury, and self-destruction by the decline in the fur trade is a deplorable misrepresentation. It tells us more about the painters than those portrayed. The aboriginals who live outside communities which engage in the fur trade are not less susceptible to alcoholism and suicide. They all inhabit a world whose dominant culture is quite incompatible with their own. It produces an alienation and an anomie which no resurrection of the fur trade could begin to cure.

The aboriginal faces the dilemma of all proud peoples determined to maintain their heritage and yet desirous of sharing the wealth produced by an alien culture. It is not possible to both maintain the traditional values of a culture inimical to the competition of commercialism and at the same time to enjoy the attributes of the commercial culture. Native people reject the commercial culture in favour of their own but are permanently tempted by its fruits.

No recognition of, or the deepest empathy for, the aboriginal dilemma could, however, justify the approach taken by Barber or the defenders of the fur industry in general. Barber acknowledges that, statistically, only one-tenth of one per cent of fur coming into the international market comes from native communities. Yet instead of logically recommending that aboriginal peoples ought to be treated as an exception, Barber assumes that if a legitimate argument can be made in favour of one-tenth of one per cent then it ought to apply by extension to the remaining 99.9 per cent. The furrier's interests are therefore promoted by an appeal to the plight of the native peoples and the Inuit—who would profit far less from a resurrection of the fur industry than would the furriers themselves.

If we accept Barber's 'official' figures and extrapolate from the international to Canadian pelt production, the total *maximum* annual loss to native communities would be $500,000—taking the trade at its record height, assuming trapping had since ceased completely and assuming that Indians received the full value for each pelt sold. We are confident that in reality the current loss to the native community is considerably greater, as much as 15 million dollars if we assume 50 per cent of trappers to be native and the average native trapper income to be the same as average trapper income. If we assume only 29 per cent of trappers to be native the loss would be less than nine million. This is ignoring overhead, which will naturally have decreased somewhat with the reduced activity. Our best guess—reading between the lines of all the conflicting statistics—is that the current income decrease from the height of the fur trade amounts to some $50 a year for each native man, woman and child, and certainly not more than $100. However, if the fur industry is concerned to protect the interests of the threatened native communities it would certainly be appropriate to have the relevant garments labelled as 'trapped by natives'. But that, no doubt, would bite into the incomes of those the industry is really concerned to protect: the furriers themselves.

The success of the opponents of the fur industry against vested economic might has been so remarkable that social scientists who imagine that economic elites always dominate societies should make a detailed study of the campaign. The reality is that those who have nothing to gain economically are winning—though the increasing strength of the Oriental market should give them cause for concern. They cannot afford to rest on their laurels. While it is deplorable that some of the more radical protesters have thrown ink on expensive fur coats, taken scissors to them, publicly ridiculed the wearers, and committed acts of vandalism against fur retailers, we also recognize that by so acting they have succeeded in arousing the public consciousness. It is one of the unfortunate characteristics of humanity that its moral sensibilities are most effectively aroused by immoral behaviour. We are confident that if sensibilities had not been there in the first place, lurking beneath the surface of consciousness, no amount of propaganda, nor any amount of rational discussion, would have served to create the awareness that the wearing of fur is a moral issue.

The successes of the anti-fur campaign are such that the proponents of fur are constantly looking for the economic motives behind the campaign. We have heard and read remarkable accounts of purported Marxist terrorism using the fur issue to overthrow the foundations of capitalism! Sometimes the activists are depicted as dupes in the service of competing economic interests—though what those interests are we are never told, and indeed have been unable to guess what they might be. On other occasions the activists are described as power-hungry opportunists determined to carve a self-important niche in the annals of history—or at least the current politics of Canada. In fact, they are simply passionate people trying to redress a grievance, to make a moral statement. And if that means seeking political power to do it then political power must be sought. And if some of them become self-important in the process we cannot see how this differentiates them from those who seek power, status and importance by the more customary channels.

Between 1988 and 1989 total Canadian pelt production reduced from over four and half million pelts to just over three million—a one-third reduction. Total pelt value declined from $123 million to under $76 million—approximately a 40 per cent reduction. Trapped fur declined from 3.3 million to 1.5 million pelts—a reduction of 55 per cent and a saving of 1.8 million animal lives. The value of trapped pelts declined 48 per cent and ranched pelts almost 29 per cent, though the number of ranch animals killed slightly increased. The detrimental effect to the Canadian economy has been tempered by the fact that fur imports have decreased from $160 million to $102 million, a reduction of over 36 per cent.

According to a 1989 opinion poll conducted by *Parent's Magazine*, 85 per cent of Americans are opposed to the use of animals to produce a fur coat. While we would have serious reservations about the accuracy of such a poll it gives clear indications that the public is unreservedly on the side of the anti-fur activists. No longer do major game shows give away fur coats as prizes. At least six of the major retail outlets for fur in Canada have resolved not to sell, including the Hudson's Bay Company which began it all! Of course, vast numbers of middle-class women, and a few men, have fur coats, but they are now usually kept in closets, not on the back. After all, what's the point in wearing a luxurious fur if people look down on you rather than up to you?

It has been suggested that the decline in the fur trade and the resultant plummet in retail prices may open a new avenue by providing a much broader market for lower priced goods. But that is based on a misunderstanding. The current reduction in prices can only be temporary, as the furs are being sold below cost price. Unless fur prices rebound *and* volume increases (for overheads remain relatively constant whatever the number of furs sold) the furriers will have no alternative but to go out of business or diversify.

The Canadian federal government has become so concerned at the state of the fur industry that in 1990 it decided to enter the business itself. The Agricultural Products Board, which has customarily entered the market to buy surplus farm products such as pork and grapes, agreed in 1991 to purchase 650,000 mink pelts to assure that mink ranchers got paid for their products. The intention was to sell them at auction to recover the costs. The federal government has long supported the fur industry through the Department of External Affairs, which has fought, and continues to fight, the European anti-fur lobby, and through the Department of Indian and Northern Affairs, which assists native trappers. But Agriculture Canada's involvement is new. In 1990 the department paid $11.7 million in grants to mink and fox breeders which were augmented by provincial subsidies—close to $7 per pelt in total in Ontario. Prices are in fact below the cost of production. The irony is that while the public chooses not to spend its discretionary income on fur it is required through taxation to provide subsidies to those whose products they deem morally unworthy of purchase.

According to *The Globe and Mail* (April 9, 1991), Alan Turner, a spokesperson for Agriculture Canada, claimed the fur-trade problem to be temporary, caused by world overproduction and not by lower demand or the effects of the anti-fur lobby. It strikes us as strange that one can talk of 'world overproduction' as the sole problem if six out of every ten traders listed by the British Fur Traders' Association went out of business between 1985 and 1990, when the number of fur stores in the Netherlands has declined from around 400 to 32, when Harrods of London has ceased to sell furs, and when Italian furriers announced a 50 billion lira loss for 1989. Does that not suggest that just *perhaps* there was a decline in demand! And when Canadian fur ranchers increase their production by only 11 per cent over three years but the price declines by 65 per cent would that not suggest some reduction in demand! Anyway what does overproduction mean other than supply exceeding demand. We wonder whether to doubt the integrity of our federal officials or put it down to the fact that they failed Economics 100 abysmally. Either way our confidence in our government is eroded—and no less in the business sense of fur-farmers who continue to overproduce when prices are substantially down, unless they know that big brother will bail them out, via the pockets of the taxpayers of course.

And if the anti-fur lobby has not reduced demand, why does the federal government threaten to remove the charitable status of Humane Societies which campaign even minimally against the fur trade? The insistence of Revenue Canada was that a balanced picture of both sides must be given. It is curious that there is no equivalent insistence that the Canadian Cancer Society present the views of the tobacco industry. Nor should there be. Why does the Ontario S.P.C.A. receive caustic and condemnatory letters from fur-farmers and representatives of the fur industry if they do not believe the anti-fur lobby is having an effect? If federal officials and the fur trade are right and it is only current overproduction which is the cause, the law of supply and demand will solve the problem in a very short time. We can only wait and see. But we know where our money is. We will not be investing in a fur farm or a trap-manufacturing company.

Chapter Ten

Animals in Entertainment: Racing, Riding and Fighting

Any coward can fight a battle when he's sure of winning.
— George Eliot, *Janet's Acceptance*

As our ingenuities diminish the amount of time and effort to be expended on providing the necessities of life so the opportunities for leisure activities increase. Throughout history animals have been frequently employed as a means to make that leisure time 'enjoyable'—from the circuses of the Roman Empire through bull- and bear-baiting, cock, dog, and bull-fighting, dog- and horse-racing, to rodeos, the modern circus, zoos and aquaria. Animals provide entertainment in films, television and on the stage.

No one could doubt that much of the 'entertainment' has been destructive—both of the animals and of all semblance of human decency. Yet the fact that animals in entertainment have frequently been demeaned, treated without consideration, and far worse, should not blind us to the fact that it is possible in principle for animals and human entertainment to be compatible. We do not hold to the view that animals should of necessity be left undisturbed by humans in their primordial natural habitat. In that case we would have to oppose the keeping of pets, which we believe can be of the greatest benefit to both human and animal. Certainly, other things being equal, the animal should be left to its primordial nature and its habitat, but we should not rule out a priori the possibility of a satisfactory human-animal relationship in the entertainment of humans.

Our experience, supported by an abundance of social science research, suggests that the more admirable of human characteristics are engendered and enhanced by contact with, and enjoyment of, the animal realm. If compassion, caring and a sense of veneration among humans toward animals and nature in general are encouraged by the entertainment then that entertainment has the most positive of values. It should itself be encouraged.

However, human entertainment, even if uplifting and worthwhile entertainment, is only valuable if it is neither cruel to the animals, nor disturbing to their dignity. Humans have a right to enjoy animals in entertainment only when there is a compensatory benefit to the animals—only when there is sufficient evidence that the animals derive a measure of satisfaction and enjoyment from the enterprise too.

161

If we lose animals from mutually advantageous entertainment we would also lose some of that potential for awe and reverence which contact with the animal realm gives us. Our sense of the community of sentient beings would diminish. We would lose an important element of that awareness which makes us better and more responsible human beings—a sense of ourselves as sharers of this planet with duties toward its constituents which go beyond our obligations to our fellow humans. Indeed, the entertainment must involve an earnest respect for the nature and dignity of the species employed, not merely for their sakes, but because to fail to do so would deprive us of the legitimate sense of well-being and sentience awareness. We would once again be exploiters. The question, of course, is whether there are entertainment activities which either do, or can, consider the interests of the animals as well as humans.

The antithesis to the question is easier to answer. There are undoubtedly many forms of 'entertainment' which are both utterly destructive of animal interests and are equally arousing of the most injurious and least healthy appetites among the human participants and spectators. We find it difficult to conceive of any explanation which would serve to begin to justify cock-fighting, dog-fighting, bull-fighting, or any analogous activities.

Yet in various parts of the world these 'sports' enjoy great popularity. Must we conclude that those who 'enjoy' such activities are lesser human beings of more 'primitive' and 'barbaric' natures than our own? In fact, some 'primitive' societies have demonstrated a far greater sense of belongingness within the world of nature. While our social, cultural and economic environments influence our attitudes, not far beneath the conscious surface of all of us lies a recognition of the rights of sentient beings. And 'rights' was the term customarily employed by Humane Societies over a century ago. Thus in an 1888 publication of the Toronto Humane Society—a society supported by the mayor and elders of the city and with three Doctors of Divinity on its board—we read that appropriate legislation since 1641 has been "proceeding more clearly upon the principle that animals have *rights*, which it is the province of the legislature to recognize in its laws, and of the courts to protect by judicial proceedings."[1] The term 'animal rights' is not the exclusive property of the radicals nor a reason for moderates to be wary when they encounter it.

Cock-fighting remains a popular pastime in South America, Mexico, Puerto Rico and some of the Caribbean islands as well as the Orient. It is an ancient form of 'amusement', having been practised in early Persia, Greece and Rome. In many places where it is practised it is

---

1 J. George Hodgins, ed., *Aims and Objects of the Toronto Humane Society* (Toronto: William Briggs), p. 12. Emphasis in original.

illegal, but enforcement is often ignored, the appropriate officers being spectators at the match! We have seen commonly acknowledged cock-fight arenas in jurisdictions where the practice is formally illegal. Even where the law is enforced the match is treated like an illicit poker game—a surreptitious inquiry leads to directions to the clandestine court. The fighting cocks are routinely equipped with steel claws to maximize the injuries and contests are customarily conducted to a deathly conclusion, although local custom may dictate the refusal or inability to fight further as an acceptable finish. In the Dominican Republic, for example, it is not unusual to witness street-strutting youths proudly and publicly displaying their champion cocks along with the offending metal appendages. It is clear that the community status is vested in the ownership of the victorious cocks. And so is wealth—for the purpose of the contests is as much gambling as fighting. Cock-fights are still not uncommon in various parts of the United States, although they are illegal in almost all jurisdictions. Massachusetts was the first U.S. state to forbid cock-fighting in 1838. Britain did not follow until 1844. In Canada today cock-fighting is a relatively rare activity but not unknown. Entry is carefully controlled. In a small southwestern Ontario town early in 1992 a cock-fighting arena was discovered by police and humane society officers just before an event was to commence. The joke of a fine imposed by the court—a mere $100 to the organizer of the cock-fight and owner of the arena—will scarcely serve to discourage the activity when a single cock may be valued at several hundred dollars.

Like cock-fighting, dog-fighting is frowned upon by all with even a vestige of sensitivity. But that may have promoted rather than hindered the activity among those with a macho mentality. People are inclined to choose their canine companions as an extension of their own personal-ities—or rather of what they want the public recognition of their personalities to be. We should be more wary of the owners of Pit Bull Terriers, Doberman Pinschers, and German Shepherds than of the dogs themselves—fine animals as they indeed are. On one occasion in the Dutch West Indies we photographed a mechanically pressed car licence plate bearing a representation of a Pit Bull Terrier and the words 'Good to the Bone'. We can only wonder about the personalities of persons who would display such a plate, but we can have no doubt about the threatening image they wish to project. This is not to say, of course, that there are no responsible and sensitive owners of such breeds. There are many. But they too must be concerned by the aspersions cast upon themselves through the irresponsibility of those who purchase their pets as subliminal weapons.

Certainly, a number of breeds have been wilfully developed for the sole purpose of fighting. And while dog-fighting has a lengthy accepted history, it is illegal in all jurisdictions in North America today. Nonethe-less it still exists, although it is reported far more often than it occurs.

In Ontario the inspectorate of the O.S.P.C.A. receives occasional reports of the activity but extensive investigation has failed to substantiate the allegations in recent years—with one exception in Brampton.

There are not infrequent calls to outlaw certain breeds deemed dangerous, and many local authorities have attempted to take steps to proscribe the ownership of those breeds. More often than not they do not carry through. Not only is it effectively impossible to relate the purported offending characteristics to the offending breed as a whole but the purportedly most offensive breed varies from decade to decade.

Today the despised dog is the Pit Bull. It is this 'breed' which is called the 'fighting dog'—which it is—and which today is blamed for all that is bad in the canine world. A decade ago it was the Doberman, before that the German Shepherd and before that the Rottweiler. While it is certainly possible to ascribe a significant number of vicious attacks to the Pit Bull—or to dogs which bear a significant resemblance—many of the breed are docile. There is a most unfortunate tendency to ascribe to the breed as a fixed characteristic those traits which will be brought out if the animal is raised carelessly, cruelly or with intent to display these characteristics. Whatever we may read, temperament cannot itself be bred—though genetic characteristics which have a bearing on temperament can be. For example, Pit Bulls are said to have an undue amount of L-tyrosine in the Reticular Activating System—a scientific way of saying they may be more easily aroused. Moreover, it is said that Pit Bulls are more than usually sensitive to, and may produce higher levels of, endorphins—another part of brain chemistry—which could make them less sensitive to pain and actually enjoy it. There is, however, no evidence that this is more true of the Pit Bull than of a number of other breeds. Moreover, if this has become an inherent characteristic of Pit Bulls how is it possible that so many of the breed do not display the characteristics which have supposedly been bred into them? This simply tells us that there is a significantly greater risk from some breeds than others, but not very much about which particular dogs or breeds are the most dangerous.

The name Pit Bull is itself not very appropriate and indeed quite confusing, since at least three breeds have the fighting characteristics attributed to the Pit Bull. The American Staffordshire Terrier, first registered with the American Kennel Club in 1935 under the name of Staffordshire Terrier (the name was altered in 1972) is, in essence, a cross between a bulldog and a terrier that was developed in the 1860s and introduced into North America a decade later. The bulldog from which it was bred—bearing little resemblance to the modern bulldog—was the dog bred in England until the early nineteenth century to bait bulls. These animals were known in the U.S. as Pit Dog, Pit Bull Terrier, later American Bull Terrier. This is the animal which is the scourge of old ladies and young children.

Or is it? Pit Bull Terriers certainly have had an unfortunate history "in the pit as gambling tools," to quote the American Kennel Club. But another breed, the Bull Terrier, which dates back to 1835, has been described by the American Kennel Club as the "fighting dog or 'gladiator' of the canine world." This breed has two varieties, white and coloured.

Then there is the Staffordshire Bull Terrier, which was registered with the American Kennel Club in 1974. This breed finds its progenitors among those bred for bull- and bear-baiting in the Elizabethan era and for fighting in early nineteenth-century England. The Staffordshire Bull Terrier—which of the three breeds here mentioned resembles the popular image of the Pit Bull the least—was refused registration in Britain until 1935 because of its reputation as a fighting dog. On the other hand, the Bull Terrier—which resembles the image of the Pit Bull the most—received official recognition by the English Kennel Club in the third quarter of the nineteenth century, presumably because it was deemed less warriorlike in its qualities.

Which, then, is the notorious, dangerous, malicious and malevolent Pit Bull? How much must it resemble one of these breeds to be recognized as one of those creatures so vicious that it must be restricted or destroyed? How could anyone ever prove that a particular dog was a Pit Bull or not?

In the summer of 1991 the British required all of the *American* strain of Pit Bull Terriers in Britain destroyed, a sentence later reduced to neutering and muzzling and being insured because of a number of vicious attacks by the breed. It was, of course, totally disloyal of the English owners to purchase American dogs in the first place! Anyway, the British would never have credited such evil of one of their own breeds. It would have been the fault of the owners. But foreign dogs and unpatriotic owners were fair game! We are confident that the attacks will not cease by the elimination of one strain of one breed.

The reality is that organized dog-fighting and vicious dog attacks cannot be eliminated by the destruction of a breed or even of several breeds. Most dogs can become cruel and vicious either by being mistreated themselves or by being trained to be cruel. Certainly the power, arousability, and tenacity of some breeds make them potentially more dangerous, but all breeds can be further bred to reduce the likelihood of negative characteristics, and all breeds are potentially loyal, friendly and considerate. The potential viciousness must be instilled and brought out by their human owners, either intentionally or in ignorance.

Dog-fighting and viciousness against humans can only be effectively controlled at the level of the owners and the individual dogs. As long as certain breeds possess a ferocious image and as long as owners choose to project their own undesirable attributes through their dogs the problem will remain. If it can be demonstrated which of the breeds—at the present that means which variety of Pit Bull, tomorrow it will mean something else—is potentially lethal the appropriate requirement may well be a couple of generations of cross-breeding. To sentence a breed to genocide does not in and of itself face the problem, and merely gives the lie that a solution has been found. It would not be a great difficulty to induce genetically the potential for the offensive and offending characteristics into some other breed. The solution lies rather more readily—if one is to be found at all—in curbing the offending and offensive characteristics of those who would want to own a lethal weapon. If one variety of 'Pit Bull' is removed from the aggressive warrior ranks we will soon have to turn our attention to the related breed, and, if they are expunged, maybe to the Doberman, and thereafter . . . what? the hunting dogs?

Bull-fighting was introduced to Spain by the Moors somewhere around the eighth century. From Spain it spread to Morocco, Southern France and Portugal. The Spaniards introduced the combat to South America where it remains popular in Mexico, Peru, Colombia, Venezuela and Ecuador. *Banderilleros* or *peones* help picadors and matadors to kill the bulls. Around 4,500 a year are killed in the arena in Spain at the present time. An average of almost three bull-fights a day are held. These are the figures provided by Desmond Morris. "Each year more than 17,000 bulls are tortured to death in Spanish bull rings," is the claim of the World Society for the Protection of Animals—which adds, "Drugged, blinded, and repeatedly stabbed, the bulls suffer unimaginable pain in the name of entertainment." Again we encounter conflicting statistics. But even if we accept the more modest ones, the terror remains appalling.

The bulls are goaded, pierced by short lances, and finally killed by a swordthrust to the neck. In Spain today the height of ambition for a youth is still to be a matador. Indeed, the state provides free education and training for budding matadors who have shown significant promise. In Portuguese-style bull-fighting the animal is not put to death in the arena.

It could scarcely escape notice that the most obviously cruel 'entertainments' are more pervasive in South America, Asia, and Southern Europe than in North America and Northern Europe. And that fact requires an explanation. Four factors apparently affect sensibility toward animals: economics, culture, socialization and rationalization. With regard to the exploitation of animals in 'entertainment' economic conditions influence the amount of leisure time available and the disposable income to be expended. The less disposable income there is, the greater the likelihood of expenditures being devoted to the least expensive of 'sporting' activities such as cock-fighting. However, it is the oppressiveness of the economy (or the society in general) which encourages those who are oppressed by the more powerful in turn to be oppressive of the less powerful. Those whose well-being is disregarded by economic iniquities are in turn likely to disregard the well-being of less powerful sentient beings. Oppression breeds resentment, which is in turn oppressive. However, economic oppression alone is an inadequate explanation, since women, who have been more oppressed than men, have customarily had a higher sensitivity toward animals. Grey Owl's wife, Anahareo, rejected trapping earlier and more readily than her English-born husband. And while it would be foolish to generalize from a single instance their story is not unrepresentative.[2] Economic relationships have to be understood within the context of a culture.

Cultures in which the mastery of nature is considered laudatory will usually have an inherent disregard for the nature they master. Paradoxically, though, as mastery is achieved, they produce an embarrassment of riches which, having satisfied most needs and many wants, permits recognition of the rights of the oppressed—including oppressed animals—since the oppression is no longer as necessary to the satisfaction of needs. Moreover, the mastery of nature with the consequent satisfaction of needs—or perceived needs—permits far greater time for many to enjoy a liberal education in which moral sensibilities are heightened. It may also provide more time to engage in exploitative ventures. Thus within any one culture over time the attitudes to animals will vary considerably. The length of time they have prevailed will affect the difficulty or ease of changing them.

The culture of a society—which is in some significant respects a reflection of the economy—will promote a certain set of attitudes toward animals at any given time and will thus create the context, the boundaries, within which legitimate beliefs will operate. And since most of us most of the time want to belong, want to feel an integrated part of our society, we are constrained to maintain the beliefs accepted by our compatriots. Those beliefs will reflect a number of factors: the belief system conducive to the maintenance of existing economic and political relationships, the religious foundations of the society and the prevailing educational and moral myths. One's sense of acceptance, status and well-being within a society is affected by the degree to which one conforms. However, it is possible to achieve one's identity and

---

2 See Gertrude Bernard (Anahareo), *Devil in Deerskins* (Toronto: New Press, 1972). Grey Owl was the pseudonym of George Stansfield Belaney (1888-1938) who devoted his talents to the cause of conservation of wildlife. He married an Iroquois, was adopted as a blood brother by the Ojibway and passed himself off as an Indian even though he had no Indian heritage.

status by belonging to a group whose norms do not correspond to the dominant values but which itself fulfils the function of integration for its adherents. While difficult, it is possible to step outside the dominant norms provided society is not monolithic but contains competing groups expressing different values. When acceptance of the diversity of legitimate values is itself a value of the society the psychological pressures to conform are somewhat diminished—or rather the pressures to conform to the predominant societal values are replaced by the pressures to conform to the values of one's parochial group.

When we are being socialized to a set of values by our parents or early school educators we are acquiring the context of our actions and beliefs. Parents and educators possess the esteem and authority to have us gladly accept the wisdom of the values they impart. If one's father enjoys 'sport' fishing—or cock-fighting—or if one's teacher preaches the virtues of hunting—or the glory of bull-fighting—it would be most unusual to do any other than accept the imparted values. Of course, if there are effective competing agencies of socialization—as there frequently are in pluralistic societies—then the monolith is breached. If parents impart one value, teachers a second and the media a third then our own sensibilities develop independently.

Once one has come to engage in a particular activity, be it cock-fighting, hunting, fishing or whatever, then one is less likely to be convinced by argument or evidence which may otherwise be compelling. We rationalize by giving greater emphasis to evidence and argument supportive of our amusements. Sensibilities are thus acquired far more readily when one has nothing, or little, at stake.

Generally, then, we may expect that the more oppressive an economy, the more monolithic and rigid a culture and the lower the level of liberal education, the greater will be the tendency to cruel and invasive entertainment. Moreover, it is likely to be the most oppressed—at least of the males—and those with the least liberal education who will participate in these entertainments. As these conditions are changed so all societies and all individuals are more likely to respond to the empathetic sensibilities which lurk just beneath the surface of the human mind.

It is not always easy to decide just where entertainment begins and ends. For example, while religious practice may be in and of itself a very serious activity it gives rise to, or often encompasses, entertainment. We noted in the first chapter the origins of religion with regard to animals and the less than happy consequences for even the worshipped animals of Egypt. And certainly animal-sacrifice religions are scarcely conducive to animal interests. There are other religions, though, closer at hand, which treat animals rather differently. In the United States there are a number of Christian sects—the most bizarrely named being 'The Dolley Pond Church of God with Signs Following'—in which the deadliest and most venomous of rattlesnakes, among others only slightly less lethal, are ritually caressed by the dedicated believers. The trance into which the participants appear to enter apparently makes them less vulnerable; in reality, since snakes must avoid at all cost wasting their venom on anything other than potential food, they do not bite the worshippers, who, in their icy trance, appear to pose no threat and are an unappetizing source of nourishment (there are occasional embarrassing mishaps). Such animals are not exactly a source of entertainment, but they are certainly being used to satisfy some kind of human desire. We wonder how different the worshippers are from the stripper enveloped by a python or boa-constrictor, titillating her audience with both purported sensuality and purported danger. Such exhibitions are not cruel to the snakes within the current Canadian legal definition of cruelty but we wonder what possible benefit there could be to the entertaining or the entertained. And when the stripper employs a pig as her co-artiste we are rather dismayed that the act is stopped because it is offensive to public decency rather than a crime against the swine.

If the relationship between religion and entertainment is obscure among the Dolley Pond enthusiasts it is more obvious in other instances. In Sri Lanka the 2,500-year-old spectacle of the Perahera may still be seen. Some 40 magnificent elephants belonging to the Temple of the Tooth take part in a mile-long night procession, mounted by headmen and their attendants, while masked devil-dancers perform their gyrations, and the enthralled crowd raise a thousand torches as they view the grand march. By all accounts it is an imposing spectacle. When the elephants are not in use for these festal purposes they are kept on the estates of the district chiefs. The Sri Lankans tenderly care for their beloved elephants. Surely, this use of animals as entertainment must be acknowledged as beneficial to both human and beast.[3]

Apart from the dog and the cat, humankind's closest relationship to the animal realm has been to the horse. There is many a father who has encouraged his daughter's love of the horse, often at great and troublesome expense, for as long as the daughter loved her horse she would have no interest in young men. Some forms of entertainment are distinctly preferable to others—at least from a father's perspective.

We have used the horse in warfare, as a means of transportation, to pull the plough and the stagecoach, to hunt the fox—and quite simply to ride for the sheer joy of it. When we exchanged the horse for the machine at the onset of the Industrial Revolution we also lost the close relationship that often existed between employer and employed. Certainly, though, in the early industrial age horses were often treated with habitual cruelty, and perhaps even more habitual ignorance. In the

---

3 See H.W. Cave, *Golden Tips: A Description of Ceylon and its Great Tea Industry* (London: Cassell, 1904), pp. 77-79.

1888 *Aims and Objects of the Toronto Humane Society* the first 10 pages on animal abuse are devoted to "Cruelty to Horses," and of the list of the "Prevalent Forms of Cruelty" which the "Society will seek to prevent," two are generic, five refer to animals other than the horse, and six refer specifically to horses. The horse was, to the late Victorian, what the cat and dog are to us today. In fact, in the list of 13 prevalent cruelties the dog is mentioned only once—the clipping of ears and tails—and the cat not at all. It was the horse which was the apogee of the animal to the Victorian.

The horse today is a relative rarity. Once—well within the memory of some of us—the horse was the hustler and bustler of our city streets, the mainstay of the farmyards and the deliverer of milk, bread and other perishable provisions. Today horses are still to be seen working in large numbers among the Waterloo County Mennonites and the 'Pennsylvania Dutch'. But to all intents and purposes the mechanical and electronic age has changed the horse from an instrument of production to a source of entertainment.

The principle of the animal as source of entertainment should not disturb us. If some anthropologists once thought of a distinguishing characteristic of humans as *animal ludens*—the game-playing animal—anyone with the slightest knowledge of domestic and wild animals will know that many of them, too, love to play. Playfulness is most notable among the young—as it is with humans—but at all stages of life animals at play are at their most delightful, for themselves as well as for us. Who could doubt that the horse loves to run, jump and frolic? They seem perfectly content to have rider astride, provided they are treated with compassion and care. If the love of the young rider for the horse may seem to exceed the love of the horse for the rider we are content to accept that there is a mutual respect and a mutual benefit.

Unfortunately, if the life of the horse as companion, ridden for pleasure and a little excitement, is a generally happy one, the life of the racehorse is far less so. When big business or the excessive desire for human success intervenes sensibility takes a decided backseat, if it gets any seat at all. This should not be read as any aversion to big business. We believe that business is the source of many of the advantages as well as the disadvantages of the modern world. And where it is the source of disadvantages it is also a prime source of the solution to those disadvantages. If the quality of life in the West is in many respects superior to that of the Third World it is not primarily because of colonialism or oppression of the working classes or the availability of resources—as political radicals insist—but because of the superiority of the commercial ethic in solving problems. All too often the ills of the disadvantaged are blamed on exploitation. The underlying assumption is that the removal of the exploitation will remove the ills. History teaches us it will not. When the Romans withdrew from their Empire the lot of the former imperialized *and* imperialists worsened for a millennium. But if it is appropriate to curb the excesses of commercialism to protect the employees, the environment or even the business world itself it is no less important to restrict those excesses to protect animals in entertainment. We make these points because it is not unusual to find the animal welfarist maligned as hiding a distaste for capitalism under the cloak of a concern for animals.

When large sums of money or merely a sense of human achievement are at stake, the participants are inclined to put success, both financial and personal, above all else and to the detriment of everything else. We have then grounds to be concerned. If amateur as well as professional athletes are willing to use steroids to further their performance, knowing the almost certain damage to their own long-term health, we have reason to believe that the desire to succeed needs to be curbed. If the desire for success results in voluntary damage to oneself how much more willing are we to damage others?

The sum of $13 million has been paid for a young racehorse, and one million is no longer a rarity. Racing stables are multimillion-dollar businesses, and businesses which are at considerable risk. Some of the more famous are in financial difficulty, threatened with bankruptcy. Unless one's horses win, and win big and often, the costs of the enterprise will exceed the income. Unless one's horses win substantial prize money neither stud sales nor stud fees will match the costs. The pressure to succeed means that the horse comes to be treated solely as capital—the means of producing wealth. It is equivalent to the industrialist's machine.

Just as industrialists treat their machines with consummate care and attention so too the owner treats the horse. It is pampered, well-fed and treated with every consideration for its health. Yet both are primarily concerned with what the machine or the horse can produce. Thus the horse matters not as an end in itself but as an instrument of production. If it does not win the major prizes, if its offspring do not fetch more than the cost of maintenance, the horse must be relegated to the industrial scrap heap.

Commercial competition may well be advantageous to the consumer. Competition tends to improve quality and/or decrease price. Individual capitalists may lose in the competition and be compelled to change their mode of production. Workers may be required to find alternate modes of earning a living. But on balance, we believe, capitalist competition produces a standard of living far in excess of that of other systems of production even though its excesses require regulation both in terms of providing a more equitable distribution and in diverting capital to areas where competition is ineffective, e.g., in the making of parks, and the protection of the environment. What distinguishes ordinary business competition from horse-racing is that the instrument of production is a machine not a sentient being.

Some will insist that not the machine, but the human worker, is truly comparable with the horse in this analysis. Labour, not machines, are the source of value, as John Locke informed us at the end of the seventeenth century, long before the anti-capitalist pronouncements of Karl Marx. Locke, Ricardo and Smith employed the labour theory of value to support competition not oppose it. We accept in part the relevance of such assertions though we think the comparison with the machine somewhat more appropriate in current racing circumstances. Whether we make the comparison with the machine or the human worker though, the points are not dissimilar and the conclusions to be drawn about relevant action identical.

If the appropriate comparison is with the machine, then the animal is being treated with utter disregard for its inherent dignity, its appropriateness to being considered as an end in itself, and horse-racing in its present form is perhaps unsalvageable. If the appropriate comparison is with the human worker then we must recognize that the horse should be entitled to the same *kinds* of consideration (not the same consideration) as workers have been in providing laws to protect their interests against misuse, and that much needs to be done to protect the racehorse.

Few would deny that the sight of competing racehorses rounding the turn heading for home is an enjoyable one, and one which in principle does not seem to be injurious to the interests of horses. Galloping horses appear to be thoroughly enjoying themselves. And while some at the racetrack may be there for the gambling rather than the entertainment provided by horse and jockey there is no doubt that many are enthralled by the sport itself. After all, we enjoy witnessing athletes competing in the Olympic Games without having to wager on which competitor will triumph.

The racehorse gallops at speeds of up to 40 miles per hour. The heartbeat of a horse at full gallop can increase from 25 beats a minute to 250 beats a minute, an astounding tenfold increase. The human heart beats at around 72 times a minute and in a professional sprint rises to perhaps somewhat in excess of 200 beats, a mere three, occasionally four, times the norm. While human athletes adjust their training and restrict frequency of competitions so as to maximize the explosiveness of their performance on the most important occasions the restrictions for racehorses are far more severe. An over-raced horse risks an enlarged heart, serious health problems and an early demise. They are thus restricted for most of their day to a narrow stall, isolated from any relationship with other horses and are prohibited free exercise. To be sure, they are exercised, but it is a rigorously controlled exercise, designed not for the general well-being of the animals but solely to maximize their racing performance.

Horse-racing has been documented as far back as 1500 B.C. in Egypt. It has been practised in a more or less organized manner since the twelfth century in England. It has provided great pleasure for countless people. The racetrack was the early source for some people of respect for the animal realm. It would be a pity to lose the sport because the racing world is not willing to clean up its own act. There are already some activists demanding the abolition of horse-racing, but if the horse-racing world takes its own steps the threat from the radical world can be readily averted.

Why, for example, was the use of the whip not outlawed long ago? It is one thing to pat the rump smartly to give a direction, another to whip the horse painfully as it approaches the final furlong. Of course, the racers tell us that the whip is merely to encourage and does not hurt the horse. Yet one need only see the reaction of a horse to a whip cracked strenuously on the hide to know the pain that is felt. Surely abolishing the whip would be no detriment to the sport. All would still start on equal terms. But, we are told, some horses need the whip to improve their performance. Apart from contradicting the claim that the whip does not hurt, we should note that if the whip is needed the horse is gaining no benefit from its participation and should not be involved in the competition. If the horse is not to be treated as a machine or a slave the whip must go.

Even more disturbing is the condition of the horses once their racing days are over, unless they are able to command respectable stud fees. Customarily racehorses whose money-earning days are at an end are euthanized. The sole reward for perfectly healthy animals which have provided enjoyment for many thousands of spectators and no mean income for their owners, trainers and jockeys is an early grave. How can owners with any concern at all for their horses permit this to happen? This is not an unfortunately rare and random occurrence, but the decided policy of many owners which affects the majority of racehorses. What can one think of racing organizations such as the American Thoroughbred Racing Association which do not require as a condition of membership and participation that healthy retired animals be put out to pasture as *minimal* common decency requires?

If the same organizations were to require regular free exercise, the companionship of other horses, and to regulate the occasions on which the horses could compete, then the racing world could avoid the embarrassment it will soon face from the activists. It is no defence to say that these requirements would marginally reduce the effectiveness of performance. So does the prohibition against human steroid use. The races would still be fair and just as enjoyable. And if they have any genuine concern for their horses the owners will do it for far better reason than to escape public condemnation. Unfettered competition almost rang the death knell of capitalism. It took the wise regulatory steps of the Disraelis, Roosevelts and R.B. Bennetts of this world to save it. It would be a shame if the benefits of horse-racing were lost because of present but unnecessary iniquities.

It should be noted that the conditions we have discussed are those at the highest echelons of horse-racing, not the lowest. At the lowest, doping, the racing of unfit animals and direct cruelty to the animals are manifest. The anti-inflammatory and pain-killing drug Butazolidin is injected so that they can run when lame or injured. There are, of course, regulations to control such practices and they certainly succeed in reducing them. But if improvements are instituted at the top they will surely filter down, not least by increasing the level of expectations.

There are other uses of horses for entertainment as well as thoroughbred flat-racing. Harness-racing is especially popular in North America in the smaller towns with small tracks. In Britain steeple-chasing continues. But such events as the Grand National at Aintree are a positive detriment to the well-being and public stature of horse-racing. Deaths and serious injuries to the horses from the crashing falls are not uncommon. If flat-racing can be defended with substantial amendments, steeplechasing cannot. The danger to the horses is too great and it does nothing to further the human-animal bond.

Showjumping, polo and eventing are difficult to assess. While they are very taxing for the horses and in increasing order of likelihood apt to cause injury to the animals, they nonetheless encourage the closest human-animal relationship. There can be little doubt that in most cases the animals are as exhilarated by the experience as the riders. If we accept the view that pain and suffering to the animal are the only criteria to be considered in determining the acceptability of a practice then showjumping, polo, and eventing are indefensible. But if we recognize that the higher order animals are truly like human beings and revel in activities which extend their capacities then we must broaden the criteria. Certainly, eventing courses must be designed to minimize the potential for serious injury. But let us acknowledge the very real pleasure the horses derive from their participation and the stimulus it provides to a true recognition of the qualities and character of the animal world. Of course, some will ask how we can know what horses enjoy, whether they really feel pleasure in such activities. The answer is simple—the same way we know whether humans are really enjoying themselves. We judge from their behaviour on the basis of experience. And no one doubts—other than a solipsist or a cynic, we suppose—that we can make satisfactory judgements about human behaviour.

Greyhound-racing falls in principle into the same category as horse-racing but our experience of the conditions in which Ontario S.P.C.A. inspectors have found greyhounds leads us to fear that it is in practice very difficult to defend at all. The haunting images of the emaciated creatures which have had to be destroyed foster little hope in us that greyhound-racing could ever be revived to an acceptable condition. Although greyhounds do not chase live rabbits at the track, by all accounts they are often trained with the use of live rabbits which they are allowed to catch. This apparently increases their ardour and exertion at the track—though one of our parents used to tell the story of a day he was at the track and the mechanical rabbit stopped in mid-course. The greyhounds continued their race not one whit distracted. Still, the way they congregate around the pseudo-rabbit at the end of the race suggests that they have an expectation of something other than a piece of machinery. And despite the requisite pre-race veterinary inspections we are convinced that difficult to detect under- and/or overfeeding or drinking can readily affect performance to determine the outcome.

Animal rights groups have claimed that there are 20,000 registered racing greyhounds in the United States today. They estimate also that only one in five of those bred for racing becomes good enough to be registered. The remaining 80,000 are "either killed, sold for laboratory experimentation, or turned into constant breeding machines."[4] We are told that 100,000 rabbits—and some kittens—are brutally killed every year in the training of the dogs. After their approximately four years of racing life the successful greyhounds are consigned to the same fate as those who failed to become successful.

For those who think that these are merely the prejudiced figures of radical groups intent on destroying greyhound-racing, figures from an article by Jack McClintoch in the June 1991 edition of *Life* serve to confirm at least the general tenor of the animal rightists' claims. There we are told that a racing greyhound from the age of 18 months is confined to a three-foot by three-foot wire-mesh circle day and night. Four times a day it is taken out "for a pit stop." Twice a week it runs a 30-second race. "At least 50,000 dogs a year become 'unusable' . . . at least 30,000 surplus dogs a year are killed," McClintoch tells us, and "few in the greyhound trade are comfortable with these facts, but almost everyone seems to accept them. More are bred each year than can possibly be used. The fastest are trained to race, some are sold into medical research—where greyhounds are prized for their tolerance of pain. Many kennels still use the grisly method of training their dogs with live rabbits, which are inevitably caught." Whether we are talking about the killing of 30,000 or 50,000 or 80,000 greyhounds every year does not make any difference to the abject and inhumane horror that greyhound-racing undoubtedly is.

If horse-racing is the sport of kings—or at least of the nobility and gentry—dog-racing has been of humbler origins. In its beginnings in

---

4   Edward F. Dolan, Jr., *Animal Rights* (New York: Franklin Watts, 1986), p. 114.

Britain it was the working man's sport and has remained predominantly so both there and in North America. In our egalitarian and democratic era it would soothe our prejudices to report that the working class treats their racing animals better than the middle and upper class. Unfortunately it is not so. The number of former racing greyhounds scheduled for destruction is so great that small groups of dog lovers have organized themselves in racing towns to find new homes for these unwanted former stars of the track. Gloria Sanders of the Greyhound Pets of America estimates that 6,000 a year are adopted. Unfortunately they have often been so ill-treated that many do not make good pets. If greyhound-racing is to be rescued from its impending doom at the hands of a distressed public the fraternity must undergo a veritable metamorphosis. "Going to the dogs" is an unfortunately meaningful phrase.

There is an unwritten rule among many Canadian Humane Societies that while rodeos may be generally criticized for the abominations that they are one should show some discretion in opposition in the west. They have become such an indigenous part of the culture, expressing the Albertan red neck self-image, that some Humane Societies consider only their grossest excesses subject to denunciation (although the Calgary Humane Society itself has shown great fortitude in its explicit opposition to the famous Stampede). Many Humane Society organizers think that to suggest that rodeos are destructive of the finer nature of both human and animal would be to risk losing sorely needed funds and general public support from western sympathizers. 'Tradition' and 'cultural heritage' are concepts used not merely to justify aboriginal trapping practices but also to glorify the worst of the aura of the Wild West, although in fact very little which takes place in a rodeo bears more than a merely superficial resemblance to anything which ever happened in 'wild West' history.

In 1924 in England the managers of London's Wembley Stadium—best known for its presentation of the 1948 Olympic Games, scores of international soccer matches and as the permanent venue for the annual English Cup Final—staged an impressive rodeo. They were promptly prosecuted under the Cruelty to Animals Act. In 1990 on the occasion of the annual Calgary Stampede Leon Adams, Oklahoma horse trainer and Stampede stalwart, expressed the view that the "Lord gave us animals. They're for our use, our subjugation. We're here to be the kings of the earth." We might have some qualms about Adams's biblical exegesis. We might express some dismay at such wanton psychological need to dominate. But most of all we should wonder why, 66 years after the Wembley prosecution, the Calgary Stampede is as popular as ever, as unscathed as ever, and almost as downrightly barbaric and cruel as ever. If moral sensibilities toward animals lurk just beneath the surface of all our consciousnesses, for some that surface is as concrete. Once we have come to enjoy an event our rationalizations serve to bury even the most compelling of humane sentiments.

The *facts* that, according to the organizers, the Calgary Stampede serves to inject "between $80 million and $90 million into the local economy every year" and that "more than one million people travel to the fair each year" are impressive. They certainly serve to persuade Albertans that it would be economically foolhardy to abandon their milch cow, to borrow an inappropriate metaphor. We have already expressed the view that we have misgivings about 'official' statistics. How many of the 'travellers' are resident Albertans whose expenditures at the Stampede are merely money that would otherwise be spent in other parts of the local economy?

In fact, 'official' figures of this kind are customarily grossly misleading. In another Canadian city 'official' statistics tell us that 600,000 visitors to an annual week-long event inject millions of dollars into the local economy. There are fewer than 2,000 hotel beds in the whole region and they are not all fully booked. How are these staggering figures reckoned? Each time a person enters an establishment related to the event that person counts as a visitor. So if a group of half a dozen locals attend three establishments every day for six days—and many do more than that—that counts as over a hundred 'visitors'. Many local businesses unrelated to the festivities report their lowest week's income for the year. In fact what the festivities have produced is not a major injection of capital into the local economy but a significant redistribution of it. The Calgary Stampede does not seem very different. Albertans should not fear that the demise of the Stampede would have an inordinate impact on their economy. Before they allow their financial fears to mask their humane sentiments Albertans should recalculate. There would be a loss, but only a small part of what the organizers tell us. 'Official' statistics are as much a part of the hoopla as the events themselves.

'Rodeo' is derived from the Spanish noun meaning 'a going around', hence its use for a cattle-ring. The rodeo has its origins with the *vaqueros*, the sixteenth-century Mexicans who wore leggings and used ropes to herd their Spanish conquerors' cattle, a practice documented as far north as Santa Fe when it was a Spanish possession. In Charles Darwin's *The Voyage of the Beagle* an 1834 entry tells us that among the haciendas in the valley of Quillota, Chile, "once every year there is a grand 'rodeo' when all the cattle are driven down, counted, and marked and a certain number separated to be fattened in the irrigated fields."[5]

---

5 Charles Darwin, *The Voyage of the Beagle*, ed. Leonard Engel (New York: Doubleday, 1962), p. 258.

From an occasion for stocktaking the event turned into a celebratory event in which the participants demonstrated their prowess. The practice proved so popular that in 1852 the new state of California enacted a statute to the effect that "every owner of a stock farm shall be obliged to give yearly one general rodeo."

But it was William Cody's 'Buffalo Bill's Wild West Show' that gave the rodeo its public and highly artificial popularity among those other than the cowboys themselves. Beginning in 1883, and spurring numerous competitors, the Wild West Show stimulated American, European and (not until the turn of the century) Canadian interest in a spurious imitation of a rapidly dying custom. The rodeo as spectacle is a farce loosely based on a reality. It is not a continuation of a tradition which relates to the practices of cattle ranchers and cowboys in American, and still less in Canadian, history.

In fact it was an American cow puncher, Guy Weadick, who first brought the rodeo to Calgary—and not until 1912. In 1923 the Calgary Exhibition and Stampede was born. It is almost comical at a time when Canadians are trying to discover an identity which differentiates them from Americans that the highly artificial, American-conceived, instituted and developed rodeo should be justified as an inherent and indigenous part of the western Canadian heritage. While it is true that new societies may more readily institute new 'traditions' it should strike us as odd that such a 'tradition' should have no historical antecedents and be decidedly foreign in origin.

Unlike horse-racing and akin to bull-fighting the rodeo does not depend on any significant co-operation between man and beast but on brutal domination. In 1986 at the Calgary Stampede an horrendous accident during a chuck wagon race resulted in the death of nine horses. This, according to the organizers, was indeed a calamity but was an occurrence beyond anything previously experienced and was not indicative of the nature of the events generally. While that is true, and while improvements to chuck wagon racing have been made, at the following year's Stampede three animals were euthanized and one horse died after collapsing in a race. Two other horses were injured but survived. In 1988 one horse collapsed and died and three other animals were injured. In 1989 two calves had to be euthanized. And these figures reflect only the obvious injuries which could not be hidden. Moreover, the Calgary Stampede is the most efficient and professionally run rodeo in Canada. We shudder to think what happens at the lesser events.

There are approximately 65 professional rodeos held annually in western Canada involving the 700 cowboys who are members of the Canadian Professional Rodeo Association (C.P.R.A.), together with the American professionals who also take part in the events. Most of them are part-timers who make a slim living from their public appearances.

However, the top 10 per cent who travel the U.S. and Canadian rodeo circuits are reported to earn between $30-35,000 a year, the top income being in the region of $160,000. Ralph Murray, the general manager of the C.P.R.A., claimed in 1990 "There's no question about it. The rodeo is growing. It's because it's entertainment for everyone." It certainly isn't entertainment for the animals. Nor is it entertainment for anyone who is aware of the grotesque practices which occur out of public sight.

Not surprisingly, animal welfare advocates have been trying to outlaw rodeos for decades. They have provided us with lurid descriptions of the horrors perpetrated during these events. Rodeo organizers tell us that such reports are the wild-eyed imaginations of naïve animal lovers who have more concern with animals than humans and who lack both the knowledge and experience to make rational judgements about rodeos. "Nobody knows what makes horses buck," they tell us. "In approved rodeos they are not starved, nor tormented, nor stimulated into bucking; they buck for the love of it."

In 1990 a major rodeo was planned for Ontario, to be held at Toronto's Sky Dome. The Toronto City Council was inundated with many letters from individuals and several substantial briefs from animal welfare organizations demanding that the event not be allowed. Council was also briefed by the rodeo sponsors and organizers. The Neighbourhoods Committee of Council requested the city's Medical Officer of Health to "report back on rodeo practices, and whether such practices could be deemed cruel to animals." The private letters to Council expressed indignation and moral outrage. So much for Mr. Murray's view that the rodeo is "entertainment for everyone." The briefs from the animal advocate groups were replete with solid evidence of the barbarism. For such people the report of the City's Medical Officer of Health was so mild that it seemed to ignore much of the evidence placed before it. His report was a careful and cautious document dealing with what was beyond evident doubt. Nor did he concern himself at all with the question of whether rodeos were morally reprehensible. He was asked to consider only "whether such practices could be deemed to be cruel to animals" and this he did within the context of a dictionary definition and the Canadian Criminal Code. Lest we be accused of possessing 'wild-eyed imaginations' let us go no further than the Medical Officer of Health's Report.

Dr. P.R.W. Kendall acknowledged unequivocally that "most activities seen during Rodeo exhibitions bear little, if any, resemblance to the skills once employed by working cowhands." In discussing the animals' participation in the events and whether they involved pleasure, he noted that "In most rodeo events this is clearly not the case, since devices such as electric prods, sharpened sticks, spurs, flank straps and other rodeo tack must be used in order to induce the animals to react in a way that will make certain events 'exciting' for the spectators."

The Medical Officer recognized recent guidelines that have been instituted which are intended to prevent animal abuse but concluded that "even in some of the sanctioned rodeos these guidelines are at times deliberately and conveniently ignored." In discussing the broken legs incurred in calf-roping events, he added, "Unseen damage that is not obvious, i.e., injuries to the neck muscles, internal bruising, or haemorrhaging, or bruising of cartilage in the larynx and trachea, are not necessarily evident during the competition."

He describes the use of spurs "to stimulate a bucking behaviour" and of two cinches, the second of which is a belt "tightened around the flank and sensitive parts of the horse." His conclusion is that, "The flank strap tightly cinched provides pressure on the lumbar nerves, which are particularly sensitive, and to the groin. Frequently a shock or two from a 'hot shot' or cattle prod, together with the irritation from the flank strap, has the horse flying out of the chute." So much for the official rodeo claim that "Nobody knows what makes horses buck . . . they buck for the love of it." They buck in fact in an attempt to avoid the pain. All bucking events, according to Dr. Kendall, "use irritants of one form or another to make the animal buck."

All this, one should note, is a description of the rodeo at its best and after substantial alterations had been made to attempt to improve the rodeo's image. Moreover, it only considers what can be demonstrably proven and not those far worse occurrences which many suspect are legion.

In his summary, Dr. Kendall states that in terms of a dictionary definition of cruelty "one must conclude that most rodeo events have that potential [to cause injury, grief, or pain], therefore can be considered 'cruel'." He notes the option that "legal recourse exists under the Criminal Code which provides an opportunity to prosecute in the event that the legal definition of cruelty is met." Kendall does not say that such a definition is met, although he clearly implies that the limits are reached if not crossed. And those limits, we must remember, are so weak that non-lethal bull-fighting is permitted, along with steel-jawed leghold trapping!

The departmental lawyers advising Dr. Kendall would have been very wary to draw the logical conclusion that rodeo practices fulfil the legal definition of cruelty, since the Criminal Code they were considering is a federal law. Had a legal opinion been advanced that rodeos were legally cruel this would have brought pressure to use the department's lawyers' arguments in a case against the Calgary Stampede in Alberta. There is considerable reluctance among many animal advocates to press such a case. The law is weak and if the case is lost the ammunition to the arsenal of the Stampede would be of great detriment to the animal cause. The Stampede would be able to claim that it has the law on its side in the battle for public opinion.

And public opinion will accept a great deal of cruelty until it is made consciously aware of a reality of which it remains largely ignorant. Rodeos are still shown on television occasionally and, surely, so the public imagines, what receives the blessing of private and public broadcasting authorities cannot be barbarous and cruel. No doubt broadcasting authorities today would be unlikely knowingly to project a healthy image for an activity which borders on illegality and transgresses all bounds of human decency. But they too are sometimes ignorant and their sensibilities are equally in need of arousal. In fact in July of 1991 the Canadian Broadcasting Corporation devoted two hours of Sunday evening prime time to the Calgary Stampede as well as a substantial proportion of its afternoon three-hour "Sportsweekend" program. Even the venerated C.B.C. still thinks of an activity with such harm to animals as a 'sport'.

Anyway, historically, television and film have been less than kind to the animal, although increasingly today public television especially is producing and airing films on wildlife which stimulate the greatest public awareness. Even in the world of theatrical fiction the British program "All Creatures Great and Small" serves to provide an entirely unsentimental view of the sensitive reality of domestic and farm animal life just over half a century ago. Although set in the Yorkshire dales of northern England its appeal is just as great to North American audiences. One must remember that many of the animals are 'actors' whose behaviour is artificially contrived for the occasion. It would be unwarranted to assume that since animals have been treated sometimes without due care and consideration in the world of video entertainment that it is not possible to justify animal involvement in such entertainment at all. The questions which need to be asked include, Does the representation serve to promote or demean the animal? Does the animal itself derive benefit from its performance? Does the representation serve to increase or decrease human sensibility toward the animal?

Once upon a time, so stories of a doubtful past always begin, horses and sheep were driven over cliffs and plunged to the water below to make a better movie. Animals have been shot and killed in movies because it was less expensive than to sedate them. While such stories abound about the early film industry they are probably exaggerations. Still, there is no doubt that cattle were caused to stampede for motion pictures. And stunt horses have traditionally been misused. The most common and decidedly dangerous stunt involves the 'running Ws'. Ropes are stretched from the saddle to the front hooves of the horse and attached with clamps. The rider triggers the ropes at the appropriate moment and horse and rider come crashing to the ground. Horses have frequently been injured and not infrequently had to be euthanized because of such stunts.

In 1939 during the filming of *Jesse James* a horse had a greased plank pulled out from under its hooves, causing a 40-foot plunge to its death. Since that time the Hollywood Office of the American Humane Association has undertaken direct and immediate surveillance of the use of animals in the production of films. And certainly in the last few years there has been considerable co-operation between film directors and the representatives of Humane Societies. Unfortunately, though, when scenes need to be shot which involve potentially inhumane usage, the filming is moved to Mexico.

In 1986 Animal Performers Canada was instituted to protect animals in films produced in Canada. Unfortunately, due to shortages of funds, despite the strenuous efforts of the Kitchener-Waterloo Humane Society in particular, the organization became moribund in 1988. Its remaining funds were transferred to the Canadian Federation of Humane Societies, where the organization still nominally exists, although inactively, until some generous benefactor revives its fortunes. During its short practical existence there was genuine co-operation from the film industry. The organization's misleading name did not help, however, for more calls were received from those anxious to place their animals in movies than from any other source.

Until quite recently animal training, whether in the circus or for film, was based on a little bit of affection and a great deal of fear. In training lions, tigers, elephants, bears or even dogs, the rule was to dominate, to force into submission. There must be master and mastered. There could be no other way, so it was thought, if the animal was not to turn on its trainer and was always to do as it was bid. Truly the animal was merely a means, human entertainment—with its resultant profit—the sole end.

Changes in the film industry in recent decades have been of the greatest benefit to the animal—in part because public consciousness has driven directors and producers to adopt a more humane attitude but also because a new generation of animal trainers has a much greater sensitivity to its charges. This should not lead us to an unduly optimistic belief that there is no longer any cruelty to animals in the production of films or that animals are always treated according to their natures or their inherent dignity. But it does mean that they are customarily treated with a consideration for their interests which was absent in the past.

The doyen of Hollywood's animal trainers is Ralph Helfer, winner of 18 PATSY awards for the best animal performances on the screen, and supplier of animal performers to over 5,000 movies and television programs. His book *The Beauty of the Beasts: Tales of Hollywood's Wild Animal Stars*[6] is full of the ambivalence we have witnessed throughout

---

6 (Los Angeles: Tarcher, 1990).

the history of animal welfare. But it is an ambivalence which reflects a progressive step in the dialectics of change.

Helfer replaced the traditional training through fear with what he calls 'Affection Training' in which love, patience, understanding and respect are the instruments of instruction. It would be easy enough to suggest that these are mere words and words are cheaper than deeds. But no one who has witnessed Helfer with one of his animals could doubt that he was involved in a relationship with the animal. If the animal was not an equal, it was certainly an object of admiration and veneration. His animals are not instruments but ends, creatures whose inherent worth Helfer acknowledges and promotes.

Wherein, then, lies the ambivalence? Helfer keeps a large stock of a great variety of animals away from their natural habitat for the primary purpose of providing animals for the motion picture screen. The film appears to vie with the animal for significance. One wonders how his stunts with the likes of ostriches, ducks and pythons can really be to the benefit of the animal. He covers the head of the ostrich with a hood. He has the scent glands removed from skunks. One suspects that he sometimes treats his animals as though they were human rather than according to their own natures, although one cannot doubt that he treats them with respect. One has cause for concern at his desire to try "to get animals when they were very young—even before their eyes had opened." But ambivalence, we suppose, is the nature of humankind, and Helfer's ambivalence is an aspect of necessary progress. For if the use of animals on the movie screen and on television is to continue, it is far better that it be in the hands of those who are, however incompletely, on the side of the animals.

It would not only be impractical to demand the abolition of the use of animals on the screen but decidedly detrimental to their potential interests. The movie screen and the television screen can be, and have been, used to demean and degrade the animal realm. But in the hands of those who care they provide the most effective media to promote the welfare of animals and have the potential to promote the requisite sensitivity for which humans have the capacity if they are offered the knowledge and means.

Helfer's own words portend the happiest possible relationship between the human and animal world. His desire is to train animals "so that they would enjoy performing as much as the viewing public enjoyed watching them." He understands the necessity of a *reciprocal* relationship. "I wanted to be able to know an animal's world *and to let it know mine.*" When he talks of respect, he talks of "mine for him, *and his for me.*" Of course, the cynic will tell us that actions speak louder than words. And so they do. Helfer's actions are reasonably impressive, but his words stand even more importantly as a clarion call to action for all who follow.

The more radical would ask why Helfer would want to train animals at all, since that is to divert them from their true nature. Still, he wants to "achieve an animal's co-operation through true respect—now that would be an achievement worth devoting one's life to." He recognizes the intellectual differences between animal and human but understands, as so few do, including many animal liberationists, that "In the realm of emotions, animals and humans share a common ground."[7]

Helfer demonstrates a depth of awareness which eludes many animal advocates. "How wonderful is the ability of animals to accept their problems! No moaning, no self-pity—just acceptance and quiet dignity. He [a lion] sees with his third eye, and the roar of his voice answers questions unknown to us to ask . . . animals listen to one perfect voice—nature's voice—and do as it bids them."[8]

In Helfer's perceptiveness and sensibility lies the route to understanding and promoting the community of sentient beings. If we must retain our concern for the treatment of animals in cinema and television entertainment we must also recognize that the attitudes of people like Helfer and his followers augur for a happier animal experience.

Chapter Eleven

Animals in Entertainment:
Zoos, Aquaria and Circuses

The Camel's hump is an ugly lump
Which well you may see at the zoo;
But uglier yet is the Hump we get
From having too little to do.
     — Rudyard Kipling, "How the Camel
       Got his Hump," *Just-So Stories*

By the time of World War II zoos and aquaria were regarded as places to take the children for a day of amusement—the promised elephant ride and the ice cream cone being of as high a priority as any educational benefit derived from a perusal of the inmates. As often as not it was a way of idling away the day when there seemed little of importance to do.

Already in Victorian times the functions of zoos and aquaria must have appeared a little uncertain to their visitors. It is instructive to read the travellers' guides which were so popular in the period. Baedeker's guides were the most famous and the most commonly consulted by the avid traveller. Wherever one was inclined to go Baedeker was sure to have a guide to follow—and if there was a zoo or an aquarium Baedeker was sure to mention it.

In Baedeker's *Northern Germany* of 1897 the description of the Berlin *Tiergarten*—the animal gardens—tells us far more about the setting than about the animals. We read that it

> is the largest and most attractive park near the town . . . and covers upwards of 600 acres in ground [The London Zoo had less than 40]. It is enlivened by several sheets of water, and combines the character of a natural forest with the trimmer beauties of a public park. The pleasant parts are the *Seepark* [marine park] . . . where numerous skaters display their skill in winter.[1]

Sure, skaters are fine, but what of the marine life? Not a word. What follows is a description of six statues to be found in the park. One warning should ring familiar to modern city dwellers. "The remoter parts of the Tiergarten should be avoided after dark." Next follows a

---

1 Karl Baedeker, *Northern Germany* (Leipzig: Karl Baedeker), pp. 85-86.

185

mention of five more statues before we finally read, "Opposite the Seepark . . . lies the Zoological Garden . . . opened in 1844. It now contains one of the finest collections of animals in the world." Even though Baedeker provides us with 14 more lines of description of the zoo the sole mention of the animals is a passing reference to "perhaps the best collection of monkeys in Europe." Instead we are told about the "well-laid out grounds," the concerts and the architecture, as well as, of course, a few words about even more busts. We are told that the Antelope House is "in an Arabian style (with a large scene in majolica, from a design by Meyerheim)" and that the Elephant House is "a gaily-coloured structure resembling an Indian pagoda." Clearly, the art, the architecture and the landscaping are of greater significance than the animals for Baedeker and his travellers. The animals may have been of passing interest but they were truly the province of the curator and his team of scientists. For the visitor the animals were, apparently, an amusing sideline to the cultural experience. Berliners today probably appreciate their zoo somewhat more. As a consequence of bombings and the destructive street battles which culminated in the capitulation of Berlin in May of 1945 only 91 of the 12,000 animals survived. Today the 84-acre zoo is one of the most popular Berlin haunts, attracting close to three million visitors a year (more than double that of London Zoo but some 800,000 less than San Diego), and has one of the largest collections of wildlife in the world.

The use of the word 'collection' twice in Baedeker's description is informative. When we use the word 'collection' today of a group of animals we are probably thinking in terms of the accumulation. The Victorians thought very much in terms of accumulating. Collecting the biggest, best, rarest and most was an intrinsic part of the intense national rivalry which plagued the nineteenth and earlier twentieth centuries—and is with us only somewhat diminished today. National zoos were policy instruments of national aggrandizement.

But we should not imagine that there was no serious interest in the animals on the part of the zoologists and naturalists. They scoured the extremities of the earth for the objects of their investigation. They earnestly desired to understand animals but only in the same manner that they wanted to understand the formation of rocks and exotic vegetation. This is, indeed, what differentiates the 'modern' zoo from the earlier animal collections. Beginning with the founding of the London Zoo in 1826 a primary purpose was the increase in scientific knowledge—partly for its own sake, partly to put animals to human use, but also to demonstrate national superiority.

Provided the assisted nation was not a serious competitor in the power stakes, international co-operation for scientific purposes was evident in zoological studies. Again Baedeker's guides are informative. In Baedeker's *Southern Italy* of 1883 we read that:

> The Neapolitan Aquarium [open in 1874] contains such an abundant stock of curious marine animals of every description, that it is perhaps the most interesting establishment of the kind in the world. Among the contents are 6-8 varieties of cuttle-fish (the feeding of the large *Octopus* is interesting), a number of electric rays (which visitors are permitted to touch so as to experience the shock from which the fish derives its name), numerous beautifully coloured fish of the Mediterranean, a great many kinds of living coral, beautiful Medusae and crested blubbers, many extraordinary-looking crabs and crayfish, pipe-fish, etc.[2]

Clearly, the fish and crustaceans are themselves the focal point of interest here. Presumably the architecture is less than impressive and there are no statues to be described—though Baedeker does describe the nearby architecture and statues at greater length than the fish. We are told of the 1872 founding by a German scientist of the 'Zoological Station' (the scientific context for the aquarium), of the large subsidies contributed by the German government, and a lesser one by British naturalists. Even here the zoological interest is subordinated to an instrument of national political influence!

We are told further of its funding by European governments—and the University of Cambridge—"for the privilege of sending naturalists to make use of the advantages of the institution." In the nine years between the aquarium's founding and the publication of the 1883 edition of Baedeker's guide, about 150 foreign naturalists had prosecuted their investigations there. The Station published "extensive periodical proceedings" and provided scientific data for museums and laboratories. "In various ways [it] has fairly asserted itself as the central point for the study of marine biology."[3]

While zoos and aquaria were open to the public to provide useful entertainment—the handling of the rays should not go unnoticed—their primary purpose was a scientific one. It is customary today to criticize zoos and aquaria for keeping their charges in unnatural conditions, quite contrary to the inmates' nature and to their psychological health. We should not forget, though, that in their origins they provided us with a wealth of zoological knowledge without which our modern sensibilities would have been less easily derived and they introduced millions to a wonderful world of flora and fauna they would otherwise have never known. Of course, we must regret the mastery of nature on which the collecting was predicated and no less must we regret the intent to mould the animals for human purposes. Moreover, we must acknowl-

---

2 Karl Baedeker, *Southern Italy* (Leipzig: Karl Baedeker), p. 85.
3 Ibid., p. 86.

edge the diminution of the quality of scientific data acquired in such unnatural habitats. But we should not reject the idea of zoos and aquaria for past unconscionable performance alone or, for that matter, for current iniquities. We must recognize that sanitized, tiled, steam-heated cages with their concrete floors and iron bars that could be readily cleaned were designed to protect the animals from disease and provide them with the warmth they required.

The extensive collections of animals for public display begun in the early nineteenth century were not the first 'zoos'. The first 'zoo' must have been Noah's Ark. Indeed, most books on zoos make some reference to the ark—four recent zoo books having 'ark' in the title. If we accept the seventeenth-century Irish Bishop Ussher's biblical dating system the ark must have been built 4,461 years ago! Taking the Bible literally Ussher calculated that the world was created in 4004 B.C. He also calculated all the intervening events. Some editions of the St. James Bible used Ussher's dating until well into the twentieth century. Ussher's unscientific dating should not be dismissed as irrelevant, however erroneous, for prosecution witnesses relied on Ussher to denounce not just the theory of evolution but almost all modern science in the Scopes trial in Tennessee in 1925. It would be unwise to forget how recent our serious understanding of animals and their relationship to humankind really is. If nineteenth-century zoo and aquaria curators lacked awareness of the nature of wild animals in the eyes of their modern critics, in their own age they displayed an awareness of the importance of the animal realm that was decidedly irrelevant and inappropriate in the eyes of many of their contemporaries. When as early as 1907 the German naturalist Carl Hagenbeck began to replace bars with moats and concrete floors with something resembling a natural habitat he was frowned upon by many as a crank with strange notions about the significance of animals.

Ignoring the ark, we find the earliest extensive animal collections in ancient Sumeria, Assyria, China, Egypt, Greece and Rome. The Egyptian menageries were in part an adjunct to worship, in Greece and in Rome they were adjuncts to the slaughter of the amphitheatres and in China they were an adjunct to hunting. What they shared in common was that they were displays of wealth and power—which does not differentiate them substantially from the 'modern' zoos of the nineteenth century.

There is evidence of a royal animal park in the city of Ur in Sumeria almost 4,300 years ago—less than two centuries after Ussher's dating of the ark! Just over a thousand years later Assyrian rulers were exchanging exotic animals—at least when they weren't at war with each other. A little later than that—around 1000 B.C.—the founder of the Chou dynasty in China, Wu Wen, had an animal park laid out. It was intriguingly called the Garden of Intelligence, but we have been unable to determine the significance behind this provocative name. Aristotle's pupil, Alexander the Great, installed what was probably the first public zoo at Alexandria in Egypt in the third century B.C.—although private royal menageries, filled by animal expeditions in surrounding territories, had existed for 1,200 years in the country of the pharaohs. In the fifth century A.D. the Eastern Roman Empire boasted a zoological collection at Constantinople (modern day Istanbul) of lions, giraffes, elephants, monkeys and water buffalo. All of these animal collections were just that: collections. They sometimes had subsidiary purposes but they were all intended as a glorification of the ruler's acquisitory prowess.

Although the earliest Chinese zoos existed 3,000 ago it was only with Kublai Khan, the great Mongol conqueror of the thirteenth century, that they were developed to a significant size. It may well be inappropriate to describe Kublai Khan's menageries as zoos at all. In reality they were game ranches: worlds of predator and prey in miniature. Prey was provided for the predators while men preyed on the victors. Providing a 'zoo' was simply hunting made easy. Instead of having to seek out the prey in their natural habitat—where the hunted stood a chance—the 'brave' warriors were provided with the opportunity to kill without having to go to energetic lengths.

The sixteenth- and seventeenth-century voyages of discovery stimulated private and even royal animal collections in Europe, although a few had existed from the earlier Middle Ages consisting of animals from the 'known' world. Once the 'unknown' world was known, everyone who was anyone had to demonstrate that fact by possessing a few exotic animals. Even itinerant pedlars proved the worth of their goods or the sweetness of their music by the companionship of a Barbary ape (which is in fact a monkey not an ape) or a Capuchin monkey. The fact that no one knew how to provide for these animal aliens—most soon became diseased and died—did not deter their popularity. New voyages soon brought back more. Kings and nobles began to extend their private menageries—seeking ever rarer and more varied stock. If we are to believe modern psychiatrists there are also rather more personal explanations for collecting. Montreal analyst Nathan Wisebord has claimed it to be an outgrowth of toilet training: "The bowel movement is the only thing a small child can really call his own." It has also been explained as a fetish to assuage the anxiety of separation from a loved one, a substitute for sexual experience or sublimation of sexual dissatisfaction, and as an aspect of the commodity fetishism of the possessive individualism of capitalist society. Rather more prosaically it may simply reflect a desire to demonstrate one's superiority over others.

No European royal menagerie ever began to rival that of Montezuma, the early sixteenth-century Aztec emperor. His enormous collection of birds and beasts was managed by some 600 keepers! "500 turkeys were killed every day to feed his birds of prey alone, and it was rumoured that his larger cats (pumas and jaguars) dined regularly on human flesh."[4] His menagerie included crippled, dwarfed, hunchbacked and albino humans. Lest we are tempted to imagine the Aztecs some kind of morally inferior barbaric race let us not forget that Albert the Great considered pygmies to be sub-human. And St. Albert is revered as a humanitarian scholar with a pronounced scientific interest in nature. Moreover, circus 'freak' shows were popular in North America and to a lesser extent in Europe well into the twentieth century.

Although we can find something approaching the idea of the 'modern' zoo in Vienna, Madrid and Paris in the late eighteenth century—the last under the watchful eye of the famous French naturalist Baron Cuvier—it was the founding of the London Zoo in 1826 which presaged the predominantly scientific and educational direction of the zoological garden. By the 1870s the first American zoos were instituted in Philadelphia and Cincinnati while Canada opened its first zoo at Halifax, Nova Scotia, in 1847. But although the administration saw their zoos as scientific establishments, the visitors—whose entrance money was necessary to fund the science—went there to escape the doldrums of city life, to find some colour to mask the drabness, and only occasionally to fill and expand their minds.

We are right to question whether modern zoos and aquaria fulfil useful and worthwhile functions. But it would be untoward to fail to recognize the void they filled, and sometimes continue to fill today. With the rapid growth of urbanization and industrialization from the nineteenth century onward increasing proportions of the industrialized world lost all contact with wildlife. Only the occasional rat or mouse, a number of domestic horses, dogs and cats, and numerous sparrows and starlings constituted the animal world of the urban dweller. Even moths adapted their camouflage to match the grimy surroundings. The zoo managed to maintain a tenuous relationship between the city dweller and the magnificent world beyond—even if it was an artificial, psychologically cruel and scientifically misleading picture the urbanite was given.

Do modern zoos or aquaria provide an environment beneficial to the animal? And, if not, can they be constructed to do so? Since the 1950s it has been increasingly recognized that the traditional zoo with iron bars and concrete floors constitutes a world which is damaging to both the inmates and the prison visitors. They still exist. Yet since the 1950s considerable effort has gone into providing a surrounding more compatible with the animal's nature.

---

4   Morris, *Animal Contract*, p. 42.

One of the wisest of animal observers and erstwhile curator of mammals at the London Zoo, Desmond Morris, has written of the traditional conditions at that most famous of wildlife collections:

> Anyone studying these wretched creatures could observe that their behaviour had become hopelessly abnormal. Many became pathological overeaters, growing immensely fat and unhealthy. One bear literally ate itself to death, dying of suffocation from the pressure of fat and gobbled food. Others became pathological pacers, walking neurotically up and down in a bizarre, stereotyped pattern of movement that eventually wore a track in the surface of their enclosures. Still others became dung-eaters, self-mutilators, or self-starvers. Aberrant sexual behaviour became commonplace, some animals even attempting to copulate with their food bowls, or with other totally inappropriate species with which they were housed. There is something grotesque about a squirrel trying to bury a nut, a wild dog trying to dig a hole for a bone, or a wildcat trying to cover its faeces, when they are all scratching at concrete floors.[5]

Would it be possible for a zoo visitor to get an accurate image of the nature of a bear, a squirrel, wild dog or cat from such viewing? What if a scientist were to analyze the eating or sexual behaviour of a species from such evidence? The image is distorted, the science is science fiction. The whole is an unjustifiable exploitation. But even if the circumstances are improved can there be a benefit to the animals? Can there be zoos without bars supportive of both human and animal natures? Can zoos promote an awareness of the interdependent community of sentient beings?

It could be said that even by posing the last question we are assuming too much. We are assuming, our detractors will say with perhaps a little justification, the possibility of Isaiah's fanciful peaceable kingdom in which (Isaiah 11, 6-8)[6] wolves, lambs, leopards, kids, calves, lions, oxen, children and asps lie down together. No, we are not quite

---

5   Ibid., pp. 44-45.

6   Whether Isaiah believed that his peaceable kingdom might ever be more than a wild fancy is impossible to divine. What should amuse us is that various biblical commentators have not even thought the passage to be about animals at all. Thus, for example, in John Brown's 1778 exegesis, verses 6-9 of Isaiah 11 are interpreted to mean "Through the abundant spread of his gospel in the world, and the saving instructions of his Spirit, shall the most mischievous and untractable sinners of mankind be rendered meek, gentle, peaceful, and harmless" (*The Self-Interpreting Bible* [Glasgow: Blackie, 1834], p. 612). No wonder Christianity is interpreted as a man-dominant religion! Even the biblical passages about animals aren't really about animals!

that naïve but we do believe that the human-animal relationship ought to be promoted rather than hindered, that humans can have meaningful and eminently worthwhile relationships with a broader variety of animals than the domesticated species, and that where such possibilities exist we should not a priori dismiss them because in a perfect world all animals would live undisturbed in their natural native habitats. Let us not forget that in that 'perfect world' horses, dogs and cats would be returned to their wild state too. And we believe that at least some horses, dogs and cats, as well as humans, benefit from the current arrangements.

The reality is that it is extremely difficult to convert existing zoos to the requirements of ethical treatment without reducing the variety of animals. Many zoos are smaller than London's pitiful 36 acres, and even in Berlin's former 600 acres only a very small proportion was ever devoted to the animals. Modern zoos must be on the outskirts of major cities, in the countryside, or restricted to a smaller variety of compatible species. Moreover, in converting zoos, one is always inclined to cut cost corners and adapt. Nothing but a total restructuring will do. It is far better to sell the existing valuable city property to developers, purchase less expensive land outside and begin afresh—if one is to begin at all. But at least now that we understand the social nature of many species of wild animals so much better they may be successfully bred. No longer is it necessary to rape the wild to stock the enclosures. Already by 1986, 90 per cent of mammals entering zoo collections were bred in captivity.

Some zoos have received substantial praise from those who think that zoos perform a valuable service and, transformed, can be good for animal and human. Desmond Morris is particularly impressed by Arnhem Zoo in the Netherlands, the Monkey Jungle in Florida and the San Diego Zoo in California, but he notes that of the 1,007 zoos in the E.C. only 218 were registered in the *International Zoo Yearbook*.

Many of the unregistered zoos are reported to display ignorance of everything necessary even to contemplating a zoo—animal, organizational and financial needs. European ignorance, in our experience, is more than matched by North American ignorance—where, at the level of the private zoo, good old North American 'know-how' knows not even what to ask. Unfortunately, North American business ingenuity does not possess the gift of Ralph Helfer's animals, answering "questions unknown to us to ask." Running a zoo requires, like all major enterprises, substantial capital, considerable administrative and entrepreneurial ability, and the relevant subject expertise. But zoos require something else—a reciprocal respect with the animals and a willingness to put their interests at least on a par with the interests of the public, and often above them. Almost all those who possess the entrepreneurial capital and capacity lack the necessary respect. Almost all those who possess the respect lack the capital and/or the skills. And the few who have them both are always tempted to forgo the respect when business problems arise. Cutbacks are at the expense of the animals, since the alternative is to lose both the business and the animals. For these reasons good zoos—with some notable exceptions—usually are public enterprises supported by taxation, at least at their founding, and afterwards by zoological society members and gate receipts.

Even public enterprise is no bar to bad zoos. A number of small towns in Canada and the U.S. have public parks with small 'zoos'—though they are not usually called that. They have a few deer, perhaps several goats, donkeys, peafowl, guinea fowl, rabbits, hares and even domestic hens. The animals are loved by the townspeople, cared for by the city personnel and tended by a veterinarian whenever there is the slightest call. But they are often inappropriately sheltered, rarely have adequate space for their species needs or the potential for privacy, and sometimes lack social companionship. Love is simply not enough. And expertise is too scarce and expensive—the knowledge of the local veterinarian is inadequate. The animals do not display the neurotic characters of the cement floor pacer but the ennui of some of them is apparent to all who care to look. On the positive side, it is a delight to see the hens scamper and peck as they once did in the barnyard, the donkeys and goats have as much freedom as the farmer used to accord them, and the rabbits and hares often have a mound which they may use as a warren. The deer, though, and other exotics requiring substantial space, must go. In response to criticisms, such public parks have reacted quickly to dispense with the display of totally inappropriate creatures. And while one is bound to have qualms about the children feeding the animals inappropriately, the joy on the youngsters' faces makes up for a great deal. There is still a place for the local 'wildlife' display if the species are carefully chosen and feeding is restricted. Farm animals in fact may be the most appropriate residents.

What is it, then, that zoos like that at Arnhem possess which makes them so special? Each area is especially designed to meet the needs of the animal by replicating the natural habitat as far as possible. The tropical enclosure is kept at appropriate heat and humidity throughout the year. Filled with tropical vegetation, streams and waterfalls, it is traversed with paths which permit the visitor to watch but not invade. Reptiles, birds, fish and butterflies—some 1,500 in all—enjoy a life remarkably similar to that of their native habitat, constantly but always quietly observed. They continue their life uninterrupted. They stimulate awe and reverence in their human admirers.

A second venture at Arnhem is the chimpanzee colony. Again the zoo replicates the natural habitat, except for the feeding and the weather—the second of which, we suppose, is significantly less harmful than for the tropical zone emigrant to Montreal or New York. The animals live in complex social groups, much as they would, say, on the Ivory Coast. They inhabit an island, separated from the humans, and appear content, never bored and genuinely at home. They live a life practically indistinguishable from that of their natural habitat, breed successfully, and remain unthreatened by the human population explosion and the risk of poachers in their native land. The visitors can watch and know that they are experiencing much of the real life of the most intelligent representatives of the great apes. Researchers can study and know that what they see is the complex, and charming, social life of humans' closest relatives.

As far as we can tell, here is an example of a zoo in which everyone gains, human and animal alike, even though one may express concern that zoo animals have to be fed rather than be required to forage. It should disturb us all, though, that Arnhem is very much the exception rather than the rule among the smaller zoos. Of course, this zoo succeeds precisely because it keeps human and non-human animals apart. It prohibits, rather than promotes, the human-animal relationship. But it also promotes that veneration and understanding which are the prerequisites of a responsible and caring relationship where such relationships are appropriate, where they promote the interest of human and animal alike. Yet Arnhem is not one of the world's 'major' zoos. It does not even receive a mention in the listing of such zoos in Maier and Page's *Zoo: The Modern Ark*,[7] although 75 others are described in some detail.

Again, let us express some concern at the unreliability of the basic data, of simple statistics we encounter in studying zoos. It is not unusual to read in reputable scholarly books written in defence of zoos of the greatly improved conditions, the scientific expertise employed and the admirable attitudes toward the animals. But when we read from the same source of the 600-plus zoos in the world and compare that figure with Desmond Morris' 1,007 in the 12 member states of the E.C. alone we have reason to wonder about the data we receive from the most reputable sources. These things may not matter much in themselves. But how can we trust the judgements of the experts if they are so careless about basic information? Must we judge zoos solely by the 600-plus registered facilities or must we inquire into the 2,000-plus unregistered animal enclosures? Many defenders of zoos want us to judge all zoos by the standards of the best.

We must be as wary of the conclusions of the experts as we are of their figures. If there is one lesson we have learned in conducting the research for this book it is that the honest, careful and impartial person, wanting to make honest, careful and impartial judgements on the basis of sound argument and evidence, should not expect to find them on the

---

7   Franz Maier and Jake Page, *Zoo: The Modern Ark* (Toronto: Key Porter, 1990).

side of 'authority'—whether that be the 'authority' of government, the research establishment or the representatives of zoos. We must wade through the conflicting material and make judgements for ourselves—and that applies as much to the reader of this book analyzing our data, evidence and argument as it does to anyone else.

There can be no doubt about the extensive variation in quality both among the major zoos and between such zoos and their smaller counterparts. Conditions in some are notoriously bad, and in recent years have contributed to giving zoos in general, including the better ones, a bad name. There has been a growing belief that even the best zoos are relics of an unfortunate past in which the animals are unwilling and unjustifiable prisoners. "It's a good zoo, but it's still a zoo," is a refrain frequently heard from a significant proportion of zoo visitors. On what basis, then, do zoos defend their continued existence?

The answer we get is threefold: conservation, research, education. With the development of scientific knowledge in recent decades, predominantly in the last 20 years, zoos have become the repositories of the expertise necessary to save endangered species, to revitalize threatened species through improvements to the genetic pool and to reintroduce animals expelled from their natural habitats by agricultural and industrial development. But if that is true why then do zoos display the large numbers of relatively common but 'interesting' species present in every major zoo? In part the answer is educational: to provide the public with the opportunity to study such animals. But the greater reality lies in the concept they enjoy using among themselves—'charismatic megafauna'. Only if they offer the big cats, pythons, grizzlies and the like will visitors pay the ticket price which provides the funds to engage in the conservation and research. And if the 'charismatic' animals are bred in captivity, looked after according to their species needs, and visitors are not permitted to cross the threshold of proximity which invades the inmates' tranquillity, this may well be a perfectly reasonable price to pay to ensure that the devastating encroachments of humankind on wildlife habitat do not utterly destroy our natural heritage.

Today reputable zoo managers recognize the need to provide a place for privacy for their charges. Most species need the opportunity to be free from the peering faces. The animal's 'flight distance'—the distance at which it will flee an approaching human—must be respected. Since animals spend much of their time foraging, wherever possible food must be hidden so that it is sought. It is unnatural to provide a wild animal with unearned food—thereby depriving it of one of its predominant activities in the wild—so every effort must be made to replicate that activity. Unfortunately, that can never be done for the large carnivores. Even if, say, one were to introduce a live zebra into a lion's area there would be no hunt—merely a short chase. And this would be as distasteful as it would be unnatural. There is no means of replicating the hunt for the large carnivores in captivity. It is an obvious problem, but one rarely discussed in books written in defence of the zoos.

Since most zoo animals have their dinners supplied, it is important to ensure that they are provided with the opportunity for compensatory natural activities. Structures similar to tree branches are successfully provided for apes. But the lion has so little to do that it is likely to sleep for 20 hours in a day—admittedly not inordinately more than it does in the wild. For the lion the stalking of the prey is a major and communal activity. Its absence can be said to make the zoo lion not a real lion at all. It is true that most cats are sprinters, not long-distance runners like the canids and thus may not *require* as much space, even though in practice they tend to use a lot of space. They hunt at night, awaiting their prey in the branches of an appropriately placed tree. Yet lions and the other major cats, which cannot be made to be truly at home in the zoo, are among the prime 'charismatic megafauna' whose presence provides the attraction to the public to spend its money at the zoo. The extensive area used by the great cats in the wild reflects their hunting needs. In zoos since the meals are provided the large natural territory is not a necessity. Still the customary partial acre any one species is allotted is less than that with which it feels comfortable. Again, though, the fact that almost all such animals are now bred in zoos means that they are not deprived of a habitat to which they have become accustomed.

The better zoos now make every effort to provide as natural a habitat as is feasible in zoo surroundings. This ensures that animals are active and doing the things they find interesting, and that the zoos must have several animals of the same species, and sometimes of other species too, interacting communally in adequate and quality space. This they have succeeded in doing for the ungulates, the monkeys and several others. But they invariably fail for the cats, and even the best zoos often provide inadequate space for fish, reptiles, amphibians and birds. A jaguar's predation area (over 25,000 acres) in the rain forest exceeds the acreage of the world's major zoos combined and is only slightly less than the total 35,000 acres (approximately) of all 600-plus registered zoos. It is not unusual to see fish which almost fill the tanks in which they are displayed. A single tropical fish may cover in a single day in its natural habitat more area than is devoted to all the fish in the zoo. Yet even where every effort is made to replicate the natural habitat for, say, alligators, as is done so admirably at the Metro Toronto Zoo, neither the mode of feeding nor the space allotted compares to the life of the creature in the wild.

A number of zoos have either purchased land for their sites outside the city limits—the Metro Toronto Zoo has 710 acres and the Calgary Zoo 439—or have developed 'satellite' zoos at some distance from the main 'campus'. London Zoo, for example, which covers only 36 acres, has developed a related complex at Whipsnade which occupies 580 acres. Only the Miami Metro Zoo—740 acres—exceeds the Metro Toronto Zoo in area, although both pale in comparison to the 1,820-acre Wild Animal Park operated by the San Diego Zoo, and to the 3,000-acre Salmonier Nature Park at Holyrood, Newfoundland. However, only 100 acres of Salmonier have to date been developed. Salmonier keeps only species indigenous to Newfoundland and Labrador. The present establishment constitutes only 30 species of mammals, reptiles, amphibians, birds and fish, and numbers no more than 80 animals altogether.

In 1989 there were 3,558 animals at the Metro Toronto Zoo, excluding invertebrates, of which there were 83 species. By 1991 there were over 4,000 animals from over 100 species. The 84-acre Berlin Zoo numbers approximately 8,600 vertebrates and 6,000 invertebrates. There are 1,563 mammals from 276 species, which compares with Toronto's 1,002 from 106, indicating a greater recognition at Toronto of animal social needs. The Miami Metro Zoo, which has only developed its Asian and a portion of its African exhibits, has 267 mammal specimens from 76 species among its 1,033 vertebrates. The largest North American mammal collections include the New York Zoo's 1,729 specimens, San Diego's Wild Animal Park's 1,450, the San Diego Zoo's 1,310 and the Chicago Brookfield Zoo's 1,340. London Zoo has 1,403 mammals on its 36 acres! Of course, such statistics are only significant as an indication of overcrowding if it can be assumed that most zoos keep similar proportions of animals in relation to size and space needs. A zoo specializing in rodents would need less space than one which housed mainly elephants and giraffes! Nonetheless, most of the major zoos keep such a similar variety of species that the statistics are prima facie indicative of the attention given to species' space and social needs. Certainly, the modern rural or suburban zoo has a greater opportunity to give consideration to such factors than do the city zoos of, say, London, Berlin and New York.

Clearly, the amount of money available plays a preponderant role in determining how many animals may be kept. The amount of space, especially quality space, is an important factor in determining how many animals *ought* to be kept. Only if animals have enough space to feel at ease, to feel in tune with their natures, will they usually breed—a statement confessedly more true of some species than others. But this is especially true of ungulates, which need to roam freely and in herds.

Tamarins (small monkeys) live their natural lives in extended families. They learn to raise their young by assisting parents with their offspring; and without that experience they are inadequate to raise their own. The golden lion tamarin of Brazil is fussy about choosing a mate. Jealous mothers reject pubescent daughters from the immediate territory. Unless there is extended and appropriate space resembling in at least some respects the rain forests of Brazil, the tamarin will be decidedly unhappy and incompetent. Unless its species needs are met there would appear at first glance to be no excuse for keeping it in a zoo. And, of course, similar stories can be told of countless other species.

Today breeding is one of the most important functions of a zoo. Animals are bred so that zoos can be stocked with animals without raping their natural habitat. Of equal importance is the breeding of rare, threatened and endangered species, some of which are now extirpated in their native lands. Yet since any resulting inbreeding will produce a degenerate species, there is now an extensive and highly successful co-operation among zoos, primarily within North America and within Europe (to cut down on costs and to minimize travel trauma) but also occasionally between continents. Shipping animals between zoos significantly improves the genetic stock and lowers the incidence of illness and premature death that were once a commonplace among zoo-bred animals.

The International Species Inventory System, started in 1977, had accumulated data on 2,400 species in 326 zoos in 36 countries by 1989 and is constantly expanding. The loss of land to agriculture, poaching, war and the general problem of pollution in all its manifestations have threatened and continue to increase the threat to world wildlife. It is estimated that one-quarter of all the species in the world are today threatened by loss of habitat. The loss of the world's rain forests is the major, but by no means the sole, problem. If threatened species are to be maintained, and at some point returned to their natural habitats, zoos and wildlife parks must preserve, protect and breed. Yet there is no point in breeding a pusillanimous and degenerate population. Animals must be bred for genetic diversity. Hence the need to maintain the I.S.I.S. data bank and to cross-breed among zoos.

A jaguar with its 25,000-plus acre habitat may in principle be an inappropriate animal to keep in a zoo, but if it is not kept and not successfully and healthily bred there will soon be no jaguars left at all, for its natural rain forest habitat is being daily decimated for agricultural land to feed South America's impoverished and undernourished population. The golden lion tamarin needs more space than almost any zoo can allot but it has been successfully bred and returned to the wild, as has, for example, Przewalski's horse—a donkey-like horse of the Mongolian plains. Moscow Zoo led the way in rescuing the horse, once thought extinct, and returning captive-bred specimens to their natural habitat. One could repeat the story of a number of species. Without zoos the world's stock of wildlife would be in even more danger than it is. Although zoos may not always be able to keep a species as its nature demands, if it is not kept at all the species will not survive.

The American Association of Zoological Parks and Aquariums (A.A.Z.P.A.) began a species survival program around 1980 and today accords special treatment to 50 species to prevent their threatened extinction. Included are 8 primates (from black lemur to gorilla), 10 carnivorous mammals (from the cheetah to the spectacled bear), 14 hoofed mammals (from rhinoceros to okapi), 12 birds (from the Humboldt penguin to the palm cockatoo) 4 reptiles, 1 amphibian and 1 invertebrate. A.A.Z.P.A. coordinates the efforts in North America to create a genetically sound pool of these imperilled animals. In Europe the International Union of Directors of Zoological Gardens has instituted a similar program. While one may legitimately question whether the zoos of the world provide the appropriate environment for some species it is undoubtedly a better environment than none at all. If some unthreatened species continue to live an inappropriate life in even the better zoos the answer lies in more funding and more space. The zoo's task of educating the public to the need is the prerequisite of a better world for the zoo animals.

One of the major success stories of the Species Survival Plans is that of the tigers. By 1988, 100 Siberian tigers had changed residence in North America at least once to improve their genetic diversity. Although breeding tigers has never been a problem, inbreeding was, to the extent that, by 1986, 47 of the 207 Bengal tigers in European zoos were deemed too inbred to be permitted to breed further. What was necessary was a program to ensure that the gene pool was healthy. But the program has been so successful that there is now an excess of zoo tigers. The answer cannot lie in merely stopping the breeding—that would soon mean a population of geriatric tigers and would also limit the necessary genetic diversity.

Of course, there is a limit to the amount of zoo space which can be devoted to tigers. The space is already too cramped for their species needs. What, then, is to be done? There is no more available space so the population cannot be increased. There is a need for greater genetic diversity and an appropriate age distribution, so breeding must continue. Logically—at least if individuals matter less than the species—older, excessively inbred tigers must be euthanized. If not, then each tiger will have even less space than now and the zoos will be even less capable of meeting species needs. It is a deplorable dilemma and one to which there is no humane solution. Whether we treat animals as individuals and accord them individual rights or treat them as species and accord them communal rights is one of those disturbing ethical problems to which we shall return.[8] Those who are in principle opposed to zoos must ask themselves whether their elimination would truly serve the animals' interests. They should ponder whether a concern for the continued existence of threatened species should require us to devote

---

8 See below, pp. 245ff., 268ff., 286ff. and 300ff.

more not less of available space in North America to those imperilled on the sea of human population expansion.

To date zoos have succeeded in reintroducing only a limited number of species to the wild. A successful solution to human population problems is a prerequisite of doing much more. Until then they must be kept in zoos. However, we should be aware that, in addition to Przewalski's horse and the golden lion tamarin, there have been remarkable successes with the Arabian oryx and the Arabian race of ostrich, with the scimitar-horned oryx, the addax, wood bison and Père David's deer. Much else is under way, from the Guam rail through the nene—Hawaiian geese—to the Rothschild's mynah, from Mallee fowl to the bearded vulture. One zoo—the Jersey Wildlife Preservation Trust—is devoted almost exclusively to building breeding groups of endangered species with the ultimate intention of restocking a revived world's flora with its fauna.

Although it is preferable to produce offspring according to the dictates of love and lust, captive animals often cannot breed freely, due to the limitations of the zoo setting. Gorillas and clouded leopards, for example, have some rather rigid mating rules—the former requiring its partner to be a compatriot known since infancy, the latter requiring the partner not to be so. Thus zoo scientists now engage in embryo-transplanting and artificial insemination with the intent of protecting threatened species and will go to inordinate lengths to ensure a live birth, including transplanting a zebra embryo into a horse, a bongo into an eland, and a gaur into a Holstein cow. In this way they saved the black-footed ferret from certain extinction and ensured a continued existence for a number of other species. Although embryo-transplanting sometimes involves putting an animal from one species at serious risk by implanting the embryo of an alien animal, the question, again, to which there is no simple answer, is whether the rights, say, of a Holstein cow are less than those of the gaur species.

Cheetahs have been found to be one of the most inbred wild animal populations ever discovered. The total world population of cheetahs is around 20,000. This figure includes a subspecies which has been found to be slightly less inbred. Since cheetahs breed very poorly in zoos, a cross subspecies artificial insemination might correct some of the genetic weaknesses caused by excessive inbreeding. Without it, the cheetah is doomed to early extinction, or at least to a species life of genetic weakness. Some zoos have had a limited success with cheetah breeding by the more amorous route—including the African Lion Safari at Cambridge, Ontario, the Paris Zoo, the Windsor Safari Park in England and the Dublin Zoo. But if the genetic structure is to be diversified artificial insemination appears to be a necessary route.

Of course, to support such conservation a great deal of research is necessary. And most of the major zoos are involved in such research.

But none is more involved than the American National Zoo in Washington, D.C. The zoo is a division of the Smithsonian Institution and was founded to preserve the bison from extinction. Today it is immersed in behavioural and ecological research, particularly on tigers, rhinoceroses, elephants, primates and bird migration. The investigations have influenced ecology and economic development policy in Nepal, Sri Lanka and Central America. The zoo is a leader in the field of veterinary biomedical science and the relationship of fauna to flora. Indeed, the zoo which is seen by the public is but a necessary appendage to the valuable research. Many major zoos, from Metro Toronto Zoo's involvement in the artificial propagation of endangered cat species to Cincinnati's work on insects, are involved in advanced zoological research which is unwitnessed by the public, although its consequences are often seen in the health and variety of the animals on display.

While public entertainment is still the most prominently visible role of the zoo, it hides much of inestimable scientific value to the animal realm behind the public mask. And we trust that no one objects to the entertainment provided it is beneficial overall to the animal realm and that constant efforts are being made at improvements. The evidence is that immense improvements have been made in even the most antiquated of zoos.

In our view the London Zoo is hopelessly overcrowded. Yet since it could not expand outwards, it has expanded up and down. Upwards, it has developed a 'free-flight aviary' which, while still a cage, allows birds the choice of numerous habitats. Perhaps it should be called *freer* rather than free flight, but it is certainly an improvement on what is unfortunately still the customary mode of keeping zoo birds. Downwards, it provides an underwater observation area—as does the Metro Toronto Zoo—to observe the polar bears enjoying their aquatic adventures. In addition, the London Zoo is heavily involved in research into genetics, disease control, reproduction and nutrition—all of some value to the animal but perhaps of greater value for the management of wild species. Yet the life expectancy of the London Zoo is limited since lack of adequate gate receipts has persuaded the directors to close the venerable institution if new funding cannot be found.

In recently constructed animal collections, such as the Metro Toronto Zoo and the San Diego Wild Animal Park, development has taken place on zoogeographic lines, so that flora and fauna are grouped according to their natural habitats. Moreover, extensive use is made of railways to transport the visitors, which allows the animals, especially some types of ungulates and wolves, a healthy sense of isolation from their observers. More and more, the modern major zoo succeeds in giving great weight to animal considerations without impeding, and often improving, the visitors' entertainment.

Since, in addition zoos ensure the maintenance of threatened wildlife, they are far more beneficial than detrimental to the animal realm. Metro Toronto, for example, houses and breeds about 50 endangered species, including lowland gorillas, Sumatran orangutans, African elephants, mandrills, Przewalski's horse, snow leopards and Puerto Rican toads as well as many not yet threatened but likely to become so, such as the grey-cheeked hornbill, the caracal (a type of lynx) and the South African oryx.

If one of the functions of a zoo is to entertain it is, of course, preferable that the entertainment be accompanied by education. The most immediate objective is to educate the public about the animals the zoo tends and to arouse and extend public sensibilities toward them. While the appropriate atmosphere in a zoo or wildlife park will induce respect, a carnival atmosphere will stimulate a consideration of animals as instruments of humankind's amusement. Unfortunately, zoos or wildlife parks frequently leave the impression that the animals have been brought together merely to titillate. An atmosphere conducive to respect and learning is a prerequisite of an adequate zoo.

In recent years the educational aspect of zoos has been extended to include instructing the public on the general ecological devastation facing the modern world. Most of the larger, responsible zoos now have displays explaining the effects of the loss of the rain forests on the native animal population. Chicago's Brookfield Zoo exhibits three different rain forest regions simulating the flora, fauna and weather—including artificial thunderstorms. New York's Bronx Zoo recreates an indoor Asian rain forest—with rain. In Washington's National Zoo the interrelatedness of soil, plant, invertebrate and vertebrate realms is stressed, demonstrating the urgent need to respond to the destruction of the world ecology, which poses the greatest threat to humanity's future.

Zoos have a major role in demonstrating how ecological problems are devastating habitats, without which they cannot survive in the wild. To take but one of many examples, global warming is eroding the ice caps—apparently far more in the Arctic than the Antarctic. Seals, walrus and polar bears are seriously threatened. If the erosion continues the only place, perhaps within half a century, that polar bears or walrus will be found is in the zoo. By teaching zoo visitors about these animals and their natural habitats, and how they are being destroyed by humanity's environmental disasters zoos will make their own continued existence indispensable.

Jake Page has written that, "There are some very bad zoos." We concur. He continues, "These are relatively few and found less and less often. It is probably fair to say that the terrible zoo is an endangered species."[9] We beg to differ. If Page is referring to the 600-plus registered zoos he has a point, if a slightly exaggerated one. For example, one Ontario animal park has clipped vultures attached to a tree branch, incapable of movement. But what of the 789 unregistered zoos in the E.C.? What of the even larger number of unregistered and uncounted zoos in North America? What of the many hundreds of unregistered zoos elsewhere in the world?

The most significant problem with the 'minor' zoos is that many develop out of the private interest, and often the private collection, of the owner who, almost without exception, has none of the necessary attributes of a zoo manager. The private entrepreneur lacks the capital, the training, the expertise, and often even the respect to run a zoo.

What do we find in such zoos? Cages far too small for the animals to turn around in. Filthy conditions—feces and debris. Animals alone with no companionship. Inadequate shelter. Overweight, unhappy, insane, bored animals. Disease. Lack of personnel. A polar bear with insufficient water to submerge in. A skunk in a double cage barely able to turn. A disturbed, excessively confined timber wolf. A beautiful bird alone in a tiny cage. All these points were made in letters to animal welfare organizations about zoos in Ontario.

Starting in 1986 Zoocheck Canada began to investigate conditions in Ontario zoos. Zoocheck found the letters to have erred on the side of generosity to the zoo owners. It would serve little purpose to list all the sins committed—though they are legion and sickening. Although there are some well-kept small private zoos the vast majority are totally inadequate.

In many jurisdictions there are no, or absolutely minimal, regulations explicitly relating to zoos. They may be minimally controlled by cruelty to animals legislation but often by little or nothing more. And even where there are relatively stringent regulations they are difficult to enforce if the matter is left to the S.P.C.A. inspectorate. Knowing minimum requirements for different species is beyond the knowledge of most inspectors, as well as most zoo owners. Ownership, regulation and inspection require a very scarce commodity—professional expertise. It is surely in the interests of professional zoo administrators to be involved in the regulation of those establishments which tend to give zoos per se a bad name.

Ontario, at present, like the remainder of Canada, has no specific regulations to cover zoos. Legislation has been prepared but its day—or year!—of implementation is constantly being put off. Indeed, one has reason to be concerned that the provincial government may not get around to implementing its legislation at all. Certainly there is an evident lack of haste, and so much else seems of higher priority. In the

---

9 Maier and Page, *Zoo: The Modern Ark*, p. 119.

interim the abominable conditions continue in Ontario, elsewhere in Canada, and much of the world. Yet even with appropriate legislation the problems are only diminished, not eradicated, unless and until an effective, professional and expert enforcement agency is established.

The Zoo Licensing Act of 1981 provides some protection for animals in captivity in Britain—although it does not provide the same degree of sensibility found in the 1986 experimental animals legislation. In the United States the Department of Agriculture sets minimum care standards for zoos on a par with those for animal experimentation—although fortunately it hasn't concluded that lions, tigers and elephants are invertebrate or cold-blooded! In Canada there is no special legislation at all. While conditions are far from perfect in each of these countries, zoo animals in Canada are afforded the least protection.

For a zoo to be even minimally acceptable it must provide space appropriate to the species. It must provide appropriate barriers—which differ according to species. Flooring, the capacity to roam, protection from potential injury, appropriate climate conditions—a special problem for tropical animals in Canada—privacy, shelter, companionship, recreation, medical attention, appropriate food, cleanliness—all these are necessary for any zoo. And they differ from species to species. In fact the small zoo—the 'roadside zoo' as it is pejoratively called—needs not just one expert but many if it is to house a variety of animals.

We saw earlier in this chapter what happened even at the famous London Zoo when animals were kept in conditions inimical to their nature—conditions which changed very much for the better. Unfortunately, those conditions and similar neurotic animal behaviour are still to be found in abundance in the 'roadside zoos'.

What are the behavioural characteristics of animals being inadequately kept? A recently introduced animal may rush around madly, throwing itself against bars or fences in its frantic attempts to escape. After a while it may fall into a state of sullen stupor. For this reason alone it is necessary to restrict zoo animals to the captive-bred unless some overriding ecological disaster indicates otherwise.

Neurotic animals may refuse to eat, or refuse to stop eating. They may be abnormally aggressive at the approach of feeding time or if they cannot escape the unwanted attention of the visitors. Similar behaviour may occur from overcrowding, separation from a companion or inability to escape a fellow inmate. At its worst, neurosis exhibits itself in stereotypical cage-pacing, rocking or immobility.

Animals may also be seen to be acting 'irrationally', i.e., their behaviour becomes inappropriate to the situation. They are denying their instinctual nature. Excessive sexual activity, masturbation and Morris's example of copulation with the food bowl are all consistent with this loss of intrinsic nature. Self-mutilation is the extreme form of this behaviour. This may also be brought on by inadequate diet and disease.

Both abnormal mother-child relationships and prolonged infantile behaviour, or even regression to such behaviour, may occur if the environment and social relationships are totally inappropriate. Cannibalism has been known in such circumstances. All these are the more extreme—but not altogether uncommon—types of occurrence. The most common is simply apathy. When a social animal is separated from relatives and companions it can sink into a deep apathetic depression in which it really ceases to be an animal at all.[10]

To keep animals in circumstances conducive to such behaviour is more than a sin. It ought to be a crime. There can be no excuse for running a zoo which permits such conditions. It is animal exploitation at its very worst. Good zoos may foster conservation, research, education and human sensibility, but bad zoos not only are a form of animal exploitation, they also encourage it in their visitors. There is no sense of awe, no veneration of nature, in watching an apathetic caged beast. This becomes debased amusement, not healthy entertainment, teaching disrespect at worst, pity at best. It is little different from watching human prison inmates in the exercise yard. The only enjoyment is that one isn't one of them.

If there are good and bad zoos there are only bad and worse circuses. The very principle of circus entertainment is to encourage animals to act contrary to their nature. The animals become objects of fun, even of ridicule. One may be titillated to think how clever they are—although the circus attempts to portray the cleverness of the trainer, not the animal. Clever or not, the animals are depicted as substitute humans or ferocious beasts tamed by the courageous trainer. They are never depicted as the animals they are.

We have abundant evidence that many circus animals are trained cruelly and kept cruelly, but cruelty by intent is not at issue here. The consequence for the animals is bound to be detrimental, whatever the intent. It is not uncommon for a touring circus to visit 250 or more towns on consecutive days. This means that every day the circus animals—bears, tigers, lions, elephants and the like—must be moved from one town to another in inadequate transportation. When zoos transport large animals they do so with as much care as possible, as short a distance as possible, and as infrequently as possible, knowing the potential trauma to the animal. The circus transports its animals maybe

---

10 We are grateful to Rob Laidlaw and Holly Penfound of Zoocheck Canada for providing the information on which the above four paragraphs are based.

200-300 times in a year. There is bound to be considerable suffering. Moreover, once the circus has reached its destination there is no possibility of finding appropriate accommodation for its animals. They must be kept in the same inappropriate, cramped cages in which they were transported. While the better zoos have eliminated the cage, the circus still maintains it—and with less space than even the bad zoos accord their animals. And when the circus animal has reached the end of its performing days there can be no retirement in the circus. It must be killed or sold to a roadside menagerie.

What matters beyond any cruelty is that the animals are portrayed entirely as something other than what they are. They inspire curiosity, perhaps amazement. But they are compelled to act in a manner totally destructive of respect. It should not surprise us that in a number of European jurisdictions circuses are no longer permitted to contain animal acts. It is encouraging to find a few North American municipalities taking the same course of action, most recently the City of Toronto in the spring of 1992, although that decision, at the time of writing, is being appealed by Ringling Brothers. We find it disturbing that Canadian police associations collect donations—often using professional fundraisers, who take a substantial portion of the funds—to send disadvantaged children to the circus. We respect their motives but are convinced that there are many better ways of providing worthwhile entertainment for children. If animal entertainment is a priority, a day at a good zoo would be distinctly preferable—or at one of those admirable circuses which no longer include animal acts. In fact, knowing of their decline in reputation, circuses are attempting to resurrect their image by associating themselves with worthy charitable organizations in the towns they visit and making modest contributions—apparently in the area of $2,500—to the organization. Of course the circus expects to recoup more than that as a consequence of its improved image and increased attendance.

The Roman satirical poet Juvenal said that the Roman people "limits its anxious longings to two things—bread, and the games of the circus." But Juvenal was referring to the chariot races and the gladiatorial and animal combats in the circus. All the Roman circus and the modern circus have in common is the name—which simply refers to the ring in which the events are performed. While the modern circus had its era of great popularity—between 1880 and 1920—it never rivalled the Roman circus for the attention of the people. Still, in the late nineteenth and early twentieth century, rural and small-town dwellers awaited the arrival of the travelling circus with the same air of expectation encouraged by the visit of the medieval fair. It was an occasion for recreation and merriment. It was always associated with mildly licentious amusement rather than with the at least somewhat educational expectation of the visit to the zoo.

In fact the modern circus began in the very late eighteenth century with the performance of equestrian feats in a horse ring strewn with sawdust. By 1830 travelling circuses with clowns, acrobats and performing animals were touring England and America. The two-ring circus was instituted in 1869 and the three-ring circus a few years later by James A. Bailey. Britain retained the one ring, believing the confusion of the three-ring circus was what it has proverbially become. Bailey joined with P.T. Barnum, who ran what was labelled "The Greatest Show on Earth." But then Barnum is best known for his statement, "There's a sucker born every minute." The greatest suckers, of course, were those who paid to see his "Greatest Show," for Barnum knew there was as much sleight of hand as genuine artistry. Barnum died in 1891, Bailey in 1907. Barnum and Bailey's was then purchased by the Ringling Brothers, and in 1919 the two circuses were combined under the joint names. Thereafter the circus declined to its current sorry state.

The heyday of the circus was the period of the late Industrial Revolution, when humanity's alienation from nature was at its peak. It was the time when an elephant's foot was most highly prized as an ashtray base, when the plumes of exotic birds were the most desirable material for a hat, and when dead armadillos made the most 'attractive' shopping baskets. It is difficult to judge whether increasing human sensibilities played any role in the decline of the circus. We would like to think so but are inclined to doubt it. Probably the advent of cinema and later of television were more important factors. On the other hand, as circus audiences have dwindled so zoo attendance has increased, to the level where it has been claimed that the zoo is the most popular form of entertainment in North America. However, to put that claim in perspective, we should note that attendance at 81 Toronto Blue Jays home baseball games is almost triple the number of visitors to the Metro Toronto Zoo in a year. But then the Blue Jays are the most avidly watched home team in baseball.

Perhaps what has always differentiated the zoo from the circus is that the former has traditionally been seen as respectable, whereas the circus has always had something suspicious, something less than wholesome, in its appeal. No disgruntled young Turk ever wanted to run away and join the zoo! The greater respectability of the zoo reflects in no small measure the manner in which the zoo was seen to treat its charges with greater respect than did the circus. When the circus is in town the Humane Society can expect to receive several complaints about the treatment of the animals. The complaints it will receive about the zoo will almost always refer to the roadside menageries.

Much of what we have said about zoos applies equally to public aquaria. Unfortunately, since fish do not grimace or cry in pain and since their cold-bloodedness has—inexplicably—led many to assume they do not feel pain in the manner of mammals, they have traditionally led their captive lives with even less consideration. Certainly, even today and even in the better zoos and aquaria, fish do not receive the consideration their species needs would indicate. No doubt the fact that they share much less with humans than do mammals has had a lot to do with the way they have been treated. They do not suckle their young, do not play in an immediately apparent manner, and most importantly, neither 'speak' nor display apparent emotion.

Aquaria have in fact never had the appeal of the zoo itself, although they have a long history. The Chinese have had a special regard for the goldfish which goes back centuries—but not millennia, as we find with mammals. The Romans and Egyptians are known to have had aquaria but they never received the attention of the menageries. For the Romans, fish did not fight. For the Egyptians they did not possess characteristics deemed worthy of worship. The Egyptians prayed to animals as 'unexceptional' as the dung beetle and the frog but could never find a fish to bow down to.

In part the reason we have had less interest in fish may simply be that they are under water, making them less readily visible than mammals, birds and even amphibia in their natural habitat. Removing them from water will kill them (though it takes a sturgeon, for example, four days to die out of water).

While Sir Francis Bacon had some interesting observations on fish in his *History of Life and Death* of 1633, and Izaak Walton's *The Compleat Angler* of 1653 was ostensibly about fish, the former was dedicated to the prolongation of life in general and the latter to the fish's death. The late sixteenth and seventeenth centuries witnessed a great interest in natural history. Aelianus, Bacon and Topsell were the authors of popular general natural histories, while Aldrovandus, Barker, Dubravius, Gesner and Salvianus were well-read writers on fish. However, much of the information they gave about fish was derived from the study of dead fish or what could be readily witnessed in freshwater ponds and streams.

The subtitle of *The Compleat Angler*, perhaps the best-known book ever written about fish, is instructive: *Or the Contemplative Man's Recreation*. The volume is as much about contemplation as fish, and the parts about fish are as much about rivers, ponds and lures as about the fish themselves. There is nothing about sea life in Walton's book and not a great deal in the others either. A serious study of salt-water animals had to await the invention of glass—or rather, since glass was invented 4,000 years ago, glass of sufficient strength to withstand the immense pressure of water. Without glass the underwater activities of deep-sea fish simply could not be witnessed. Public aquaria only became feasible with the development of glass of sufficient strength to function as walls for the tanks in which fish were kept.

It was not until well into the nineteenth century that such a capacity was developed. The first glass aquarium was constructed in 1853 at the London Zoo in Regent's Park, 26 years after the zoo was first open to the public. Thereafter the study of sea life was greatly facilitated, culminating in the construction of the scientifically invaluable Neapolitan aquarium in 1874.

Criticisms of aquaria have, however, been levelled far more at the keeping of sea mammals rather than fish. Whales, dolphins, sea lions and sea elephants are treated not according to their natures but as circus performers, being trained to amuse by clever but unnatural tricks. Their dignity is offended. Moreover, they lack the space they need to live anything approaching a natural life. They become objects of amusement, of idle curiosity. The spectators are offered a picture of these wonderful social and free-ranging creatures entirely offensive to their reality.

The defenders of the sea circus claim they are defending endangered species. Superficially that is a fine defence. Certainly, in Canadian coastal waters the gray whale and walrus have already been extirpated, and the sea otter, bowhead whale, right whale and beluga whale are endangered. The humpback whale is threatened, while the blue whale, fin whale and Sowerby's beaked whale are rare or vulnerable. But none of these creatures is a prime object of display in the sea circus. The animals are chosen because of their performance potential. But even if they were chosen for protective purposes they would be somewhat better off—perhaps not a great deal because of space restrictions—in an aquarium where their trainability was not the object of idle amusement.

The Vancouver Aquarium is the only aquarium per se which is listed among the major zoos of the world in Maier and Page. The 1.2-acre site houses 25 specimens from seven species of sea mammals along with 87 reptiles, 101 amphibians, 46 birds and 8,407 fish. The aquarium is extensively involved in breeding programs for killer whales, sea otters and many fish. While one may regret the lack of the space the sea mammals require, the aquarium's conservation work stands as a ready justification for its existence. The same cannot be said for the charismatic megamarines of the sea circus, including Vancouver Aquarium's own sea circus. To be sure, attempts are made at breeding but only for the purpose of providing new entertainers for the sea circus performance.

The admirable public concern for the plight of the sea mammals arises predominantly not from their use as circus performers but from the fishing and pollution menace. Driftnets are used to drag the ocean for food, but these nets succeed also in killing dolphins, whales, turtles, seals and birds, and push many species to the point of extirpation. It is estimated that 6.5 million dolphins have been killed by tuna fishermen using purse seine nets.

Whales, of course, are still hunted despite the serious threat to their very existence, and they are still captured from the wild for public display in aquaria. The Canadian government shows little reluctance to grant permission to aquaria, predominantly American ones, to capture these magnificent beasts, even though it is known that this captivity seriously harms the extensive whale pod family life and that very early death is a likely consequence of the capture.

Sea trash dumped from ships and boats—and that left on the beaches by holiday-makers—wreaks havoc on the marine population. The U.S. Coast Guard estimates that recreational boaters dump an average of 1.5 pounds of garbage per person into the water on each trip. Seventy-five tons of trash are left on Los Angeles beaches every week. Boating and beach-going cause untold harm through plastic and other non-biodegradable pollution, making the marine habitat an unsafe place for the marine population. It is perhaps, though, a pity that most concern is expressed for the sea mammals and scarcely ever for the fish.

When Edgar Allan Poe wrote of the "perfumed sea" he had not encountered modern pollution. Neither do Shakespeare's "silver sea," nor Wordsworth's "immortal sea" reflect the reality of the modern ocean. The words of William Whiting's sonorous hymn, "O, hear us when we cry to Thee, For those in peril on the sea" must be sung anew for those in peril *in* the sea.

Chapter Twelve

Of Farms and Factories

Forth issuing on a summer's morn to breathe
Among the pleasant villages and farms
Adjoin'd, from each thing met conceives delight.
       — Milton, *Paradise Lost*

As a work of art, I know few things more pleasing to the eye,
or more capable of affording scope and gratification to a taste
for the beautiful, than a well-situated, well-cultivated farm.
       — U.S. Senator Edward Everett, 1857 address

There is an eighteenth-century nursery rhyme which many of us chanted as children about the sheep in the meadow and the cow in the corn. Many of us retain idyllic images of bustling barnyards with scurrying fowl, the contented cow lazily chewing the cud, and the sheepdog expertly rounding up his charges. Our nursery rhymes and romantic recollections enjoin us to regret the passing of these bucolic scenes. It is truly a paradise lost. But it is not long gone. The television series "All Creatures Great and Small" still conjures up the pleasing picture of farm life half a century ago.

The new picture is of farm factories with veal calves in crates, chickens in cages no bigger than themselves, and cattle which are scarcely allowed to move. As we drive the highways we witness the transportation of squealing pigs, tightly penned turkeys and morose cattle. We know from respected colleagues of the unbridled terror of the slaughterhouse and we know, and are told, we must go to see for ourselves. But we won't. We simply don't have the stomach for it.

Disturbing as the modern picture is—and it is heart-rendingly drawn in several books which touch on intensive farming—it is neither entirely accurate nor without its benefits, at least for humans if not at all for the animals. And few of the books or chapters which are critical of intensive farming paint the other side of the picture. To be able to make a reasoned judgement, the other side must be given its hearing.

Before we do so, let us state that, unlike many who have written on intensive farming, we are not vegetarians. Perhaps, we are told, if we visited an abattoir we would be. And perhaps that is just one of the reasons we choose not to go, though we have enough other cowardly reasons already. We readily confess that our meat-eating habits are a reflection of a personal ambivalence which has its counterpart in the history of ambivalence we have sketched throughout this book

We like our meat to be pre packaged in cellophane, bearing as little resemblance to the outward appearance of an animal as possible. We are happy that words like 'beef' and 'pork' are used rather than 'cow' and 'pig'. The lack of a direct reference to the animal makes meat more palatable. We draw the line at ordering veal, even though we know that in many restaurants we'd be getting pork anyway. We couldn't choose a live lobster from a tank but have no difficulty enjoying it served anonymously. We occasionally feel sufficiently guilty that we will order a vegetarian meal and we make a conscious effort to eat lower down the food chain. But we remain constant if not dedicated carnivores.

We have read the arguments in favour of vegetarianism and find them appealing. We have read the arguments in favour of a meat diet and consciously find them less than compelling. But they serve as adequate rationalizations for our continuation to dine on appetizing meals which contain the flesh of animals. And, yes, we understand that these rationalizations do not differ in principle from those which hunters employ to justify their 'sport' and trappers to support their part-time livelihood. Though they do not differ in principle, they do, we believe, differ in fact, for meat-eating can be defended far more readily. Still, our carnivorous habits reflect an ambivalence which is not always consistent with our sensibilities. We are singed by Beaumont and Fletcher's words in *The Lover's Progress*: "Deeds, not words shall speak me." We *feel* what the Irish poet Oliver Goldsmith meant when he wrote, "They pity, and they eat the objects of their compassion."

The readiest defence for carnivores lies in attacking the integrity of the vegetarians. Leonardo da Vinci wouldn't eat meat but he killed animals for his art. George Bernard Shaw cheated on his principles to prolong his life. Seventh Day Adventists won't eat meat but their religious practices fail to consider secular human needs. Adolf Hitler was a vegetarian. But such caustic critique will not do, for every criticism can be matched by dozens of counter-examples—from Tolstoy to Gandhi.

Vegetarians will point out that studies have shown that carnivores suffer more heart attacks. Meat-eaters will reply that since vegetarians tend to concentrate their lives around the maintenance of their health it is not surprising they are more immune. Moreover, such statistics do not compare vegetarians with sensible, moderate health-conscious meat-eaters but include all those who eat excessively, eat too much fat, carbohydrates, salt, etc., etc. It is not a question of whether vegetarians are healthier than others but whether vegetarians are healthier than health-conscious non-vegetarians. And the moderate meat-eaters insist that it is they who are decidedly healthier.

Vegetarians will point out that such athletes as Paavo Nurmi and Edwin Moses reject meat. Meat-eaters will reply that these are the exceptions that prove the rule. Proportionately, there are more meat-eaters than vegetarians among top athletes, but that, too, may be explained by factors other than the type of food consumed. Vegetarians will insist that changing to a vegetarian diet will allow people of less developed countries to be more readily fed. Carnivores will tell you that vegetarianism would require even more of the rain forests to be devoted to food production. Moreover, they will insist that a healthy vegetarian diet requires the expenditure of a great deal more time on acquiring food and eating it, thus cutting down on the time available for all the other important aspects of life. They will insist that an adequate vegetarian, or even mainly vegetarian, diet requires such planning, foresight and expense that it is only feasible for the affluent.

So the debate rages. We do not have the expertise to make a sound judgement. Nor, we believe, do many of those who pontificate so eloquently on the matter. For now, the jury must be out. Still, it can be said without fear of contradiction that North Americans and West Europeans would be healthier by reducing their meat consumption and by eating on a regular basis lower down the food chain. For now, at least, meat production is an important aspect of modern society and needs to be investigated.

Desmond Morris's claim is that, "There is nothing shameful about killing animals as a source of food. What is shameful, however, is the manner in which we treat many of them before we kill them."[1] No doubt intensive farming has changed the world of the country farm into an agribusiness in the same manner that industrialism scarred the face of the nineteenth century. But we should not forget that the long-term effects of industrialism have been vastly to improve living standards for almost all the inhabitants of the industrialized world, despite the environmental devastation that industrialism brought in its wake. And if President Hoover promised "a chicken in every pot," that is what modern agribusiness has brought about. Agribusiness is the agricultural equivalent of industrialization. Modern agricultural methods may have been everlastingly detrimental to the food animal, but they have also made meat affordable on a regular basis to all but the very poor. The question we must ask is, how do we change the horrifying conditions of food animals so that the vast majority of humans do not also suffer? But since Western Europeans and North Americans already eat far more meat than is good for them, perhaps the solution is not as difficult as it appears. Higher meat prices—and a great deal more health educa-

---

1   Morris, *Animal Contract*, p. 115. For a defence of meat-eating, see Morris, *Animal Contract*, pp. 112-15. For the case for vegetarianism, see Singer, *Animal Liberation*, pp. 159-83.

tion—may be to everyone's ultimate benefit. Still, with the amount of 'junk food' eaten in North America, education will be no easy task. Europeans eat as much junk food, but it is more in the pastry and cream than in the meat line.

The death—or at least serious sickness—of the traditional family farm has not been caused entirely by agribusiness methods. Extensive health and safety regulations also rang the death knell of those wonderful rural scenes—which are still depicted on dairy product packages, meat containers and television commercials. Is it merely our fanciful imaginations that even the manure and rotting hay smelled better then? Certainly, there is a tendency to romanticize that lost past. Farm animals were not always well cared for, disease was often rampant, the veterinarian may only have been called as a last resort, and knowledge of farm husbandry was decidedly less.[2] Health controls became vital for both animal and human and it was they as much as agribusiness which forever altered the structure and conduct of the traditional farm. Many remain convinced, though, that healthier methods produced less tasty food! But fundamental changes to modern intensive methods will not automatically bring back the beauty of Senator Everett's "well-situated, well-cultivated farm," unless we are willing to risk health as well.

In general, then, modern agribusiness methods produce less expensive and more rigorously disease-controlled food. Is this a sufficient defence for the modern conditions? Let us deal with the second point first, for its use as a defence by agribusiness is a chimera. It is certainly true that modern health and safety regulations will not permit a return to the sometimes unsanitary conditions of farming half a century ago. But small private farms continue to exist, as well as those run by the adherents of traditionalist religions, and they have no difficulty in meeting modern regulations. They have certainly had to make adjustments, sometimes unpalatable adjustments, but their farms meet all health requirements without having to engage in the techno-logical husbandry revolution. In fact, in 1988 legislation was passed in Sweden which required grazing rights for cows, larger cages for chickens and separate bedding and feeding places for pigs. Reports suggest no

---

2   The term 'husbandry' is interesting, reflecting gender divisions and their relationship to animals. Husband meant initially both the tiller of the soil and a man joined to a woman by marriage. The economic relationship was implied in the language. The later 'husbandsman' was originally two words 'husband man'. In the 'husbandsman' form it came to be associated exclusively with agriculture. 'Husbandry' meant initially the administration of a household as well as a farm and again reflected the male dominance. After the seventeenth century the use of 'husbandry' was generally restricted to agricultural management, then later extended to include all animal management, as in zoo and aquarium 'husbandry'.

detrimental (and probably positive) animal and human health consequences.

High-tech farming is based on the principle of maximizing production at the least possible cost—an admirable principle with regard to business provided it is not at the undue expense of employees and animals. Employees, and the workings of the market, can look after the employees' interests. Unfortunately, the animals do not have the same protection. No one has taught them about trade unions or the laws of economics. As we saw with horse-racing, the efficiency of entrepreneurial methods are to be commended, provided, and to the extent that, they treat the animals as ends in themselves. There is, however, a difference. And that is that the very purpose of farm-animal production is to kill the animal raised. If it had not been raised for food it would have had no life at all.

This does not simply accord humans the right to do with the farm animal as they wish. After all, if we were to follow that line of reasoning, it would mean that parents would be entitled to treat children in any manner they see fit merely because they had given their offspring life. Desmond Morris suggests that we treat farm animals—and indeed all animals—on the basis of a social contract. He claims that "we must ensure that the animals we kill for our food live the best possible lives before they die. Anything less is a betrayal of the Animal Contract."[3] Most philosophers today agree that social contract theory is inadequate either to explain or justify obligations. Nonetheless, to think of ourselves as in a reciprocal contractual relationship with the animals we use may be considered a valuable heuristic device. However, if we accept that philosophical approach, our obligation to the farm animal during its lifetime is even greater than for animals we do not kill, since our use of the animal deprives it of its life. The farm animal always makes the ultimate sacrifice. If we wish to consider our relationship to animals to be of a reciprocal contractual nature, then our obligations to farm animals during their short lives is of the highest possible order.

The reality of our treatment of farm animals is the very reverse. In intensive farming the only time any consideration is given to the animals is when it is profitable to do so. Competition and new technology have produced significantly less expensive food, at least when considered as a proportion of disposable income. If the product were an automobile or a toy we should rejoice in the fact. Unfortunately, it is a sentient being which is treated in the same way as an automobile or a toy. Farm families once treated their stock with at least a modicum of respect, but modern farming techniques now *require* that no respect at all be given.

Some 30-odd years ago, one of us lived for a while in a German village, staying with friends. Every day the family geese would be taken

---

3   Morris, *Animal Contract*, p. 115.

for a walk, following each other in a decided awareness of their station in life. Each goose knew its social relationship to the others. Occasionally we would pass another walker with his own geese on a narrow pedestrian bridge. In passage the geese would get mixed up, but always at the other end the right geese in the right number—and we think the right order—would emerge. We were proud of *our* geese. They mattered to us.

A pig lived in an extension of the house. It was treated with cordiality and a degree of friendship. Geese and pig were, however, destined for the dinner table—though, fortunately, we had left before the day of reckoning arrived. During their lives the geese and pig were treated with respect and accorded a healthy measure of dignity. This is what we think Morris means by the obligations of the animal contract. On larger farms with many animals, the relationship, the respect, must have been diminished but it still existed. In modern factory-farming conditions there is, and can be, absolutely no respect, no consideration, no caring. The animal is nothing more than an object of production. It can be no different from a piece of steel or a piece of plastic. It cannot be, and is not, treated as a creature with feelings.

While any semblance of an animal contract would require extra consideration for farm animals, legislation in many jurisdictions explicitly and intentionally gives them less. In the United States the Animal Welfare Act we discussed in Chapter Six lays down certain standards for animal cages—absolutely minimal by any criteria of the most elementary humaneness—but explicitly it exempts from inclusion cages for animals being reared for human consumption. Similarly, in Britain the 1954 Protection of Birds Act lays down minimal cage sizes—no bigger than to allow a bird to stretch its wings—and then adds that the regulations "shall not apply to poultry." Truly farm animals deserve less consideration than others in the eyes of our legislators!

Even in Sweden the 1988 legislation only requires cage sizes to be increased marginally right away. However, by 1997 battery-type poultry cages will be eliminated completely in Sweden. (Battery cages are interconnected units housed in tiers.) By 1994 they will be outlawed in the Netherlands, and each hen will be entitled to 1,000 cm^2 (approximately 155^2 inches) of living space, and must have access to nesting and scratching areas. In Switzerland battery cages have already been eliminated. By 1995 all 12 E.C. countries will be required to allot a minimum of 450 cm^2 (just less than 70^2 inches) to each hen. The 21 member countries of the Council of Europe are *advised* to eliminate battery cages by 1997 but, as we saw in our discussion of animal experimentation, the European Parliament has neither compulsion nor enforcement powers. It is curious to note that while Britain has led the way in general animal cruelty legislation and in protection for experimental animals it has lagged behind its European counterparts in protection for factory animals. It has been suggested that British parliamentarians might care for animals but care rather more for their breakfast. In reality, though, British legislation has been delayed for further study because the government was dissatisfied with the proposals brought before it. Legislation can be expected in Britain prior to the 1995 E.C. implementation date. It is already illegal in Britain to force moult hens (a practice in which they are temporarily deprived of food, water and light which brings about the loss of old plumage and the growth of new, which, in turn, stimulates the hens to lay more eggs), though the practice continues unabated in North America.

To put the European cage and space sizes in perspective, research conducted by the British Houghton Poultry Research Station concluded that a hen needs 1,681 cm^2 of space (approximately 260^2 inches) in order to be able to turn around with ease if kept in a single bird cage. The European proposals are progressive, but they scarcely begin to replicate traditional farm conditions.

European progress is slow and considerate of only the most primitive of poultry needs, but North America is still in the dark ages. On second thought, that's unduly harsh to the dark ages, for then poultry ran and fed at will, engaged in their complex 'pecking order' societal relationships and lived a full life before they became dinner. In North America the customary space in which the whole life is spent varies from 300 cm^2 (46.5^2 inches) to 375 cm^2 (58^2 inches). Even more cramped conditions are common, although industry producer organizations recommend a tiny 48^2 inches (310 cm^2)—less than the size of this page![4] Animals in such conditions can perform not a single one of the activities which makes them what they are. They cannot stretch, walk, scratch or nest and they cannot engage in the complex social activity which is their nature. Unless remedial action is taken immediately, only Swedish, Swiss and Dutch hens will be hens in any meaningful sense by the end of this century—and even they won't be the hens we knew in the barnyard. North American hens will still be the distressed, neurotic, even insane creatures they are today.

Agribusiness interests tell us that only "happy, well-cared-for animals can be productive." They are productive, ergo intensively farmed animals are happy, well-cared-for animals! We can think of no more outrageously false assertion made by any representative organization. The misleading assertions of the research establishment pall into insignificance when compared with this blatant—and knowingly blatant—falsehood. Presumably, for the agribusiness interests all is fair in love, war and profit. A few random statements by industry representatives should suffice to convince. "The breeding sow should be thought

---

4 The legislative and space information on which the preceding paragraphs are based is derived from Singer, *Animal Liberation*, pp. 110-12.

of, and treated as, a valuable piece of machinery whose function is to pump out baby pigs like a sausage machine." Thus spake not Nietzsche's Superman but an agribusiness corporate manager. "They hate it! The pigs just hate it." That is the view of a pork producer on tail-docking. "We have discovered chickens literally growing fast to the cages"—i.e., their claws become welded to the bars. That came from the president of a national poultry organization. In a British farming magazine we read that "The modern layer is, after all, only a very efficient converting machine, changing the raw material—feeding-stuffs—into the finished product—the egg—less, of course, maintenance requirements."[5] If the animals are "cared for" they are cared for in the same way an industrialist looks after a machine—no more than is absolutely necessary for it to function efficiently—and the *sole* function of the farm animal is to produce food at the least possible cost. It is no exaggeration to say that no other factors enter into the equation.

If intensive farm animals are 'happy' why do so many of them die not from physical illness but from stress? Why, when cage sizes for poultry or pen sizes for veal or compounds for pigs are under discussion, is the only consideration one of increasing profitability? Why do animals lose so much weight after castration, debeaking, dehorning and the like if they are anything less than totally distraught? (To be fair, it must be mentioned that these practices also occur in extensive farming.) Search as we might we have been unable to find a solitary instance of a factory-farming organization concerned with the inherent dignity of, or cruelty to, a farm animal. Cruelty is only considered when that cruelty decreases productivity. We eschew hyperbole and we have tried to give a balanced picture throughout this book but we have honestly been unable to find one redeeming feature in the way in which factory farm animals are treated.

We can only remain carnivores by deliberately ignoring all the evidence or shopping carefully—and expensively—for food which is not intensively farmed. The reality is that we manage to conceal from ourselves what it is that we are eating. It is a remarkable aspect of psychological denial that we manage to consume flesh without reflecting on the unconscionable cruelty which has been committed in providing us with our meal. We know the enormity of the facts and worry about them *between* breakfast and lunch and *between* lunch and dinner. At lunch we may eat salami but not pig. At dinner we may have a steak but not cow. Even when it's chicken or lamb—why society has been less concerned to conceal the animal origins of these creatures we do not know—we never think of the debeaked, solitary, neurotic, cramped creature we are eating but simply a drumstick. We conveniently forget

---

5   These quotations—and many more like them—are documented in Singer, *Animal Liberation*, pp. 95ff.

the conditions under which fresh lamb is shipped from New Zealand. If we thought about it at all we would probably be happy to eat domestic fresh lamb or New Zealand or Welsh frozen lamb, for of all farm animals, lamb is less cruelly farmed than the others (though recent Australian practices are decidedly retrograde). But the truth is that somehow at feeding time we are conveniently able to dismiss the matter from our minds. What a complex thing the human mind is! We must constantly remind ourselves—human decency and dignity require it—that the minds of the farm animals which are tortured in their millions every day differ from ours only by degree. We cannot conceive of any legitimate moral principle which could permit intensively farmed animals to be treated in the manner they are.

What, then, is all the fuss about? How are they treated? Where, indeed, shall we begin? Perhaps with cattle for, save for the sheep, they have a better life than most intensively farmed animals. It is often assumed that dairy cattle are the best treated. In fact, beef cattle have the best lives—being given six months of comparative freedom before perhaps 30-35 per cent in Canada, 70 per cent in the U.S., are shipped off to feedlots where they are fattened for consumption. Still, even here they may have 70 square feet of space and the company of others before they are slaughtered at around 14 months of age.

Many remain on something approaching a traditional farm, though many of these suffer from excessive unshaded exposure to the sun in summer and undue cold in the winter. And where they are kept indoors this results in overcrowding. At one time beef cattle lived some two years before slaughter. Now with 'improved' feeding they can reach the appropriate weight in almost half the time. Yet the 'improved' diet consists of eating grain rather than grass. This is ruinous to the cattle's well-being. Their stomachs are unsuited to the diet, but to mix the grain with the roughage the cattle needs would slow down the weight gain. Everyone recognizes that beef cattle need grass to be healthy, but few farmers will give it to them. To do so would be to lose out in the highly competitive market conditions. Farmers simply cannot afford to do what is almost universally acknowledged as necessary to the health of the animal. Governments must legislate to require all producers to meet relevant standards. We say that this requirement is 'almost universally acknowledged', for industry lobbyists trot out the old canard that only healthy animals put on weight. Weight productivity is a prime indication of well-being. Scientific study after scientific study has proved this false. In fact scientific study is superfluous. Common sense would tell us how absurd the proposition is. The fact that an animal puts on weight is no indication of its health, as is evident merely by looking at pathologically obese zoo animals and human beings.

Still, beef cattle are better treated than any other regular meat source, other than lamb. Should we, then, eat beef to the exclusion of pork, veal and poultry? If our sole consideration were the treatment of the animal the answer would be an unequivocal yes. Unfortunately, as we all know from widely publicized medical reports, we consume far too much red meat for our own health. Moreover, excessive European and North American beef consumption has been absolutely devastating to the world environment. Moral decisions are often remarkably complex!

Raising livestock, predominantly cattle, accounts for some 85 per cent of topsoil loss with resultant wetland deterioration in the United States. More than one acre per individual—260 million acres in all—have been cleared to grow crops not for human consumption but to feed livestock, again predominantly cattle. That one acre produces only 250 pounds of beef but several thousand chickens or tens of thousands of pounds of vegetables or fruit. The same land can produce 10 times as much poultry or up to 20 times as much vegetation for human consumption. Over half of all water consumed in the United States goes to watering fodder for livestock, again predominantly for cattle. Livestock grazing destroys much of North America's ability to sustain wildlife by converting land usage. And, believe it or not, cattle flatulence is a major air pollutant with long-term detrimental effects to the environment. Despite these problems governments, in Europe especially, continue to pay farmers to overproduce beef, i.e., to produce even more beef cattle than the European beef lovers can possibly consume. Despite their own beef overproduction the European Community, in conjunction with the World Bank, purchases great quantities of beef from Botswana for purely political reasons. The requisite fencing of Botswana cattle acreage reduces dramatically the habitat and passage of native wildlife. Of course, it can be retorted that humans matter more than the animals. Sure, but the consequence of considering such *immediate* human interests is large-scale, perhaps irreversible, damage to the human environment. Unless we put the environment first there will be no humanity left to consider in a not very distant future.

Since poultry consumption is so much less devastating to the environment, should we not greatly reduce beef consumption and eat chicken instead? Unfortunately, poultry are the worst treated of all farm animals. To protect the environment through switching to more poultry consumption would be to inflict even greater misery on the world chicken population.

Today some 98 per cent of chickens consumed in North America come from factory farms. They can be divided into broilers—which we eat directly—and layers—whose eggs we eat. They are both kept in total confinement, with broilers crowded together in large sheds (about 60-90,000 at a time is the customary figure) and layers in the battery cages we previously described, usually three to five in a cage piled three or more cages on top of each other. The cages for layers are slanted to allow the eggs to roll forward—which puts constant stress on the hens—and there are no perches to allow the birds to rest. They are so frustrated that they claw and peck at each other, lose their colour, develop brittle bones, and find themselves unable to stand. Moreover, they live their lives in semi-darkness—a measure designed to minimize their stress so that they will not damage the other birds. They are de-beaked—a painful procedure also designed to minimize damage to other birds—often twice in their lifespan for layers, once for broilers.

While 15 or more years is the natural lifespan of a domestic chicken, factory-farm stress reduces that to about one year for a layer. During the year the distraught and exhausted layers produce increasingly fewer eggs. At this stage they are often force-moulted—deprived of sustenance and light—a shock which kills some and convinces others to lay more. When they are no longer able to produce eggs efficiently they become pet food or chicken soup, having lived maybe 7 per cent of their natural lifespan and never once having been permitted to behave as a natural chicken should. But even that's better—or perhaps worse, dependent upon whether a life of hell is considered better than no life at all—than the fate of the male. Shortly after hatching males are disposed of, usually by being unceremoniously dumped into plastic bags until they die from suffocation from the weight of those dumped on top of them. The alternative is to gas them. If we thought of the conditions under which the mother hen survives no doubt our breakfast eggs or our supper omelette would not be quite so appetizing.

Broilers live for some 8 to 10 weeks of fattening before being slaughtered. They live not much more than 1 per cent of their natural lifespan. They are debeaked and have their toes clipped with a hot-knife machine—to minimize the damage caused by the incessant fighting their accommodation engenders—constantly fed and then shipped to the slaughterhouse where they share a few minutes of terror—following the hardship of the journey—before their misery is brought to an end. No wonder slaughterhouses have a rapid turnover in staff. When we see the complex community relationships of poultry on a traditional farm and compare them to the existence of the factory-farmed chicken we have no alternative but to purchase free-range poultry and their eggs. To do otherwise would be to condone conditions which are far worse than those endured by rodeo cattle, circus animals, roadside zoos and even farmed fur-bearers. Of all the crimes committed by humankind against the animal kingdom the treatment of intensively farmed poultry is the worst. If we think of ourselves as more civilized than the Roman hordes who slaughtered the animals in the amphitheatre we must think again. A future kinder, gentler and more humane generation will look back with abject horror on our incredible cruelty to the poultry world—and consider us decidedly less humane than the Romans.

If one enjoys milk, butter and cheese—and we certainly do—one is compelled to give consideration to the treatment of dairy cattle. Fortunately, only some 50 per cent of dairy cows are intensively farmed, but we haven't found a method of determining which half the milk, butter and cheese we purchase comes from. Perhaps the best way is to look at the idyllic farm conditions depicted in the advertising of dairy products and then purchase the products of the competitor. Those who protest too much are probably the worst sinners. Certainly many consumers would respond positively to advertising campaigns which promoted the source of their products and demonstrated that their cows were not intensively farmed. Indeed, if consumers demanded it the producers would respond—and, if necessary, adjust their sources accordingly. Public purchasing pressure is an instrument producers readily comprehend.

Conditions for intensively farmed dairy cattle are distinctly preferable to those for poultry. On many farms—but by no means all of them—80 to 120 cattle are kept in a single barn, remaining in their stalls throughout their lives, often being tethered by chain leashes. Such cattle are forced to stand on slatted floors so that their feces and urine will disappear—or partly disappear anyway—through the slats. Since farmers used to put cattle grids on the roadways because hoofed animals would not cross them, we can imagine how cows feel about the slatted floors.

What is worse, however, is that the cattle are made to breed continually, usually by artificial insemination. This applies to those which are allowed a little wandering as well as the tethered ones. Cows only lactate after calves are produced, usually for about 10 months, so to keep them producing milk they must be constantly calved. With milking twice a day the cycle of pregnancy and lactation wears the cow out after about five years—a fraction of its natural lifespan of perhaps 25 years. It is then slaughtered for pet food or hamburger meat.

The life of a dairy cow, bad as it is, is distinctly preferable to that of some of the cow's offspring—the veal calf. To escape the possible charge of being melodramatic and in order not to dwell on grizzly details, we have refrained from graphic description of some of the horrors of intensive farming. Nonetheless, even the most hardened of hearts must recoil at a simple description of the conditions in which veal calves are kept and for which there is no possible justification in terms of decreased food costs, health or even better-tasting meat. The sole purpose of raising white veal, or milk-fed veal as it is sometimes called, is the colour.

When calves are barely 48 hours old they are customarily removed from the presence of their mothers—what a waste of good milk to use it on the calves whose gestation stimulated it! This is highly traumatic for both mother and infant. Of course, modern dairy cows produce far more milk than is good for the calf—but that does not justify complete separation of mother and infant. At the time of separation the calves are divided according to gender. The dairy farmer keeps the potentially better milk producers. The males and the poorer quality females are shipped off to become veal, unless the females are destined for the beef cattle market.

The white veal calves survive from three to four months while they are kept permanently in stalls into which they barely fit so that they cannot turn, even to dissuade visiting insects or to lick themselves. They are fed on artificial milk—musn't waste the real stuff—with a high fat content and absolutely no iron. They are, in other words, intentionally and maliciously deprived of everything necessary to their health. Indeed, it is precisely the debilitating anemia brought about by these conditions which produces the sickly white meat colour demanded by veal lovers. The calves are even deprived of hay on which to rest for they would eat the essential roughage—but then that would change the colour of the meat. It would only be a slight change but that would disturb the aesthetic picture—not the taste at all—for the culturally refined white veal eater. White veal calves used to lick their iron bars to get just a taste of the essential mineral they need. But that too was taken away from them and replaced with wood or plastic. Having been fed until they reach the totally unnatural weight of around 300 or more pounds (136 kg) in about 14 weeks they become the meal of culinary *aficionados* who can't possibly imagine the grotesque suffering that produced the meat they are so appreciatively consuming. It should scarcely surprise us that countries such as Britain and Sweden have outlawed this abominable cruelty, though even they have only somewhat improved conditions. In North America these conditions, which would have appalled Neanderthals, continue without apparent concern among civilized national, state and provincial legislators.

The 1987 European Parliament resolutions not only recommended the phasing out of battery cages within 10 years, but also the abolition of veal crates and the deprivation of iron and roughage to veal calves. The measure was passed by 150 votes in favour with none against and two abstentions. Any political scientist would tell you that such practical unanimity is scarcely ever encountered unless the evidence is over-whelming and incontrovertible. None of the members of the Parliament who represented predominantly agricultural countries or agricultural areas within their own country could bring themselves to oppose passage of the resolutions. We believe that no single piece of evidence could demonstrate more conclusively that, freed from the pressures of agricultural industry lobbyists, all legislators would come to similar conclusions.

Nor did the European Parliament restrict its resolutions to veal and poultry. They also insisted that sows should not be kept in individual stalls or on tethers and that the castration of male pigs and routine mutilations such as tail-docking should cease. In the view of the European Parliament the pork-producing industry was no better than the other agricultural producers.

In intensive-farming conditions, after breeding a sow gestates for about 100 days, usually kept permanently in a stall scarcely any bigger than herself. As she approaches the end of pregnancy she is transferred to a farrowing stall, where she is even more constrained. Shortly after birth the piglets are removed from the mother—naturally they would suckle for about two months—so that the sow can be bred again. Up to a dozen or more piglets are placed in a pen about 10 x 12 feet (3 x 3.7 m) and fed until they are ready for slaughter. The conditions are so cramped that, as with poultry, the animals become immensely distraught and fight—hence the castration and the tail-docking, the one to diminish aggression, the other to remove the object most readily attacked. After some five months they are slaughtered, although their natural life span would be 10-12 years.

We should be aware that pigs are intelligent and highly social animals, about as intelligent as the average dog. They make good pets—a practice quite common in New Zealand—and have none of the dirty characteristics of which they are customarily accused, unless, of course, they are kept in unsanitary conditions and have no alternative. In factory-farming conditions they customarily suffer from what is known as 'porcine stress syndrome'—at its worst this results in "rigidity, blotchy skin, panting, anxiety, and often—sudden death."[6] How would we feel if our canine friends were kept this way? Surely, there can be no greater excuse for treating a pig in such a manner than there would be, say, for a basset hound or a spaniel. And if we take Morris's animal contract seriously there is even less excuse, for we demand of the pig the ultimate sacrifice—its life.

Mutilation of farm animals is common. Debeaking, dehorning, tail-docking, and even castration are customary practice—and they are normally (though not always) undertaken without anesthesia. Farm-industry lobbyists always insist that these are undertaken for the benefit of the animal. Indeed, we have recently received correspondence at the Ontario S.P.C.A. from the Ontario Farm Animal Council telling us that such practices *and* research to minimize them are for the benefit of the animal! We haven't been able to work out how the two are compatible. In one sense, of course, the industry lobbyists are right. These things are done to minimize harm to the animal—harm which is brought about precisely and almost universally because farm animals are kept in conditions which are totally destructive of their nature, their physical health and their psychological well-being. Of course, every industry

---

6 *Farm Journal* (May 1974). Quoted in Singer, *Animal Liberation*, p. 122.

lobbyist also knows that the reason such practices are undertaken is to minimize damage so that profit will not be harmed. They know equally that giving the animals appropriate space, allowing them to socialize, and not depriving them of their offspring or parents immediately after birth would make the procedures quite unnecessary. What the 'research' to curtail these methods amounts to—e.g., breeding hornless cattle—is a means to keeping the farm animals in the same deplorable conditions without suffering the financial losses brought about by 'accidents' which are caused by these conditions.

It is not always farm-industry lobbyists who defend modern intensive farming conditions. Everyone who purchases the products does so whether it is intentional or not. And yet others write to defend such practices because they believe they are genuinely of benefit. For example, Frank Hurnik, Professor of Farm Animal Behaviour at the University of Guelph, Ontario, has numbered as "significant benefits" such factors as "inexpensive food for consumers, reduced seasonality of marketed products, better animal protection against adverse weather conditions and predators, and improvements in animal disease prevention."[7] Professor Hurnik's defence of the modern farm industry seems significant because it is the only one we could find not written by an agricultural columnist or a lobbyist. The first claim is undoubtedly true. The second factor refers, presumably, predominantly to fruit and vegetables. We wonder why it was included in an article about animal rights and intensive farming. There have been marginal adjustments to meat availability from intensive farming but few suffered unduly in the past from lack of particular meats at certain times of the year. The third factor is a partial but misleading truth. Farm animals have indeed been bred to withstand adverse weather conditions. But providing them with adequate protection from the elements and predators would be far more readily accomplished by providing them with better fencing around their enclosures and a safe place at night rather than permanent incarceration. The fox may no longer be able to get into the chicken house but give the chicken a choice between present misery and the risk of being the fox's supper and guess which she would choose!

The fourth factor is, again, a partial but misleading truth. Certainly, farm animals may receive better medicine to ward off illness, but the drastic reduction in their lifespan makes disease no great concern—especially when modern farming conditions ensure that both psychological and physical illness are a permanent part of the animals' lives. What is most notable about Professor Hurnik's defence of modern farming conditions is that none of the benefits to animals—to the extent that they *are* benefits to animals—are consequences of intensive

---

7 Frank Hurnik, "Improving Animal Rights has Costs for Humans," *Kitchener-Waterloo Record*, July 22, 1991, p. A7.

farming. Better medicine and greater safety for farm animals are quite independent of whether animals are farmed according to traditional or modern methods.

Still, one might be impressed that an independent academic specializing in farm-animal behaviour could reach such conclusions supportive of modern farming techniques. One's respect for Dr. Hurnik's objectivity might be diminished, however, when one discovers that he is a farmer as well as an academic.

Again, though, we return to the question of cost. Modern farming methods have undoubtedly decreased the cost of meat. Is that worth the great harm to the animals? Even if one were to argue that animal interests don't matter at all, the case against modern methods would still be insurmountable. The great need for concentrated intensive meat production is because of the huge increase in meat consumption. The annual per capita meat consumption in the U.S.A. is 111 kilograms. In Canada it is 70 kilograms. In India it is 1 kilogram. While malnutrition was once a major problem in India it is far less so today—without increasing meat consumption. Almost every nutritionist would insist that North American meat consumption, especially red meat consumption, could be more than halved without harming health. Indeed, most would insist that it would be highly beneficial to health to reduce meat consumption by that much. As everyone is aware, Europeans and North Americans are significantly overweight. Health considerations would again indicate a significant reduction in both meat consumption and consumption of other less healthy foodstuffs. Eating lower down the food chain, especially more fish, would be of dietary benefit. If meat consumption were drastically reduced, the price of meat would rise—because intensive farming methods would be less beneficial to the farmer—but the overall expenditure on food would actually decrease. Eating more sensibly would actually save money. In fact, one could argue that a decrease in the cost of meat was precisely what stimulated vast increases in meat consumption to the decided detriment of health in the Western world. If prices were to increase and consumption consequently decrease, the benefits to health would be substantial.

The benefit to the environment would also be of great significance, largely because agricultural land now used predominantly for livestock foodstuff would be returned to more beneficial usage and because the drastic waste of water on producing such foodstuff would be decreased. The wetlands would begin to return. Consideration for the interests of animals is not necessary to recognize that intensive farming methods have resulted in a deterioration of human health and the health of the environment. Professor Hurnik points to benefits derived from intensive farming, but it is not difficult to recognize that the balance is overwhelmingly on the other side. And that does not require us to become vegetarians—which may or may not be advantageous to human health. It requires only that we reduce meat consumption substantially both in our own interests and those of our environment.

Of course, the benefit to the farm-animal realm would be incalculable. The case for a very significant reduction in meat consumption is one of those rare instances where a cost-benefit analysis does not apply. It is not a question of balancing the human interest against the animal interest. Both human and animal gain alike. One must have some concern for the loss to the farmer, but the farmer who will lose the most is not the individual farm owner but the huge agribusiness corporations—which are often subsidiaries of chemical corporations or insurance companies. Indeed, the small farmer would gain by informed and concerned consumers making knowledgeable choices about their purchases based on the conditions under which the meat was produced.

Chapter Thirteen

Companion Animals

Brothers and sisters, I bid you beware
Of giving your heart to a dog to tear.
> — Rudyard Kipling, *The Power of the Dog*

I had an aunt in Yucatan
Who bought a Python from a man
And kept it for a pet.
She died, because she never knew
These simple little rules and few; —
The snake is living yet.
> — Hilaire Belloc, "The Python,"
> *More Beasts for Worse Children*

Outside of personal relationships, there is no greater joy for a human than developing an association with a pet, a companion animal. But what animal? Dogs and cats have been humankind's most common companions—the former for at least 12,000 years and the latter at least 4,500 years. Yet not only dogs and cats have served as pets. Amerindians tamed moose, bear and more. Today people have monkeys, cougars, wolves, lions, pythons—as well as hamsters, mice and rabbits—as pets. Even cockroaches, spiders and beetles have been treated as pets of a kind. And ferret- and hedgehog-keeping are now being promoted.

To begin to ponder the purpose of a companion animal one must first consider what is meant by a pet or a companion. According to the *Concise Oxford Dictionary* a pet is a tame animal treated with fondness. A companion is an associate *in* or a sharer *of*. The essence of both 'pet' and 'companion' is a relationship involving affection and/or belonging-ness. Companion and owner form a communal relationship. Since a relationship involves feelings both *toward* and *from*, the qualities and characteristics of each partner determine what kind of relationship is possible.

Humane Societies generally deplore the keeping of 'exotic' pets—a practice which is proliferating. Most of this opposition is based on eminently sensible reasons: the potential danger to the public; the inappropriateness of the surroundings in which the animals are kept; and the impracticality of getting relevant veterinary attention. Inspectors of the Ontario S.P.C.A. have been called upon when pythons have escaped into apartment water systems, when cougars have been taken for walks in public parks and when wolves have been kept penned where children can poke their arms through the fence. Nonetheless, it should not be assumed a priori that the keeping of 'exotic' pets—i.e., pets which are not the customary pets—is always inappropriate. The question is whether such relationships can be of benefit to both human and animal.

Whoever coined the phrase "leading a dog's life" clearly had no experience of the dog as companion animal in a responsible human family environment. A dog's life can be extremely rewarding—both for the dog and its owners. But can the same be said of a python or a tarantula? Clearly the motives of people who own such exotics are suspect, however objectively beautiful a python may be judged to be. We find it difficult to understand such ownership as anything other than an unhealthy attempt to make a statement about oneself—unless perhaps the owner is a herpetologist or an arachnologist. And the statement made is a less than self-complimentary one. Clearly no relationship between owner and beast is possible in any mutually satisfactory manner.[1]

The ownership of a Capuchin monkey or a wolf or perhaps even a lion may be said to fall into a different category. Capuchin monkeys are sometimes trained to be the "hands and legs" of quadriplegics. As our closest relatives, monkeys are certainly capable of a satisfactory relationship with humans. They can and do develop affectionate and comfortable associations with their owners. Domesticated wolves often have a very similar relationship to their owners as do dogs—all of which are, of course, descended from wolves. There are several well-documented stories of playful and positive human-lion relationships—Ralph Helfer's with Zamba[2] is perhaps more positive than that of Daniel in the lions' den, since Daniel merely escaped.[3] Nonetheless, monkeys,

---

1   Some animal advocates object to the use of the term 'owner'. No living being, they claim, should be owned, since being owned is as detrimental to animals as it once was to slaves. Domestic animals are in fact owned in law. To use any other word would be to fail to recognize the legal relationship. We do not object to the term on philosophical grounds either, since people tend to be more responsible toward that of which they have pride of ownership. Some of our friends in fact tell us they feel owned by their pets. And that, we believe, is quite appropriate. There should be mutual ownership between animal and keeper provided ownership is felt in the sense of common belonging.

2   Helfer, *The Beauty of the Beasts*, chap. 4.

3   Dan. 6. It is not so unbelievable that the lions did not harm Daniel. One human in their company would not necessarily disturb them if he did not provoke. Nor should it surprise us that the lions later "brake all their bones in pieces" of Daniel's accusers' wives and children. The presence of large numbers would of itself be a disturbance to the pride. And we are not told what else the intruders

wolves and lions are social creatures who need the company of their own kind, need an environment suitable to their nature (monkeys, for example, must have trees or substitute trees to climb) and need expert veterinary care. They are better off in their natural environment. Still, as their environments are threatened or if some haphazard event brings human and animal permanently together, a mutually beneficial relationship is possible if the owner provides a suitable environment and relevant expertise is available. We are certainly not promoting such relationships, except where there are evident benefits, as in the instance of the quadriplegics. The motives of those who would wish to own monkeys and lions are only somewhat less suspect than those of the tarantula keeper, and species needs can scarcely ever be met. Only in special circumstances can the relationship be beneficial to the animal. Unfortunately, those are almost never circumstances in which exotic pets are currently kept. Nevertheless, the very special relationships which may be enjoyed between dogs, cats or ponies and their owners are not necessarily restricted to such customary companions. Should we think otherwise, there is a danger that we will believe that a special responsibility may be owed to domesticated species but scarcely any at all to those we deem 'wild'.

Indeed, in principle, if almost never in practice, such exotic pet-keeping may be preferable to keeping a gerbil on a treadmill, colourful fish in a tank or a bird in a gilded cage. White mice, hamsters, gerbils and the like are certainly deserving of respect and consideration, but we do not see how their presence in a home is likely to encourage such attitudes. They may help instruct children in some mysterious manner about the wonders of nature, but there are readier ways of doing that. Certainly such animals do little to encourage a sense of community with, or respect for, other species, and the attention devoted to them is usually very short-lived. Unfortunately, our experience suggests that the reason for possessing such animals is merely the desire to possess for its own sake. The animal is merely a new toy to be discarded when the next whim comes along. Of course, such motives are sometimes involved in the purchase of dogs and cats, too, but the animals bring such joy and meaning into families that the initial unsavoury motive can be rapidly overtaken.

Caged birds and tanked fish are often little more than decorative furniture. Their colourfulness adds to the setting. Still, budgerigars which are given daily freedom to fly a little, are spoken to often, and

---

may have done—shrieking, running in fear or whatever. Certainly Daniel's deliverance was no proof of the presence of the angel nor his accusers' demise that of the inferiority of the Persian religion. It should amuse us again though (see above, p. 191) that John Brown's 'explanation' of the meaning of the story makes no reference to animals (*Self-Interpreting Bible*, p. 772).

encouraged to perch for a little social comfort on the owner's shoulder are better off than the clipped macaw in the zoo—especially if there is a pair of the home dwellers. And if there is a spacious tank without overcrowding, privately owned fish are better off than their zoo or public aquaria counterparts, too. Still, they would undoubtedly be better off in their natural habitat.

There are, however, exceptions to almost every rule, and some people do develop meaningful relationships with birds, white mice, hamsters and on occasion even fish. But pet-keeping is only justifiable if the animals derive some benefit from being kept. Unless there is some human-animal relationship or unless there is otherwise some threat to the animal, the keeping of pets cannot be justified.

Provided the animal kept as a companion is the right one for the circumstance, the advantages to both human and animal are without measure. While the advantages for the human are more readily demonstrable, few could doubt the apparent advantages to the animal as well. That is, of course, provided the animal is not treated cruelly, with disregard for its interests or as some creature which it is not—a substitute human, for example.

If the statistics one reads are to be believed, there are about 57 million cats and 52 million dogs in the United States, almost 7 million dogs and over 6 million cats in Britain, about 2-1/4 million dogs and just over 2 million cats in Canada. Since the U.S. population is approximately four times that of Britain and nine times that of Canada, the United States has a significantly higher proportionate pet population than Britain, and Canada comes a distant third. In Canada almost one in every four homes has a dog, and more than one in every five has a cat. In the United States more than one in every two homes has a dog and more than one in every two has a cat. Well over three-quarters of homes have one or the other (or both). These figures constitute a remarkable testimony to the popularity of the companion animal.

Clearly, given the costs of keeping pets as well as the considerable inconvenience they cause, some significant benefits must be derived from the companionship of species other than one's own (there are slightly over one million non-dog or cat pets in Canada and, we assume, proportionate numbers elsewhere). Indeed, cats and dogs, dogs especially, have come to accept our way of life as theirs. If dogs meet while being taken for a walk they will greet each other, sniff a little, wag their tails and depart, showing a decided preference for the company of their owner than for their species compatriot. Their loyalty is beyond measure. After a scolding they will forgive the injustice and cuddle up for affection. Only if they are left alone far too long will they refuse to forgive for a while—and that is only because they pine for the affection of those with whom they have a sharing relationship. They constantly give to their human companions, demanding only in return a pat, a friendly word and some food.

Dogs offer many of the benefits of a human relationship while demanding only a small part of the sacrifices which human familial relationships require. It should not surprise us that a 1991 book, *The Unofficial U.S. Census*, reported that of the 41 million U.S. dog owners 13 million claimed their attachment to their animals as close as that of a best friend, 6.2 million as close as a child and 4.2 million as close as a spouse; 28.5 million buy Christmas gifts for their pets and 9.8 million celebrate their birthdays. A similar poll in Britain suggested that 10 per cent preferred their pets to their partners, 20 per cent thought them more important than their children, and about 35 per cent considered them more important than their jobs. (Incidentally, if the 52 million dogs and 41 million owners are accurate figures for the U.S.A., that would indicate just over 1-¼ dogs per owner. It is generally preferable that companion animals have species companionship but that applies rather more to cats than to dogs, whose communal world has become practically indistinguishable [except, of course, for breeding] from that of the owner.)

The bright side of the companion-animal human relationship is very bright indeed. Unfortunately, there is also a dark side. Every Humane Society shelter and every animal pound euthanizes *unwanted* pets week after week after week. The employees come to have a significant disregard—downright distaste even—for these abandoners of animals which ought to have become intrinsic members of the family. The reasons given for the abandonment are legion in their variety and ingenuity. What they usually amount to, though, is that these people don't care enough and aren't responsible enough. There is a story which is current in Humane Society circles of the lady who gave up her cat because she changed the colour of her furniture and the colour of the cat clashed. The story is—presumably—apocryphal but it reflects the manner in which some people treat animals as an expendable and renewable resource rather than as individuals. The animal is merely an extension of their own personalities, and as their whims wander, so their animal 'requirements' are adjusted. It is estimated that some 13 million dogs and cats are destroyed in the U.S.A. annually and almost a million in Canada.

Some Humane Societies go to significant lengths in checking out potential owners before agreeing to sell. Yet this is a route fraught with hazards, for not only is it sometimes difficult to determine the potential responsibility of an owner—though it does help eliminate the very worst—but a denial often means that the animal which would have been adopted must die. And just as we refuse to visit the slaughterhouse, so too, we will not watch the animals being euthanized. We know how heart-rending it is without having to see it performed. We don't believe that watching a child being beaten would make us despise child-beaters any more than we already do. We don't think watching a dog or a cat being killed would make us any more sensitive to its plight or more empathetic to the veterinarians or Humane Society employees who perform these unpalatable tasks.

In the Western world there are many thousands more animals than potential owners. When one purchases a dog or a cat from a breeder or a pet store the animal is—usually at least—capable of producing many more animals, the vast majority of which will be unwanted. Most owners, of course, do not intend to breed their animals—it just 'happens'. The answer, of course, lies in 'spaying and neutering' as it is customarily called. (We are not sure why both words are used— 'neutering' seems to cover both genders adequately. 'Sterilization' is even better.) In order to reduce the numbers of unwanted pets Humane Societies have been actively involved for almost two decades in promoting the sterilization of pets, to avoid having to euthanize so many of them.

Naturally, sterilization is a relatively expensive procedure—around $100 at the veterinary clinic—and many are unwilling, or unable, to add that amount to the cost of animal purchase and maintenance, especially where many of the public see it as a practice which detracts from the animal's nature, making the female less feminine and the male less masculine. In fact the procedure diminishes the more aggressive aspects of behaviour and makes the animals more loving and lovable, although the fact must be faced that this alters the true nature of the animal. Sterilization is only beneficial to cats and dogs because humans have first required and now allow cats and dogs to reproduce wantonly. Humane Societies advocate the procedure, and many are willing to refund a part of the purchase price if evidence of sterilization is produced. Some Humane Societies' veterinarians are willing to offer lower rates for animals purchased from the Society. And yet other Societies hold Spay-Neuter Clinics where the procedure is performed very inexpensively and in certain cases free.

This is just one of the occasions where the interests of Humane Societies and the interests of the veterinary profession are at odds. In a 1980 poll of veterinarians conducted by the Michigan State University College of Veterinary Medicine there was strong agreement that veterinarians should promote pet sterilization. A substantial majority, however, believed Humane Societies should not be permitted to hold low-cost spay-neuter clinics. It is scarcely surprising that the veterinarians should hold this view. Low-cost clinics cut down on their own income—and veterinarians as a whole are not very highly recompensed, at least not in relation to their years of medical training. Moreover, they argue, with some justice, that low-cost clinics do not substantially increase the number of procedures performed but merely encourage those who can afford to have the minor surgery conducted at the veterinary clinic to choose the less expensive alternative. Clearly there is some merit in the veterinarians' views. Nonetheless, some Humane Societies now have the surgery performed prior to adoption and add a nominal cost to the price of the animal. Certainly, such increased prices appear to have had no appreciable effect on the number of sales, and if we are not to continue to produce hundreds of thousands of unwanted animals some such policies are necessary. It is only fair, however, to develop such policies in conjunction with veterinarians. Perhaps special charitable funds need to be developed to assist the aged in particular. Certainly there are many community groups and service organizations devoted to assistance to the aged. Animals are so important to the health of the aged that this would be an eminently worthwhile project to encourage.

Radical animal rights advocates will often claim that the benefits from owning companion animals lie exclusively with the human. We find this attitude rather difficult to comprehend. In responsible homes, the game-playing of the young animals, the joyful greeting of the children returning from school, the excitement at the announcement of a walk, the purring of the contented cat snuggling on the lap are all witness to the satisfaction derived by the animal from its human contacts. Of course, there are irresponsible—and sometimes cruel—owners, but then there are irresponsible and cruel parents too. The problem faced by the companion animal is sometimes from those who vent their wrath on their pets because they are unable to vent it on their spouse, offspring, sibling or parent. We are constantly made aware of the irresponsibilities and cruelties perpetrated by pet owners. They are truly sickening.

Nonetheless, the more common problems are the result of ignorance of species or breed needs and overindulgence. For there to be a good human-animal bond the owners must take the trouble to learn about the animals' needs—such as exercise, routine and diet—and know how to judge the animal's language—body or vocal. If animals are to benefit as much from the relationship as humans then the humans must have more than love—though that is indispensable. They must also have knowledge and respect. And respect implies an understanding that the animal must be considered as an end in itself with specific species and breed needs, not merely as an instrument of human entertainment. Present circumstance requires us not to forget the animal's need for attention. As we write these pages a cockapoo is constantly jumping on the table, licking our hands—always the writing hand—and lying across the pages to divert our attention away from the writing and toward him! We don't think it's the content of the book he objects to. He does the same when we do the crossword puzzle.

Pet-keeping is, of course, no modern phenomenon. It has a venerable history which goes back thousands of years. Only in the last century, however, has it become a commonplace in the Western world. We are struck by the fact that when we read eighteenth- and nineteenth-century novels there are rarely if ever any mention of companion animals. To the extent that they were present they played only a minor role in their owners' lives. Nonetheless that crusty old late Victorian Rudyard Kipling proved the exception and recognized the power of dogs to captivate the human heart, as did Sir Edwin Landseer, not by describing the dog's magnetism, but by painting it.

Companion animal ownership began to expand with the increased interest in natural history toward the close of the nineteenth century. Of course, already in the seventeenth century King Charles coddled his spaniels and self-indulgent aristocrats proudly presented their exotic pets, but we doubt that they took them for walks or cleaned up their feces. In fact, in the West, the close interrelationship between humans and beasts developed out of the relationship with the working animals—horses for transport, dogs for hunting and herding and cats for mousing and ratting. When affectionate human-animal relationships are mentioned in the novels of earlier centuries it almost always arises out of the close human-animal bond derived from a working partnership.

Thus, when Richard Martin first introduced legislation into the British parliament in 1821 to protect animals from cruelty, it was the horse which was the object of compassion. Martin was at first ridiculed in Parliament, reporters being unable to record the debate with any accuracy because of the ribaldry which ensued. There were convulsions of mirth, preposterous exclamations that Martin would want to legislate for dogs and cats next! If it seemed ridiculous to legislate the protection of horses how much more absurd it was to suggest that humankind should be restricted in the manner in which it treated animals which were of a lesser working necessity. And when the British S.P.C.A. was founded in 1824 its predominant concern was to protect horses from the cruelty inflicted by those who worked them.

In *The Descent of Man* (1871), Charles Darwin wrote: "Man scans with scrupulous care the character and pedigree of his horses, cattle, and dogs before he matches them; but when he comes to his own marriage he rarely, or never, takes any such care." We are not sure Darwin is quite right in the latter part of his statement. Hindu arranged marriages, the comments of Xenophon and Theognis in classical Greece on the importance of wise choices, aristocratic prohibitions against unions with commoners, church and state requirements against familial inbreeding, the traditional dire threats about the consequences of inter-racial marriages—now diminished but customarily still whispered by members of all races—suggest that Darwin was exaggerating human *insouciance*. Still, it has been suggested, without any attempt at comedy, that marriage choices are often made in a state of insanity. Yet it is undoubtedly true that significantly more care has been given to the breeding of animals in order to develop characteristics appropriate to a particular task. Horses have been bred variously for speed, jumping ability and for strength. Dogs have been bred for different kinds of herding, a wide variety of species-specific hunting and fetching, and for fighting. More recently they, and cats, have been bred solely for certain looks deemed appealing. Indeed, the groups of dogs under which the American Kennel Club lists the various breeds include sporting dogs, hounds, working dogs, terriers, toys and non-sporting dogs. (The term 'toy' should raise eyebrows, but it is just a synonym for miniature.) Clearly, the first four categories consist of breeds developed for specific purposes totally unrelated to their suitability as a companion per se—and some for purposes quite unsuitable for a home environment. Neither of the other categories were developed specifically for their appropriateness as a companion animal. Yet all today are companion animals—and many suit the role admirably.

One sometimes reads that there are over 400 breeds of dogs and 50 breeds of cats today. There may well be if one uses methods of calculation which count very similar breeds in different countries as separate breeds. In fact the American Kennel Club lists 126 breeds, almost all of which are registered breeds. Human owners tend to display a special affection for a particular breed. They see themselves less as dog owners than as *aficionados* of borzois or beagles or basenjis. We must ourselves confess a special attachment to bassets, cocker spaniels, Birmans and British Blues. In fact, though, mongrels generally make better companion animals than purebreds. They are less highly strung, more malleable, more loving—in short, less self-important. They have greater genetic diversity and fewer breed-specific traits, e.g., the desire to hunt—and are thus more amenable to a life where companionship, walking and playing constitute the highlights of life. The characteristics of a particular breed may, however, be relatively rapidly changed if they are judged—as some should be—quite inappropriate for a comfortable life of human companionship. The British bulldog—which gained popularity as the district attorney's constant companion in the television series "Jake and the Fatman"—is a case in point. The breed was developed for the nefarious practice of baiting bears. But when that was outlawed in the 1830s the dog was rapidly bred to eliminate its viciousness but to retain its loyal, resolute and equable character. Still, all in all, mutts make better pets, especially if they are to be the companions of children. If a purebred is chosen it should be chosen with an eye to its inbred characteristics in relation to the environment it will inhabit, including the people.

Unfortunately, many people still choose their breed of dog as an extension of their personalities—which probably means that, taken as a whole, corgi owners are nicer than the owners of Dobermans. (We expect a letter of commendation from the Queen but for all the

Doberman Pinscher owners who want to pillory us let us explain that if you have read this far in the book you are not one of those we are describing. Of course, the Doberman in the right hands is a fine dog. In the wrong hands it can be used as a lethal weapon.) What is most important is that any potential purchaser should be sure of the customary characteristics of the breed and its source. Naturally, we would prefer that people bought their animals from the Humane Society shelter or the public pound. That would save a lot of very fine animals' lives. But we acknowledge that it is a practice we have not always followed ourselves. So we can scarcely urge it as indispensable on others. Nonetheless we do so urge, our own practices notwithstanding.

One of the greatest injustices perpetrated today is that committed by the so-called 'puppy mills'. Their actions are a crime not only against the animals they breed without an ounce of concern for their well-being but also against the owners—especially against their children, who soon lose the friend they have rapidly come to love to disease or genetic fault. Puppy mills breed their bitches to the point of death from physical exhaustion—just as hog breeders do with their sows. The puppies are removed from their mothers far too soon—with attendant effects on their personalities—and they are so inbred and in such unhealthy surroundings that they very frequently have both serious illnesses and disastrous genetic defects. Even if such animals survive they will almost never make good companions.

Although it is easy to condemn puppy mills in general, it is difficult to determine which breeders need to be monitored by appropriate and enforceable legislation, or to be shut down entirely. Puppy mills often sell their animals through pet stores, or they advertise them in newspapers as though they were private sales, and the dog is usually brought to the potential purchaser's home. If a visit to the breeding establishment is permitted, the potential purchaser is prevented from seeing the conditions in which the animals are kept. Of course, if the conditions are witnessed a formal complaint can be made and the premises inspected. Otherwise, Humane Societies can do little, since entry can only be gained if there is demonstrable evidence, not merely well-founded suspicion, of an offence. Some jurisdictions now require that anyone selling more than a certain number of animals in a year, say 10, are required to have their premises regularly inspected. Moreover, vendors are required to pay all legitimate veterinarian expenses to combat illness for a period of a year, provided those illnesses were not contracted after purchase. If the animal has an incurable illness or an avoidable physical defect the purchase price must be refunded in full. If this does not immediately prevent the breaking of a child's heart it would at least dissuade pet stores from selling animals from non-reputable breeders and seriously discourage the puppy mills from maintaining their unsavoury practices. Indeed, some U.S. states now bar all live animal sales from pet stores. Until all jurisdictions have such legislation, the problem will continue. Even then the excessive breeding of bitches and the problem of excessive inbreeding will only slowly diminish.

As we have said, specific breeds developed out of the use of working animals for particular purposes. Today we are thankful that those years are predominantly behind us. Yet, while there was considerable cruelty in many instances, it was the relationship which grew out of the respect for the working animal as well as the hunting partner which led to the generally greater recognition of our responsibilities toward the animal realm. Dogs that were bred to hunt, to retrieve or to herd derived satisfaction from their tasks and were rewarded by their masters for their successes. When the animal performed its tasks well not only was it rewarded with a suitable tidbit but it aroused a respect and admiration in the owner which over time extended to animal life in general. Dogs need activity and the challenge of performing their tasks well if they are to be healthy. And if they perform those tasks with skill and dedication they stimulate their owners to treat them with the respect which is a prerequisite of a healthy relationship.

Unfortunately, horses were generally bred for more laborious and generally less skilful tasks, and hence failed to arouse the admiration and respect of their owners, and still less of the employees who were required to work them as though they were machines. It is not surprising, then, that nineteenth-century animal protection legislation and the activity of the early Humane Societies were directed predominantly toward the protection of horses. The hunting horse, however, was a partner in the chase. Co-operation between rider and horse was essential to success, and the hunting horse aroused respect and its activities stimulated a close relationship between the rider and the ridden. On the other hand the mere drudges, pack asses, were *sometimes* respected by their drivers despite the lack of skill, as were camels. Elephants were almost always respected by their mahouts—even though the initial training of elephants left something to be desired. The customary method was to have one person act cruelly to the elephant. The second person would then drive off the first and present themselves to the elephant as a friend and rescuer.

Just as the incipient age of egalitarianism brought an end to slavery, if not to racial oppression, so too it encouraged the recognition that all dogs and all horses, not merely the special ones, deserved respect. Although it failed to end the mistreatment or the oppression, it stimulated people to greater sensibilities, which developed rapidly until the period of World War I. However, the two world wars, and especially Nazi atrocities and the lingering oppression of imperialism, required a concentration on human rights and needs. Only with the publication of

Peter Singer's *Animal Liberation* in 1975 were minds once again turned to the oppression of animals.

It should be emphasized that the kinds of attention devoted to animal interests are merely an extension of the deep concerns one must have for oppressed peoples. Just as we must respect those of other nationalities and other races, so too we must be considerate of the interests of animals. This does not mean that human and animal interests or rights are the same. They are not. What it means is that the kinder, gentler society in which we all profess to believe requires that we also treat all sentient creatures with respect and consideration.

Even those who care not a jot for species other than their own must recognize the great benefit that companion animals provide—for the blind, the deaf, the infirm, the ageing, the incarcerated. Moreover, respect for animals developed in youth is a decided hindrance to later anti-social behaviour directed against other humans. And those who benefit from animal companionship benefit the most when they have an affection and respect for the animals themselves.

There is an abundance of documented evidence that those who commit crimes of violence against other humans are likely to have previously treated animals cruelly. This appears to be especially true of serial killers. We are not suggesting there is some causal relationship, i.e., that cruelty to animals somehow *causes* cruelty to persons, but we think that courts and law enforcement agencies should treat cruelty to animals in a far more serious manner than they do. In the interests of deterrence and rehabilitation of such criminals, authorities should recognize the potential with which they are dealing. We also think that, to the extent aggressive behaviour can be limited by socialization and education, encouraging greater respect for, and positive attitudes to, animals also encourages more considerate behaviour toward humans.

One of the greatest benefits for adults in visiting a responsible zoo or wildlife park lies less in watching the animals than in seeing the awe and respect on children's faces—unless, of course, that respect has been marred by attitudes learned from parents. Even then the wonder may overcome parental insensibility. Certainly, that kind of awe and respect can only increase reverence for life in general. Even greater long-term respect for the rights of others is derived when the child has a meaningful relationship with a companion animal. It is not surprising that even St. Thomas Aquinas, who otherwise thought animal interests of no importance, recognized that considerate behaviour toward animals promoted considerate behaviour toward humans.

Sometimes attitudes toward companion animals may be somewhat bizarre. Everyone knows of the eccentrics who keep a houseful of felines and spend more on feeding their cats than themselves. Every now and again we read of a cat—why cats more than dogs we do not know—being left a considerable amount of money by a devoted but now departed owner. In fact the cat has been treated to a great amount of mysterious idolatry and not merely by ancient Egyptians. Nowhere is the mystery of the cat better exemplified than in literature. Edgar Allan Poe's *The Black Cat* is redolent with images of the mysterious power of the cat. Poe's admirer, the mid-nineteenth-century French poet Charles Baudelaire, claimed a spiritual kinship with the cat. And T.S. Eliot's mystical cats have now been popularized in Andrew Lloyd Webber's musical production. For some, especially in the Middle Ages, the cat was a symbolic representation of sorcery and the darker side of nature. For the vast majority of cat owners, though, the cat is simply a proud, self-possessed, independent but loving and lovable ball of fun.

The dog has received less mysterious but more consistent admiration as a loyal, courageous and attached partner. Although there are numerous exceptions, owners seem to fall into categories of 'cat people' and 'dog people'. Each has its committed adherents, who are often willing to castigate the claimed qualities of the other. Although cats and dogs differ clearly in their natures both, in different ways, provide the greatest benefits to humans, especially to those who are in some manner deprived.

One of the most successful activities undertaken by Humane Societies is the pet visitation program whereby pet animals are taken on visits to hospitals, nursing homes and clinics. Some hospitals now run their own programs and employ pet therapists. Some independent organizations—such as the Pet Access League Society (P.A.L.S.) of Calgary, Alberta—devote themselves to providing such a service—in the P.A.L.S. case with some 300 volunteers and 400 pets. Prisons now find animal visitation a most effective form of rehabilitation. In fact a London hospital began using animals for therapy in the 1700s, but the practice was discontinued and not resurrected until the 1960s.

What is so therapeutic about having a pet? No one knows for sure but the available evidence suggests that many pet owners feel that pets can be trusted while humans are thought to give only if they get something more in return. Seniors who have become withdrawn respond to pets, and visits from family pets have been demonstrated to increase recovery rates in patients, especially for patients recovering from heart attacks. Pets not only seem to care, they also give the deprived, the aged and the sick something to care for. Pets make one feel that one matters, that one has a purpose, a continued role in life. They comfort with touch, make us feel needed and, apparently, make us feel safe. Certainly, there is undisputed evidence that those among the aged and the infirm who have pets live longer than those who do not. And, of course, there are still working dogs today—seeing-eye dogs and hearing-ear dogs—which not only fulfil practical and essential roles for their owners but provide them with companionship and comfort as well. Moreover, studies have shown that for adults and children in wheelchairs the companionship of a dog forms a social bridge to the able-bodied.

It is not, however, only the aged and sick who benefit from the companionship of an animal. Children often feel that if nobody else understands them, the dog will. If a child has been scolded and feels alone the dog or the cat will help overcome that loneliness. The pet's love is unconditional and invariable—as long as it is not treated cruelly. For the adult who has had a bad day at the office or a tiff with the spouse the pet is an undeniable comfort. Moreover, for the lonely, pets make human contacts much easier. If you take the dog for a walk everyone wants to stop and chat. If you walk alone you are usually left alone. And some research has suggested that children argue less and co-operate more when a pet is around.

That humans benefit from animal companionship is beyond dispute. In a responsible home environment pets benefit substantially, too. More than 80 per cent of pet owners consider their companion animals to be family members. They describe their animals in terms of 'love', 'affection', 'companionship', 'trust', 'loyalty', 'need', and 'care'. They are sensitive to the animals' feelings and believe their animals to be sensitive to their own human feelings. At its best, the relationship between human and companion animal constitutes a community of sentient beings. For those who believe that animals other than companion animals are entitled to similar respect and consideration the task is to extend that communal sense beyond its present bounds.

Certainly, we are convinced of the great potential benefits of pet-keeping to both keeper and kept. However that conviction tends to encourage us, and most animal welfarists, to downplay much of the darker side of pet ownership. There is an enormous amount of animal suffering inflicted by breeders attempting to instil an unnatural conformity to artificial standards with little concern for the genetic consequences. Overfeeding, improper feeding, neglect and isolation are often inflicted on pets by careless, ignorant or irresponsible owners. We must bear in mind that, for example, budgerigars are social birds and able fliers, that guinea pigs are essentially social, and that practices which ignore such facts must be of essence cruel to the animals. We must ask how many fish die in transportation to the pet store. We must ask how many puppies are handled to exhaustion by children who want them to play at all times. If pet-keeping is potentially beneficial to both humans and animals that potential will not be achieved unless we concentrate on changing attitudes and providing appropriate education.

Chapter Fourteen

The Community of Sentient Beings

> . . . a very miracle
> Of fellow feeling and communion
> — Alfred Lord Tennyson,
> *The Lover's Tale*

Ralph H. Lutts, professor of Environmental Studies, Audubon Society museum director and author of *The Nature Fakers*, insists that "Our obligation to pets is not a useful guide to understanding our obligations to wild animals."[1] Pets are treated as individuals. Wild animals must be treated as a part of their ecosystems. There "is no need to value and care for individuals. Death and life are opposite sides of the same coin . . . 'nature [is] indifferent to its creatures' suffering'."[2] He writes further that "Caring about the welfare of individual wild animals is not enough if one wants to preserve, conserve and protect wildlife . . . it takes knowledge as well as feeling and love to protect deer."[3] He warns us of the danger of the sentimental "notion that death has no place in nature." Lutts places himself on the side of science, nature, realism and knowledge against the sentimentalism he derides in animal rights and animal welfare advocates.

Discomforting as Lutts's assertions may be, he is making some telling points, though perhaps with not quite the force he imagines. Our obligation to pets does differ somewhat from our obligation to wildlife because of the community relationship we enjoy with our companion animals. Because humankind has so damaged the planet we inhabit, if we are to save it we must consider the interests of our ecosystems as prior to that of individual wildlife. Both zebra mussels and ring-billed gulls pose a serious environmental threat at present in or around the Great Lakes. But we must not forget that it is the human population explosion and humankind's interference in nature which has brought about most of such problems. If we do not succeed very rapidly in decreasing the human population there will be no ecosystems left to be concerned about. There can be little point in putting the importance of our ecosystems above that of individual wildlife if we do not also place it above that of humankind's right to breed at will and overpopulate—

---

1 Ralph H. Lutts, *The Nature Fakers* (Golden, CO: Fulcrum, 1990), p. 195.
2 Ibid., p. 196.
3 Ibid., p. 198.

244 Animal Welfare and Human Values

with the consequent devastation to our own as well as the wildlife's habitat. Lutts recognizes only a part of the ecological problem, and by far the less damaging part at that. It is certainly true that we must look beyond the welfare of the individual animal toward species and ecological interest. But it is equally true that, to the extent that species and ecological interests are not incompatible with the interests of the individual animal, then the individual is of paramount significance.

We must certainly recognize the necessity of the cycle of life and death in nature and we must restrain our natural propensity to side with one animal—a bird perhaps—over another—say a snake—when the one has chosen the other for a meal. We must indeed not interfere. And we must recognize that the bug is as important to the ecology as a rabbit. But we must also avoid assuming any unnecessary suffering or death as somehow nature's will. Of course, as Lutts says, one needs knowledge as well as feeling and love. But let us not forget that we need feeling and love as well as knowledge. Those who claim they have the knowledge sometimes lack the affection. The animal world is in large part a world of predator and prey. We must accept this as a part of nature's necessity. We must not misrepresent nature's beauty. But we must accept the killing and the suffering *only* when they are a part of nature's necessity.

When we read Dr. Lutts's admonitions we wonder at their purpose, where they are leading. We are not left long in the dark. In the guise of science and realism we are once again being offered a defence of hunting! Lutts tells the story of how the removal of over 6,000 predators from Arizona Kaibab National Forest between 1906 and 1923 pushed the number of deer from 4,000 in 1906 to 100,000 by 1925, and by 1927 more than half had died of disease and starvation. The predators had, of course, been removed to "ensure good hunting." It was the lack of predators which had brought about the huge increase in deer population which in turn over-browsed and over-ate the vegetation. "Recent hunting debates," Lutts tells us, "suggest that animal rights advocates have not learned this lesson."

But what is the lesson? Obviously Lutts thinks that the lesson is that predation is necessary in nature. And so it is. But there are other lessons to be learned too. First, that authorities should not have interfered with the roles of predators and prey to promote the interests of the hunter. Without both interference with the natural order of things *and* hunting the balance of nature was being harmoniously maintained. It is clear that the authorities lacked the knowledge to intervene in a manner that was not ecologically damaging. And the activities of hunters were unnecessary to the maintenance of a sound environment.

Second, despite the activities of hunters for whom the policy was instituted the disaster still occurred. Hence the claim that hunting restores the balance is invalid. It was the desires of hunters which upset the balance in the first place. Third, such stories are almost always about deer, or perhaps beaver, rarely about other species and, of course, it is deer which are most avidly hunted—and beaver which are frequently trapped. Lutts gives us two more examples of the need for hunting—both about deer. Why, we wonder, are such stories never about porcupines or about shrews? In reality it is because the problems are caused by humankind's unnatural intervention. No one has bothered to remove the porcupine's predators—since porcupine are not customarily hunted other than for control purposes—and an imbalance has not arisen.

It can, however, be legitimately argued that humankind's disturbance of the environment through deforestation and other atrocities brought about by the human population explosion now requires intervention to maintain stable and balanced animal and habitat relationships. That is, indeed, an unfortunate consequence of the human population increase. But even if we were to have the knowledge of precisely what was required, hunting would not be the answer, for hunting is based on humankind's lowest appetites. What is needed is veneration, and hunting—except where it is required for food—is destructive of veneration. If we are to maintain appropriate population sizes and nature does not offer a ready solution, the answer lies in sterilization, not killing. Some progress has already been made in developing sterilization darts. They should be rapidly perfected. Then if hunters really believe that it is the skill not the killing which motivates them, let them hunt with sterilization darts not bullets.

The prime lesson we should learn from Lutts's accounts is that hunting usually disturbs rather than promotes the balance of nature, and the 'resource management' to promote the 'harvest' for hunters fails to produce a satisfactory solution. If the problem were not one caused in large part by hunting one would expect the predicament to arise with equal frequency among non-hunted species. It is incumbent upon us to note that nature has its own way of dealing with these hunter-made ecological problems. As Lutts points out, by 1927 the deer population had been more than halved by disease and starvation. Given time, nature has a solution even to the avarice of the hunter. The hunter created the problems. But it did not need the hunter to solve the problem. Hunting to promote the interests of the hunter and hunting to solve the problems caused by the hunter are equally ignorant of nature's laws. If we must intervene because ecological considerations require it we must ensure that the intervention is one that considers the whole of the ecology, not merely that which affects the immediate selfish human interest. Culling may be an occasional necessity but it can never be justified to uphold human dominance over nature. The human is an intrinsic part of the natural order. To pursue the immediate human interest at the expense of the health of the whole planet is to destroy the human environment as well as that of the animal and plant realms. We must consider all life as a part of one interrelated community with a common interest. We can no longer afford to consider human interests outside of the interests of the remainder of the planet.

It is precisely because Lutts and others take the unwarranted step of using 'science', and 'realism' and 'environmental concerns' to defend hunting that animal advocates are inclined to ignore the significance of the assertions on which the hunting argument is predicated, i.e., the recognition that individual animal, species and ecological interests may be incompatible on at least some occasions. And if that is so we cannot simply look philosophically at questions of animal rights solely in terms of the right not to suffer, as the animal liberationist insists. We might add, though, that similar considerations require us to recognize that we can no longer afford to think in terms of the human right to live as one pleases provided one does not interfere with the rights of other humans to live as they please, which is in essence the classical liberal creed. Today we must acknowledge that doing as one pleases has occasioned an ecological catastrophe. Today we *must* think primarily in terms of our responsibilities not our freedoms, our obligations not our choices. And our responsibilities are not merely to the human community but to all life on this planet and even to the planet itself.

Humankind has come late to its recognition of the ecological disaster it has perpetrated. Increasingly, though, since the early sixties, it penetrated our consciousness and by the early nineties it has become the paramount Western concern. It is this recognition which has led such ecologists as Ralph Lutts to insist that we cannot afford to view animals in terms of individual rights. At the same time other ecologists, Warwick Fox for example, tell us that we should be "moving away from human-centredness."[4] This, of course, leaves us with a paradox. We must recognize ourselves as a part of the interrelated planetary whole with commensurate obligations to all life, but the interest of the whole requires us to over-ride the individual rights of animals. The argument is persuasive—though we must insist that, if it is to go uncontested, it also implies that the interest of the whole requires us to over-ride the individual rights of humans. Others whose concerns are more mundane and anthropocentric claim that we should forget the plight of animals and concentrate on ridding the world of the exploitation of humans. Yet others insist on the need to extend human rights to the animal realm. These competing conceptions of the good are complex and involve perplexing philosophical problems to which we shall return[5]—though not without considerable trepidation as to our ability even to begin to

---

4   Warwick Fox, *Toward a Transpersonal Ecology* (Boston: Shambhala, 1990), p. 3.
5   See below, Chapter 15.

weave our way through the maze. For now we need to ask whether there can be a community of sentient beings in which rights and obligations are interrelated.

A community is a body which shares certain interests in common, has a common purpose, a common belongingness, as a consequence of which the members have certain obligations to each other. Clearly we share life with all living things, including plants and micro-organisms. Yet any obligation we may have to the latter can only come from an intellectual recognition of rights or interests. We do not share a fellow feeling with plants or micro-organisms although we may revel in the beauty of a particularly attractive flower or tree. There is no sense of community with plants and organisms except in the limited if important sense of a recognition of the interrelatedness and interdependence of all living beings. We may well have obligations to all life and even more to all sentience, but we may have even greater obligations to those with whom we share a felt relationship, to those who are members of any one of the many felt communities to which we belong, all of which have interconnecting relationships to each other.

Family is our most tightly knit community, though, in the Western world especially, individualism and social and occupational mobility have diminished the traditional concept of family. Still, even in the West it is commonly acknowledged that we have greater responsibilities to, and a greater sense of sharing with, members of our families: our offspring, spouses, parents, siblings and close or even sometimes distant relatives, than we do to and with others. Since 80 per cent of pet owners have been reported as considering their companion animals as family members, there can be little doubt that there is a feeling of common belonging, of community, with animals.

If not to the same degree as family, we feel greater obligations to our compatriots in a work environment, in a political or sporting or service association, in a church community or a nation than to those who do not belong. This is because we share a part of our identity with them as well as our interests. Of course, we feel differing degrees of identity—and differing degrees of commonality—dependent upon the significance of the particular group or association to our own individual identity and in differing degrees as circumstance and issues alter. We tend to feel a greater sense of belonging to the extent that the association is under threat. There is a greater fellow feeling among, and more consideration toward, fellow nationals in a time of defensive, and sometimes aggressive, war. But at all times we have to balance our differing community relationships as their differing interests are in conflict. It is thus that we recognize that our decisions concerning what is right and what we ought to do are influenced by the significance to us of a particular community and its relationship to other communities to which we belong.

Our sense of obligation to our companion animals is greater than to wildlife because of the communal relationship of the companion animal to us. Our fellows in the human community are, to most people, of greater significance than the animal realm in general because we share more with other people than we do with other animals. Our sense of commonality—of community—with the animal realm is increased by our recognition of the threat it faces from the cruel and the careless.

We are not suggesting that our sense of community is the only factor which affects our obligations—our moral consideration for other beings—but that it is an important one. The question we wish to raise is whether it can be extended legitimately to non-human animals. It is an important question because, as we have seen in each of the issues we have discussed, our degree of fellow feeling with animals, our sensibilities toward them, are prime factors in determining answers to each of the questions. Each requires a balancing of certain human interests with certain animal ones for us to come to a conclusion. What we feel we owe to the animals in considering their interests depends in large part on how much we feel we are like them and, perhaps what is not quite the same thing, how much they are like us, i.e., how much we *share* as animals. Prima facie the more we share the more we owe. It is in part a question of balancing the competing interests of our differing community relationships and the greater, or lesser, sense of belonging we have with the animal realm, especially with those parts which we feel closest to ourselves. The degree of the sense of belonging materially affects the balance.

Historically in fact community and universality or equality have been viewed as antithetical to each other. As our conceptions of rights and equality have been extended to encompass those previously excluded so we have become inclined to think in universalistic and egalitarian terms to the exclusion of the more parochial and community-oriented terms. This, it seems to us, has been a grievous error, since it ignores the reality of our concrete relationships to specific others.

It has, of course, been appropriate to extend our moral awareness to the inappropriateness of race or gender or ethnicity as barriers to, say, education or equal consideration before the law or designations of moral worth. And it has been right to extend our moral considerations to other animals, too, if not in the same manner as our extension to other humans. But it has been inappropriate to do this at the expense of belongingness, of fellow feeling, of community, with specific others to which we owe our identity as social creatures. In reality it is certain humans, not humanity, we love, certain animals, not species, we number as friends. This is not a bar to our respect for all of sentient life but it reflects the reality of social life. The concentration on universalistic and egalitarian criteria of 'the public good' has led us into the realm of abstraction and logic at the expense of concreteness and feelings. When we deal in universalistic and egalitarian concepts everything is made the same. When we employ communitarian concepts we are led to recognize the differences.

Peter Singer tells us in the preface to his *Animal Liberation* that he and his wife "didn't love animals":

> We tried to explain that we were interested in the prevention of suffering and misery; that we were opposed to arbitrary discrimination; that we thought it wrong to inflict needless suffering on another being even if that being were not of our own species; and that we believed animals were ruthlessly and cruelly exploited by humans, and we wanted this changed. Otherwise, we said, we were not especially 'interested in' animals. Neither of us had ever been inordinately fond of dogs, cats, or horses in the way that many people are.[6]

Admirable as Singer's concerns are to eliminate suffering and cruelty they are the concerns of a philosopher, of a logician. They are concerns expressed because he believes the *logic* of morals requires it, not because he has a fellow feeling with the animals. As Friedrich Tönnies, the philosopher of *Gemeinschaft*, averred, love is the essence of community. What we derive from universalism and egalitarianism is impartiality, and impartiality is always at the expense of the partiality we feel toward our specific loved ones. Morality requires our recognition of a certain kind of equal consideration for all, but were we to predicate our behaviour solely on such a consideration we would be deprived of our essentially social and communitarian natures. If all are to be treated equally we must lose the love inherent in our most significant relationships.

In the final analysis if we rely on universality, impartiality and equality we are nothing other than Hobbes's autonomous individuals. Hobbes would then be right that only the other animals are social. In fact not only are humans social but each individual's identity is affected by social relationships. This is especially so in a sound marriage—something increasingly difficult to achieve in highly individualistic Western society. But it is what Oscar Wilde meant when he wrote that "in married life three is company and two none." Numerous Christian marriage ceremonies refer to a "mystical union" and to two being "made one." What is meant is that in an essentially shared relationship our identity, our conception of ourselves, our self-recognition are materially altered. And if no other relationship affects our identity as much as that of a marriage there are many relationships which do impinge on what we see ourselves as. Thus our feelings, our emotions, our partialities do, and should, impinge on our attitudes and behaviour

---

6 Singer, *Animal Liberation*, p. ii.

toward others. Impartiality, universality and equality are not enough. Shared relationships are the very source of our feelings. There must be some balance between the impartial logic of morality and the moral attitudes inspired by partial relationships.

This is important to the consideration of animal welfare issues because, as we have seen throughout this book, the degree to which one believes one ought to seek alternatives to animal experimentation or to eliminate hunting or to treat farm animals better is materially affected by our degree of identity with the animals at least as much as by the logic of moral consideration.

Peter Singer's views and those of the animal liberationists in general are predicated on considering humans and other animals as in some manner morally equal. What we have suggested throughout this book is that non-human animals are entitled to a great deal more respect than they are customarily given even though they may not be morally equal. This is largely because all sentient creatures are, in differing degrees, entitled to our consideration because we share so much with them. In some cases, as with companion animals, our and their identities are materially affected by the relationship. In other cases, we owe consideration because we extend the consideration we feel we owe to those who are a part of the relationship to all who share characteristics in common with those who are a part of the relationship.

For Singer, the principles he expresses are "demanded by reason, not emotion."[7] For us, the principle of consideration is demanded by emotion, by feelings—which are, anyway, not inconsistent with reason. Indeed, they are the starting point of rational considerations. We use reason to develop, refine and order our sensibilities. Reason, reflection, introspection are an important part in a search inside of ourselves for, and a raising to consciousness of, the inner feelings which constitute our human nature. It is reason which elucidates and refines the moral sensibilities which constitute the essence of our moral nature. Reason is necessary to the expression of morals but reason does not discover our morality. It merely elucidates our natural compassion.

Jean-Jacques Rousseau tells us there are two principles which motivate human behaviour: self-preservation and compassion. Following Francis Bacon, and Bernard Mandeville in *The Fable of the Bees*, Rousseau tells us that when our self-preservation is not at stake we have a "natural compassion" toward others "which the most depraved moral habits can destroy only with difficulty."[8] Compassion is "a natural

---

7   Ibid., p. iii.
8   Jean-Jacques Rousseau, *Discourse on the Origin and Foundations of Inequality Among Men* (1755), in *Rousseau's Political Writings*, ed. Alan Ritter and Julia Conaway Bondanella (New York: W.W. Norton, 1988), p. 28.

sentiment which [moderates] the activity of self-esteem in each individual."[9] For Rousseau, compassion was spoken "directly by nature's voice" and was anterior to reason. Indeed, reason—at least the 'reason' of the Enlightenment and of the age of science and learning—moved us further away from our natural moral sentiments. Reason hindered rather than expressed our natural compassion. And it is no exaggeration to claim that this natural compassion exists in animals other than humankind. The eighteenth-century Scottish philosopher David Hume tells us that a horse will naturally step over a sentient object it finds in its path. In a wildlife park it is not uncommon to find a lion and a tiger snuggling up together. If properly introduced to each other dogs and cats will show considerable compassion for the interests of each other. Cynthia Moss in her *Elephant Memories* tells us how elephants will go out of their way to avoid hurting, even though one swipe of the trunk could kill a 1,000 pound cow. And far more, of course, animals will demonstrate the greatest concern for members of their own species—provided, as Bacon, Mandeville and Rousseau tell us of humans, their own preservation is not at stake. If this natural compassion constitutes the essence of human morality—and we would claim that it does—then other animals as well as humans have a significant moral sense. The more complex animals not only share reason and emotions with humankind but morality as well.

We would in fact claim that, despite Singer's assertion that his principles are "demanded by reason, not emotion," his principles too are predicated on feelings. Moreover, we would not only claim it to be true for Singer but for all moral theory—whatever the protestations about reason rather than emotion. Singer asserts his principles by quoting from Bentham on the question of who possesses rights. Bentham asserts that the question of moral agency is not whether the agent can reason or speak but whether it can suffer. Neither Bentham nor Singer ever proves this. Indeed proof is impossible. The truth of Bentham's assertion is tested by application of the principle to various instances. In the final analysis we are asked to accept or reject the principle by determining whether its implications are in accord with our intuitions—ultimately our feelings and emotions. Reason is employed to determine how we ultimately *feel* about suffering by analyzing various instances of the principle's application. The principle is acceptable if it is in accord with those deepest understandings/feelings within our nature, rejected if it is not. And the means of rejection is by consideration of whether there are instances in which the principle does not seem to apply. However, even if we do find such instances—one of which we have already mentioned with regard to ecology[10]—this does

---

9 Ibid., p. 29.
10 See above, pp. 246-47.

not require us to consider the principle completely inapplicable. It would merely imply that it is not the sole applicable principle. As we shall argue in the next chapter,[11] there are several appropriate and not always compatible principles which apply. And that makes consideration of human as well as animal rights an extremely difficult task.

If community and morality are somehow dependent on feelings, we are required to ask about the nature of the human-animal community, for we have already suggested that the degree of obligation is affected in part by the degree of belongingness, of fellow feeling. And we tend to feel most strongly for those with whom we share something important to us. Clearly, we share less with the animal realm in general than we do with other humans. Our sense of attachment, of responsibility, is affected further, however, both by the reciprocity of the relationship and the compassion we feel most strongly for those we consider oppressed.

Community, by definition, cannot be a one-way street; it requires a degree of mutuality. A community requires *fellow* feelings, i.e., all members of the community must have feelings toward each other. In a lesser sense, of course, all a community needs is a commonality, a sharing of interests in common in some significant manner. Were we to treat the concept in that manner it would go without saying that there is a community not merely of sentient beings but of all life—for all life has a common interest in the continued existence of this planet. What we are more concerned with here is a shared feeling toward each other. For there to be a community in that sense animals must have an attachment to humans as well as vice versa. None of us would deny such an attachment in the case of companion animals. But how much further can such an attachment go?

A community need not be a community of equals. The most close-knit traditional human communities have had rigid hierarchical structures with the greatest inequalities. A family relationship is a complex interdependence of differing levels of authority. In the Chinese extended family this requires a veneration for grandparents as well as parents. Even in the modern Western family where there may be a spousal equality, that usually implies different authority relationships with regard to different matters. But even if that is not so there is a hierarchy among siblings. Moreover, infants, the mentally handicapped and the senile belong to a family—are a part of the community—as much as any other.

Equality is not at all a necessary attribute of a community. What matters is mutual need and a feeling of affection, of belonging. And humankind has received considerable affection from cetaceans (especially dolphins), the felids (especially lions), the canids (especially wolves), the great apes (chimpanzees, gorillas and orangutans),

---

11 See below, pp. 265-66.

elephants (especially Indian elephants) as well as the more customary companion animals. The community of sentient beings is not merely a feeling from humankind toward other species but *from* them too. And experience indicates that such fellow feeling can extend well beyond the customary companion animals. In fact pigs, skunk, moose, raccoon, bear, deer, dolphins, whales and many more have entered into constructive and affective animal-human relationships. If that is so, then, as we have extended our natural affection for those closest to us to a recognition of universal human rights, so too, we should extend our affection for specific animals to the realm of sentient beings in general. But just as our responsibilities are greatest to those closest to us in the human community and secondarily to the oppressed, so too our responsibilities toward the animal realm are greatest to those with whom we share the most and secondarily, in accord with Gandhi's dictum, to those who are the most helpless and the most exploited. It is in fact our exploitation of the animal realm historically—and currently—which has hindered a more extensive communal recognition.

The fact that the community of sentient beings is not a community of equals may increase, rather than decrease, our responsibilities. Just as we have a greater responsibility to infants, the mentally and physically handicapped, and the oppressed than to humankind in general, so too we have greater responsibilities to the animal realm when it is mistreated than when it is treated well.

Oliver Goldsmith said of Samuel Johnson's attitude toward a hapless soul, "he has become miserable, and that insures the protection of Johnson." Gandhi extended the same principle to animals. "The more helpless a creature, the more entitled it is to protection by man from the cruelty of man." We owe protection to the oppressed not because the logic of morality requires it but because of our natural compassion which applies to the animal realm in principle less than to humankind in general but more than to those unoppressed humans who do not require our protection, to those who have no need of our compassion. And the relationship between our responsibilities to humans and to animals is affected by the degree of similarity we perceive between the human and the animal realm. Given a recognition of the essential similarity between human and animal, our natural compassion encourages us to treat animals as intrinsic members of one of our communities.

But if that is so, why, historically, have we not done so? It is in part because Western understanding has been 'scientific' and 'parsimonious'.[12] Western science has been motivated by only one of Rousseau's two motives. Compassion has been subverted by self-preservation and self-interest, even if sometimes 'enlightened' self-interest. It is to

---

12 For a discussion of the concept of parsimony, see above, p. 41.

literature rather than to science and philosophy to which we must look for a recognition of humankind's relationship to the natural world. Yet even literature from the age of Milton until Romanticism avoided 'nature' and the expression of emotion.

The classic school of literature shunned as vulgar all exhibitions of strong emotion and enthusiasm. Everything had to be orderly, serene and, in short, classical. Nature, if it was mentioned, was neat, tidy and clean. It wasn't 'natural' at all. The classic school corresponded to the school of scientific thought. Truth was clear, cold and unemotional. Beginning in the mid-eighteenth century, however, there began a movement toward a recognition of the power of imagination to perceive a reality deeper and more meaningful than that known to the physical senses alone. Sometimes, of course, Romanticism exceeded its own boundaries, exhibiting *unbridled* passion and *uncontrolled* sensibilities—passion and sensibility not grounded in experience and beyond subjection to reason. But always it added a profound spirituality to the timid world of the mundane. Sometimes it was excessively sentimental but always it inspired an appreciation of nature and its spiritual significance.

The poetry of the Romantic movement was the poetry of wonder and mystery. It offered answers to questions which science and classicism did not know to ask. The nature it admired was not the neat, ordered nature of the manicured garden but the wild and mysterious nature beyond human control. No longer was nature admired because it was useful to humankind but because it involved the recognition of a world of mystery and imagination beyond human self-satisfaction and self-interest.

What Romanticism did above all else was to place humankind within the world of nature and extolled our relationship with, rather than our dominance of, the rest of the sensible world. It described emotions with care and detail and raised sympathy for others over self. At its worst it exhibited a tasteless lack of restraint. At its best it demonstrated a splendid confusion of pathos and sagacity, irony and passion. Of course, the scientific mind would consider the confusion merely disorder. But for the Romantic the confusion merely demonstrated a deeper understanding of reality. Charles Caleb Colton summed up the Romantic attitude in his *Lacon*: "Man is an embodied paradox, a bundle of contradictions." Radical political doctrines sought to transcend the contradictions. Science ignored the contradictions because to acknowledge them would be to eschew order (although its recent appreciation of chaos theory may permit science to overcome its traditional limitations). Romanticism revelled in the contradictions because it recognized them as the inexorable, ineradicable human condition.

In modern parlance we are apt to equate Romanticism with the unreal and the absurd. But in fact that is only because prevalent conceptions of the real depend upon a very limited view of the human mind and fail to comprehend humankind's empathetic character which, if unrestrained by cynical science, reaches out to the whole of nature, knowing that it belongs within but is also its apex—at least for some matters and for some of the time.

It is the Romantic attitude coupled with Darwinian science which leads to the recognition of the human place within nature. They encourage us to recognize our similarities to the animal realm. Peter Farb writes in his *Humankind* that:

> Scientists now know that the chasm separating humans from animals is not so wide as it once appeared. Some animal species have evolved a rich communication system, while others make and use tools, solve difficult problems, educate their young, live in complex social organizations, and apparently possess an aesthetic sense. So any definition of human uniqueness obviously would have to be based on differences in degree.[13]

Now some have argued that this is an inappropriate way of looking at the animals, simply giving them the status of inferior and defective humans. Warwick Fox, for example, insists that "just as there are lots of things that humans have more of or do much better than many other animals, so the reverse is also true."[14] And John Rodman claims that such comparisons degrade animals by failing "to respect them for having their own existence, their own character and potentialities, their own form of excellence, their own integrity, their own grandeur."[15]

Fox and Rodman's points are well taken. Yet the point does not have to be that animals are like humans but not as good, although we acknowledge that is how such statements are frequently perceived. It is certainly worth emphasizing the sonar system of the dolphins, the speed of the cheetah and the pronghorn, the flight of the birds, the grace of the felids, the power of the elephant, the protectiveness of a myriad of animal mothers, and so on.[16] But that is in fact saying that in these respects humans are like animals but not as good. What should be stressed is that despite the differences one should recognize with Honoré de Balzac that "There is but one animal. The Creator [or nature, or evolution, if one prefers] used one and the same principle for all organized beings." And it is a principle which allows for fellow feeling among members of that organization.

---

13 Peter Farb, *Humankind* (St. Albans: Triad, 1978), pp. 12-13.
14 Fox, *Toward a Transpersonal Ecology*, p. 15.
15 "The Liberation of Nature?" *Inquiry* 20 (1977): 94. Quoted in ibid.
16 A reading of Desmond Morris's *Animalwatching* is to be heartily recommended to those who want to understand the remarkable achievements of animals.

Following in the steps of the literary Romantics came the nature Romantics of the late nineteenth century. Such naturalists as Ernest Thompson Seton, Charles G.D. Roberts, William J. Long and Jack London stimulated Canadians and Americans to an awareness of the wonders of the wilderness. They roused an environmental and endangered species protection movement which has only in recent years been rekindled. Unfortunately they sometimes 'romanticized'—in the pejorative sense of that term—the activities of wildlife and described their behaviour in inappropriately excessive and inaccurately anthropomorphic terms. Occasionally—but not always—they left the impression that nature was a place without struggle, fear or pain. Nature consisted in nobility and beauty—which it does—but there was little of the other side of the coin. Predation was rarely mentioned—nor were the lice, fleas, worms and parasites which infested the noble and beautiful.

In 1903 an article by John Burroughs appeared in *The Atlantic Monthly* denouncing the 'sham naturalists' who invented 'facts' and who described the world of nature as they wanted to see it, not as it was. The debate raged in newspapers, magazines and books for about four years. The avid hunter Teddy Roosevelt jumped on the Burroughs bandwagon. In the short run the 'science' and 'realism' of Burroughs won out over the fellow feeling and communitarian spirit of the nature *lovers*—to the lasting detriment of humankind's recognition of its relationship to the world of the beasts. Burroughs represented the behaviouralist, mechanistic, abstracted, atomistic perspective on understanding; Ernest Thompson Seton and his associates, the communitarian, involved and activist alternative. For Burroughs and his behaviouralist followers animal behaviour is to be understood as instinctive and conditioned. For Seton it is creative and rational. Despite Seton's exaggerations, as Noel Perrin has written, "the experience of the past eighty years tends to support Seton more."[17] Even Ralph Lutts, who takes the side of science against sentiment, begrudgingly acknowledges the contribution of the 'nature romantics' to our understanding of wildlife. In fact the whole of the modern ethological approach to animal behaviour supports the methods of the so-called 'nature-fakers' and 'sham-naturalists' even if we must, along with Burroughs and Lutts, recognize that the latter took undue liberties in their reporting of 'facts' and even if they were sometimes more story-tellers than they were chroniclers of natural conditions.

It is decidedly inappropriate to disregard the findings of the nature romantics because they imposed their values on the wildlife they studied. This is after all precisely what the behaviouralists and mechanists do too. Their paradigm is one of a world which is self-

---

17 Noel Perrin, "Introduction," in Ernest Thompson Seton, *Wild Animals I Have Known* (Harmondsworth: Penguin, 1987) (original edition 1898), p. xiii.

serving and self-preserving. But, as Rousseau recognized, that is only half the story. There is also a natural compassion which, we have suggested, exists in the animal as well as the human realm. To understand nature is to understand both its self-centredness and its compassion.

It is unfortunate that the term 'Romantic' has received such a bad press. It is customarily employed to mean unpractical, quixotic, dreamy and remote from experience. Like the term 'animal rights' it has come to be used as a term of abuse despite its venerable history. But if we recognize that the Romantic is one who understands that there is another side to nature beyond the simplistic behaviouralist one, that imagination as well as analysis is a source of understanding, that we are an intrinsic part of nature and not outside it, that we are creatures of other-regarding passion as well as self-interest and reason, then we can come to recognize that the Romantic image is closer to reality than the barren world of scientific parsimony.[18]

After Darwin and the Romantic school of literature no one has done more than the great ape ethologists to stir humankind's recognition of similarity to creatures other than ourselves. Some of these ethologists—most notably Jane Goodall, Dian Fossey and Biruté Galdikas—have also become a part of the ape communities they have studied. There can be no substitute for reading their own words if one wants to understand the relationship of the famous ape ladies to their animals, although Sy Montgomery's *Walking with the Great Apes*[19] is a fascinating second-hand account. But we will try to give a short sketch, however inadequate it must be.

The essential difference between the relationship between ourselves and our companion animals or livestock and that of the ape ladies with their chimpanzees, gorillas and orangutans is that the former is decidedly on our terms and the latter on the animals' terms. Pets and livestock have entered our world. Louis Leakey's researchers have entered the world of apes. (Louis Leakey was the paleontologist who sponsored and found the funding for the pongid studies.)

The researchers set out to create a privileged trust between themselves and their apes and each in a different manner succeeded. Their feelings toward *their* animals developed rapidly into belonging and love. Each proudly reports the engaging characteristics of the beasts they study. Each, as Montgomery writes, "is firmly convinced that the animals she loves are the best. For they do love them. It's a love as deep and as passionate as the love one has for a child or a spouse or a lover; but it is a love unlike any other."[20]

---

18 Again, on parsimony, see above, p. 41.
19 Sy Montgomery, *Walking with the Great Apes* (Boston: Houghton Mifflin, 1991).
20 Ibid., p. xix.

Of course, this may diminish the impartiality, the objectivity, of their findings. If one is involved with one's research subject then one's objectivity suffers. While that is true, one has to be impressed with the degree to which each of the researchers has limited the extent of the problem. Still, many scientists insist that this is a serious detriment to their studies. They are in danger of becoming the late twentieth-century 'nature fakers'. Being involved, being committed, sharing, all interfere with the search for truth. There is some merit in such criticism. However, it fails to recognize that it is precisely by becoming involved that one extends one's horizons, one recognizes patterns and characteristics that would otherwise be missed, one sees beyond the external behaviour to the intricate world of the apes' emotions. While there is a danger that one may inappropriately impose one's own feelings on the apes there is an even greater danger in distanced understanding that one will not recognize the complexities and depth of emotions for what they are. On balance the ape ladies have demonstrated that their approach is superior to that of the 'objective' scientist, at least in the understanding of primates in the wild. Through understanding, in the sense of feeling at one with, our knowledge of the behaviour of the apes has been greatly enhanced. One cannot understand fully without empathy for the life of the ape. If there are 'scientific' dangers in being inside rather than outside one's study there are even greater 'scientific' drawbacks in being outside—one will simply not share, and hence not fully understand, the emotions and the creativity one is witnessing. After all, we can only fully understand other humans by recognizing in them aspects of their personalities we understand in ourselves. This is not to say that we possess identical characteristics, merely that we share in differing degrees in our own natures and propensities what we see in them. Our understanding of other humans depends upon our successfully recognizing similarities *and* differences, but differences which develop from a certain underlying similarity. And so it is with understanding the apes. What should astonish us is that the similarities are far greater than we might ever have imagined—including aspects of behaviour we might find less than appealing (instances of rape among both the chimpanzees and the orangutans, for example). However, Goodall also describes the chimpanzees' significant sense of self as individuals, and their sense of humour.

Goodall describes the intellectual and emotional similarity of chimpanzees to humans. The games of the young, the greetings of the mature, the relationship of mother to child are in many respects almost identical to ours in their basic structure. Goodall claims to have learned a great deal from a chimpanzee named Flo—all the researchers named their apes—on the art of motherhood. She describes the stresses brought on by the loss of a loved one. "Flint," she said, "died of grief."

Dian Fossey wrote of "sharing something with the gorillas," of Digit as being her friend and of the cohesion of the gorilla family unit (far stronger than with chimpanzees, somewhat stronger than with the orangutans). One feels especially when reading Fossey that our language is always inadequate to describe the animal-human bond, although the same sense comes across in the other account as well. This is in large part because the language we employ to describe emotion and belonging was developed in an era which recognized only the self-interested side. Our language is predicated on a behaviouralist approach to understanding. It is inadequate to express fully the sentiments of community, sharing and belonging. Certainly, our language makes it easy to work within the behaviouralist paradigm, difficult to express oneself adequately outside of it. Thus it is that Fossey was always aware that she lacked the tools to describe what she implicitly understood. It was not Fossey's fault, but the circumscription of language designed to express an individualistic mode of conception.

Leakey chose women to conduct the research because he believed that women are both "blessed and cursed," according to Tita Caldwell, "with sensitivity and intuition that only one in a million men have."[21] In Western culture 'manliness' was traditionally understood as competitive, striving and individualistic, whereas 'womanliness' has traditionally implied sharing, altruism and belongingness. Certainly, the ape ladies have brought these qualities to bear in their studies. In Goodall's communications with the chimp she named David Greybeard she tells us that "the soft pressure of his fingers spoke to me not through my intellect but through a more primitive emotional channel: The barrier of untold centuries which has grown up during the separate evolution of man and chimpanzee was, for those few seconds, broken down."

Of course, our language is inadequate to express what Goodall experienced. But even more importantly it should be recognized that an impartial uninvolved approach, requiring 'objective' scientific evidence could never have permitted Goodall, or ourselves via Goodall, to understand the significance of the event. It can only be comprehended through intuition and imagination and as a mysterious but meaningful part of the animal-human bond.

Aristotle tells us that when there is envy or contempt there can be no friendship and that community depends on friendship.[22] There are, according to Aristotle, many varieties and different qualities of friendship with different purposes.[23] What Goodall, Fossey and Galdikas have with their apes is a very special form of friendship in which there is no remnant of contempt of the human for a 'lower' species but a

---

21 Ibid., p. 83.
22 Aristotle, *Politics*, V, xi, 7.
23 Ibid., VIII, passim.

community relationship in which questions of higher and lower are never raised. It is a bond. As Helfer says of the animals alone, but we might add of the apes and their human friends, they "listen to one perfect voice—nature's voice—and do as it bids them."[24] While it is an interspecies association it is one entirely in accord with nature. It reflects the extent to which the animal-human bond may be developed. Moreover, as David Greybeard's actions indicate, it is not a one-way street.

It is, we are now increasingly and rightly told, the lens of theory and methodology that clouds vision, not the focus of empathy. The 'trimates', as these researchers are now sometimes called, have discovered a wealth, a richness, of knowledge denied to those who remain scientifically uninvolved. They have stimulated others, almost entirely women, to enter the same kinds of relationships to gain *both* kinds of understanding: Alison Jolly with lemurs, Barbara Smuts and Shirley Strum with baboons and Cynthia Moss with elephants—the only one of Leakey's researchers to enter the non-primate field. Men, Leakey believed, soon lose patience with their study. They enter the field, discover what they want to know and move on. Women retain their loyalty and their dedication—Goodall now for over 30 years.

Biruté Galdikas, the least well-known of the trimates, said of Dian Fossey after one of her well-known tantrums, "I didn't realize at that time that Dian was a gorilla." The only way to explain Fossey's behaviour was to recognize that she had accepted the rank orderings of gorilla society. She had, to all intents and purposes, become one of them. Neither Goodall nor Galdikas, despite their love for *their* apes, have given up their humanness. They have established relationships with, but not become one, of the apes.

Galdikas waited eight years before she saw an orangutan use a tool. The patience required is phenomenal. She witnessed and described the rape of adult females by subadult males—a not infrequent occurrence. She is the most 'scientific' of the three—she co-authored a fascinating paper on the use of different food sources by males and females in both orangutan and chimpanzee colonies and suggested that this could well be the origins of the division of labour—hunting males and foraging females. Despite this she always self-confessedly puts the orangutans, and her relationship with the orangutans, above science.

Because of their relationships with the animals each of the ape ladies puts the interests of her own ape colony above that of other members of the species and the colony species above other species.[25] The relationship is a truly communitarian one. For the triumvirate the apes became their extended families. Each has a sense of belonging

---

24 Helfer, *The Beauty of the Beasts*, p. 45.
25 See Montgomery, *Walking with the Great Apes*, Sec. 3, pp. 193ff.

which requires greater responsibilities to those with whom one shares the community than to others, and to those who most closely resemble the characteristics of the members of the community more than to animalkind in general.

Now, of course, it could be readily argued that apes as our closest evolutionary relatives are more appropriate for a human-animal relationship than species which are more distant from us. And there is, of course, some truth in this. Clearly, a relationship with, say, a spider would be rather fanciful and scarcely meaningful, although we may still treat the spider's web-building capacity with appropriate awe and learn from its tenacity, as did Robert the Bruce. Still, we know from our relationships with companion animals that non-primate relationships can be both meaningful and productive, as we saw in the previous chapter. Moreover, R.D. Lawrence and Farley Mowat have written extensively on their relationships with wolves. There is beauty and depth in the relationship between Ralph Helfer and his lion, Zamba. And Cynthia Moss feels herself a part of the elephant world even if it is not at all to the degree of Dian Fossey in her gorilla world.

While one should not make too much of brain sizes it is still worth noting that the brain-to-body size measurement of the human is some three times that of the chimpanzee but only 40 per cent greater than that of the dolphin. It is seven times that of the dog, which is slightly greater than that of the wild pig and the cat. Immediately below the great apes and the rhesus monkey comes the elephant, some 70 per cent larger than the dog and some 30-odd per cent smaller than the chimpanzee. Clearly, given the established relationships with the great apes and with dogs, brain size would suggest the possibility of the greatest human-animal bond with dolphins and elephants. Whales, fox, camel and walrus are a little more 'intelligent'—not the right word but we can't find another—than the dog. Horse, sheep, ox, mouse and rabbit, in descending order, are somewhat less so. Only the watery habitat of the dolphin has hindered an even greater human-animal co-operation than has frequently been noted. Because of that habitat a meaningful ongoing relationship has been hindered.

In her book *Elephant Memories*[26] Cynthia Moss describes 13 years of life with an elephant family in Kenya. She describes their antics, frolics, social organization and the trauma of death in a manner entirely reminiscent of human behaviour and emotions. She differs from the trimates in that she does not see herself as a part of the community but "in the role of voyeur, not as a participant."[27] Still, from the very beginning of her study she developed a strong attachment to her animals long before they got to know her. She started naming them,

---

26 Cynthia Moss, *Elephant Memories* (New York: Ballantyne, 1989).
27 Ibid., p. 16.

which, as she wrote, "is a fascinating phenomenon and a surprisingly powerful process. Somehow by naming something one possesses it, almost creates it. At the same time one feels a closer relationship to that thing."[28] And that is an awareness one cannot derive from studying external behaviour in the 'objective' manner of the behaviouralists. After about four years in Amboseli a dying elephant apparently attempted to communicate her distress to Moss and around the same time she was charged by a bull who wanted to keep her away from the females in estrus. Never, however, despite a passing acquaintanceship with her elephants, did Moss ever enter into a closer relationship with them. We know from the relationship between the mahouts and their Indian elephants that a close-knit relationship is possible. But Moss wanted to know the elephants in *their* social relationship. To have entered it would have been to change it. Despite this she developed the strongest feelings, the greatest sensibilities, toward her elephants. But it was never a reciprocal and hence communal relationship. There can be love and affection both within and without the communal relationship. Sy Montgomery felt—and expressed—love toward the emus she studied even though she never entered their world. They aroused an awe, respect and fellow feeling without her ever belonging.

Communal relationships certainly enhance our sense of obligation toward other species but, as we have seen, it can also exist without them. Moss, Goodall, Fossey and Galdikas were all very protective of the interests of *their* animals, especially when those animals were threatened by the behaviour of other humans. The natural sense of compassion is increased by the relationship to the animals, especially if there is a reciprocal communal relationship but very significantly without it if there is a naming of the individual animals, which mysteriously increases one's attachment.

If the trimates developed such a special communitarian relationship with the apes and if millions do it with their companion animals and have a special sense of compassion toward the animals which 'belong' to them—and we are using *belong* in the sense other than that of ownership—then it appears that all animals are entitled to an earnest consideration for their interests.

If that is so then the cattle, deer, pigs, fox and mink are entitled to a similar kind of consideration for their interests to that which Moss and the ape ladies give to the objects of their study. It is not always easy to determine how far down the evolutionary scale one must go before the entitlement decreases substantially—the snake, the cockroach, the amoeba? Whatever that point may be, clearly all complex animals are entitled to a great deal more consideration than they customarily receive in hunting, trapping, farm management, entertainment and even

---

28 Ibid., p. 36.

frequently as companions. Their essential biological, emotional, rational and moral similarity to humans makes it logically appropriate. Their dignity as fellow animals entitles them to it unless the self-preservation of their predators or the most pressing ecological considerations require it—and even then absolutely no more than is required. Still, we must acknowledge that the natural human compassion does not appear to extend equally to all animals. No one cares for the protection of the zebra mussels in the same manner that all with a vestige of sensibility care about threats to the wood bison or the deer. Animal liberationists will often tell us this is inappropriate, that "all animals are equal," as Peter Singer avers. We are not convinced. Nor, however much Singer wishes to persuade us to the contrary, was his philosophical mentor Jeremy Bentham. In the *Deontology* Bentham tells us that "We deprive [animals] of life, and this is justifiable—their pains do not equal our enjoyment. There is a balance of good."[29]

29 Quoted in W.E.H. Lecky, *History of European Morals from Augustus to Charlemagne*, 2 vols. (New York: D. Appleton & Co., 1875), 1: 47.

Chapter Fifteen

The Philosophy of Animal Rights

> In practical matters the end is not mere speculative knowledge
> of what is to be done, but rather the doing of it. It is not
> enough to know about Virtue, then, but we must endeavour to
> possess it, and to use it, or to take any other steps that may
> make us good.
>
> — Aristotle, *Nicomachean Ethics*

Aristotle's precepts are admirable if we know wherein goodness lies. If
we lack the speculative knowledge of what is to be done, Aristotle's
advice is to imitate the *spoudaios*—the mature person of practical
wisdom. But how do we know who is the *spoudaios* when persons of apparent integrity and wisdom differ so widely in their interpretation of
animal welfare issues? We have no alternative but to investigate the
speculative questions even though we feel temperamentally unsuited to
it. In some moral issues sound practical judgement comes easily. The
issues are clear, and the answers are equally clear—even though the
philosophical justifications for those answers may be difficult to
determine. Unfortunately, animal welfare issues do not fall into the
readily resolved category.

The philosophical problems are abstract. The cases are concrete.
And we would prefer to deal with the concrete cases by recommending
the development of sensibilities—emotions refined by reflection in
relation to compassion. But that is unfortunately insufficient when there
is little basic consensus on the degree to which animals are entitled to
moral consideration or on whether they are all entitled to the same
consideration.

The perhaps insuperable difficulty lies in the competing and perhaps
permanently conflicting factors which must be considered in determining animals' right to ethical treatment. There is both the very possession
of life and the quality of life to be considered. There is the possession
of sentience and the degree of sentience. Moreover, purposiveness,
rationality and self-awareness all play a role. The complexity of
community, social interaction and kinship all deserve some attention.
Further, species versus individual interests, species endangerment and
ecological considerations must all enter into the equation. Somehow
they must all be balanced and a judgement made on what action best
fits the balance. It is a truly daunting task. Moreover, human capacity
to make sound judgements, however limited, may exceed the human

capacity to provide philosophical answers to such complex questions. Sound judgements are easier come by than sound justifications. We are reminded once more of Chief Justice Mansfield's wise admonition to his judges (above, p. 76). He thought their capacity to make just decisions significantly superior to their capacity to give an adequate justification for those decisions. But no one has given anyone else the authority to make those decisions in the animal welfare questions, and thus their very principles must be discussed.

What is clear in consideration of animal welfare issues is that what is customarily being discussed is the *comparative* rights of animals, but when it comes to writing philosophy it is usually the abstractions alone which are discussed. We must confess to being perplexed by philosophical discussions unless we know their practical implications in conflict of interest situations. No one, we suppose, believes that a mouse cannot be distinguished from a stone. No one believes the stone has rights. The rights of a mouse to be and live as a mouse are usually accepted, provided, say, the mouse has not invaded a human home and is munching on the provisions or eating a hole in the skirting board. Immediately the question arises whether the human right to be rid of the 'pest' is greater than that of the mouse to its unhindered life. If raised at all, the question has usually been answered in favour of the right to a spotless kitchen. As a consequence of the increased sensibilities aroused by the animal rights movement the question is now at least raised. Even those who raise it usually suggest that if the mice cannot be removed harmlessly they should be fed something which sterilizes them, or should be killed painlessly. No one seems to consider the mice to have the right to their unhindered life in the human home. Thus there are seen to be competing rights, and the human rights outweigh those of the mice, although the mice may also be given some consideration. Those who champion the rights of animals have implicit—and occasionally explicit—criteria for distinguishing a hierarchy of animals, and hence different levels of animal rights.

Just as Hobbes and Locke, conferring "equal" rights on "the people," included only those they deemed industrious and rational (as C.B. Macpherson convincingly demonstrated[1]) so too animal rights advocates, when they talk generically of the rights of animals implicitly (occasionally explicitly) accord preference to some animals over others. Thus the rights of a dog inflicted with fleas are implicitly assumed to be of greater merit than those of the fleas. Indeed the comfort of the dog is preferred over the right to life of fleas. The shelters of even the most radical humane societies, those in which the doctrines of animal rights are most rigorously espoused, are regularly disinfected to eliminate

---

1   C.B. Macpherson, *The Political Theory of Possessive Individualism: Hobbes and Locke* (Oxford: Clarendon, 1962).

fleas, lice, cockroaches and the like. Clearly, for the proponents of animal rights not all animals have equal rights, any more than all humans were accorded universal rights by the early classical liberals. And that is so despite the customary expression of those rights in the language of universal and egalitarian rights.

Most animal liberationists would readily concede a good part of this. Peter Singer, for example, considers sentience to be the determining factor. If the animal does not feel pain it has no rights. In 1975 he concluded that drawing a line between a shrimp [which is an arthropod] and an oyster [a mollusk] is as good a place as any to make a determination of sentience.[2] By 1990 he had somewhat changed his mind. "While one cannot say with any confidence that these creatures do feel pain, so one can equally have little confidence in saying that they do not feel pain."[3] The point remains. For Singer animals have the right to "equal consideration" if they are sentient.

For Tom Regan, the doyen of American animal rightists, the relevant factor is what he calls "the subject-of-a-life-criterion"—a criterion which is met by individual animals which have:

> beliefs and desires; perception, memory, and a sense of the future, including their own future; an emotional life together with feelings of pleasure and pain; preference—and welfare—interests; the ability to initiate action in pursuit of their desires and goals; a psychophysical identity over time, and an individual welfare in the sense that their experiential life fares well or ill for them, logically independently of their utility for others and logically independently of their being the object of anyone else's interests.

For Regan, the animals which have rights are "mentally normal mammals of a year or more."[4] Clearly, Regan's position is far less universal than that of Peter Singer. Still, for both, once the criteria of inclusion have been met rights are extended to the animals in a universal and egalitarian manner. There is no attempt—at least no consistent and unequivocal attempt—to offer criteria of distinction or discrimination or gradation among animals, including human animals, which fall into their respective categories of moral entitlement.

What strikes us immediately about Regan's classification is that while many mammals possess in some degree or other the criteria he outlines some possess it in far greater degree than others. To take one example, it is clear that some mammals live predominantly not so much

---

2   Singer, *Animal Liberation*, 1st ed. (1975), p. 179.

3   Ibid., 2d ed. (1990), p. 174.

4   Tom Regan, *The Case for Animal Rights* (Berkeley: University of California Press, 1983), pp. 243, 278.

as individuals but as members of herds. When antelope sense the presence of a lion they react in unison, as a group; in fact, they appear to act so as to promote the overall well-being of the kin group rather than that of any individual animal. Thus while chimpanzees have a decided sense of self as individuals, lower species of wildlife appear to regard themselves as extensions of others rather than as individuals. We have some hesitation in accepting that Regan's criteria really apply to the animal realm as it is. We are not sure whether even the chimps would fit Regan's criteria. The criteria appear more to reflect the view of animals as incomplete humans of the era of human individualism—a characteristic which is not even essentially human but merely a particular cultural type of human. Now we do not wish to suggest that wild animals lack individuality. Certain species are decidedly solitary—bear, woodchuck and leopard, for example—and even gregarious herd animals undertake actions which refer only to individual needs and inclinations. What we want to emphasize is that for all species, including the human species, a concentration on individuality alone will fail to comprehend the complete nature of the animal.

It is quite compatible with both Singer's and Regan's claims, we shall argue, to conclude that all animal life has inherent value but where the interests of one sentient being are threatened by the interests of other sentient beings, some kind of preference is required, some kind of hierarchy has to be introduced. The recognition of animal rights thus implies that all—or at least most—animals have an inherent right to life and to the prevention of unnecessary suffering which will stand unless countered by a stronger and incompatible claim, unless countered by a greater right. The pertinent questions, then, are asking what stands as a legitimate counterclaim, and what criteria we employ for distinguishing the levels of rights.

In addition we need to ask if criteria we apply to animals are similar to those we apply to humans. Prima facie, there appear to be some discrepancies. For example, while it is generally agreed that it would be unjust to condemn an innocent person to death for murder in order to protect some perceived community interests—e.g., if the failure to apprehend the real culprit were tearing the societal fabric asunder—it would be equally customary to ignore the criteria of individual justice in considering, say, whether to cull a bison herd in order to hinder the spread of an infectious sickness. The overall interests of the bison community and the protection of other species would usually take precedence over justice for an individual bison. Thus we are inclined to judge animals—other than those with which we have a personal relationship—by collective or species or ecological criteria, humans and companion animals by the criteria of individual justice.

The classical argument for animal rights is to be found in Peter Singer's *Animal Liberation*. He bases his claims on the traditional liberal conception of equality of rights. He contends that if it is wrong, as is now commonly acknowledged, to discriminate on the basis of gender or race then it is equally wrong to discriminate on the basis of species. He points out that equality is a moral idea, not an assertion of fact.

Singer cites the eighteenth-century utilitarian Jeremy Bentham to the effect that "Each is to count for one and none more than one," and quotes from the *Introduction to the Principles of Morals and Legislation*: "The day *may* come when the rest of the animal creation may acquire those rights which never could have been withholden from them but by the hand of tyranny." Bentham reasons that if "the blackness of the skin" does not give us a right to exploitation, neither does the number of legs, the amount of reason, or the degree of conversibility:

> A full grown horse or dog is beyond comparison a more rational as well as a more conversible animal, than an infant of a day or a week or even a month old. But suppose the case were otherwise, what would it avail? The question is not, can they *reason*? nor, can they *talk*? but, can they *suffer*?[5]

Nevertheless, Bentham was not writing about the equality of animals with humans—nor even probably about the equality of black slaves—but about their inexcusable exploitation. There is no evidence to support the claim that when Bentham averred that "Each [is] to count for one" he meant that non-human animals were to be included. Indeed, had that been his intention, he would have recommended voting rights. And, of course, animal liberationists do not intend such an interpretation. They should certainly remember Bentham's insistence that depriving animals of life is justifiable and that "their pains do not equal our enjoyment."

What Bentham meant, we surmise, is that since animals have the potential for suffering their interests must be considered. Nowhere can we find that he writes or even suggests that they be given *equal* consideration. Peter Singer claims that "Although Bentham speaks of "rights" in the passage I [and we] have quoted, the argument is really about equality rather than about rights."[6] We certainly concur that Bentham was not writing about rights in any meaningful sense, for his description of "natural rights" as "nonsense" and "natural and imprescriptible rights" as "nonsense upon stilts" is notorious. Nonetheless, we can find no reason to believe he was writing about equality either. Unfortunately, Bentham does not continue with his thoughts about the status of animals.

---

5   Bentham, *Principles of Morals and Legislation*, 17, 4, b, p. 282. The quotation in Singer, *Animal Liberation* (2d ed. [1990], p. 7) is slightly incorrect. Singer has "they" instead of "the case." Bentham has "conversible," Singer "conversable." We point this out not to be pedantic but because Bentham is quoted so often via Singer that the words might as well be as Bentham wrote them.

6   Ibid., p. 8.

The now frequently cited passage is in fact but a part of a footnote referring to the practices of "the Gentoo [Hindu] and the Mahometan religions" where "the interests of the rest of the animal creation seem to have met with some attention." In the body of the text Bentham is merely bemoaning the fact that jurists have "degraded" the animal realm "into the class of *things*." What he appears to be objecting to in the footnote is "Cruelty to animals." He believes they are entitled to legislative protection, though they should still be eaten. But nowhere does he indicate that they are entitled to anything more than protection from cruelty. Singer has certainly succeeded in enhancing Bentham's reputation as the champion of animal rights and animal equality but, so far as we can discover, without a great deal of justification—though, we might add that when *The Principles of Morals and Legislation* was first published in 1789 *any* consideration for the interests of animals had to be welcomed. Still, as we saw earlier, both Burke in 1756 and Hume in 1751 might more justifiably be applauded for quicker recognition.

Singer notes that although there is a degree of consensus among philosophers in recognizing the basic moral principle of giving some form of equal consideration to the interests of others, very few of them have extended the principle to the members of other species. He claims that Jeremy Bentham did recognize and extend this principle to other species[7] and concludes that we must give equal consideration to the interests of all beings with the capacity for suffering "or, more strictly, for suffering and/or enjoyment or happiness."[8] But this amounts to a misleading double appeal to authority. First, Singer appeals to the authority of the "Many philosophers and other writers" who have espoused the "principle of equal consideration" but who, it is acknowledged, do not extend the principle beyond humans and who, if asked, may well refuse to do so. Second, Singer appeals to the authority of Bentham who, we have suggested, gives no indication that he accepts the principle ascribed to him. This appeal to authority is significant because Singer offers no other justification for the principle. He does give us the impression that "reason, not emotion" demands it. However, he does not indicate *how* reason demands it. What is significant is that the principles he espouses, rather than being principles demanded by reason, we shall be arguing, are but principles demanded by the ethics of liberal individualist society or, more properly, the principles of the values of that society as fleshed out by reason.

Singer insists that, in the determination of rights, the principle of equality requires that the suffering of one being be treated equally with the like suffering of any other being. He quotes such eminent authorities as the neurologist Lord Brain and the scientist Richard Serjeant to

---

7   Ibid., pp. 6-7.
8   Ibid., p. 7.

the effect that animals—at least the higher species—have minds and experience pain in like manner and to a similar degree as ourselves. Two things need to be noted about this. First that there is an acknowledged difference between the lower and higher species in terms of pain. Second, that Bentham, and Singer in his statement of principle, write about suffering, not pain. While there may be some correlation between suffering and pain, the former involves the reflective faculties of the cerebral cortex, which suggests that the potential for suffering is significantly more developed in humans and decreases as mental complexity decreases. Pain is located in the diencephalon, which is well developed in many more animals but is still differentiated, if less obviously, according to organismic complexity. Thus, even if we accept the principle that "the suffering of one being be treated equally with the like suffering of any other being" this implies that we treat humans as more significant than monkeys, monkeys as more significant than dogs, dogs as more significant than oxen, and oxen as more significant than rabbits. Moreover, if we restrict ourselves to 'suffering' we have no reason to be concerned about the shrimp, and not much to be concerned about the squid. Singer tells us that "when the United States Defense Department finds that its use of beagles to test lethal gases has evoked a howl of protest and offers to use rats instead, [he is] not appeased."[9] Yet on his own principle he should be somewhat appeased for rats must suffer less than beagles. Even if we allow Singer to sneak in 'pain' by the back door we should still recognize that this requires that we treat those animals with greater potential for pain as more significant than those with less. Any consideration of suffering must lead us to the conclusion that treatment of different species must be differentiated, following Singer's principle of 'like suffering', according to the degree of mental complexity.

What, then, might be the import of Singer's concept of 'speciesism'— a "prejudice or attitude of bias in favour of the interests of members of one's own species and against those of members of other species"[10]? Of course, one cannot support 'prejudice' or 'bias' but that is because the concepts themselves contain a negative connotation. But Singer's own principle of 'like suffering' requires that we prefer the interests of the human species over those of other species. Singer's own principle leads us in the direction of the speciesism he so roundly condemns. To take Singer's precepts seriously would appear to require us to give far less consideration to non-human animals than would Bacon's principle of compassion or Gandhi's claim that "the more helpless a creature, the more entitled it is to protection by man from the cruelty of man." We do not for a moment want to suggest that

---

9 Ibid., p. iii.
10 Ibid., p. 6.

Peter Singer has a lack of consideration for animal interests. We know that is not so. We are merely concerned to show how difficult it is for even the most accomplished of philosophers adequately to give formal expression to those sensibilities toward animals which Singer in fact feels. And we recognize full well how much easier it is to detect inadequacies in philosophical statements than it is to offer something to replace them which does not contain even greater inadequacies of its own.

At one level Singer appears to want to incorporate these kinds of criticisms into his philosophy. Indeed, he avows that "a rejection of speciesism does not imply that all lives are of equal worth." He holds, like Regan, that "a life of a self-aware being, capable of abstract thought, of planning for the future, of complex acts of communication, and so on, is more valuable than the life of a being without those capacities."[11] He goes further and acknowledges that neither he, nor any other prominent animal liberationist, holds "the right to life of a human being with mental capacities very different from those of the insect and the mouse"[12] as only equal to those of the insect and the mouse. For Singer, suffering requires equality of consideration, the right to life does not. Or, perhaps the capacity to suffer is simply the sole criterion by which we should differentiate our treatment of other beings, which means we should give preferential treatment to the human over the chimpanzee over the cat over the mouse and so on. Would this then mean that if human suffering is diminished by experimentation on chimpanzees such experimentation is justified provided we have a realistic expectation that the amount of human relief is greater than the chimpanzee's pain? Or that if experimentation on, say, 10 humans produced relief of suffering for, say, 50 chimpanzees, the degree of pain being more than offset by the degree of relief, then the experiment would be justified? We think that is probably the logical implication of Singer's argument, but he is never too clear. If this is so, then Warwick Fox would be wrong to imagine the animal rights approach of Regan as "more restrictive" than that of the animal liberationist Singer[13]—which merely reflects the difficulty of getting the various approaches in perspective.

Mental complexity does not affect equal consideration in the case of suffering—or does it and Singer doesn't want to tell?—but overcomes equal consideration in the case of the value of life. It is not always clear just what the implications of Singer's principles are, but prima facie, these two are incompatible. If the suffering of a dog in a medical experiment will save the suffering of a human is it justifiable? In his

---

11 Ibid., p. 20.
12 Ibid., p. 271.
13 Fox, *Toward a Transpersonal Ecology*, p. 165.

chapter on animal experimentation Singer skirts such questions. He rightly tells us of cruel and clearly unjustifiable experiments but never gives us a clear-cut answer to the central question. What we need to know explicitly is whether the mental complexity of a human affects the question of the right to life. If yes, we have to wonder what Singer's chapter title "All Animals are Equal" actually means. If not, we have to wonder what it is that makes the difference.

In fact what Singer's words seem to imply is not at all that "All Animals are Equal" but that all pain and suffering are equal, i.e., that X amount of suffering in a human is equal to X amount of suffering in a horse. This would be equivalent to Bentham's *"felicific calculus"* in which appropriate action is determined by calculating projected amounts of pleasure and/or pain. The appropriate action is the one which maximizes the former and minimizes the latter. But as John Stuart Mill argued effectively in his *Utilitarianism* (1863), there are different *qualities*, not merely quantities, of pleasure. Conversely, there must be different qualities of suffering. If, as Mill argued, the cerebral pleasures are of greater merit, so the suffering of more cerebral beings are more worthy of avoidance. In that case the sufferings of humans are worse than the sufferings of chimpanzees which, in turn, must be worse than the sufferings of rodents. Unfortunately, Singer never makes it clear in his writings where he stands on such issues.

If Singer is less than clear, some of the other animal rights advocates are decidedly confused. The prominent American animal rights writer Michael W. Fox gives the lie to Singer's claim about the beliefs of "other prominent animal liberationist" writers. In his *Inhumane Society*, Fox states that "all life is equal. It is unethical to value any one life over any other"—the dog over a flea we wonder! He sees "humans and other animals as coequal, morally equivalent."[14] On the other hand, Fox tells us that the "ecological ethic takes precedence over an individual's right to life" and that "the culling of animals . . . can be justified ethically."[15] Fox's earlier and later statements in the same book clearly imply that ecological considerations permit us to exterminate excess human population and that people may be legitimately 'culled' where their existence is a threat to the ecology (which, of course, it is almost everywhere!). We doubt, of course, that Fox quite means what he says but this clearly indicates the difficulty of espousing abstract principles without checking them against practical implications. We doubt that Fox would really advocate the slaughter of a few million Chinese or North Americans or the decimation of the population of Bangladesh or, say, even the forced sterilization of most Brazilians or Belgians, but that is

---

14 Fox, *Inhumane Society*, pp. 98, 210.
15 Ibid., pp. 230, 231.

what the logical implications of the abstract principles he espouses would suggest.

Equality, Singer tells us, is a moral idea, not an assertion of fact. Facts, Singer avers, will have no bearing on the equality of rights to which race and gender—and now species—may not be a bar. Of course, if Singer really considers racism, sexism and speciesism to be alike then we will have no alternative but to interpret him as arguing that each species must be treated equally. The fact of differing species' mental complexity will not allow us to distinguish our behaviour toward them on that basis. The *fact* that intelligence does not differentiate blacks from whites, women from men is a factor in the recognition that racism and sexism are morally wrong. But Singer does not appear to want to accept that. For him the fact that individual blacks, whites and women may be less intelligent than others and that this fact does not affect the requirement for equality is sufficient for him to assert that facts do not affect the issue of equality. Yet, paradoxically, for Singer, it is precisely the *fact* of greater mental capacity which requires us to ascribe preferential rights to the more complex species on the question of the right to life. On the one hand the fact of inequality is irrelevant to the issue, on the other hand it is the determinant in the issue. Why the difference, we are never told.

Singer notes that the "basic principle of equality does not require equal or identical *treatment*; it requires equal consideration. Equal consideration for different beings may lead to different treatment and different rights."[16] But if speciesism is truly analogous with racism and sexism does this not imply that one may then ascribe different rights to different races and genders? Of course, it may be appropriate on occasion to treat races and genders differently in order to maintain or achieve equality of race or gender. To claim, however, that different rights as ends rather than means were appropriate would in fact be to deny the essential equality of consideration. If humans and other species may have different rights does this not mean that humans and other animals are unequal in principle unless these rights are merely a temporary means to achieve equality? Now, of course, one could well retort that only women can have the right to an abortion and that does not mean that men and women are not equal. But is this not saying that the *fact* of a gender biological distinction does not interfere with the overall equality which is predicated on the *fact* of a similar mental complexity between men and women? The "different treatment and different rights" must surely mean something decidedly different in relation to different races and genders than it does in relation to different species.

---

16 Singer, *Animal Liberation*, p. 2.

By acknowledging that "different treatment and different rights" among species may be appropriate, is that not conceding precisely what is at issue? If the mental capacity of humans accords preferential rights, requires different treatment, does this not imply that there is a differentiation of rights according to a hierarchy of species? And does such an approach not lead us inexorably in the direction of treating other animals as means rather than as ends? And since suffering, distinguishable from pain both in duration and reflectiveness, varies in relation to the mental capacity of the species, then rights must be differentiated according to species on that issue too. If what is at issue is only the total amount of suffering then this could well lead to a significant disregard for the interests of less sentient creatures. It would imply, for example, that we should choose to use rabbits rather than mice in animal experimentation.

Even some animal rights philosophers have seen Singer's utilitarian approach as too restrictive. It balances interests, but fails to consider the "separateness" of individuals. Indeed, this is the objection made to utilitarian philosophy in general by such eminent critics as John Rawls and Robert Nozick. Tom Regan and Paul Taylor extend Rawls's and Nozick's considerations to the case for animals and suggest a more egalitarian treatment of animals. But this in turn involves viewing animals as 'individuals' as 'individually separate' and one may object that this ignores the reality of human social life and far more that of the essentially non-individualist lives of, say, the rhinoceros or the deer or the wolf. One is tempted to think that those who write about animal rights base their considerations on their knowledge of companion and farm animals, whose lives are decidedly different from the communal nature of much wildlife. To treat animal rights in terms of individual separateness is to ignore their sense of themselves as an element of a whole, including those animals which are somewhat solitary. If we are to treat animals according to their own essential natures, it is inappropriate to employ criteria which apply only to the highly individualistic human of the age of science and technology. Even human individuals in individualistic society have essentially shared relationships which affect their own conceptions of themselves in a manner other than as mere individuals. And if that is so for humans it is far more strongly so for the remainder of the animal kingdom.

The reason inequalities of fact are so often considered irrelevant to equality of rights is that it is rightly deemed inappropriate to dilute the basic human dignity of other humans according to their class, beauty, intelligence, race, etc. Not that facts do not affect the issue, simply that *these* facts do not affect the issue. Whether different classes, races and genders are reasonably similar in mental and moral capacities is relevant. If Caucasians had one-third the mental capacity of Orientals and lacked the capacity for moral virtue we would consider these facts relevant. If racism *means* the discrimination of treatment on the basis of race this hypothetical distinction of capacity would justify racism. If racism, on the other hand, implies *arbitrary* discrimination this hypothetical distinction would not justify *arbitrariness*. No fact could justify arbitrariness, but that is because of the nature of arbitrariness. In the case of racism and sexism what is objected to is that people sometimes do make arbitrary distinctions, i.e., they consider the person's skin colour or gender as indications of lesser intelligence or cultural inferiority. Because they are wrong in their assumptions they are wrong in their attitudes and behaviour. In this case the facts do not justify different treatment and different rights. Yet in the case of animals the distinctions of facts with regard to intelligence do justify, on Singer's own acknowledgement, different treatment and different rights. Speciesism is not only justified but Singer himself is a speciesist. Now, of course, it will be retorted that what speciesism implies is that one should not make arbitrary or unjustified distinctions. But that can only mean that one should take into consideration the relevant differentiating facts in determining how to treat animals. And who would deny that? The point is that there are relevant differentiating facts—unlike the cases of racism and sexism—and the task is to determine what they are.

For Singer, the sole consideration is the degree of pain—at least most of the time. Sometimes it is 'suffering' and sometimes the quality of a life—which, we suppose, could be decided by applying the criterion of potential for pain or suffering. By contrast Tom Regan suggests there is an "inherent value" to all beings "who have an *individual experiential welfare*, logically independent of their utility relative to the interests or welfare of others." He acknowledges that a line has to be drawn somewhere and concedes that "where one draws the line between those animals who are, and those who are not" to be included in the category is certain to be controversial.[17] Once an animal is included in the category, distinctions of potential for pain or suffering are irrelevant. What matters is the "inherent value" of each and every animal.

We have two concerns with this approach. First, it treats the animal realm, again, as though it were composed of individual animals in the same manner that modern Western human society consists of individual persons. From our experience we would suggest that much wildlife does not see itself in terms of "individual experiential welfare" but in terms of itself as the natural extension of others, as part of a cohesive whole whose individual interests cannot be separated from the group interest. We would, moreover, suggest that is probably also how primitive humans saw themselves, and how modern humans would see themselves

---

17 Tom Regan, "Ill-gotten Gains," in Langley, *Animal Experimentation*, pp. 29, 38.

if modern conditions had not so warped their natures that they became mere autonomous individuals.

The second concern lies in Regan's concession that a line must be drawn somewhere. Regan is conceding that all within count equally, those without not at all, with regard to "inherent value." But the drawing of the line anywhere would suggest that there are degrees of value and that would suggest distinction of treatment along some continuum. We would certainly not regard the rights of a spider or a mosquito as equivalent to those of, say, a fox but we do feel that they have some kind of value. We will kill a mosquito if it is biting though we would prefer to discourage its presence. We do not kill spiders in our home but we do remove them. This is not a thought-out philosophical respect for the rights of mosquitos or spiders but merely a natural distaste for killing.

What we find frustrating about the writings of such eminent philosophers as Singer and Regan is that they tell us so little about the relationship of their abstract principles to concrete reality, and we are unable to assimilate them to our experiences without being so informed. We can only fully understand abstract principles if we can test them against our feelings, our intuitions. This does not mean that such abstract principles cannot inform, or extend, or alter our feelings. They decidedly can, but only when we understand them for what they imply.

As Edmund Burke said before he acquiesced in a principle, "I must see the things, I must see the men." Does the fact that a chimpanzee is in closer biological and evolutionary relationships to humankind than to gorillas or orangutans affect how we treat them or not? Does the companionship of a dog bestow more entitlement to consideration on it than a camel we do not know, even though camels may have more reason than dogs? Or must we treat a sheep and a horse with equal consideration? If so, why, and if not, why not? Again as Edmund Burke opined:

> I do not put abstract ideas wholly out of any question because I well know that under that name I should dismiss principles; and that without principles, all reasoning in politics, as in everything else, would be only a confused jumble of particular facts and details, without the means of drawing out any sort of theoretical or practical conclusion.[18]

Nonetheless, he also insists that it is "Circumstances" which "give in reality to every political principle its distinguishing colour and discrimi-

---

18 Edmund Burke, "Speech on the Unitarians," in *Works* (London: Bohn, 1854-57), 6: 112-13.

nating effect."[19] Unless we know how the principles apply in practice, in particular circumstances, on specific occasions, we do not truly know the principles. And we feel we are always left hanging by Regan and Singer. Since we do not know how to apply their principles, we do not really know their principles.

It is, unfortunately, left to others to apply the principles and when we read how they are applied we are far from satisfied. For example, to return to Michael W. Fox and his *Inhumane Society*, we find the claim in favour of the egalitarian and against the utilitarian view. Having renounced utilitarianism he claims to replace it with "enlightened self-interest"[20]—which, of course, is a principle directly associated with the doctrine of utilitarianism! He claims that, "To accept *any* form of violence against animals on the grounds of human necessity is, in the final analysis, chauvinistic and patronizing."[21] Yet in the very next sentence Dr. Fox offers locust plagues and rabid dogs as instances where violence may be justified. He tells us "there is no hierarchical principle, which, in its insecurity and ignorance—and above all, its *emotional insensitivity*—causes so much suffering to those in the weaker strata of human society and to the animal kingdom."[22] Later he insists "that all animals of similar sentience should be given equal and fair treatment."[23] Not only does he not recognize this as an aspect of the utilitarian doctrine he has denounced but he does not seem to realize that the implication of treating animals equally if they have similar sentience means treating them differently if they do not have similar sentience—which is supportive of the "hierarchical principle" he has repudiated. He claims to espouse "natural law, following Hobbes and Locke"[24] but does not seem to understand that Hobbes and, to an only slightly lesser degree, Locke are usually presented as ringing the death knell of natural law, replacing it with natural rights. More importantly, natural law principles are entirely inconsistent with the principle of "enlightened self-interest" on which Fox claims to predicate his philosophy.

Finally, Fox tells us that "what is ... needed in animal rights philosophy [in addition to the concern with suffering] is reference to kinship, animals' intrinsic value, and concern for the environment."[25] Indeed it is! What Fox does not tell us—which is precisely what we need to know—is how these competing individualistic, communitarian

---

19 Edmund Burke, *Reflections on the Revolution in France* (London: Dodsley, 1790), p. 92.
20 See Fox, *Inhumane Society*, pp. 12, 100, 210, 231.
21 Ibid., p. 100.
22 Ibid., p. 221.
23 Ibid., p. 228.
24 Ibid., p. 221.
25 Ibid., p. 222.

and ecological considerations—all of which are prima facie in opposition to each other—may be made compatible. As soon as we leave the
realm of abstract philosophy animal rights advocates are unable to
locate that philosophy in any manner adequately in relation to practical
questions of the consideration of animal interests.

Now it could be said that we are being decidedly unfair, that we are
taking but a single case. While that argument may have some merit we
would point out that Tom Regan described Fox's book as a "brave
book . . . that unmasks the powerful professional and corporate interests
intent upon plundering the earth and enslaving the other animals with
whom we share it, in the name of 'progress'." And Ingrid Newkirk,
National Director of PETA (People for the Ethical Treatment of
Animals) went even further, claiming that "In every generation there
comes a book that forces society to re-examine its own fundamental
values. *Inhumane Society* is just such an explosive book for the
1990s."[26] Certainly, the most prominent animal rights advocates seem
to find Fox's philosophy adequate.

Paul Taylor has argued that Regan's case for inherent value fails to
demonstrate an equivalency between human and non-human but that
nonetheless the case for animal rights may still be rescued. Taylor
suggests that Regan's respect principle subsumes a moral right
(belonging to inherent value) which is tautological:

> If this is how we are to construe what is owed to an
> individual as its due, then *to accept the respect principle
> is already to accept the existence of a moral right*, a moral
> right belonging to any individual that has inherent
> value. Consequently the respect principle cannot
> constitute the validating ground for such a moral right.
> By laying down the normative requirement that respect
> for an individual's inherent value is owed it as its due,
> the moral right to such respect is implicitly being
> asserted by the principle. According to Regan's argu-
> ment the respect principle was supposed to be the
> rational basis for the moral right of any being having
> inherent value to be treated with respect.

In place of inherent value, Taylor offers us "basic rights," which consist
of:
1. Security-rights ("the rights of each individual to be protected from
   being killed, raped, assaulted, tortured, or otherwise made the victim
   of direct physical abuse"),

---

26 Regan's and Newkirk's comments are from pre-publication reports to the
publishers printed on the book's dust cover.

2. Liberty-rights (the right to be "unhindered by others in the pursuit of one's legitimate [morally permissible] interests"),
3. Autonomy-rights (including the right to privacy), and,
4. Subsistence-rights ("the right to biological survival and right to a level of physical health at least sufficient to enable one to actively pursue one's legitimate interests").[27]

According to Taylor these are rights shared by both humans and animals.

Again, however, we note the individualist orientation of Taylor's categories and the fact that they are inconsistent with ecological considerations. We wonder whether the right not to be killed means that we should interfere in nature's predation and save the bird from the snake. We wonder whether the right not to be raped implies that we should intervene in the world of the chimpanzees and orangutans. We ask ourselves what the term "legitimate interests" means and whether it implies that legitimate interests are the same for humans and animals or differ along some continuum.

Taylor does help by telling us that, "we must conceive of rights as *protecting those conditions essential to the right-holder's existence as the kind of being it is*. Whatever conditions are essential to making it possible for such an entity to realize its welfare are those to which it has a moral right."[28] Nonetheless, this still begs the question of what "kind of being it is." We suggest that there is a variety of different kinds, very few of which have the individual self-conception on which Regan and Taylor have predicated their arguments.

Certainly, we concur with Taylor when he states:

> We not only respect them but deem them worthy of our respect in virtue of their being the kind of entities they are (namely, having the characteristics that enable them to satisfy the subject-of-a-life criterion). Next, we could specify those conditions in their lives and their environment that must be realized if they are to exist as beings of that kind. If they have inherent value as the kind of beings they are they have the moral right to exist as that kind of being. Our duties toward them follow as a consequence.[29]

However, we would still respect them if they failed to possess "the subject-of-a-life criterion." Moreover, we doubt that this philosophy is needed to demand respect. We respect them and deem them worthy of respect because it is a part of our intrinsic and essential human

---

27 Paul Taylor, "Inherent Value and Moral Rights," *Monist* 70, 1 (1987): 23, 26.
28 Ibid., p. 27.
29 Ibid., p. 29.

nature—human nature untainted by those aspects of civilization which destroyed Rousseau's noble savage.

The criticisms we have so far adduced do not, however, get at the heart of the failing of animal rights philosophy. Ultimately, the philosophy fails because it does not recognize animal society for what it is—a world of conflicts of interest. It is a world where human and non-human animal interests conflict *and* where non-human and non-human animal interests conflict.

On Singer's analysis we assume that there are occasions where the amount of relief of pain brought about by animal experimentation would be sufficient to justify the pain inflicted on animals. On Regan's 'subject-of-a-life criterion', as supported by Taylor, this is less likely. At least on Singer's analysis we understand what would count as justification if it were possible adequately to measure pain, though this becomes substantially more problematic once 'suffering' enters the equation. With Regan and Taylor we do not know what, if anything, is allowed to enter a cost-benefit analysis, though we know that the life of a mouse has, in some manner, less significance than the life of a human. What we have no understanding of from any of these writers is where the snake and the bird fit in. Prima facie, to follow Taylor is to deny the snake what it needs to survive. So far as we can tell the philosophy of animal rights only bears on the human-animal relationship and not always helpfully at that—and signifies nothing about the nature of the vast majority of the animal realm. Certainly, animal rights philosophy is a decided hindrance to our ability to deal with the vastness of the ecological problems we now face. On the basis of Singer's, Regan's and Taylor's analysis it is inconceivable that we could find any justification for moral decisions which required the culling of animal populations unless we were willing to do the same with humans. And it would lead us to the inappropriate conclusion that we must interfere in the occasionally cannibalistic and rapacious world of the chimpanzees—a duty we would possess if we belonged to that world but a right which we lack if we don't.

Chapter Sixteen

The Philosophy of Animal Protection

> I could never free myself from the feeling that warm-blooded creatures were akin to us and not just cerebral automata. Consequently I cut demonstration classes whenever I could. I realized that one had to experiment on animals, but the demonstration of such experiments seemed horrible, barbarous and above all unnecessary. I had imagination enough to picture the demonstrated procedures from a mere description of them. My compassion for animals did not derive from Buddhist trimmings of Schopenhauer's philosophy, but rested on the deeper foundations of a primitive attitude of mind—on an unconscious identity with animals.
>
> — Carl Gustav Jung, *Memories,*
> *Dreams, Reflections*

Jung recognized the primal sympathy we feel for the animal realm. It is a very part of our nature to identify with those who are like us, and the more like us the greater the identity—other things being equal. Experimentation is not to be rejected per se, unnecessary experimentation is. Philosophy is not necessary to a demonstration of the justice of a fellow feeling with the animal realm. It is a part of our primitive essence, gradually eroded as we have achieved our mastery over nature. This identity with nature, with the world of the animals, does not deny our carnivorous nature (Jung was not a vegetarian). It means that we treat nature with the awe and respect to which it is entitled.

What Jung is indicating is that the compassion Rousseau ascribes to his noble savage is still with us, although the advance of civilization, of industrialism, of technology and its attendant egotistic individualism has stripped us of the better part of our noble primitive heritage. It is that same propensity which the Europeans found in the North American Indian during the early voyages of discovery but which they diminished by making the Indian dependent upon killing for trade and profit rather than for food and raiment. Still, as Rousseau understood so well, we cannot return to our primitive natures, we cannot unlearn what we have learned. Moreover, to try to do so would be to lose the cultural advances we have made—the diminution of racism and sexism, for example. We must, as in all things, attempt to achieve some balance, retaining the best of what we have gained while resuscitating the best of what we have lost. It is no easy task, but what it takes is the stimulation to sensibility rather than philosophy.

Is there, then, no role for philosophy? Indeed, there is. But it is less to discover ultimate truth than to give order and compatibility to those truths which lie deep within us, to distinguish the self-preservation from the altruism, the compassion. But unless we can raise those truths to the level of consciousness, there is no appropriate material with which philosophy is to work.

By 1685 the French under Louis XIV had ameliorated the condition of slaves. By 1807 the British had abolished the slave trade but slavery itself was not abolished in the British West Indies until 1833, and in the United States slavery continued until 1865. We should not imagine, however, that the end of slavery implied any recognition of racial equality. Indeed, as we have seen, in the 1870s Charles Darwin was still writing about the chiefly emotional but partly rational differences among races and Charles Kingsley could still describe Dyaks as beastlike.

Even those who thought kindly of other races did not consider other races equal. Late nineteenth-century travel books are replete with mildly amusing though deplorable racism. Orientals, for example, are depicted as kind, polite and pleasant (if always 'inscrutable') but rationally, or at least culturally, inferior (presumably because they used explosive powder to make fireworks rather than to charge weapons, and while they produced porcelain centuries before Europeans they neglected industrialization and marketing!). Many who criticized the conditions in the Alabama cotton fields deplored the manner in which the blacks were exploited but certainly did not consider them equal to the whites who employed them. Indeed the white plantation managers were condemned because *they* should know better. The blacks could not. In the Western world a general recognition of racial equality did not begin until after the Second World War and is still very far from complete. Even today many Orientals and East Indians as well as whites consider blacks racially inferior—both in intelligence and in culture. Such attitudes remain a lingering part of traditional belief systems. What is at issue is a matter of *fact*. And, of course, reputable research has demonstrated that there are no relevant distinctions among races with regard to native intelligence or capacities. The point is that no similar research could possibly demonstrate that animals are equal in intelligence or capacities, though in some capacities they are distinctly superior. When blacks and Orientals were considered inferior those with respect treated them honourably and with dignity but not with equality. What is similar about animals is that they are entitled to be treated with honour and dignity, according to their intrinsic natures. What is different is that they are not, and cannot be in any meaningful sense equal. They are entitled to just but not equal treatment which respects their nature as the animals that they are. And, as we shall suggest, justice for animals does not imply equality or equal consideration but proportionate consideration.

It is worth recalling the charmingly well meant but today quite unacceptable words in R.D. Blackmore's *Lorna Doone* on the character of woman: "her nature is larger . . . although her mind be smaller."[1] In 1865 such words signified the height of respect. And we can readily smile at the lyrics to Gilbert and Sullivan's *Mikado* of 1885, "that singular anomaly the lady novelist, she surely won't be missed." Women were fine creatures in their place and acting according to their nature, but how unfeminine to invade the proved prerogative of men!

Thumbing the pages of the early eighteenth-century magazine *The Spectator*, we find Richard Steele informing us disdainfully in his "Care of the Female Sex" that "Discourse for their entertainment, is not to be debased but refined," that he will "endeavour at a style and air suitable to their understanding." He tells us of "the thoughtless creatures who make up the lump of that sex."[2] Know thy station and thy true nature, woman!

In his "Catalogue of a Lady's Library" Joseph Addison acknowledges the lady in question to be "improved by learning" and notes "how much more valuable does she appear than those of her sex, who employ themselves in diversions that are less reasonable though more in fashion." Nonetheless, since woman "is so susceptible of impressions from what she reads" the lady's library would have been better stocked with books which "have a tendency to enlighten the understanding and rectify the passions."[3] Women should be more intellectual than they are, but not too much more, for they do not possess the reason of men! The condescension is infuriating but we should not fail to recognize the protectiveness, care, concern and compassion which are present along with the sexism. Women possess reason, but not enough of it that men do not need to take care of their interests! There is a kind, considerate, protective and respectful racism and sexism as well as the even more pernicious variety. We can ask no more than for a kind, considerate, protective and respectful speciesism.

Both Addison and Blackmore considered women to possess greater generosity of spirit than men, which was evidenced, for example, in their kinder treatment of animals. In that respect they were 'superior' to men, although that 'superiority' meant that they lacked the ruthless realism necessary to deal with the 'real' world! Women were to be admired for

---

1   R.D. Blackmore, *Lorna Doone*, 2 vols. (Toronto: Copp Clark, 1902), 2:208
2   Richard Steele, "Care of the Female Sex," in Alex Chalmer, ed., *The Spectator*, 12 vols. (New York: Sargeant et al., 1810), 1:109-110 (1:4, March 5, 1710-11 of original).
3   Ibid., p. 266 (1:37, April 12, 1711).

their virtuous character even though they were decidedly not the mental equals of men. Again, only in the twentieth century, and only in any significant manner since World War II, have we come to recognize that we were making *factual* errors, that the rational and emotional faculties of women and men could not be relevantly differentiated to justify gender discrimination. Facts were not only relevant to the equality of rights, to equal consideration, they were absolutely essential. Nor should it escape our attention that the eighteenth- and nineteenth-century recognition of female superiority in certain respects was not considered relevant to the determination of equal rights or equal consideration. Reason was the determinant. Indeed, precisely because women were deemed weaker, less rational and more emotional they were entitled to greater protection from the vicissitudes of life. Animals are today in a similar position to blacks and women in earlier times. What differentiates the situations, though, is that the *facts* are lacking to permit either equality of rights or equality of consideration for animals.

Peter Singer asks us to extend to all sentient beings, to members of other species, the equality of consideration which we now acknowledge as required in matters of race and gender. We are overcoming racism and sexism. Now, analogously, it is time to overcome speciesism. But Singer has failed to demonstrate that speciesism belongs in the same class with racism or sexism. The overcoming of our prior failure to recognize equality of mental capacity or of suffering in other races and in women cannot be replicated in the case of other species. Now one may well retort that it is equality of consideration that is at issue here, not equality of rights. True, but that would itself indicate that speciesism was not analogous with sexism or racism. Moreover, in the case of gender and race it was precisely the recognition of the equality of fact on which the equality of consideration was based. Without the equality of fact it was proportionate, not equal, consideration which seemed to be merited.

If we are satisfied that other species do not have similar capacities for reason and suffering why should we not continue to discriminate? What is needed is greater respect, awe and veneration and we owe that in part because of our recognition of the far greater similarity to ourselves than we previously recognized. Facts, especially the fact of evolution, are important in recognizing the duties we owe—which, because of differences in the degree of similarity, are not owed equally.

When we thought women and other races unequal to men and whites, some still recognized the respect we owed them. And some recognized also that because they were 'inferior' and could not always look to their own interests they were entitled to even more protection than white men. It is this respect and protection to which animals are entitled, but only in their relation to humans. Animals in the wild must be left to obey nature's laws. We have no right to protect one species from another merely because we have a preference. And we have no right to protect other species from humans when humans are acting within nature's necessity. Inuit, hunting for wildlife to feed and clothe themselves, have a duty toward the animal realm only to the extent that it does not hinder their self-preservation and to the extent that the health of the planet is consistent with it. Thus, for example, when threatened beluga whales are hunted one has to weigh ecological interests against those of the Inuit. The reality of ethical decisions is that they are not merely a question of upholding rights but of balancing competing rights. And rights are not all of the same merit. We should indeed treat the lives and suffering of other species with respect, compassion and protection but not with equal respect, equal compassion or equal protection.

The relationship of rights to justice is far from the simple one that animal rights philosophers would have us believe. The history of humanity is not simply one of gradual progress in the recognition and implementation of rights but one of such progress in constant tension with the maintenance of community, society and natural order. Neither human nor animal rights can be understood outside the context of community and order, although utilitarians and individualist liberals have made a valiant effort to do so, as we have seen in looking at the animal rightist philosophical writings. Now that the interests of the planet are under such threat it is relatively easy to see the limitations, for some individual rights are clearly incompatible with planetary survival. Taylor's "right of each individual to be protected from being killed," "the right to be unhindered by others in the pursuit of one's legitimate interests" must on occasion be subordinated to ecological considerations—at least in the case of non-human animals. One could anyway suggest that one might doubt the right to survival of a mass murderer or claim that wild animals have no right to be protected from interference in the pursuit of their legitimate interests by their predators. And we must surely recognize that, however much we may detest it, we must on occasion cull some animals to protect others—in the case of infectious sickness—and on other occasions cull some animals to save the vegetation so that other species may survive. Of course, such ecological considerations are necessary largely—though not entirely—because of humankind's arrogant abuse of nature, but that does not affect the fact that innocent animals must be killed. A consideration of individual rights is never enough. Moreover, we must recognize that while ecological considerations may now be paramount there has always been a conflict between individual and community rights which could never be settled by individual rights considerations alone. And if we cannot understand human rights outside the context of community it is even more true of wildlife, for their sense of community, their sense of sharing life with other species members is, we would surmise, far greater than that of the human.

Modern discussions of ethics and politics customarily revolve around the concepts of equality and liberty. But this has not always been the case. Until the seventeenth century, ethical, social and political thought was predominantly concerned with the search for order, the maintenance of community. The sense of a common belonging, a view of the self as inextricably involved with others, and interminable power conflicts, along with the difficulties of meeting basic needs, required it. Individual rights have generally been acknowledged and extended only to the degree that the granting of such rights would not irreparably harm the stability of the society and the continuity of the relationships which constitute the community. Until order and stability are secured, individual rights seem far less precious. Order was deemed the prerequisite of individual rights and liberties being meaningful and worthwhile. We are not suggesting that individual rights do not matter but that they are historically conditioned, they are contingent rights. The nature of morality arises primordially from our nature as communal beings. Individual rights, far from being the essence of morality, are contingently developed in a particular cultural setting as supplements to our essentially social nature.

It is a natural but unfortunate fact that in the days of primitive humanity no one wrote about ethics or about social and political theory. We can never know how our early ancestors conceived of their social obligations and the terms in which they saw themselves as selves. It is not until the individual emerges from the strict bonds of primitive society that writing begins, and even later that stylus is put to tablet to discuss ethics. In other words we have no records of the human mind when the individual mind was but a part of the collective consciousness. To be sure, C.G. Jung and a few others have recognized the continued role of the collective unconscious mind in human thought and behaviour, but our knowledge of it is at best severely limited. Yet in that collective unconsciousness, if we could understand it, might be found more clearly the natural morality of mutual obligations of which Rousseau gives us but a glimpse in describing the compassion of the noble savage. We might suggest that therein is to be found the essence of morality rather than in modern individualist theory.

Now, of course, it could be retorted that it is only when the human emerges as an individual and fulfils the human potential that humanity is truly achieved. Perhaps that is so, though we might hazard a guess that what is lost is as valuable as what is gained and, anyway, any understanding of the non-human animal must be predicated on a recognition of the predominantly communal consciousness which pervades all wildlife.

In the earliest writings on ethics and politics the notion of individual rights was notable by its absence. For Plato justice required a hierarchical relationship among classes in order to ensure the basic harmony of society. The question of individual rights never arose for Plato, nor indeed explicitly for Aristotle, although he complained bitterly of Plato's excessive concern for unity. Some three centuries later the Stoics were acknowledging a certain limited equality in principle of all humans as individuals, a recognition of the equal dignity inherent in all persons, a doctrine then adopted by Christianity. In St. Thomas Aquinas we encounter a recognition that there are goods which pertain to each individual as a self as well as those which pertain to membership in a community.

It was only with the onset of the age of science and commerce that philosophers began to concentrate almost exclusively on individual rights. Copying the successful method of inquiry of the natural scientists studying physics and astronomy, the early classical liberals, most notably Hobbes and Locke following Bacon, reduced matter to its simplest constituent parts in order to comprehend the whole. Thus the individual rather than the community became the object of investigation—and individualism inexorably produced a concentration on individual rights and the attendant egalitarian universalism. Only Rousseau and Herder—and to a significantly lesser degree Burke—stood out against this warping of our understanding of the essentially social character of humans and of human morality.

Recognizing the potential conflict between the private and public order, slightly later classical liberals—Adam Smith, for example—elevated the concept of Providence to a new role. It 'explained' how individual self-interest produced the public good, but even that public good was nothing other than the sum total of private goods. The French Revolution proclaimed the universal (but individual) "rights of man"—including for the first time those of blacks and women—though it believed that French civilization was the surest route to such rights and did not balk at imposing that civilization on other cultures. As the balance of power shifted, first the British Empire and then the American economic empire took up a comparable cause. The utilitarians and egalitarians followed Kant in proclaiming the principle of treating each as one and no more than one—a principle which in fact meant treating each *only* as one, as an autonomous and abstracted self, not as a creature of belonging, a member of a community. Modern rights and egalitarian theorists—including animal rights theorists—are thus representatives of a historically conditioned ethic which ignores the communal nature of humankind and animalkind. Their philosophy serves to justify the modern individualistic conceptions on which it is predicated. However persuasive and sophisticated it may be it represents but one side of the human condition and a very tiny part of the non-human condition.

While Plato was willing to grant equality to women in his guardian class—though not in the other classes—it was not as a consequence of any recognition of individual or gender rights but to promote the ends of the polis. Aristotle remained closer to customary Hellenic sexism. In his *Politics* Aristotle informs us that the "slave is entirely without the faculty of deliberation; the female indeed possesses it, but in a form which remains inconclusive."[4] He cites Sophocles to the effect that "A modest silence is a woman's crown," and Sir Ernest Barker notes that the saying implies there is a special form of goodness possessed by women which is absent in men.[5] Nonetheless, the woman has no political role. "The man is naturally fitter to command than the female, except where there is some departure from nature."[6] There is a begrudging acknowledgement of a degree of rationality in women but decidedly not to the level of the male. Their superior 'goodness' was decidedly not grounds for extending political rights, and may even have been a detriment. It is only with Machiavelli that we find expression for the sentiment that a good ruler must learn how to be bad—the idea probably preceded him by a couple of millennia. What is important to recognize is that it is reason rather than any other quality which is considered grounds for the greatest respect. Aristotle's view remained more or less uncontested until Mary Wollstonecraft argued the egalitarian case in her *Vindication of the Rights of Woman*[7] at the close of the eighteenth century. Nonetheless, gender equality was an idea so preposterous to her contemporaries that it was readily dismissed. Despite the entry of such luminaries as Germaine de Staël and somewhat later the Brontë sisters and Wollstonecraft's daughter Mary Shelley into the world of literature, most of their contemporaries regarded them as somewhat strange and distinctly unfeminine. It was only with the later nineteenth-century successes of the suffragettes that women's rights were taken seriously—although they had a short-lived flourish during the French Revolution—and even then they were often opposed by men who were otherwise enlightened.

It has been said that Elizabethan England was a paradise for women, a purgatory for men and a hell for horses. But it was said by a man and perhaps a prejudiced one at that. It has only been in the second half of the twentieth century that there has been a general acceptance of the principle of gender equality, in part because the

---

4   Aristotle, *Politics* (Oxford: Clarendon), p. 35, 1, xiii, 7.

5   Ibid., p. 36, 1, xiii, 11.

6   Ibid., p. 32, 1, xii, 1.

7   Mary Wollstonecraft, *Vindication of the Rights of Woman*, ed. Carol H. Poston (New York: Norton, 1988) (first published 1792).

commercial and technological revolutions have downgraded the importance of physical strength and required increased educational skills. And, most importantly, they have produced such a variety and abundance of skilled positions that men have felt less threatened than they once were by the acquisition of skills by women which otherwise would constitute a threat to their security, dignity and livelihood. Rights are more readily extended when they constitute less of a threat to those who already possess them. Improved economic circumstances and a more or less continuous relative internal stability and order in society have encouraged the acceptance of the rights which were always implicit within individualist ideology. It should, of course, be understood that while these rights were extended to a class—the class of women—they are not communitarian but individual rights.

Now that we are no longer threatened by wild animals, now that our herds and flocks are less subject to decimation by predators, now that we no longer compete with animals for scarce food resources, now that we no longer need their pelts for warmth, so it would appear that the time is ripe to extend rights to all sentient beings. To the extent that economic and social circumstances have made it possible to acknowledge gender rights so too it is now much more possible than previously to give far greater consideration to the rights and interests of animals. And we applaud the animal rights advocates for grasping the initiative and encouraging greater human sensibilities toward the animal realm. Where we differ from them is in philosophy and hence in the manner and proportion in which those sensibilities are directed.

Animal liberationists want us to believe that they stand at the forefront of moral progress—and they do. Just as racial and gender rights have been hard won in the enduring fight against oppression, so now one must press on to the final victory: the elimination of exploitation against the animal kingdom—and they are right. Where we differ, and differ substantially, is in what constitutes exploitation, what constitutes misuse of their rights, and to what rights animals are entitled. But we concur wholeheartedly that at present they are given far less consideration than that to which they are entitled.

It is our contention that individual rights, whether derived from the elimination of race, class, gender or now species discrimination, have been won at the expense of community and that while those rights have the greatest value there has been a considerable price to pay. Abstract rights, we would claim, can only be understood and justified in the context of a historical community. Our particular historical context—that of the age of science, technology and liberty—has produced autonomy, individuality and dignity but also alienation, anomie and loneliness. A debate has been raging now for over a decade between the liberal individualists—e.g., John Rawls and Alan Gewirth—and the communitarians—e.g., Alasdair MacIntyre and Michael Sandel[8]—on the relative merits of their cases with regard to the nature of justice. One consequence of the debate is that the notion of an abstract self as bearer of abstract prior rights has by common consent been eliminated from the discourse—but not from the writings of Peter Singer, Tom Regan or Paul Taylor.

There is now a consensus that values can only be understood in the context of a society's possession of "shared understandings." If one does not comprehend those "shared understandings" for what they are, that fact will of necessity, but unwittingly, inform the conclusions reached. Singer, Regan and Taylor subsume liberal individualist preconceptions— the "shared understandings" of Western liberal democracies—within the concepts they employ and thus provide us with an account of the logical implications of Western liberal individualist thought and nothing more. What they produce is a grand tautology—an informative, sophisticated, perceptive and sometimes brilliant tautology, but a tautology nonetheless. They begin from the assumption that each must be treated as one and no more than one, and from the assumption of the value of the autonomous individual. They demonstrate the logical consequences of those egalitarian and individualistic preconceptions—but tell us nothing about whether those assumptions are worthwhile. If, as we have suggested, the kind of society on which those assumptions are predicated produces anomie, alienation and loneliness as well as autonomy, individuality and dignity it is well worthwhile to question the assumptions.

The doyen of early communitarians, Friedrich Tönnies, tells us of community, of which the purest form is family, that it is ruled by love, not abstract justice, biological ties, not a social contract. By contrast, for Jeremy Bentham, wedded to individualist utilitarianism:

> The community is a fictitious *body*, composed of the individual persons who are considered as constituting as it were its members. The interest of the community then is, what?—the sum of the interests of the several members who compose it.[9]

There can be no clearer example of the problem of following the scientific analogy by reducing everything to its simplest parts in order to understand the whole. Society can *then* only be understood as an

---

8 John Rawls, *A Theory of Justice* (London: Oxford, 1972); John Rawls, "Kantian Constructivism in Moral Theory," *Journal of Philosophy* 77 (1980); John Rawls, "Justice as Fairness: Political not Metaphysical," *Philosophy and Public Affairs* 14 (1985); and much more on the liberal side. On the communitarian side the more important have included Alasdair MacIntyre, *After Virtue* (Notre Dame: University of Notre Dame Press, 1981), and Michael Sandel, *Liberalism and the Limits of Justice* (Cambridge: Cambridge University Press, 1982).
9 Bentham, *Principles of Morals and Legislation*, 1, 4, p. 12.

association of individuals. Social relationships can *then* only be understood as using others to pursue individual ends. Love, indeed, can *only* be understood as mutual individual lust or as the satisfaction of individual needs. What it cannot be understood as is a sharing of the self.

For Bentham—and indeed for all thoroughgoing liberal individualists—there can be no essentially shared relationships, those relationships "which penetrate so deeply as to constitute the identity of the separate selves involved." Such a relationship is one "whereby two separate selves become redefined in their identities as one through the relation with the relation (as union rather than contract) coming to constitute what were once separate selves as one shared self."[10] Anyone who has loved another deeply will know precisely what is meant. And so will any parent. Moreover, this essentially shared relationship exists for the infant prior to becoming a separate self. The self is initially shared with a parent and only develops a separateness later.

While this essentially shared relationship applies most obviously to family relationships and affaires de coeur, it also applies, if in lesser degree, to communities, nations and people, citizens and bearers of traditions, as Michael Sandel points out.[11] In fact, in time of war, one may share one's national identity with a love and passion more commonly restricted to familial relationships. Consistent liberal individualists are precluded from understanding such essentially shared relationships. This does not mean that they do not so understand. It means that they must unwittingly step outside the consistency of their paradigm to do so. For those who would count each as one and no more than one there can be no understanding of the possession of an identity beyond the autonomous self. They are precluded from understanding loyalty, love, patriotism—in a word, community. They are precluded because either their assumptions or their explicit pronouncements deny its existence.

For individualists—those who conceive of society as a sum total of individuals—there can be no conflict between the public interest and the sum total of private interests. Only individuals are real and only individuals have interests. The "community" is a "fictitious body" which can only be understood through its autonomous individual constituents, not the individual through community relationships. While this is a hindrance to the understanding of relationships in individualistic Western society it is an absolute bar to comprehension of the collective world of the wild animals—a world of the collective rather than the

---

10 Patrick Neal and David Paris, "Liberalism and the Communitarian Critique: A Guide for the Perplexed," *Canadian Journal of Political Science* 23 (1990): 426, 427.
11 *Liberalism and the Limits of Justice* (Cambridge: Cambridge University Press, 1982), p. 179.

individual consciousness. The abstract autonomous self is the ultimate reality for consistent liberal individualists, and while a few modern individual rights theorists such as Rawls and Gewirth have made some progress in overcoming the implications of that untenable position, it continues to inform their understanding. More importantly, from the perspective of the animal rights issue that understanding of the self dominates the thought of such animal rights theorists as Singer, Regan and Taylor. None of this would matter if it did not prevent them from understanding morality from a different perspective—that of belonging.

Already in the eighteenth century David Hume hinted at the impossibility of the individual rights position, not by noting that rights were historically conditioned, as modern communitarians do, but by reference to the nature of our birth. We are members of a family, Hume tells us, before we are individuals. Hume does not take the thought any further, unfortunately, but we can readily recognize that if we follow the scientific analogy, as do such diverse thinkers as Bacon, Hobbes and Bentham and their modern individualist successors, and reduce wholes to their simplest parts then, at least in one sense, the simplest part is not the autonomous individual but the dependent individual. At birth the infant possesses and develops its feelings, its needs, its love and its obligations toward its parents, especially the mother, on whom the infant is dependent for its life. We acquire our earliest values in relations to another with whom we have an essentially shared relationship prior to any development of individuality. Our essentially shared relationships exist prior to any possibility of an autonomous individual and prior to contingently shared or contractual relationships. It is in this context that we develop our values, our love, our obligations and our loyalties.

Our ideas of justice and rights—what we owe and what is owed to us—develop out of our belongingness in the family community. Our very conceptions of justice thus develop not in abstract, egalitarian and universalistic terms but in the particularism of the family. The justice—the giving of each person his or her due—of the family is both conceptually and chronologically prior to universal notions of justice. We owe our responsibilities and duties first to those to whom we owe our lives, and parents feel the greatest responsibility and duty to those to whom they have given life. But it is a duty not felt as an imposition but as love. It is the source of our compassion for all who need protection, but none are entitled to it as much as our offspring.

As we develop as social individuals so we extend the responsibilities we owe to parents first to siblings and members of the extended family, then to those who share membership in our wider communities and ultimately to humankind in general and in some cases to other species. Rights are indeed the converse of those responsibilities, for any right of one person implies the responsibility of another. Of course, rights ultimately become more complex than this but only as they are filled out by individualist philosophers investigating the logical implications of rights. They believe they are analyzing a thing in itself but what they are investigating is a value derived by extension from the nature of essentially shared relationships.

Our sense of justice extends from those with whom we have essentially shared relationships—those relationships which affect our very identity, our conception of who we are—to those with whom we have contingently shared relationships—which do not penetrate the identity of the self—and extends in decreasing order of significance. We do not think of ourselves as autonomous units but as the spouse of A, the parent of B, an Anglican, a Canadian, etc. But why, then, do we have the greatest compassion, not in order of proximity to the essential identity of ourselves, but often to those in greatest need of protection? It arises, we would surmise, from the fact that we feel the greatest urge to protect our loved ones, especially our offspring, precisely when they have the greatest need of protection. Because they have the greatest right to protection—right as the converse of responsibility—when it is needed, so we have the greatest responsibility to provide it, and so it is extended from those with whom we have the most essentially shared relationship to all.

It is a matter of no small moment that since there are always many in need and their interests are rarely in accord, social and ethical life constitutes constant social conflict, balancing our love for those closest with those in greatest need of compassion. The requirements of universal rights and community are in constant tension. What should be clear is that, with the exception of companion animals, our relationship with the animal kingdom is even more 'contingent' than our relationship to humanity as a whole, though because there is great exploitation of animals there is also a significant need for our compassion.

Of course, we will be told that to base morality on such conceptions is to commit the error pointed out so well by David Hume, that we are deriving an 'is' from an 'ought', or that we are committing the naturalistic fallacy made famous by G.E. Moore. But we are not saying that 'good' *means* 'compassion' or 'love', merely that these are instances of it. While we cannot *define* good in terms of natural qualities, this is no bar to saying that 'good' behaviour consists in or relates to the fulfilling of certain needs or acting on certain sentiments. These 'goods' are known to us as a part of our unconscious identification with others, including the realm of animals, but it is not an equal identification. Their woes are our woes but in differing degrees of significance.

We are impressed by the line of argument taken by Aristotle, Richard Hooker and G.E. Moore. The good is simple and known directly. In Aristotle's terms ethical values are known by *nous*—rational intuition. The philosophical part of the inquiry involves discriminating our compassion from our feelings of self-preservation and giving order and ranking to the different circumstances in which humankind's basic conceptions of self-preservation, love and compassion apply. Individualist and egalitarian philosophers think solely in terms of the universal application of rights, failing to recognize that the very values they proclaim arise directly out of the communitarian relationship.

Now the relativist will tell us this is all fanciful nonsense—the product of over lively imaginations. The values of any society are, Marx believed, an ideology developed to protect the interests of those who dominate. We would not doubt that there is a tendency for such self-serving principles to be socialized and advanced. But if Marx had really believed his own pronouncements he would then have understood the futility of change, for it could only bring self-serving pronouncements on behalf of the new rulers. Other cynics such as Hobbes, Machiavelli and Bentham believed the art of politics to lie in ensuring a form of societal organization in which the interests of the rulers and the ruled coincided as far as possible, so that when the ruling class pursued its interests the interests of the ruled would also be served. We do not doubt the significance of such assertions. But they are predicated on understanding only one side of human character—the self-serving side—which surely has predominated in the age of individualism. But it is only one-side of human nature, and the continued presence of the other—albeit in diminished form—is witnessed in all forms of service, stewardship and compassion, not least, and perhaps most, in the compassion extended toward the animal realm for, perhaps with the exception of companion animals, it can *only* be adequately explained in terms of our natural propensity to protect and to alleviate the suffering of others.

But let us see how the relativist gives a different interpretation of values, telling us how values are derived merely from self-interest. To return to C.B. Macpherson's interpretation of classical liberalism, the ideas of such thinkers as Hobbes and Locke are depicted as arising in defence of the interests of the newly emerging middle classes (or, what amounts to the same thing, became popular with the middle classes because they were useful to those interests). Hobbes and Locke, especially the latter, wrote in terms of universal rights, the rights of the people, but meant only the rights of those they deemed industrious and rational, i.e., the owners of property, the middle classes. Now we might note initially that if Hobbes and Locke were promoting the interest of a particular class it was not the promotion of personal interest but the promotion of interest which they *shared* with others.

In arguing against the privileges of the aristocracy and landed gentry the language employed was the language of universal rights. Now *even if* the intent was to promote the interests of a particular class, the logic of the language employed required the rights to be extended beyond that class. Over time individualist and universalist logic prevailed and rights were more or less universally extended. The implications of a value system predicated on the supremacy of the individual prevailed. But it should be recognized that they were derived from the consideration of the interests of those with whom an interest was shared. If liberal conceptions of rights were initially class-restricted, those conceptions were sufficiently persuasive to liberal thinkers that rights were gradually extended by direct reference to those rights which initially enfranchised only a select few. The *fact* that industry and reason were not class-restricted required the extension of the rights once the *fact* was recognized. Again we can see that the differing attributes of people were deemed essential to the determination of rights. Facts are vital to deciding which rights, what degree of consideration, are justified. All are considered, but only a few are considered sufficient on the basis of differentiating facts. Over time the facts were re-evaluated and, over time, all adult humans were included within the category of relevant right-holders. Non-adults were still excluded because they were deemed to have insufficiently developed reason, insufficient experience and too little at stake. Even within liberal 'universal' conceptions of franchise rights 'facts' are employed to diminish the universality of applications—to minors and the incarcerated, for example. In the case of non-human animals the facts are such that we need to consider their relative rationality—and other factors—in determining how they should be treated. We are not sure to what degree this is in accord with Singer's notion of "different treatment and different rights." Our difficulty with Singer is that we can never be sure what "different treatment and different rights" we are to accord. Consideration of the potential for suffering alone does not seem enough.

What seems of particular relevance in the case of liberal universal rights is that, ignoring the criticism of its historical contingency, it would appear to imply that all must be considered of inherent value but that differentiating facts, particularly with regard to reason, will determine how much value they are accorded. We do not think that this necessarily distinguishes our views in this regard from those of Singer and Regan. Where we differ, though, is in noting that these differences imply frequent conflicts of interest and that where those conflicts occur greater consideration must be given to the more rational and the more complex. What reason alone can never determine, though, is how we can resolve those conflicts. Only our sensibilities can do that. And that involves giving the greatest reign to our natural love and compassion—but they too must distinguish among those with whom we have essentially and contingently shared relationships. In the final analysis we are left only with judgement.

Love, loyalty and friendship are the essence of community. They imply preferential treatment for those with whom we share the communal relationship, those who are a part of the common belonging, over outsiders. They are prior—logically and chronologically—to, but the source of, our recognition of universal rights. Liberal individualist thinkers only recognize the universal. But we can only make the case for universal rights as an extension of particular rights. In our consideration of appropriate action we must find some balance between the two—and whereas liberal individualists always give preference to the former our understanding of society suggests greater weight than is customary in philosophical discourse ought to be accorded the latter.

Even if liberal individualist discourse in modern society concentrates almost exclusively on universal and egalitarian rights we can see that in practice both principles are recognized. Most espouse the idea of equal educational rights (although some have been quick to point out that they may lead to an oppressive meritocracy which is no more preferable to traditional class exploitation, if they are not balanced by other rights. Others note that in the static rather than occupationally expanding society they are the source of a debilitating conflict, pushing the less capable downwards at least in terms of their expectations). To the end of equal educational opportunities, the polity provides more or less equal educational access and provides assistance for the financially disadvantaged to profit from higher education. Some will, of course, insist that not enough is done, that schools in some areas may not be on a par with schools in other areas, that more grants and loans should be given to students from impoverished backgrounds, etc. The dissatisfied claim that the principle of equal educational rights is not being adequately pursued. Those in authority will not object to the principles on which the claims are based. Indeed they will also espouse them. But they will point to the practical difficulties of persuading teachers to move to less popular areas—the principles of equality and liberty are here in conflict—of finding the funds without harming the economy, etc. All—or almost all—acknowledge the same principle.

Yet everyone also acknowledges that children from homes with loving, responsible, knowledgeable parents will always have greater educational opportunities than those from disadvantaged homes. The only way to create a genuine equality of educational opportunity would be to remove children from their parents shortly after birth and to have children raised by the state. Now no one (other than Plato for his guardian class) proposes such a solution. And the reason is, quite simply, that while we do indeed enjoin the principle of equal educational opportunity we also consider the love, caring and nurture of the family as a wholesome part of a healthy community, and an intrinsic part of a just society. Particularistic love and universal justice are in conflict, and we balance the competing principles as adequately as our practical wisdom will allow. Moreover, in reality, there are not two but many competing principles whose relative merits our circumscribed 'prejudice' what is now customarily meant. He was referring to the habits of mind which are "the wisdom of ages" and preferable to the brilliant abstractions of philosophers. For Aristotle and Burke how we do feel is a prima facie indication of how we ought to feel which stands unless countered by further evidence and reason. How we do feel is prima facie evidence of the content of our moral collective unconscious minds.

Humankind's attitudes to the animal kingdom are thus the starting point of understanding our obligations. There is substantial evidence that highly communal and pre-literate societies have a greater sense of identity with the animal realm than have more individualistic societies. Generally, though, the animals that are respected the most, that are treated with awe, are those which possess the 'most admirable' characteristics, e.g., those that are courageous, care most for their own family members, display the greatest amount of cunning, etc. Those that are admired and respected the most possess characteristics worthy of imitation. They also respect those they fear.

Today, beyond our concern for domestic animals, we appear to give the greatest consideration to those threatened with extinction or extirpation from a particular habitat. This is a part of our recognition of nature's diversity and interrelatedness and our awareness of the ecological dangers we are facing, although it should be noted that even among vertebrates we show distinctly more concern for the plight of, say, the humpback whale (which is only threatened) over the salish sucker (which is endangered). Of course, consideration for the interests of threatened or endangered species usually requires the preference of their interests over those of other species. If we are to apply our conception of individual human rights to animals then, of course, we would be prevented from considering overall ecological interests at all. We must conclude either that the ecological considerations are inappropriate or that animal rights differ in some manner from human rights.

Ecological considerations have in fact led us in two different directions simultaneously. On the one hand, as we have come to recognize the problems the planet faces, we have come to find it necessary to protect some species by harming others, to kill some animals of a species in order to assist the healthier ones, and the like—to apply collectivist criteria, criteria by which the interests of the whole differ from that of the sum of the individuals. On the other hand, as we have come to recognize ourselves as an integral part of the animal world, sharing a common threat to our well-being, some come to have a genuinely shared relationship with animals, or at least some relationship where little or none existed before. Just as in wartime we feel a greater common bond as a consequence of a common purpose so, too, under a threat to our common environment we feel a common belonging,

minds are inadequate to discern. What we are always left with is
necessity of making a judgement—an intricate balancing act involv
differing and competing collectivist and individualist principles. Wl
reliance on universal principles of justice alone may make
judgement easier it is not then a judgement which gives due weigh
community.

If we are required constantly to balance competing principles in
decisions concerning appropriate action with regard to humans, th
no less true, and indeed adds complicating further considerations w
determining appropriate action toward animals, for we cannot cons
our moral actions toward other animals outside of our moral act
toward humans. Excluding our relationship with our companion ani
and the trimates with their respective primates—especially Dian Fc
who 'became' a gorilla—R.D. Lawrence with his wolves and sir
situations, the animal-human relationship will most frequently be
of a contingently shared relationship, i.e., one which is less signif
to one's identity than are close human community relations
However, the compassion owed to exploited animals increases
consideration for them to the very extent that they are exploited.
they, however, not exploited, the compassion would require less
consideration of their interests and our greater natural compassic
humans would prevail. Personal, social and political decisions r
us to use our judgement to balance competing claims. The rec
question involves asking where our responsibilities toward anim
into the competition.

It is now an axiom of philosophical discourse that a knowle
facts has no bearing on what is right. Indeed, it was precisely i
recognition that Peter Singer claimed equality a moral idea anc
fact. Unfortunately, we have no way of referring to the fact of c
ing legitimate values co-existing in tension other than by refer
facts. Thus while we acknowledge that facts, intuitions, knowl
how we do feel, subjected to rational analysis, cannot *prove*
good, or just, or right, they can provide us with evidence. T
prima facie *indications* of goodness, justice and rights which stan
countered. While Plato ridiculed popular opinion, Aristotle und
that it was our necessary starting point, although he understood
that it was only a starting point which rigorous analysis might re
For Aristotle, Plato was too brilliant and too reliant on
individual wisdom, for while that brought great truths it also
the greatest errors. Edmund Burke wrote of the prejudic
"renders a man's virtue his habit." He tells us that "prejudice
reason, has a motive to give action to that reason, and an
which will give it permanence."[12] Of course, Burke does not

---

12 Burke, *Works*, 11:359.

albeit in a weaker way. As we come to share a relationship with animals, as we come to feel a sense of common belonging, so it becomes increasingly difficult to ignore criteria of individual justice. This is especially so when we have a personal and durable relationship with the animals concerned. But if we wish to protect the environment we cannot afford to comply with the sentiments of justice we feel. We are truly, once more, on the horns of a dilemma.

The closest traditional relationship of human to animal has been that with the working animal, and the degree of respect awarded—and in a subsidiary sense earned—has related to the animal's capacity to perform its tasks. Relatively recently, the dog has been introduced to new tasks: the seeing-eye dog and hearing-ear dog, for example. It has become their nature to perform the tasks allotted to them. And what we admire in the working dogs' capacity is something we perhaps mistakenly regard as intelligence, for scientific data based on brain to body size suggest the dog to be less 'intelligent' than the camel and the walrus. The difference, we suppose, is that the camel is less willing to do our bidding and the walrus scarcely at all. Canine compliance may have a lot to do with our respect. Certainly, in a working relationship the essentially shared features of community can be felt in like manner and to the same degree as in a companion relationship. In fact working animals, especially hearing-ear and seeing-eye dogs, function in both capacities.

Animals which display a positive response to human attention tend to arouse a warm response in us—from the budgerigar through the dwarf rabbit to, most of all of course, the cat and the dog—while animals which appear to possess few emotions, or, more realistically, don't display them in the manner humans recognize, or don't display them toward humans, receive less approbation.

And certainly those animals we deem beautiful or attractive find a readier response. Those who think beauty is simply in the eye of the beholder should read Cynthia Moss's account of the agreement among her acquaintances on which of the elephants she studied were more and which were less attractive. It would be a useful scientific study to ascertain whether in mating choices among monogamous or at least selective animals their selections corresponded to human ideas of attractiveness. It would not be an easy study to conduct, but it would be useful in understanding the principles of aesthetics. Certainly, bird and cetacean singing suggests a conformity between human and animal aesthetic conceptions.

While we tend to prize intelligence in animals very highly in the abstract it seems unlikely that most people admire, respect or like animals for their mental capacities to the exclusion of—or even as much as—other characteristics such as belongingness, responsiveness, perceived virtue, possession of worthy imitable characteristics and physical attractiveness. To be sure, the perceived 'stupidity' of the ass has brought it low esteem, but that has probably more to do with its 'obstinacy'—which is simply a pseudonym for its independence—than anything to do with its mental capacities.

Some animals we tend to despise—scorpions, alligators and the like in particular. This presumably has a lot to do both with their unattractiveness and the fear they instill in us for their harmful capacities. It has even been suggested that the fear of the snake is a part of an unconscious antipathy, a residue of the collective unconscious, though we have no evidence it is so—or, for that matter, isn't so. We also tend to denigrate the pig by associating it with dirtiness, the wolf by associating it with . . . well, Little Red Riding Hood perhaps. Of course, all such denigrations are readily dismissed by facts about the real nature of pigs and wolves.

We are also inclined to have low esteem for the less complex animals—from mice (despite their 'greater intelligence' than rabbits) to amoebae—unless, as in the case of butterflies, they have some redeeming feature such as their beauty. Our low esteem of them is not, however, so much predicated on their lack of mental capacity as on the fact that they are insufficiently complex to possess the social characteristics we admire and with which we can identify, although, as in the case of mice, we might be inclined to confuse their lack of complexity and admirable social characteristics with lack of significant size.

Apart from companion animals, humans reserve their greatest affection for cetaceans and primates. Although we have slaughtered over 90 per cent of the world's whale population we have, rather late in the day, finally come to appreciate whales for the complex highly sentient beings with great mental capacity and an elaborate communication system that they are. And this is all even more so in the dolphin. As a consequence of the ethological studies of the ape ladies we have become aware of the complex and endearing social relationships of those species closest to us in evolution—as well as becoming aware of their occasional rapacious and warlike tendencies. Among all these species, though, it is not recognition of mental capacity alone which has brought about our change of heart. Other characteristics, such as the orca's singing—as beautiful in its own way as that of the songbirds we so highly prize—and socially integrative behaviour are equally esteemed. Mental capacity—with its attendant capacity for suffering—does not appear to be the superordinate criterion we employ in evaluating species, although the other characteristics we admire tend to have some essential relationship with complexity which, of course, is also relevant to mental capacity. In our evaluation of the significance of other species, perceived virtue and sociability are at least as important criteria.

What strikes us is how similarly human evaluations of the worth of animals corresponds to human evaluations of fellow humans—in terms of firstly their similarity as a species to humans in structure and complexity and secondly their intelligence, sociability, responsiveness, attractiveness and specific virtues (e.g., loyalty, courage, etc.). It should be noted that in terms of human evaluations of humans we recognize 'errors' that we make. Thus, for example, psychological research has established that educators have a significant tendency to judge academic performance in humans partly by the physical attractiveness of the student. Short, obese and ungainly students are deemed less intelligent than tall, slim and sprightly students. As a consequence, educators are—or should be—on their guard against allowing such irrelevant factors to intrude into their evaluations. Similarly, in evaluating the potential for suffering or value of life the cuddliness of the creature would appear an inappropriate criterion, although it is not at all inappropriate to our feelings toward the animal.

Throughout this book we have hinted at, and occasionally made explicit, the grounds on which we make the judgements we make. We have written about the factors which enter into judgements and, perhaps a little unkindly, have written of what we see as the shortcomings in other philosophies. But we have not laid out the principles which we ourselves espouse. We have some trepidation in so doing for they are far more the product of sensibilities, of our unconscious identity with the animal realm, than they are of any consistent and well-reasoned philosophy. They are the results of giving conscious form to sentiments we find deep in our souls. But since we have undertaken to write the book we can find no excuse for not laying bare our souls and have those principles subjected to the same scrutiny that we have given to others.

We doubt that, in Singer's terms, ants have sentience, and we are sure that they do not meet Regan's "subject-of-a-life" criterion. But we do believe that ants are worthwhile, that we have a responsibility to go out of our way to avoid harming them. As individuals they may be deemed insignificant. As communal beings their lives are very complex. Their work ethic arouses our admiration. Indeed, the intricacy, complexity and co-operation of their behaviour makes them more admirable than somewhat more complex organisms.

Worker bees kill their brothers and queen bees strive to kill their fertile daughters because the interests of the hive are greater than, and decidedly different from, the sum total of the individual interests of the bees. Newly dominant lions *and* newly dominant barnyard cats will kill young offspring sired by a previous monarch. The bees, although they are, we imagine, sentient, do not possess individual but communal value. For us to kill a worker bee would be of little or no damage to the bees. For us to kill a queen would indeed be harmful. The degree of sentience is an irrelevant factor. What matters is the communal interest. The life of the killed barnyard kitten or lion cub is deemed, by the cats' and lions' nature, as less significant than the maintenance of patriarchal relationships. (The reason cannot be the maintenance of genetic strength, as has been suggested, since the sperm strength as opposed to the amount of sperm is no less in older than younger creatures. An old male lion, cat or human is just as likely to have healthy offspring, although it is less likely to have offspring.) Even barnyard cats and lions, surely very well-developed creatures by any criteria, would seem to have a greater communal than individual self-conception and scarcely fill the highly individualist "subject-of-a-life" criterion. No, *all animal life has value, sometimes individual, sometimes communal value, and we have a duty not to harm any of it, unless our own significant and natural interests are at stake. But we have different degrees of responsibility*. At present the southern United States is infested with harmful bees. Humans have a right to take their lives—unless it can be demonstrated that there is a greater damage to the environment than benefit to human protection.

Other things being equal, *human beings should not interfere in natural predation*. They have no right to protect any one wild animal from another unless it is necessary because overall ecological considerations require it, e.g., in the case of the endangerment of a particular species. However, *since we have a communitarian relationship with our companion animals we are entitled to give them preferential treatment*. For example, if a companion dog were in danger from another animal, however much more sentient or however more readily it met the 'subject-of-a-life' criterion, we would be justified in its protection even though in identical circumstances among competing wildlife we would have no such justification.

We also, for similar communitarian reasons, have *a right to give preferential treatment, other things being equal, to non-companion animals with which we have a communitarian relationship or a potential relationship*. Thus the trimates were entitled to give preferential treatment to their apes even against the interest of humans who invaded their space.

Where the interests of animals are in conflict preference is to be given according to some synthesis of ideas of the quality of life, degrees of sentience, rationality, sociability and self or communal awareness. Explanation of this synthesis is a complex matter beyond certainly *our* individual rationalities. It is one of Lord Chief Justice Mansfield's instances where judgement is likely to be superior to the capacity to give justifications for the judgement. Normally, humans will only be required to make such judgements in such matters as animal experimentation where one is required to determine the relevant human versus animal interests and the animal versus animal interests in deciding which animals to employ. At a lower level our judgements are required in considering our behaviour toward 'pests' such as mice, spiders and other insects. It would appear reasonable to harm them only if they are inflicting some significant harm or at the very least significant inconvenience upon ourselves.

It is important to emphasize the role of judgement rather than abstract philosophy—the latter of which is beyond the capacity of most of us to develop in such a manner that it can be readily applied in the decisions we make. John Henry Cardinal Newman in his *The Grammar of Assent* of 1870 tells us that "It is the mind that reasons, and that controls its own reasoning, not any technical apparatus of words and propositions. This power of judging and concluding, when in its perfection, I call the Illative Sense." He describes it as being "parallel to *phronesis* in conduct and taste in Fine Art." *Phronesis* is Aristotle's concept of practical knowledge derived from experience and appropriate to action. This he contrasts with *sophia*, philosophical knowledge derived from reason. Russell Kirk describes Newman's Illative Sense as "constituted by impressions that are borne in upon us, from a source deeper than our conscious and formal reason. It is the combined product of intuition, instinct, imagination and long and intricate experience."[13] This Illative Sense bears some relationship to sensibility and the unconscious identity we possess with the animal world, which have been seriously impaired by the excessive rationalism and individualism of the age of science.

What, then, is justice for animals? Only the Illative Sense can tell us, and its voice is faint and indistinct in a world totally discomforted by such a non-empirical concept beyond the reach of mathematical and individualistic reason. Nonetheless, Aristotle's conception of distributive justice provides us with avenues toward an appropriate understanding. Aristotle's distributive principle has received an unpopular press in our liberal and egalitarian era, in part because it acknowledges different classes of persons, different levels of value, with some interests, notably those of women and slaves, receiving no worthwhile consideration at all. Using the traditional Greek oligarch-democrat dichotomy, Aristotle tells us that:

> Both oligarchs and democrats have a hold on a sort of conception of justice; but they both fail to carry it far enough, and neither of them expresses the true conception of justice in the whole of its range. In democracies, for example, justice is considered to mean equality. It does mean equality—but equality for those who are equal and not for all. In oligarchies, again, inequality in the distribution of office is considered to be just; and indeed it is—but only for those who are unequal, and not for all. . . . *A just distribution is one in which relative value of the things given corresponds to those of the persons receiving.*[14]

---

13   Kirk, *The Conservative Mind* (Lake Bluff, Illinois: Regnery, 1986), p. 385.
14   Aristotle, *Politics*, III, ix, 1, 2, p. 17. Emphasis added.

The relevant question for both oligarchs and democrats, Aristotle tells us (and we might add, for communitarians and individualists, for Romantics and liberals), is "who are the persons to whom their principles properly apply?"[15] To put it in more modern idiom, a just distribution is one in which more consideration is given to those whom one values more highly and some consideration is given to all. And if that conclusion is somewhat less than appealing to liberals and some communitarians with regard to persons it may be more acceptable when applied to animals, at least if we accept that there is a hierarchy of species, that some animals are less than equal to others in certain relevant respects. And just as the fact of essential equality among genders and races precludes proportionate justice in human society, so the fact of essential inequality makes it appropriate when considering animals.

Aristotle concludes that a successful constitution, a viable regime, a just way of life, must maintain a balance between the competing meritocratic and egalitarian principles. Since, unlike Plato, Aristotle rejects a natural harmony achieved through a rank subordination in society, he demands a mixed regime in which persons of mature reflective practical wisdom use their judgement to balance competing interests under the rule of law. It is a not inappropriate analogy for the treatment of animals. Fair consideration for different species, based on the differences of fact with regard to the quality of life, the capacity for suffering, mental and social complexity and self *or* communal awareness, allows for significantly different treatment and rights. Judgements about a hierarchy of animal value are a prerequisite of appropriate action toward them whenever there is conflict of interests. Clearly, it is such judgements which animal protectionists make in their concern with the plight of the dolphin inadvertently caught by tuna fishermen. They indicate a clear preference for the dolphin over the tuna.

---

15   Ibid., 3, p. 117.

Chapter Seventeen

Epilogue: Ode to Sensibility

Let us a little permit Nature to take her own way; she better understands her own affairs than we.
— Michel de Montaigne,
Of Experience, ca. 1590

While many of us have experienced something approaching an essentially shared relationship with a companion animal and have gazed in awe on confronting a large or beautiful wild animal in its natural habitat, the notion of a community of sentient beings may be considered a rather vague and ethereal aspiration, something idealistic, even irrational. It is certainly something beyond reason—but then so is love for a spouse, so are loyalty and sacrifice. Anyway, what is wrong with an ideal if it does not blind us to reality?

What we are in essence talking about is "primal sympathy," to recall Wordsworth, our "unconscious identity" with the animal realm, to recall Jung, our willingness to go out of our way to avoid harming any living animal, to recall Schweitzer. It is a part of our intrinsic human nature severely damaged by the excessive individualism of our modern age. But we are not asking for a return to the past, for not only can humankind not unlearn its historical experience, but we recognize the benefits of modernity as well as its calamities.

Romantic reaction against the age of industrialism did not disavow the benefits of commerce. Robert Southey in his *Colloquies* tells us that "the ordinary and natural consequences of commerce are everyway beneficial; they are humanizing, civilizing, liberalizing."[1] It was industrialism which marred the face of the earth. It was industrialism which destroyed human sensibilities. But all was not lost, progress was always possible in any circumstance. Southey has Sir Thomas More say to Montesinos:

> I admit that such an improved condition of society as you contemplate is possible, and that it ought always to be kept in view: but the error of supposing it too near, of fancying that there is no road to it, is, of all the errors of these times, the most pernicious, because it seduces the young and generous,

---

1 Robert Southey, *Sir Thomas More*, 2 vols. (London: Murray, 1829), 1: 197.

307

> and betrays them imperceptibly into an alliance with whatever
> is flagitious and detestable.[2]

If we have no dreams there is no road to travel. In Southey's words there is also a warning appropriate to radical animal activists. The demand for jam today is itself destructive of humankind's finer nature. What does it benefit the animals if their most benevolent protectors so debase their own altruistic nature that the principles of veneration and primal sympathy are themselves demeaned? Ends can only justify means if the means are not themselves destructive of the principles of behaviour on which the ends are predicated.

It is certainly true, as is customarily noted, that the Romantics glorified feudalism, but as William Makepeace Thackeray made it clear—in the "De Juventute" of 1860—feudalism, as the Romantics understood it, ended with the age of steam and the locomotive, not with the age of commerce. This is important to recognize because the Romantics were no enemies to the flourishing of the individual spirit and human dignity. It was the excesses they deplored. The ages of science, commerce and utility produced an enlightened mind which only in its excesses destroyed the altruistic, collective and communitarian spirit. It was this universalism, with its attendant egalitarianism, which ultimately encouraged the elimination of racism and sexism. But in its excesses it also furthered speciesism. What is so rarely recognized is that racism and sexism are of a different order from speciesism. The philosophical defeat of racism and sexism has been accomplished through the development of individualism and universalism. The reduction of speciesism will be accomplished by the recognition of communitarianism. It is not communitarianism without individualism which is required but a balance between them. We must never be willing to risk what has been gained in our desires to gain even more. Our look at the history of the status of animals indicated that while progress was achievable it was not inexorable.

If there is an overriding message to this book it is that the animals have more to gain from the development of human sensibilities than from the refinement of human philosophy. As William Cowper expressed it: "I would not enter on my list of friends,/(Though graced with polish'd manners and fine sense,/Yet wanting sensibility), the man/Who needlessly sets foot upon a worm."[3] And, as Dr. Johnson said, "Nothing is little to him that feels it with great sensibility." No one

---

2 Ibid., p. 32. Should anyone want to point out that Sir Thomas More lived in the sixteenth not the nineteenth century they should be reminded that More is resurrected for the purposes of Southey's book. We find him discussing inter alia Robert Owen's utopian socialist factory system at New Lanark, which was instituted in 1800.

3 William Cowper, *The Task*, Book 6, "Winter Walk at Noon," ll. 560-64.

knew better than Rousseau that polite manners and compassion were historically at odds. Sensibility is the readiness to feel compassion for suffering, to be moved by the pathetic, and to identify through the emotions with others. Moreover, it involves awe and reverence for things as they are in their own natures and a willingness to side with, to protect, even when those natures are not our natures and those emotions not our emotions.

As we have conducted the research for, and written, this book we have found our own sensibilities constantly developing. If we began this book on the side of the animals we close it feeling far more than ever inextricably involved in their world. We *feel* with the animals. We feel *with* the animals. We will have no greater reward than if one of our readers comes to share our own heightened sensibilities. And we can find no readier way of accomplishing that than feeling *with* the Romantics.

The Romantic reaction against the excesses of the Enlightenment involved espousing the communitarian spirit of which we have written. In origin, eighteenth- and early nineteenth-century Romanticism extended to a more imaginative plane the conservative critique of the rationalist, individualist and scientific thought which suffused the new liberal civilization.[4] However, historians of ideas have always found difficulty in delineating the disparate and sometimes contradictory elements of that Romanticism.[5] Sometimes Romanticism appears little more than a generic name for the tenets of those who rejected the artificiality and perfectibility of utopian liberal thought. However, whatever the precise contents of that Romanticism might be, it is clear that it involved the sense of community, of common belonging, of what we now call essentially shared relationships. For many of the Romantics it involved an immersion within, rather than a standing above, nature. It pitted loyalty against individual freedom, duty against individual rights and, above all, feeling against individual reason. We were not to be the lords of the earth bending nature to our will but an integral aspect of nature, rejoicing in our heritage and sharing a planet with other important, worthwhile sentient beings. The modern conservationists, environmentalists and ecologists are the natural extension of the Romantic movement.

William Wordsworth, the most popular of the Lake poets, is commonly regarded as the literary giant of the English Romantics. In his "Influence of Natural Objects" he wrote of the "Wisdom and Spirit

---

4 See, for example, Alfred Cobban, *Edmund Burke and the Revolt against the Eighteenth Century: A Study of the Political Thinking of Burke, Wordsworth, Coleridge and Southey* (London: Allen & Unwin, 1929).
5 See, for example, A.O. Lovejoy, *Essays in the History of Ideas* (New York: Braziller, 1955), especially chap. 12: "On the Discrimination of Romanticisms."

of the universe!" and of "The passions that build up our human soul."
Among his poems are "To a Butterfly," "The Pet Lamb," "The
Sparrow's Nest," "The Last of the Flock," "To the Daisy," "The Green
Linnet," "To a Skylark," "The Kitten and the Falling Leaves," and "Of
a Favorite Dog." He also wrote "Fidelity" and "Ode to Duty." Humankind's unity with nature and the elevation of passion over reason are
constant themes of his verse.

His "Intimations of Immortality" is perhaps the hymn of naturalistic
Romanticism and includes the immortal lines:

> Ye blessed creatures, I have heard the call
> Ye to each other make; I see
> The heavens laugh with you in your jubilee
> My heart is at your festival
> My head hath its coronal
> The fullness of your bliss, I feel—I feel it all.[6]

If our own technological, cynical and progressive age is out of tune with
such sentiments we can at least recognize their significance to those who
fought the losing campaign against the coming of industrialism—a
campaign incidentally now being refought by those who recognize that
submitting nature to our whim has brought us more anguish than joy.

For the Romantics too, though, the nature they enjoined us to
worship was the nature of beauty and complexity. There are no odes to
lice, no glorification of the carrot, although Wordsworth saw merit in
the weeds and Samuel Taylor Coleridge did try to arouse sympathy for
the denigrated ass:

> Poor little foal of an oppressed race!
> I love the languid patience of thy face.
> And oft with gentle hand I give thee bread.
> And clasp thy ragged coat, and pat thy head
>
> . . . .
>
> Poor Ass! thy master should have learnt to show
> Pity—best taught by fellowship of Woe![7]

To be sure, Coleridge does espouse the glory of all living beings:

> I essay to draw from *all* created things
> Deep, heartfelt, inward joy that closely clings;
> And trace in leaves and flowers that around me lie
> Lessons of love and earnest piety.[8]

---

6   William Wordsworth, *The Poetical Works of William Wordsworth* (Edinburgh: P.
Nimmo, undated), p. 301.
7   Samuel Taylor Coleridge, *The Poetical Works of Samuel Taylor Coleridge* (London:
Henry Frowde, 1912), pp. 74-75.
8   "To nature," ibid., p. 429; emphasis added.

Nonetheless, Coleridge does not seem to notice the essential incompatibility of this sentiment with his "Hunting Song" in which he glorifies the chase of the wolves, unless he regards the conflicts of interests and a hierarchy of beings as an intrinsic part of the nature he extols. Of course, wolves were so maligned in Coleridge's time that they were treated as deserving of destruction.

We can certainly recognize a similar drawing together of human with nature in modern ethology. Dian Fossey's study brought about such a close relationship between herself and the gorillas that she named them individually and even dedicated *Gorillas in the Mist* to some of her favourites: 'Digit,' 'Uncle Bert,' and 'Macho.' 'Brigit,' 'Danali' and 'Shawano' are among the names R.D. Lawrence gave to his wolves. Almost a century ago, Ernest Thompson Seton wrote of 'Lobo' the wolf, 'Silverspot' the crow, 'Raggylug' the rabbit and 'Redruff' the partridge. But as soon as relationships become so intimate, so personal, so involved, that naming, with all its attendant magic, becomes appropriate, then the possibility of making collective decisions in the interests of the overall environment diminishes. As soon as we have a sufficiently intimate relationship to confer a name we feel compelled to make decisions with regard to the named being by the criteria of individual justice. We are compelled to consider whether the individual animal *deserves* a proposed treatment rather than whether that treatment conforms to the overall interests of the species or the environment. Particularism competes with egalitarianism—and such is our nature that love usually wins out over universality. If humans and wildlife are treated by the same criteria of individual justice, then we cannot deal effectively with environmental problems—unless, of course, we become willing to treat humans by the criteria of collective justice!

Certainly, the writings of the animal rights philosophers are no help, indeed are a hindrance, to our understanding of such moral decisions. But the fact that many species have a collective consciousness, a sense of themselves as an integral part of the species, kin group or family allows us to understand that the killing of some for the benefit of the whole is not alien to their moral nature, although the harming of one species in the interest of another is more problematical. For us to be able to deal with that situation ethically we require a consciousness of a collective planetary good. It is therein that "primal sympathy" ultimately lies. And if such a collective consciousness is unlikely of achievement one can only feel dismay at the prospects for there being a future.

It is needful of recognition that the rules of behaviour—the moral rules—which prevail among non-humans, and somewhat more among humans in primitive rather than in individualistic society, are themselves collectivist.[9] Certainly, the collectivism of the ants, the bees, the barnyard cats and the lions suggests very different standards from those to which we are accustomed. But this does not mean that we should, therefore, consider it inappropriate to judge animal behaviour by moral standards, merely not by our own individualistic human moral standards. The rogue elephant is a case in point, as is the behaviour of a canine mother which wilfully refuses to suckle its young. They are breaking the moral laws of their own species.

Following Charles Darwin's evidence and argument, we see little reason to deny animals a moral sense, even though it is, of course, a far less cerebral one than our own. In humans the cerebration is necessary, for the source of our morality lies deeply hidden within our unconscious minds. As we have said, philosophizing is raising to consciousness the natural morality within our souls. In the case of animals the cerebration is less, but then they are so little removed from their primal nature that soul-searching is not necessary. Their understanding of their morals lies close to, or at, the surface. They do not need to delve.

Indeed, at the risk of being thought somewhat bizarre, we would suggest that Darwin does not go far enough, for he insists that "of all the differences between man and the lower animals" the moral sense "is by far the most important."[10] We would insist that it is only less philosophically refined. When the animal breaks the rules of its own communitarian existence it is acting immorally. When a chimpanzee or an orangutan rapes another it is acting immorally—against the rules of its own moral system. There is even a "rape grunt" of the aggrieved, a sound unlike any other in the chimpanzees' world. The victim is hurt, assaulted and degraded and acts as such. The perpetrator is aware of its crime and acts as such. This is not applying human moral standards to chimpanzee behaviour. It is applying chimpanzee standards to chimpanzee behaviour. Goodall's research has demonstrated beyond reasonable dispute how chimpanzees make rational choices among the various alternatives before them. The act of rape is a choice and a choice which contravenes chimpanzee standards of good conduct. This does not mean that forced sexual penetration per se is an immoral act. If that is the standard by which a species generates itself then it is simply a part of species behaviour, not an immoral act.

Now it could be retorted that, in the case of humans, standards are not enough. We have to apply ethical criteria to determine whether the standards are appropriate. That is true, but that is in large part because human society has so departed in its civilization from its primitive

---

9 A reading of Lamartine's novels should suffice to convince that such collective rules in human society were significantly effective not too long ago.

10 Darwin, *The Descent of Man* (New York: A.L. Burt, no date, but reprint of 2d edition of 1874), p. 110.

nature that the complex and continued circumstances require us constantly to test how our morals meet those circumstances. The animal in its more consistent social environment does not need such cerebral inquiry into its moral standards.

Giving the lie to the customary—and justified—animal rights emphasis on the essential similarity between human and animal thought processes,[11] Peter Singer insists that it is quite inappropriate to infer anything about ethics from non-human animal behaviour—which, one would have thought, is an example of the type of speciesist mentality of which Singer so vociferously complains. Certainly, it gave justification to a reviewer of the second edition of *Animal Liberation* to claim that if we accept Singer's understanding of animal ethics the whole thesis fails. Marx Charlesworth insists, in line with Singer's argument but not conclusions, that "we are the only beings in the world for whom the notion of moral values has any meaning. Animals are not responsible for what they do. We have a moral concern for them but they do not evince moral concern for each other or for us." He therefore concludes—against Singer's conclusions—that "In this crucial respect human beings simply are superior to animals. If this is 'speciesism', then so be it."[12] We cannot concur. Animals are indeed responsible for what they do, since they—or *at least* the more developed species—deliberate among options. They do indeed evince a moral concern for each other both within and without their species—they customarily choose not to injure others except where their own self-preservation is at stake, and in like manner they evince moral concern for us, especially, but certainly not solely, when a relationship has been established. The Newfoundland's propensity to rescue the drowning is perhaps the best-known example. Indeed the Newfoundland was the dog employed by the eighteenth-century Humane Society when that society was devoted in Britain to the rescue of those in peril at sea.

In fact in their relationships to humans they will come to display a fairly complex moral recognition, one which far exceeds their powers of ratiocination. To take a simple but common example, a domestic cat will display a greater degree of tolerance of exuberantly boisterous behaviour from an infant than it will from an older child or an adult. The cat will sharpen its teeth—with a degree of gentility—on an adult's finger but not on that of an infant. The cat has a primal sense of what is appropriate. But, the retort will be, that is simply instinct. No, instinct is an inappropriate word, for the cat has a number of options before it and will adjust its behaviour to meet different but not entirely dissimilar circumstances. It is, if you like, behaving according to its nature, but

---

11 See, for an oustanding and informative example, Mary Midgley, "Are you an Animal?" in Langley, *Animal Experimentation*, pp. 1-18.

12 Marx Charlesworth, *ACCART NEWS* (Australia) 4, 2 (Winter 1991): 10.

there is both an individual as well as a species nature and a moral as well as an immoral nature. Not all cats in all circumstances will make similar decisions. Anyway any attempt to use 'instinct' as an explanation of such behaviour would have to recognize that the same concept would then become applicable to similar human behaviour.

Singer insists that the failure of one animal species to consider the interests of another species, e.g., by killing for food, is irrelevant to our ethical considerations. Animals, Singer believes, "are not themselves capable of making moral choices."[13] If this were so, the distinction between human and non-human animals would be one of kind not of degree—and much of the animal rights case would carry a great deal less weight. To the contrary, in fact, animal sympathizers, Singer included, tell us that non-human animals only kill what they need to survive, that only humans kill for sport, and we are surely—and rightly—told this as a reprimand against human arrogance and insensitivity to other sentient beings. In such instances are we not in fact being told that animal morality is higher than human morality? If only humans have the faculties necessary to consider ethical questions and behave accordingly, as Singer believes, then there is an unbridgeable gulf between human and other animals. If, on the other hand, our ethical reasoning is a raising to the level of consciousness what we already know, what already exists within us as a part of our human and animal nature—and which exists in other forms in other species—then the difference between ourselves and other species is only one of degree and circumstance, even though the differences of degree and circumstance are extensive and even if only humans deliberate self-consciously about ethical issues. If we follow Singer's reasoning, we can only be ethical by moving away from our animal toward our differentiatingly human, from our communitarian toward our individual, natures—the degree of individuality of which is at least as cultural as it is human. On the other hand, if we recognize our essential similarity with other sentient beings we can better come to comprehend ourselves as members of a community—more correctly, of several hierarchically ordered communities—and thus understand our obligations to our fellow beings—both human and non-human—in a hierarchical manner.

The contemporary predominance in Western civilization of considerations of individual interests in human relationships is not of itself an indication of a greater concern with human dignity but instead reflects a particular, not necessarily superior, cultural condition and the role of liberal individualist thinkers within it. If considerations of individual justice were to dominate those of community, the belonging aspects, the most fundamental interpersonal aspects, of humankind would be rele-

---

13 Singer, *Animal Liberation*, p. 225.

gated to insignificance through the diminution and impoverishment of essentially shared relationships.

In the invocation of our primal sympathy, in giving conscious expression to our unconscious collective identity, in refining our sensibilities, so we become the best we can be both as humans and as animals. As the undeserved but necessary police force of the ecology, humans must practise the police motto of "To Serve and Protect"—but must leave wildlife undisturbed unless circumstance warrants intervention in the interests of those it is our responsibility to protect.

In refining our sensibilities it is within our souls that we must search to rediscover our unconscious identity with all of life. That identity has been blurred ever since the onset of Western civilization among the classical Greeks some 2,700 years ago. But it has never been erased. Now that we face the gravest ecological perils it is an identity more readily aroused, for present circumstances encourage us to understand it as a necessity for our own continued well-being as well as that of those who share the planet with us.

Select Bibliography

Abella, Irving. "The Making of a Chief Justice: Bora Laskin, The Early Years." *Law Society of Upper Canada Gazette* 24 (1990): 187-95.

Aquinas, Thomas. *Summa Theologiae*. Turin: Caramello, 1952.

Attenborough, David. *The Trials of Life: A Natural History of Animal Behavior*. Boston: Little Brown, 1990.

Audubon, John James. *Audubon's Birds of North America*. Secaucus: Wellfleet, 1990.

Bacon, Francis. *Essays*. London: R. Chiswell et al., 1706.

Baedeker, Karl. *Northern Germany*. Leipzig: Karl Baedeker, 1897.

—————. *Southern Italy*. Leipzig: Karl Baedeker, 1883.

Barker, Ernest, ed. *The Politics of Aristotle*. London: Oxford University Press, 1952.

Bentham, Jeremy. *An Introduction to the Principles of Morals and Legislation*. Ed. Burns and Hart. London: Methuen, 1982.

Bernard, Gertrude. *Devil in Deerskins*. Toronto: New Press, 1972.

Blackmore, R.D. *Lorna Doone*. 2 vols. Toronto: Copp Clark, 1902.

Blaikie, A.H., and J.A. Henderson. *Nest and Eggs*. London: Nelson, n.d.

Borwein, Bessie. "Life is a Miracle—But is Threatened by Disease." Mimeograph. October 1989.

Brown, John. *The Self-Interpreting Bible*. Glasgow: Blackie, 1834.

Burke, Edmund. *Works*. 8 vols. London: Bohn, 1854-57.

—————. *Reflections on the Revolution in France*. London: Dodsley, 1790.

—————. *A Philosophical Enquiry into the Origin of our Ideas of the Sublime and Beautiful*. London: Rivington, 1812.

Burnett, J.A. et al. *On the Brink: Endangered Species in Canada*. Saskatoon: Western Producer Prairie Books, 1989.

Canadian Council on Animal Care. *Guide to the Care and Use of Experimental Animals*. 2 vols. Ottawa: Council on Animal Care, 1980.

Cave, H.W. *Golden Tips: A Description of Ceylon and its Great Tea Industry*. London: Cassell, 1904.

Chalmer, Alex, ed. *The Spectator*. 12 vols. New York: Sargeant et al., 1810.

Chandler, Alice. *A Dream of Order*. London: Routledge and Kegan Paul, 1971.

Cheney, Dorothy L., and Robert M. Seyfarth. *How Monkeys See The World*. Chicago: University of Chicago Press, 1990.

Childe, Gordon. *What Happened in History*. Harmondsworth: Penguin, 1960.

Cobban, Alfred. *Edmund Burke and the Revolt against the Eighteenth Century*. London: Allen and Unwin, 1929.

Coleridge, Samuel Taylor. *The Poetical Works of Samuel Taylor Coleridge*. London: Henry Frowde, 1912.

Darwin, Charles. *The Voyage of the Beagle*. New York: Doubleday, 1962.
————. *The Descent of Man*. New York: A.L. Burt, n.d.
————. *The Origin of Species*. Harmondsworth: Penguin, 1985.

Disraeli, Benjamin. *Endymion*. 3 vols. London: Longman's Green, 1880.

Dolan, Edward F., Jr. *Animal Rights*. New York: Franklin Watts, 1986.

Doncaster, Anne, ed. *Skinned*. North Falmouth: International Wildlife Coalition, 1988.

Elsworth, Steve. *A Dictionary of the Environment*. London: Paladin, 1990.

Farb, Peter. *Humankind*. St. Albans: Triad, 1978.

Farrar, F.W. *The Early Days of Christianity*. London: Cassell, 1891.

Forsyth, Adrian. *Mammals of the Canadian Wild*. Camden East: Camden House, 1985.

Fossey, Dian. *Gorillas in the Mist*. Boston: Houghton Mifflin, 1983.

Fox, Michael W. *Inhumane Society*. New York: St. Martin's, 1990.

Fox, Warwick. *Toward a Transpersonal Ecology*. Boston: Shambhala, 1990.

Fraser, Laura et al. *The Animal Rights Handbook*. Venice: Living Planet Press, 1990.

Garbutt, Alan. "Biomedical Research: The Paperchase." *University of Western Ontario Medical Journal* 58 (2) (1989).

Gilman, John. *Report on Status and Trends in In Vitro Toxicology and Methodology Modification for Reducing Animal Use*. Ottawa: Health and Welfare Canada, 1991.

Goodall, Jane. *In the Shadow of Man*. Cambridge: Bellknap, 1986.
————. *Through a Window*. Boston: Houghton Mifflin, 1990.

Helfer, Ralph. *The Beauty of the Beasts: Hollywood's Wild Animal Stars*. Los Angeles: Tarcher, 1990.

Hobbes, Thomas. *Leviathan*. Ed. Michael Oakeshott. New York: Collier, 1962.

Hodgins, J. George, ed. *Aims and Objects of the Toronto Humane Society*. Toronto: William Briggs, 1888.

Hooker, Richard. *The Works of Mr. Richard Hooker*. 2 vols. Oxford: Clarendon, 1865.

Houghton, Walter E. *The Victorian Frame of Mind*. New Haven: Yale University Press, 1957.

Howitt, William. *Homes and Haunts of the British Poets*. London: George Routledge, n.d.

Hurll, Estelle M. *Landseer*. Boston: Houghton, Mifflin, 1901.

Hurnik, Frank. "Improving Animal Rights has Costs for Humans." *Kitchener-Waterloo Record*, July 22, 1991.

Ingold, Tim, ed. *What is an Animal?* London: Unwin Hyman, 1988.

Jackson, Thomas. *Our Dumb Companions*. London: S.W. Partridge, n.d.

Jefferies, Richard. *The Open Air*. London: Chatto and Windus, 1904.

Kirk, Russell. *The Conservative Mind*. Lake Bluff, Illinois: Regnery, 1986.

Knight, Charles. *Old England*. 2 vols. London: James Sangster, 1847.

Langley, Gill, ed. *Animal Experimentation: The Consensus Changes*. New York: Chapman and Hall, 1989.

Lansdell, Herbert. "Laboratory Animals Need Only Humane Treatment: Animal 'Rights' May Debase Human Rights." *International Journal of Neuroscience* 42 (1988).

Lawrence, R.D. "Conservation in Ontario: A Time for a Change." *Animal's Voice*. Newmarket: OSPCA, Spring 1991.

——————. *In Praise of Wolves*. London: Collins, 1986.

Lecky, W.E.H. *History of European Morals from Augustus to Charlemagne*. 2 vols. New York: D. Appleton & Co., 1875.

Ley, Willi. *Exotic Zoology*. New York: Bonanza, 1987.

Linzey, Andrew. *Animal Rights, A Christian Assessment*. London: SCM Press, 1976.

——————. *Christianity and the Rights of Animals*. London: SPCK and New York: Crossroad, 1987.

Lockhart, J.G. *Memoirs of the Life of Sir Walter Scott, Bart*. 7 vols. Edinburgh: Cadell, 1837.

Lovejoy, A.O. *Essays in the History of Ideas*. New York: Braziller, 1955.

Lover, Samuel. *Rory O'More*. London: Daily Telegraph, n.d.

Lutts, Ralph H. *The Nature Fakers*. Goldon, CO: Fulcrum, 1990.

Macaulay, Lord. *The History of England*. 4 vols. London: Longman, 1854.

Macpherson, C.B. *The Political Theory of Possessive Individualism: Hobbes and Locke*. Oxford: Clarendon, 1962.

Maier, Franz, and Jake Page. *Zoo: The Modern Ark*. Toronto: Key Porter, 1990.

Martin, Calvin. *Keepers of the Game*. Berkeley: University of California Press, 1978.

Matthiessen, Peter. *Wildlife in America*. New York: Viking Penguin, 1987.

Montgomery, Sy. *Walking with the Great Apes*. Boston: Houghton Mifflin, 1991.

Morris, Desmond. *The Animal Contract*. London: Virgin, 1990.

——————. *Animalwatching*. London: Jonathan Cape, 1990.

Moss, Cynthia. *Elephant Memories*. New York: Ballantyne, 1989.

Nash, Roderick Frazier. *The Rights of Nature: A History of Environmental Ethics*. Madison: University of Wisconsin Press, 1989.

Nature Through the Year. London: Odhams Press, 1946.

Neal, Patrick, and David Paris. "Liberalism and the Communitarian Critique: A Guide for the Perplexed." *Canadian Journal of Political Science* 23 (1990).

Paterson, David, and Mary Palmer, eds. *The Status of Animals*. Walling-ford: CAB International, 1989.

Pope, Alexander. *An Essay on Man*. London: Methuen, 1970.

Rawls, John. *A Theory of Justice*. London: Oxford University Press, 1972.

Regan, Tom. *The Case for Animal Rights*. Berkeley: University of California Press, 1983.

Rousseau, Jean-Jacques. *Discourse on the Origin and Foundations of Inequality Among Men*. New York: W.W. Norton, 1988.

——————. *The Social Contract or Principles of Political Right*. New York: Signet, 1974.

Russell, W.M.S., and R.L. Burch. *The Principles of Humane Experimental Technique*. London: Methuen, 1959.

Sandel, Michael. *Liberalism and the Limits of Justice*. Cambridge: Cambridge University Press, 1982.

Serpell, James. *In the Company of Animals*. Oxford: Basil Blackwell, 1986.

Seton, Ernest Thompson. *Wild Animals I Have Known*. Harmondsworth: Penguin, 1987.

Shepard, Paul. *Thinking Animals*. New York: Viking, 1978.

Shoemaker, Myron E. *Fresh Water Fishing*. New York: Doubleday, 1942.

Singer, Peter. *Animal Liberation*. 2d ed. New York: New York Review of Books, 1990.

Southey, Robert. *Sir Thomas More*. 2 vols. London: Murray, 1829.

Sullivan, Edward. *The Book of Kells*. New York: Crescent, 1986.

Symonds, John Addington. *Miscellanies*. London: Macmillan, 1871.

Talfourd, R. *Letters and the Life of Lamb*. London: Sisley's Ltd., n.d.

Taylor, Paul. "Inherent Value and Moral Rights." *Monist* 70, 1 (1987).

Thomas, Keith. *Man and the Natural World: Changing Attitudes in England 1500-1800*. Harmondsworth: Penguin, 1984.

Vasari, Giorgio. *The Great Masters*. Ed. Michael Sonino, trans. Gaston Du C. de Vere. New York: Park Lane, 1988.

Wakefield, Priscilla. *Instinct Displayed*. London: Harvey and Dalton, 1821.

Walton, Izaak, and Charles Colton. *The Compleat Angler*. London: Studio Editions, 1985.

Watts, Alan. *Nature, Man and Woman*. New York: Vintage Books, 1970.

White, Gilbert. *The Natural History of Selborne*. London: Cassell, 1908.

Widgery, Alban. *Interpretations of History*. London: George Allen and Unwin, 1961.

Willis, Roy. *Man and Beast*. London: Hart-David, McGibbon, 1974.

Wollstonecraft, Mary. *Vindication of the Rights of Woman*. New York: Norton, 1988.

Wordsworth, William. *The Poetical Works of William Wordsworth*. Edinburgh, P. Nimmo, n.d.

Index

Lemur, 199, 260
Leopard, 9, 191, 200, 202, 268
Lice, 256, 267, 310
Liechtenstein, 91
Life, 175
Limbourg brothers, 22
Linzey, Andrew, 129
Lion, 9, 17, 120, 182, 189, 191,
    195, 204, 205, 229, 230, 231,
    251, 252, 268, 303-304
Lizard, 23, 115
Locke, John, 53, 172, 266, 278,
    289, 296
Lockhart, J.G., 24
Locust, 278
London, Jack, 256
London Review, 52
London Zoo, 185, 186, 190, 192,
    197, 204, 209
Long, William J., 256
Los Angeles, 210
Louisiana, 115, 132-35
Lover, Samuel, 106
Lutts, Ralph H., 243-46
Luxemburg, 91
Lyell, Charles, 38
Lynx, 130, 137, 141, 146, 202

Macaulay, Lord, 19
Macaw, 232
Machiavelli, 10, 290, 296
MacIntyre, Alasdair, 292
Macpherson, C.B., 266, 296
Madrid, 190
Maier, Franz, 194
Malays, 39-40
Mallee fowl, 200
Malthus, Thomas, 38
Mandeville, Bernard, 250
Mandrill, 202
Manicheans, 16
Mansfield, Lord Chief Justice, 76,
    266, 304
Marcus Aurelius, 49
Marijuana, 148

Marmot, 143
Marquardt, Kathleen, 59
Marten, 115, 143, 145, 146
Martin, Richard, 34, 236
Marx, Karl, 26, 42-43, 157, 172,
    296
Massachusetts, 62, 116, 138, 163
Massachusetts Bay Colony, 28
Materialism, 27, 30, 40-41
Matthiessen, Peter, 116, 121
McClintoch, Jack, 175
McInnis, Edgar, 123
McKay, Barry Kent, 143
McWilliam, Ann, 59
Mechanics, 27, 28, 40-41, 256-57
Medical Research Council (U.K.),
    68
Medusae, 187
Mesopotamia, 8
Metallurgy, 9
Mexico, 106, 123, 162, 166, 177,
    182
Miami Metro Zoo, 197
Michigan State University College
    of Veterinary Medicine, 234
Midgley, Mary, 41, 313
Mill, James, 31
Mill, John Stuart, 31, 101, 273
Millstone, Erik, 80
Milton, John, 101, 211, 254
Mink, 115, 137, 141, 143, 146, 147,
    158, 262
Missouri Humane Society, 35
Mole, 153
Mongoose, 11
Monkey, 50, 102, 186, 189, 196,
    197-98, 200, 202, 229, 230,
    231, 271
Monkey Jungle, Florida, 192
Montaigne, Michel de, 26-27, 307
Montesquieu, Charles Louis de,
    10
Montezuma, 189-90
Montgomery, Sy, 257-59, 262
Montreal, 55, 193